The Collected Works of
William Howard Taft

The Collected Works of
William Howard Taft

David H. Burton, *General Editor*

VOLUME VIII

"LIBERTY UNDER LAW"

AND

SELECTED SUPREME COURT OPINIONS

Edited with Commentary by
Francis Graham Lee

OHIO UNIVERSITY PRESS
ATHENS

Ohio University Press, Athens, Ohio 45701
© 2004 by Ohio University Press
Printed in the United States of America
All rights reserved

Ohio University Press books are printed on acid-free paper ⊚ ™

12 11 10 09 08 07 06 05 04   5 4 3 2 1

Publication of *The Collected Works of William Howard Taft* has been made possible
in part through the generous support of the Earhart Foundation of Ann Arbor, Michigan,
and the Louisa Taft Semple Foundation of Cincinnati, Ohio.

Photograph of William Howard Taft courtesy of
William Howard Taft National Historic Site.

"Liberty under Law" was first published by Yale University Press, 1922.
Taft's 1924 testimony before the House Judiciary Committee appeared in Serial 45
(Washington, D.C.: Government Printing Office, 1924) (25273).

Library of Congress Cataloging-in-Publication Data

Taft, William H. (William Howard), 1857-1930.
Liberty under law and selected Supreme Court opinions / edited with commentary by
Francis Graham Lee.
p. cm. — (The collected works of William Howard Taft ; v. 8)
Includes bibliographical references and index.
ISBN 0-8214-1564-6 (cloth : alk. paper)
1. Judicial opinions—United States. 2. Law—United States—Cases.
3. Taft, William H. (William Howard), 1857-1930. I. Lee, Francis Graham.
II. Title. III. Series: Taft, William H. (William Howard), 1857-1930. Works. 2001 ; v. 8.
E660 .T11 2001 vol. 8
[KF213]
352.23'8'097309041 s—dc22
[347.73/2634]   2004005243

Dedicated to

the Taft family,

for five generations serving

Ohio and the nation

The Collected Works of
William Howard Taft

David H. Burton, General Editor

VOLUME ONE

Four Aspects of Civic Duty and *Present Day Problems*
Edited with commentary by David H. Burton and A. E. Campbell

VOLUME TWO

Political Issues and Outlooks
Edited with commentary by David H. Burton

VOLUME THREE

Presidential Addresses and State Papers
Edited with commentary by David H. Burton

VOLUME FOUR

Presidential Messages to Congress
Edited with commentary by David H. Burton

VOLUME FIVE

Popular Government and *The Anti-trust Act and the Supreme Court*
Edited with commentary by David Potash and Donald F. Anderson

VOLUME SIX

The President and His Powers and *The United States and Peace*
Edited with commentary by W. Carey McWilliams and Frank X. Gerrity

VOLUME SEVEN

Taft Papers on League of Nations
Edited with commentary by Frank X. Gerrity

VOLUME EIGHT

"Liberty under Law" and Selected Supreme Court Opinions
Edited with commentary by Francis Graham Lee
Cumulative Index

Contents

Acknowledgments, xv

Commentary by Francis Graham Lee, xvii

LIBERTY UNDER LAW

Liberty under Law, 3

**SELECTED SUPREME COURT OPINIONS OF
CHIEF JUSTICE WILLIAM HOWARD TAFT**

October Term, 1921

Volume 257

Hildreth v. Mastoras	21
American Steel Foundries v. Tri-City Central Trades Council	23
Truax v. Corrigan	30
Terral v. Burke Construction Co.	36
Wallace v. United States	37
Railroad Commission v. Chicago, Burlington & Quincy Railroad	39
New York v. United States	43
Omitted Taft Opinions	45

Volume 258

Howat v. Kansas	46
United States v. Balint	47
Ponzi v. Fessenden	48
United Zinc & Chemical Co. v. Britt	50
Balzac v. Porto Rico	52

Stafford v. Wallace   56
Omitted Taft Opinions   60

Volume 259

British Columbia Mills Tug & Barge Co. v. Mylroie   60
Atherton Mills v. Johnston   62
Bailey v. George   63
Bailey v. Drexel Furniture Co. (Child Labor Tax Case)   64
Hill v. Wallace   70
United Mine Workers v. Coronado Co.   73
Omitted Taft Opinion   78

October Term, 1922

Volume 260

Lederer v. Stockton   79
Chicago & Northwestern Railway Co. v. Nye Schneider Fowler Co.   81
Wichita Railroad & Light Co. v. Public Utilities
    Commission of Kansas   83
Freund v. United States   85
National Union Fire Insurance Co. v. Wanberg   87
Brewer-Elliott Oil & Gas Co. v. United States   90
Ryan v. United States   92
United States v. Bowman   93
Cumberland Telephone & Telegraph Co. v. Louisiana Public
    Service Commission   95
Liberty Oil Co. v. Condon National Bank   97
City of Boston v. Jackson   98
Champlain Realty Co. v. Brattleboro   99
United States v. Lanza   101
Heitler v. United States   104
Sioux City Bridge Co. v. Dakota County   106
Walker v. Gish   107
Federal Trade Commission v. Curtis Publishing Co.   108
Omitted Taft Opinions   110

Volume 261

Charles Nelson Co. v. United States	110
Pennsylvania Railroad Co. v. United States Railroad Labor Board	112
Work v. Mosier	116
Hallanan v. Eureka Pipe Line Co.	118
Keller v. Potomac Electric Power Co.	119
Adkins v. Children's Hospital	123
Omitted Taft Opinions	127

Volume 262

Board of Trade v. Olsen	127
Ex parte Fuller	131
Dier v. Banton	132
Essgee Co. v. United States	135
Work v. McAlester-Edwards Co.	137
Sonneborn Brothers v. Cureton	139
Wolff v. Court of Industrial Relations	143
Omitted Taft Opinions	148

October Term, 1923

Volume 263

Director General of Railroads v. Kastenbaum	149
Craig v. Hecht	151
Dayton–Goose Creek Railway Co. v. Interstate Commerce Commission	154
First National Bank v. Missouri	157
Omitted Taft Opinions	160

Volume 264

Puget Sound Power & Light Co. v. County of King	161
Mahler v. Eby	163
Omitted Taft Opinions	164

Volume 265

Hammerschmidt v. United States	165
Hetrick v. Village of Lindsey	167

United Leather Workers Union v. Herkert & Meisel Trunk Co. 168
Omitted Taft Opinions 171

October Term, 1924

Volume 266

Chicago Great Western Railway Co. v. Kendall 172
Tod v. Waldman 174
Panama Railroad Co. v. Rock 175
Omitted Taft Opinions 177

Volume 267

Swiss National Insurance Co. v. Miller 178
Ex parte Grossman 180
Carroll v. United States 186
Samuels v. McCurdy 194
Pennsylvania Railroad System v. Pennsylvania Railroad Co. 199
Lancaster v. McCarty 201
Brooks v. United States 203
Barclay & Co. v. Edwards 206
Western & Atlantic Railroad v. Georgia Public Service Commission 207
Steele v. United States No. 1 209
Steele v. United States No. 2 212
Cooke v. United States 213
Omitted Taft Opinions 216

Volume 268

Coronado Coal Co. v. United Mine Workers 217
Selzman v. United States 222
Maple Flooring Manufacturing Ass'n v. United States 224
Omitted Taft Opinions 226

October Term, 1925

Volume 269

Donegan v. Dyson 227

Central Union Telephone Co. v. City of Edwardsville — 230
Omitted Taft Opinions — 232

Volume 270

Maryland v. Soper No. 1 — 232
Oregon-Washington Railroad & Navigation Co. v. Washington — 236
Omitted Taft Opinions — 239

Volume 271

Booth Fisheries Co. v. Industrial Commission of Wisconsin — 240
Appleby v. City of New York — 241
Appleby v. Delaney — 244
Thornton v. United States — 245
Yu Cong Eng v. Trinidad — 248
Goltra v. Weeks — 253
Omitted Taft Opinions — 256

October Term, 1926

Volume 272

Myers v. United States — 257
Hughes Bros. Timber Co. v. Minnesota — 268
Hanover Fire Insurance Co. v. Harding — 270
Federal Trade Commission v. Western Meat Co. — 273
Omitted Taft Opinions — 274

Volume 273

Tumey v. Ohio — 275
Shields v. United States — 278
Kelley v. Oregon — 280
Ford v. United States — 281
Omitted Taft Opinions — 285

Volume 274

Morris v. Duby — 285
Federal Trade Commission v. Claire Furnace Co. — 288

Cline v. Frank Dairy Co.   291
Weedin v. Chin Bow   295
Omitted Taft Opinions   298

October Term, 1927

Volume 275

Gong Lum v. Rice   299
Segurola v. United States   303
Atlantic Coast Line Railroad Co. v. Standard Oil   306
United States v. Murray   309
Omitted Taft Opinions   311

Volume 276

Wuchter v. Pizzutti   311
Nigro v. United States   314
Hampton & Co. v. United States   319
Omitted Taft Opinions   323

Volume 277

Blodgett v. Silberman   323
Dugan v. Ohio   326
Compañia de Navegacion v. Fireman's Fund Insurance Co.   328
Gaines v. Washington   330
Olmstead v. United States   332
Omitted Taft Opinion   336

October Term, 1928

Volume 278

Lehigh Valley Railroad Co. v. Board of Public Utility Commissioners   337
Oriel v. Russell   342
Wisconsin v. Illinois   344
Larson v. South Dakota   349
Arlington Hotel Co. v. Fant   351
Omitted Taft Opinions   354

Volume 279

County of Spokane v. United States 354

Carson Petroleum Co. v. Vial 359

Sutter Butte Canal Co. v. Railroad Commission 363

Alberto v. Nicolas 367

Ex parte Worcester County National Bank 373

United States v. Fruit Growers Express Co. 377

United States v. John Barth Co. 379

Chesapeake & Ohio Railway Co. v. Stapleton 381

Old Colony Trust Co. v. Commissioner of Internal Revenue 385

United States v. Boston & Maine Railroad 388

Omitted Taft Opinion 389

October Term, 1929

Volume 280

Colgate v. United States 390

Interstate Commerce Commission v. United States ex rel. Los Angeles 391

United States v. Jackson 392

Omitted Taft Opinions 394

Appendix 1: William Howard Taft's Statement and Testimony before the House
   Judiciary Committee, 1922 395

Appendix 2: William Howard Taft's Statement and Testimony before the House
   Judiciary Committee, 1924 417

Cumulative Index 423

Acknowledgments

The author wishes to acknowledge the great support he received from Dean Brice Wachterhauser and the Faculty Development Fund of Saint Joseph's University in completing this volume. Without that support, this project could not have been completed. My long-time colleague, Professor David H. Burton, deserves thanks as well, not only for allowing me the pleasure to work on this volume, but for his support of my writing that spans almost three decades. I also want to thank my administrative assistant, Mrs. Jane Frangiosa, and two former student assistants, Charles Duncan and Peter Evich, for the less-than-glamorous work they did in assisting in the completion of this volume. Finally, I thank Ohio University Press editor Sharon Rose, whose keen eye saved me from many embarrassments and who graciously tolerated my sometimes slow replies to her queries. Any errors that remain are now only my responsibility.

Commentary

Francis Graham Lee

Of all the positions that came his way during what was to be a remarkable half century of public service, of all the offices that fell to a man who "owned to keeping his 'plate rightside up' when appointive jobs were being passed around," William Howard Taft welcomed none as much as he did President Warren Harding's offer to nominate him as the tenth Chief Justice of the Supreme Court of the United States.[1] This was the long-desired post that, at last, realized for Taft "the comfort and dignity and power without worry I like."[2] Upon being notified of his nomination, Taft reportedly said to Harding: "I love judges and I love courts. They are my ideals on earth of what we shall meet afterward in heaven under a just God."[3]

In nominating Taft as successor to the venerable Louisianan Edward Douglass White, Harding and his attorney general, Harry Daugherty, had no reason to wonder what type of judge Taft might be. His writings and speeches as an appeals court judge, law professor, and ex-president clearly set forth a judicial philosophy that would guide him for what would prove to be ten years at the helm of the Supreme Court. (From the start, Taft planned to serve ten years on the Court and then retire and take the grand tour of the world. Death would prevent him from making the voyage.)

Taft's judicial philosophy was greatly influenced by his view of himself as a faithful disciple of both John Marshall and Alexander Hamilton. As such, he was a federalist who viewed state regulation suspiciously, championed the federal government, and saw an independent and powerful judiciary as the bulwark for protecting the "vested rights" that the Framers sought to guarantee by this "more perfect union." He also viewed the independence of the presidency and its total control over the executive branch as necessary for the Constitution's system of checks and balances to work effectively. The essay "Liberty under Law," reprinted in this volume and written by Taft before he assumed the chief justiceship, presents the picture of a person who was less likely to experience the learning curve faced by many other new justices, even those who, like Oliver Wendell Holmes, Jr., had had considerable previous judicial experience before joining the Supreme Court.

Taft arrived with a clear vision of what he needed to do as chief. During his ten-year tenure he came as close as any chief justice has to achieving just that. One student of Taft, for instance, asserts that Taft, more than any president in the first third of the twentieth century, shaped the Court and, as importantly, created an aura around the Court of judicial independence and nonpartisanship that allowed the Court to weather the storms that buffeted it in the 1930s.[4]

Even as his health declined and he realized that his days on the bench were numbered, Taft could reflect on how much he had accomplished and could feel reasonably confident that his legacy would endure. In contrast, the two later justices who also arrived on the bench with definite agendas—Felix Frankfurter and Warren Burger—failed almost totally to achieve their goals. In contrast, Taft could rightfully claim to have met almost all the ambitions he had set for himself when he arrived on the Court in 1921.

Although possibly unsuited for the presidency and surely unhappy in the White House, Taft was a natural for the role of chief justice. "I am head of the judicial branch of government," he claimed in 1922.[5] Here the same attributes that doomed his term in the White House—one biographer characterized him as "a smiling Buddha, placid, wise, gentle, sweet"[6]—allowed him to establish himself as a respected and well-liked leader. As chief, he was also unusually effective in securing legislative support for those parts of his agenda that required congressional action. His three great triumphs in this arena were persuading Congress to establish the judicial conference, chaired by the chief justice; successfully lobbying through Congress the Judges' Act of 1925, a statute that freed the Court of much of its burdensome obligatory jurisdiction and stands second only to the Judiciary Act of 1789 in establishing the power of the federal judiciary; and finally, securing an appropriation to purchase land and build the current Supreme Court building—the Court's first permanent home. These three accomplishments laid the foundation for the Supreme Court as we know it today. Taft's testimony to the House Judiciary Committee, contained in this volume, shows the clarity of Taft's vision of what a modern court system needed in order to function effectively.

Taft also saw his role as chief as allowing, indeed requiring, his involvement in the process of selecting federal judges. Taft appointed six justices during his one term as president—only George Washington and Franklin Delano Roosevelt appointed more. Harding and Daugherty appear to have given Taft significant control over nominations to the federal bench and, though less successful in the succeeding Coolidge and Hoover administrations, Taft continued throughout his term to importune presidents on judicial appointments. He appears to have had some say even in Herbert Hoover's selection of Charles Evans Hughes over Harlan Fiske Stone to succeed him as chief justice.[7]

Taft's legacy also includes 249 opinions of the Court and seventeen dissents. These demonstrate both how closely Taft followed the views expressed prior to his elevation to the high bench and how Taft's views reflected the changing nature of American society in the 1920s. Taft was, particularly in his early years on the Court, a workhorse, taking many cases that the other justices were not anxious to tackle. A few examples of his patent and admiralty cases are included, but in the main they have been omitted, along with cases involving contract and salary disputes. In one of the omitted cases, Taft began his opinion: "This is an ordinary patent case. There was no reason for granting the application for a writ" (*Layne v. Western Well Works,* 261 U.S. 387, 388 [1923]). Taft's willingness to take these less attractive cases resulted in his writing a disproportionate number of the Court's opinions during his service as chief. Abraham estimates that Taft "wrote almost twenty percent of the Court's opinions."[8]

Taft as Chief Justice

Courts may have been heaven to William Howard Taft—and they must have appeared even more celestial after his four years in the White House and the disastrous presidential campaign of 1912—but the particular heaven to which Taft would quickly ascend, "affirmed with only four no votes on the very same day the nomination reached the Senate," was not an altogether happy Eden.[9] The Court had badly fractured during the final years of Edward Douglass White's tenure in its center chair (1910–21). Indeed, many of the problems that Franklin Roosevelt incorrectly alleged were afflicting the 1937 Court were present in 1921. The Court was behind in its caseload, hampered by the infirmities of certain of its members, and divided by personal feuds among others of the brethren.[10]

Taft knew all of this and saw it as a challenge to which he could more than measure up. The stamina with which he attacked the job and the skill he showed as "social leader" quickly won him a respect, admiration, and friendship from his colleagues that would endure to the end of his service on the Court.[11] This respect was evidenced by the heartfelt tribute penned for the Court by its senior member, Oliver Wendell Holmes Jr. to mark Taft's leaving in 1930.[12] Historians and political scientists have also been generally respectful of his years as chief justice. In a ranking of the first hundred justices, twelve were considered "greats" and fifteen "near greats." Taft is found in the latter category.[13] A more recent survey, limited to the justices of the twentieth century, ranked Taft fourteenth out of fifty-two.[14] Admittedly, playing the role of *primus inter pares* does appear to increase a justice's chances of being favorably evaluated. Five of the "greats" served as chief justice and two of the "near greats" also presided over the high court. In contrast, Taft is widely rated as only "average" among presidents, a conclusion in which the jovial Taft might well have concurred, having himself noted that he had "retired from the Presidency of the United States with the full and unmistakable consent of the American people."[15]

Taft seems to have quickly brought a sense of concord to the Court, although he was never fully able to rein in the unusual behavior of Justice James Clark McReynolds.[16] He was able, however, quickly to "mass" the Court, based on the philosophy of "no dissent unless absolutely necessary."[17] Early on, Theodore Roosevelt had summed up Taft's general talent for bringing consensus, noting that with "Taft sitting on the lid, everything will be okay."[18] Justices as diverse as Pierce Butler—"Dissents seldom aid . . . [and] often do harm. For myself I say: 'lead us not into temptation'"—and Louis D. Brandeis gave in to the chief's desire for consensus and held their dissents.[19]

Taft did have an aversion to dissents, but the fact was that he rarely found himself in the minority. He quickly overcame the divisiveness that had characterized the White Court toward the end of White's service. The figure below presents the voting patterns on the Court from 1922 to 1924. This period was picked because it represents a period of stability in the Court's membership. The "Index of Interagreement" was devised by Glendon Schubert in 1958 as a measure for determining the degree of interagreement in non-unanimous cases. Schubert posits .70 as high, .60 to .69 as moderate, and below .60 as low.[20] The center bloc controlled five votes. In

Table 1

Index of interagreement in split decisions of the Taft Court from 1922
(beginning 261 U.S. 86) to 1924 (ending 267 U.S. 132)

	Brandeis	Holmes	Taft	Van Devanter	Butler	McKenna	Sanford	Sutherland	McReynolds
Brandeis	–	77	61	51	51	44	54	34	41
Holmes	77	–	74	63	63	55	68	47	45
Taft	61	74	–	89	87	77	89	60	46
Van Devanter	51	63	89	–	95	78	85	67	45
Butler	51	63	87	95	–	83	85	61	48
McKenna	44	55	77	78	83	–	75	53	38
Sanford	54	68	89	85	85	75	–	72	55
Sutherland	34	47	60	67	61	53	72	–	67
McReynolds	41	45	55	45	48	38	55	67	–
Percent assent	59	70	92	93	93	80	93	69	53

Brandeis-Holmes	0.77
Center Bloc	0.778
Sanford-Sutherland	0.72

addition, Taft could count on a high level of support from Holmes. The two voted together 74 percent of the time.

The rate of dissent on the early Taft Court was dramatically lower than that of the Court in the waning days of the chief justiceship of Taft's predecessor, Edward Douglass White. The same observers, however, who credit Taft with this achievement are equally quick to note that the dissent rate on the Court jumped after 1925.[21] In large part, the post-1925 rise in dissents can be attributed to the adoption of the Judiciary Act of 1925 (the "Judges' Act"). One of Taft's most significant accomplishments (see Appendixes 1 and 2 for Taft's testimony before congressional committees on its behalf), the act eliminated many trivial cases from the Court's docket. These were cases that prior to 1926 the Court would have had to take, cases that likely would have been decided by unanimous vote. Thus, while the percentage of cases not decided unanimously does climb in the terms after 1925, the number of cases decided by full opinion also declines dramatically. If one assumes that the cases no longer heard by the Court—cases that fewer than four judges deemed to involve a "substantial federal question"[22]—would have been noncontroversial had they remained on the docket, their inclusion would have reduced the dissent rate to a level almost identical to that found on the Court during Taft's first four full years as chief. For example, if you take the average of the number of cases disposed of by full opinion beginning with the 1922 term and ending with the

Table 2
Rate of dissent on the Taft Court, by term

Term	Total dissents	Solo dissents	Total opinions	Percent dissent
1921	37	8	175	.211
1922	18	4	225	.08
1923	22	8	214	.103
1924	21	11	231	.091
1925	17	8	211	.081
1926	29	9	198	.146
1927	25	3	171	.146
1928	22	8	126	.174
1929	7	1	34	.205

1925 term, it is 219. By contrast, in 1927 the Court handed down only 171 cases with full opinions (as opposed to cases disposed of summarily). Assuming that the cases that no longer took up the Court's time as a result of the Judiciary Act of 1925 would likely have been disposed of without dissent, their inclusion would have changed the dissent rate for 1927 and made it more similar to the earlier low rates. Thus, if the Court had decided not 171 cases, as it did in 1927, but rather a number equal to the pre-1925 yearly average of 219 and if these additional cases were decided without dissent, the dissent rate for 1927 would have been .114 instead of the actual rate of .146. The former rate would have not been much different than the low dissent rate of the early Taft Court.

The later Taft Court, however, did show certain differences from the pre-1925 body. The appointment of Harlan Fiske Stone, Calvin Coolidge's attorney general, to succeed the aged and infirm Justice Joseph McKenna changed the Court's chemistry dramatically. With the accession of Stone, the last justice to join the Taft Court, there quickly developed a three-member bloc consisting of Stone and Justices Brandeis and Holmes. Unlike the Holmes-Brandeis dyad in table 1, however, this new bloc appears to have separated Taft from Holmes. The rate of interagreement between the two drops from 74 percent (high) to 60 percent (moderate, verging on low). At the same time, Justice George Sutherland begins to vote more often with Taft and the other members of the majority (center) bloc.

Comparing the earlier and later periods for dissents, one can see that Taft found himself presiding over a Court that was beginning to divide along the lines—clear liberal and conservative blocs—that would characterize the pre-1937 Hughes Court. Tables 4 and 5 show the number of dissenting votes cast by each justice. An index of cohesion is calculated for each. Following Schu-

Table 3

	Brandeis	Holmes	Stone	Taft	Van Devanter	Sanford	Butler	Sutherland	McReynolds
Brandeis	–	80	63	47	47	46	35	42	29
Holmes	80	–	78	60	56	46	46	44	33
Stone	63	78	–	67	62	62	54	55	39
Taft	47	60	67	–	91	80	78	70	60
Van Devanter	47	56	62	91	–	77	87	71	61
Sanford	46	46	62	80	77	–	71	73	60
Butler	35	46	54	78	87	71	–	83	59
Sutherland	43	44	55	70	76	73	83	–	56
McReynolds	29	33	39	60	61	60	59	56	–
Percent assent	52	63	68	94	94	84	76	75	63

Index of interagreement	
Left Bloc	0.74
Center Bloc	0.72

bert, an index of cohesion is defined as "the ratio of the mean of the included dissenting pairs, in a postulated bloc, to the mean of the total dissents of the included justices."[23] More than .50 is considered to be high and .40 to .49 is seen as moderate.

Although the results of Taft's efforts at building consensus began to fray in the late 1920s and totally collapsed after he left the Court, his administrative accomplishments continued to be felt. Indeed, few gainsay his accomplishments in this regard.[24] Even the critical Justice Felix Frankfurter said of Taft that his "great claim in history will be as a reformer," and that he had adapted the federal judicial system "to the needs of a country that had grown from three million to a hundred and forty."[25]

As president, Taft had regularly importuned Congress to proceed with various reforms of the federal judiciary.[26] As chief justice he continued in like fashion, with his great triumphs being the adoption of the Judges' Bill of 1925 and his successful lobbying of Congress for the appropriation of funds for a separate building for the third branch of government.[27] The Judges' Bill finally freed the Court from much of its obligatory docket and allowed it greater discretion in determining which cases it would hear. Earlier, Taft had convinced Congress to authorize the Judicial Conference with the chief justice, *ex officio,* as chair. Equally significant for the development of the Court in the twentieth century was the erection of the magnificent—Justice Brandeis, among others,

Table 4

	Brandeis	Holmes	Sanford	Taft	Van Devanter	Butler	McKenna	Sutherland	McReynolds
Brandeis	(3)	9	0	1	0	0	1	0	6
Holmes	9	(0)	1	2	0	0	1	2	2
Sanford	0	1	(0)	1	0	0	0	2	2
Taft	1	2	1	(0)	1	1	1	0	0
Van Devanter	0	0	0	1	(0)	2	1	1	0
Butler	0	0	0	1	2	(0)	2	0	0
McKenna	1	1	0	1	1	2	(3)	1	1
Sutherland	0	2	2	0	1	0	1	(0)	7
McReynolds	6	2	2	0	0	0	1	7	(5)
Total dissents	16	12	3	3	3	3	8	11	19

Index of cohesion

IC [left]

Holmes-Brandeis   0.644

IC [right]

Sutherland-McReynolds   0.467

Table 5

	Brandeis	Holmes	Stone	Sanford	Taft	Van Devanter	Butler	Sutherland	McReynolds
Brandeis	(9)	37	24	5	1	0	2	1	8
Holmes	37	(1)	25	3	2	0	1	2	4
Stone	24	25	(2)	5	2	0	3	6	4
Sanford	5	3	5	(0)	2	0	4	8	7
Taft	1	2	2	2	(1)	2	2	2	2
Van Devanter	0	0	0	0	2	(0)	7	4	2
Butler	2	1	3	4	2	7	(1)	15	8
Sutherland	1	2	6	8	2	4	15	(3)	10
McReynolds	8	4	4	7	2	2	8	10	(18)
Total dissents	53	41	34	18	7	7	25	27	41

Index of cohesion

IC [left]   0.677

Butler-Sutherland   0.577

thought it too grand—Grecian-style temple that engaged Taft's loving attention but that he did not live to see completed.[28] Aside from the grandeur,
Brandeis was concerned with what moving away from Congress would mean
for relations between the two branches. One wonders what relations would
have been in succeeding decades had the Court remained attached to the
Capitol.

That Taft was a success in this aspect of his role as chief justice is beyond
doubt. "[N]o chief justice thus far in our history [1992] matched his active
role in court administration, and his leadership in bringing about legislation
that gave needed discretion to the Court to control its docket."[29] The same
historian, Jonathan Lurie of Rutgers University, concludes, however, that, in
contrast to his administrative triumphs, "too often his decisions reflected a
fear of change rather than its necessary facilitation."[30] Pringle is harsher,
dubbing him "conservative, if not reactionary."[31]

A *Time* magazine observation made at the time of Taft's retirement may
have been most on target in remarking of his tenure: "Outstanding decisions: none."[32] More recently, a scholar of the chief justice has noted that
"Taft has drifted into almost total professional eclipse . . . , no more known
to the average lawyer or law student than are Chief Justices White, Fuller, or
Waite."[33] Current students of neither law nor political science are apt to be
frequently exposed to his writings.[34]

Alpheus Thomas Mason, Taft's pre-eminent judicial biographer, characterizes Taft's record as "chameleonlike."[35] Whether this characterization is
complimentary or not is, perhaps, arguable. It does, however, set Taft apart
from the other leading judicial conservatives of the period, such as Pierce
Butler, James McReynolds, Willis Van Devanter, and George Sutherland,
however "intertwined [Taft was in many regards] with the aspirations and
accomplishments of . . . the Four Horsemen."[36] As members of the Hughes
Court, these four were rarely, if ever, to change their coloration to suit current conditions, even if such conditions included the Depression of the
1930s. Taft's opinions on unions and picketing are examples of what his supporters might term flexibility. His union critics must have been somewhat
surprised and pleased by the *Tri-Cities Trades Council* case, 257 U.S. 184
(1921), only to have their worst fears confirmed in the same term in *Truax v.
Corrigan,* 257 U.S. 312 (1921).

Part of Taft's reputation as a die-hard conservative might come from some
of the outrageous comments he made during his career, especially toward the

end of his service on the Court. Taft, who was diagnosed with hardening of the arteries and who relied in his later years on Justice Sutherland to complete some of the opinions issued in his name, was fearful of what would come when he left the Court. Hoover, he felt, was just like Holmes, Brandeis, and Stone—a Progressive![37] Mason and Beaney quote a 1929 letter from Taft to his fellow conservative justice, Pierce Butler, in which Taft worried that "the most we can hope for is continued life of enough of the present membership to prevent disastrous reversals."[38] Pritchett quotes Taft during the same period as warning that "I must stay in the Court in order to prevent the Bolsheviki from gaining control."[39] Such comments, however, cropped up even in his early years as chief. Mason quotes Taft, for example, as promising to block all "socialistic raids on property rights."[40]

Surely Taft was a conservative, but in fact all the justices of the time were conservatives of some stripe.[41] Brandeis, the true Jeffersonian Democrat, feared the vice of big government, even if he did not share the Big Chief's fear of a "Bolshevik" threat to America.[42] One aspect of Taft's understanding of his role as a judge sets him apart from the likes of Brandeis and Holmes: his warm embrace of judicial activism. Taft believed firmly in the power of the judiciary to make law. In this he was akin to the great Cardozo, but unlike Cardozo and other advocates of self-restraint, Taft believed that it was not simply the right of the judge to act, but his duty to do so.[43] Cardozo would caution that judges were limited, that their task was to work within the "'interstices' of the law" and to respect precedent.[44] Taft, in contrast, boasted after his confirmation that he had "announced at a conference of the Justices that he "had been appointed to reverse a few decisions" and, with his famous chuckle, added, "I looked right at old man Holmes when I said it."[45]

This activism manifested itself not only in the number of statutes that the Taft Court declared unconstitutional—Henry Abraham, for example, identifies twelve cases in which the Taft Court voided a federal statute—but also in the way Taft appeared to ignore any factors that might have allowed a less activist Court to sustain a law.[46] In *Truax v. Corrigan,* 257 U.S. 312 (1921), Taft saw all alternative remedies for the owners of "The English Kitchen" cut off by the Arizona statute. In the much less well known case of *Wuchter v. Pizzutti,* 276 U.S. 13 (1928), Taft, in contrast to Holmes, Brandeis, and Stone, who also saw potential due process problems with the New Jersey law, saw the statute as on its face a violation of procedural due process.

In addition to his activism and his love of judicial power, and, particularly, its exercise, another major factor shaping Taft's judicial record was his admiration for John Marshall and the principles underlying the arguments in favor of the Constitution found in the *Federalist Papers*. His writings and lectures prior to becoming chief justice resonate with the influence of Marshall and Hamilton. For Taft, as for the framers, property rights were seen as the basis for individual rights, and a strong federal government, a presidency in control of the entire executive branch of government, and an independent judiciary were the means by which rights could be protected. As a disciple of Marshall, Taft was keen to defend federal supremacy from any encroachments by states on areas delegated to the federal government. As a disciple of Hamilton, he invariably rose to the defense of both judicial and executive power, seeing their preservation as essential for maintaining an effective system of checks and balances.

The influence of Marshall is noted by most students of Taft.[47] His oft-stated admiration for Marshall stemmed in part from the fact that it was Marshall who made the judiciary, and in particular the Supreme Court, a major player in the governmental process. Marshall, by his opinion in *Marbury v. Madison*, 1 Cranch (5 U.S.) 137 (1803), had moved the Court out of the shadows cast by the other two branches of government. Like former secretary of state Marshall, Taft never envisioned his career on the Court as an end to an already enviable political career but rather as the crowning capstone of that career. Both chiefs clearly relished power.

Taft's view of how the Constitution was to be interpreted was also drawn from the Marshall era. It was a Constitution "intended to endure for ages to come" (*McCulloch v. Maryland*, 4 Wheat [17 U.S.] 316, at 322 [1819]), and therefore its interpretation called for judicial craftsmanship. The "slot-machine" theory of justice, an addition best exemplified in a subsequent decade by Justice Owen Roberts's decision in *United States v. Butler*, 297 U.S. 1 (1936), which held that the duty of a judge is "to lay the article of the Constitution which is invoked beside the statute which is challenged and to decide whether the latter squares with the former," had no appeal for him.

Thus, unlike other judicial conservatives of the late nineteenth century and, particularly, those who sat with Taft on the 1920s Court, Taft rejected the positivist or declaratory theory of the law. Instead, he concurred, surprisingly, with the notions of Holmes and Brandeis as to the importance of considering the lessons learned from sociology and economics. The lessons learned, however, were often quite different for the activist Taft than for the self-restraintist Holmes and Brandeis. For Taft, "shaping the law to meet new situations [was] the Court's 'highest and most useful function.' The notion that 'judges should interpret the exact intention of those who established the Constitution' was the 'theory of one who does not understand the proper administration of justice.'"[48] Judicial knowledge of economics and sociology would help preserve the best of American institutions.[49]

In interpreting the powers of Congress under the Commerce Clause (I-8–3), Taft was likely to follow what most scholars would agree is the tradition of John Marshall. In these cases, he was apt to go along with the wishes of Congress, even if those who challenged the law invoked the rights of property or the liberty of contract doctrine. In fact, one historian says of his Commerce Clause decisions that "Taft was a decided liberal," and another speculates that Taft would have approved of Hughes's famous "switch in time that saved nine" decision in *N.L.R.B. v. Jones & Laughlin Steel Corp.*, 301 U.S. 1 (1937).[50] Had Taft's health been better and had he served longer, it is possible that the clash between the Court and the other two branches of government that occurred shortly after his death might have been less intense and that the distinctions advocated by Cardozo and Brandeis between commerce subject to federal regulation and that subject to state regulation might have carried the day.

Taft's commerce decisions frequently ignored the infamous *United States v. E. C. Knight*, 156 U.S. 1 (1895), decision of Chief Justice Melville Fuller, which had distinguished between manufacturing, a state concern solely, and commerce, which occurs afterward and is alone subject to congressional power. Instead, Taft's opinions on the subject closely tacked the stance set forth by Justice Holmes in the landmark case of *Swift v. United States*, 196 U.S. 375 (1905). He did this most notably in the case of *Stafford v. Wallace*, 258 U.S. 495 (1922), upholding for a unanimous Court the constitutionality of the Packers and Stockyards Act of 1921 and in *Board of Trade v. Olsen*, 262 U.S. 1 (1923), where Taft's liberal reading of the commerce power forced Justices McReynolds and Sutherland into dissent. Taft's opinion in the second child labor case, *Bailey v. Drexel Furniture Company*, 259 U.S. 20 (1922), obviously takes a less expansive view of federal power, but it should be noted that *Bailey* has not been overturned and that, as Justice Frankfurter would subsequently stress in an opinion that cited *Bailey*, Taft's opinion in *Bailey* had "the silent accord of Justices Brandeis and Holmes."[51]

Taft is more typical of the pre-1937 Hughes Court on issues involving state regulation of property. Here his love of the rights of private property combines with the Federalist suspicion of local majorities and how such majorities use power to violate "vested rights." *Wolff v. Court of Industrial Relations*, 262 U.S. 522 (1923), offers an example of this. In contrast, Taft's famous dissent in *Adkins v. Children's Hospital*, 261 U.S. 525 (1923)—admittedly a case involving the exercise of federal and not state power—and specifically his conclusion in *Adkins* that *Lochner v. New York*, 198 U.S. 45 (1905), was no longer viable as precedent (261 U.S. 525, at 564) does indicate that Taft's embrace of the sanctity of liberty of contract was not absolute. He did adjust a Fieldian philosophy to the spirit of the times.[52]

The "old Court," the pre-1937 Court, was generally little concerned with issues of individual rights and liberties apart from that of property and contract, nor was it interested in issues of equal protection. Given the conservative tenor of the Court, it is surprising that the process of incorporation, whereby the guarantees of the Bill of Rights are applied to the states through the due process clause of the Fourteenth Amendment, began during Taft's tenure. *Gitlow v. New York,* 268 U.S. 652 (1925), initiated this practice. Surprisingly, there was no dissent among the nine justices as to the applicability of the guarantee of free speech as a restraint on state police power.

Taft never wrote an opinion that specifically addressed the issue of incorporation, but in those cases that dealt with individual rights he never took the position that states were not bound by the Bill of Rights. In fact, in several criminal cases, Taft seems to proceed as if the states were under the same restraints with regard to criminal procedure as the federal government.

His two major decisions on matters related to the Bill of Rights are surely of a type that one would expect of a conservative jurist. One, *United States v. Lanza,* 260 U.S. 377 (1922), which dealt with the guarantee of double jeopardy, remains good law. The other, more famous one, *Olmstead v. United States,* 277 U.S. 438 (1928), which dealt with wiretaps, stood as precedent until almost the end of the Warren Court.

Taft's view of the judiciary's role—in American society and as a coordinate branch of government—is perhaps the most significant legacy of his chief justiceship. Although it is hardly likely that he will ever be rated ahead of a Holmes or a Black or even a Frankfurter, Taft's view of the role of the Court is probably more contemporary than those of any of these judges. Taft operated in a political environment in which the other two branches of government were frequently deadlocked. "Cool Cal" Coolidge might have slept a lot, as Alice Longworth Roosevelt was wont to note, but his veto pen was quite hot. The fourth party system was coming to a close, and with it the ability of government to take the initiative. In this vacuum of leadership, Taft and the Court could play a major role. Much the same as been observed concerning the Rehnquist Court in current American politics.[53]

Despite his remarks when first appointed to the bench, Taft's concern with precedent also seems contemporary and reflects the *cri de coeur* about the importance of precedent in insuring not just certainty in the law but the power of the Court issued in *Planned Parenthood v. Casey,* 505 U.S. 833 (1992), by the three justices—O'Connor, Kennedy, and Souter—whose votes determine most of the present Court's close decisions.

Finally, Taft's commitment to "vested rights" provided the basis upon which the "modern Court" moved to protect individual rights and liberties, both those found in the text of the Bill of Rights and those found in the vague contours of the Fourteenth Amendment's due process and equal protection clauses. Writing in 1968, Mason and Beaney observed that "the new interest in judicial guardianship . . . has not won full support."[54] Whether or not it had "full support," many commentators have concluded that the Burger Court was far more apt to assume the role of "Guardian Kings" than was its predecessor, and that the Rehnquist Court seems to have continued the course of sitting as a superlegislature as each June it routinely strikes down a brace of federal legislation.[55] Taft would understand.

Yet in the final analysis, Chief Justice Taft was a part of the America of the 1920s. He was the "the most influential constitutionalist of the 1920s," and his tenure as chief was hailed broadly at his retirement.[56] However different his arguments sound to contemporary ears, in reading Taft one must remember, as Archibald Cox has so eloquently written, that "while the opinions of the Court can help to shape our national understanding of ourselves, the roots of its decisions must be already in the nation. The aspirations voiced by the Court must be those the community is willing not only to avow but in the end to live by. The legitimacy of the great constitutional decisions rests upon the accuracy of the Court's perception of this kind of common will and upon the Court's ability, by expressing its perception, ultimately to command a consensus."[57]

Notes

1. Alpheus Thomas Mason, *The Supreme Court from Taft to Warren* (Baton Rouge: Louisiana State University Press, 1968), 43–44.

2. William Howard Taft to Horace D. Taft, January 28, 1900, as quoted in Henry F. Pringle, *The Life and Times of William Howard Taft: A Biography,* 2 vols. (New York: Farrar and Rinehart, Inc., 1939), 1:148.

3. Fred Rodell, *Nine Men: A Political History of the Supreme Court from 1790 to 1955* (New York: Random House, 1955), 189.

4. Donald F. Anderson, "Building National Consensus: The Career of William Howard Taft," paper presented at the annual meeting of the American Political Science Association (Boston, September 3–6, 1998), 26–27.

5. Walter F. Murphy, C. Herman Pritchett, and Lee Epstein, eds., *Courts, Judges, and Politics: An Introduction to the Judicial Process,* 5th edition (Boston: McGraw Hill, 2002), 88.

6. Judith I. Anderson, *William Howard Taft: An Intimate History* (New York: Norton, 1981), 259.

7. A. Anderson, "Building," 22.

8. Henry J. Abraham, *Justices and Presidents: A Political History of Appointments to the Supreme Court,* 3rd edition (New York: Oxford University Press, 1992), 188.

9. Ibid., 187.

10. Pringle, *Life and Times,* 2:968.

11. On Taft's stamina, Pringle writes, "Preparing for his new duties, Taft drafted a schedule for his daily life. He rose at 5:15, began work at 6 o'clock . . . [worked all day, went home], worked from five to seven, took an hour off for dinner, and labored again until ten o'clock. This would be his hour to retire" (*Life and Times,* 2:961–62). Regarding his leadership role, David J. Danelski introduced the concept that the effectiveness of the Court depended upon the functions of both task leader and social leader being performed. Although Hughes was able to perform both, Danelski argued that during the Taft Court Justice Willis Van Devanter acted as task leader while Taft functioned as social leader ("The Influence of the Chief Justice in the Decisional Process," in *Courts, Judges, and Politics,* ed. Murphy, Pritchett, and Epstein, 663–64).

12. Wrote Holmes: "We call you Chief Justice still—for we can not give up the title by which we have known you all these later years and which you have made dear to us. We can not let you leave us without trying to tell you how dear you have made it. You came to us from achievement in other fields and with the prestige of the illustrious place that you lately held and you showed us in new form your voluminous capacity for getting work done, your humor that smoothed the rough places, your golden heart that brought you love from very side and most of all from your brethren whose tasks you have made happy and light. We grieve at your illness, but your spirit has given life and impulse that will abide whether you are with us or away" (280 U.S. v [1930]).

13. Albert P. Blaustein and Roy M. Mersky, *The First One Hundred Justices: Statistical Studies on the Supreme Court of the United States* (Hamden, Conn.: Archon Books, 1978), 37–38.

14. Michael Comiskey, "Has the Modern Senate Confirmation Process Affected the Quality of U.S. Supreme Court Justices?" paper presented at the annual meeting of the American Political Science Association (Boston, September 3–6, 1998), 15.

15. Abraham reports the results from eight surveys of presidential success and failure (*Justices and Presidents,* 415–17). The Taft quote is from Herbert S. Duffy, *William Howard Taft* (New York: Minton, Balch & Company, 1930), 313, as cited in Kenneth B. Umbreit, *Our Eleven Chief Justices,* vol. 2 (Washington, N.Y.: Kennikat Press, 1969), 397.

16. "McReynolds and Brandeis belong to a class of people that have no loyalty to the court and sacrifice almost everything to the gratification of their own publicity and wish to stir up dissatisfaction with the decision of the Court, if they don't happen to agree with it" (W. H. Taft to C. P. Taft II, October 30, 1926, as quoted in Alpheus Thomas Mason, *William Howard Taft, Chief Justice* [New York: Simon and Schuster, 1965], 226). Mason here asserts that "Taft's castigation of McReynolds exceeded that against Brandeis" (226–27; see also 215–17).

17. Danelski, "Influence," 668.

18. Lawrence Martin, *The Presidents and the Prime Ministers* (Markham, Ontario: Paper Jacks, Ltd., 1982), 72.

19. The Butler quote is from Martin, *Presidents,* 72. On Brandeis, see Alexander M. Bickel, *The Unpublished Opinions of Mr. Justice Brandeis: The Supreme Court at Work* (Cambridge: Harvard University Press, 1957).

20. Glendon A. Schubert, "The Study of Judicial Decision-Making as an Aspect of Political Behavior," *American Political Science Review* 52 (1958): 1013.

21. Cf. Mason, *William Howard Taft,* 255; Mason, *Supreme Court,* 61. Danelski points out that after 1925 Taft was more likely to assign the opinion of the Court to one of the conservatives and not use the assignment as a means of winning over one of the more liberal (self-restraint-oriented) justices ("Influence," 667).

22. The "rule of four" appears to date back to 1891. After 1891 cases that came to the Court on "discretionary" writs required the vote of four justices to be added to the docket. The Judiciary Act of 1925 dramatically reduced still further the number of cases the Court had to take as a matter of right, thereby increasing the Court's discretion to determine the cases it heard. As part of Taft's lobbying effort before Congress on behalf of this legislation, Taft's chief lieutenant on the Court, Justice Willis Van Devanter, made what subsequent Courts and justices have seen as a commitment to employ "the rule of four." "We always grant the petitions [for review of a case] when as many as four think that it should be granted and sometimes when as many as three think that way. We proceed upon the theory that, if that number out of the nine are impressed with the thought that the case is one that ought to be heard and decided by us, the petition should be granted" (As quoted in David M. O'Brien, *Storm Center: The Supreme Court in American Politics,* 6th edition [New York: W.W. Norton & Company, 2003], 208). In 1988 Congress finally ended the practice that required certain cases to be taken by the Court. The current Court, as a result, has no obligatory caseload. During the 1980s the Court under Chief Justice Warren Burger appears to have relaxed the "rule of four." The result was that it was necessary only for three judges to wish to add a case. One consequence of this was a dramatic increase in the number of cases the Court heard. Chief Justice William Rehnquist ended this practice and reduced the Court's workload by over one third.

23. Schubert, "Study," 1011.

24. An excellent survey of Taft's role in modernizing the federal judiciary can be had in Robert Post, "Judicial Management and Judicial Disinterest: The Achievements and Perils of Chief Justice William Howard Taft," 1 *Journal of Supreme Court History* (1980): 50–78.

25. An unsigned editorial in the July 27, 1921, issue of the *New Republic,* written by then Harvard law professor Felix Frankfurter, sounded a very different note than had most of the contemporary press concerning Taft's appointment as chief justice. Cf., Alpheus Thomas Mason, *William Howard Taft,* 236–38. The quote is on page 15.

26. Allen E. Ragan, *Chief Justice Taft* (Columbus: The Ohio State Archaeological and Historical Society, 1937), 104–11. Ragan provides very possibly the best description and analysis of Taft's opinions of all the students of Taft's tenure as chief justice.

27. "Judges' Bill" is the popular term for what was in fact the Judiciary Act of 1925, one in a series of statutes that began with the Judiciary Act of 1789, whereby Congress, exercising its power under Article III, Section 2, regulates the appellate jurisdiction of the Court.

28. On Brandeis's opinion, see Philippa Strum, *Louis D. Brandeis: Justice for the People* (Cambridge: Harvard University Press, 1984), 354–55.

29. Jonathan Lurie, "William Howard Taft," in *The Oxford Companion to the Supreme Court of the United States,* ed. Kermit L. Hall, (New York: Oxford University Press, 1992), 856.

30. Ibid.

31. Pringle, *Life and Times,* 2:967.

32. As quoted in Post, "Judicial Management," 51.

33. Ibid., 50.

34. The leading law school casebooks carry few Taft opinions, as is the case with their counterparts in political science. Walter F. Murphy, James E. Fleming, and Sotiros A. Barber (*American Constitutional Interpretation*, 2nd edition [(Mineola, N.Y.: Foundation Press, 1995]) include only one Taft opinion: his dissent in *Adkins*. David M. O'Brien (*Constitutional Law and Politics: Civil Rights and Civil Liberties*, 2 vols., 3rd edition [New York: W.W. Norton & Company, 1997]) includes excerpts from Taft's opinion in *Olmstead* but gives almost twice as much space to selections from the Brandeis dissent. Alpheus Thomas Mason and Donald Grier Stephenson Jr. (*American Constitutional Law*, 12th edition [Upper Saddle River, N.J.: Prentice Hall, 1999]) appropriately—Mason is Taft's leading biographer—give the greatest space to Taft opinions, providing their readers with both *Stafford v. Wallace* and *Olmstead v. United States*. The sixth edition of the work (1978), edited by Mason and William M. Beaney, also contained *Bailey v. Drexel Furniture Co.* and *Adkins v. Children's Hospital*, both missing from the later edition. Taft's absence from law school casebooks is even more noticeable. Gerald Gunther and Kathleen M. Sullivan (*Constitutional Law*, 14th edition [Westbury, N.Y.: Foundation Press, 1997]) allot fifteen lines to a "summary" of Taft's opinion in *Myers*. William B. Lockhart, Yale Kamisar, Jesse H. Choper, and Steven H. Shiffrin (*The American Constitution*, 7th edition [Saint Paul: West Publishing Co., 1991]) include none of Taft's opinions.

35. Mason, *William Howard Taft*, 261.

36. G. Edward White, *The American Judicial Tradition: Profiles of Leading American Judges* (New York: Oxford University Press, 1976), 179.

37. Pringle, *Life and Times*, 2:967.

38. Alpheus Thomas Mason and William M. Beaney, *The Supreme Court in a Free Society* (New York: W. W. Norton & Company, 1968), 162.

39. C. Herman Pritchett, *The Roosevelt Court* (New York: MacMillan and Company, 1948), 18.

40. Mason, *Supreme Court*, 52.

41. Ibid., 71.

42. The fact that Brandeis did not dissent in *Wolff v. Court of Industrial Relations*, 262 U.S. 522 (1923) was not a tactical decision by Brandeis as in the case of other withheld dissents. "Warmly approving Taft's opinion, Brandeis thought it would 'clarify thought and bury the ashes of a sometime [compulsory-arbitration] boom'" (Mason, *William Howard Taft*, 253).

43. Benjamin N. Cardozo, *The Nature of the Judicial Process* (New Haven: Yale University Press, 1921), 141.

44. Ibid., 113, 93–94.

45. Mason, *Supreme Court*, 52.

46. Henry J. Abraham, *The Judicial Process: An Introductory Analysis of the Courts of the United States, England, and France*, 7th ed. (New York: Oxford University Press, 1998), 304. Included in this total is *Adkins*, from which the chief dissented. On the whole, Abraham classifies the Taft Court as "cooperative" and not challenging the other two branches inordinately, unlike, for example, the Marshall, Taney, Fuller, Hughes, and Warren Courts (373–74).

47. Cf. Mason, *William Howard Taft*, 244; Ragan, *Chief Justice Taft*, 79; David H. Burton, *Taft, Holmes, and the 1920s Court* (Madison, N.J.: Fairleigh Dickinson University Press, 1998), 147. Paul L. Murphy ("Constitutional History, 1921–1933," in *American Constitutional History*, ed. Leonard W. Levy, Kenneth L. Karst, and Dennis J. Mahoney [New

York: MacMillan and Company, 1989]) adds John Locke, Adam Smith, and the Manchester economists—William Blackstone, Thomas Cooley, and Herbert Spencer—to the list of those whose thinking influenced Taft (207).

48. Mason, *Supreme Court,* 48.

49. Ibid., 51.

50. Ragan, *Chief Justice Taft,* 119; Burton, *Taft, Holmes,* 151.

51. Mason, *William Howard Taft,* 248.

52. White, *American Judicial Tradition,* 180–81.

53. Linda Greenhouse, "The Justices Decide Who's in Charge," *New York Times,* June 27, 1999, 4. The Greenhouse article begins with the simple statement: "The Supreme Court rules." Chief Justice Taft must smile atop the pediment of his Temple.

54. Mason and Beaney, *Supreme Court,* 348.

55. The term "Guardian Kings" is taken from Mason, *William Howard Taft,* 262.

56. Paul L. Murphy, "Constitutional History,"207.

57. Archibald Cox, *The Role of the Supreme Court in American Government* (New York: Oxford University Press, 1976), 117–18.

LIBERTY UNDER LAW

Liberty under Law

An Interpretation of the Principles of Our Constitutional Government

Mr. Cutler, the public-spirited donor of this Lecture Foundation, in the letter establishing it, expressed the view that where our political system shows weakness, it fails for lack of sound education of our people:

(1) In the principles of our Constitutional Government;

(2) In the history of its development and its application to changing conditions; and

(3) In the moral standards best developed in religious teaching and not safely to be separated from university work. He, therefore, concluded that the most useful contribution he could make, to render democracy safe for the world, was to found a course of lectures to promote serious consideration by as many people as possible of the fundamental and vital elements of permanence in the Constitutional Government in the United States. I am proud to have been selected as the first speaker in this course.

Accepting the language of the gift as the text for this opening lecture, we must examine what is the true nature of our Constitutional Government as a means of judging what is needed to preserve it.

The Constitution of the United States was not born as Minerva is said to have been, full armed from the brain of Jove. No great and abiding institution ever is. It was the first written constitution of an independent nation which, after creating its governmental organization and the agencies by which it was to be carried on, imposed on those agencies effective limitations of their powers by creating machinery for enforcing most of them. It recognized the ultimate power in the people of the United States and in their name proceeded to frame restrictions upon themselves as to how they might exercise their power through their appointed or elected agencies. In independent nations, this was a new conception; but it was not a long step from the kind of popular government which the colonies, the predecessors of the states, had had in exercising their powers under royal charters. Here the framers of the Federal Constitution found the suggestion of a written and defined form of government and of the enforcement of the limitations of its power. Whenever they departed from their charters, the British Government held such departures of no effect. It was easy with this experience for the people who were the makers of the new nation to take the steps, first, of prescribing in written compact the character of the government to be formed, and, second, of imposing on themselves the formal restraints by which they should be made to keep within the terms of that compact.

The second feature of the Constitution having a novel aspect was its federal character. This was forced on the Convention. The Revolution had been won by the states who had succeeded the colonies and who, after winning independence, lived along from 1783 to 1787 under the weak articles of the Confederation in relations and conditions going from bad to worse until, in spite of the bitter jealousies between them, they joined in an effort to improve the loose bond which the articles furnished. The states would not merge themselves in one government and the federation plan was adopted to retain local self-government and sovereignty in the states and yet to create out of the people of the states a nation having all needed functions for national purposes, and presenting a unit front to the world in international matters. There had been federations before, but never one in which the central government was so clearly national, and had its life and being so directly in all the people.

The third feature of the Government under the Federal Constitution was its purely representative character. It vested the ultimate power in the people, but it secured to them the exercise of that power only through representatives. The selection of the President was not put directly in the people but in an electoral college, members of which were to be appointed by the states in any way a state thought fit. The Senate was made up of two representatives from each state, large and small, and was not to be directly elected by the people but by the state legislatures. The House of Representatives was the only branch of the Government whose members were to be chosen directly and in numerical proportion by the people. The judges were to be appointed by the President and so were all the executive subordinates of the

President. It is true that since the Constitution was adopted, the Electoral College, which was created in order that its members might exercise their judgment as to the man to be selected as President, has in fact lost this power and is only an instrumentality for registering the people's vote as between previously ascertained candidates with a weight proportioned to the population of the states. The members of the Senate, too, are now directly elected by the people.

The slightest study of the history of the framing of the Constitution shows that the members of the Convention in large majority thought that the permanence and safety of the new government required provisions which should prevent a change of policy to meet every temporary wind of popular passion. The checks and balances between the popular will and its ultimate control created by our Federal Constitution are greater than with most popular governments. The rigid term of four years, by which the Executive remains in power no matter how strongly the people may give their verdict against him in the mid-term Congressional election, the six-year term of each of the Senators, arranged in three classes, so that only one-third of the Senate can be changed every two years, and even the certain full two years of each House of Representatives, however great the change in popular sentiment in a year, all make a contrast to what is called Responsible Government, like that in Great Britain, France, Canada, and other countries. Certainly, we are not a pure democracy governing by direct action, and the great men who framed our fundamental law did not intend that we should be.

The Constitution makers had it in mind to secure individual liberty, the right of personal and religious freedom, of property, and the pursuit of happiness. These include the right of labor and of contract, and the protection against deprivation of any of them save by due process of law. This protection was granted primarily against the National Government and many forms are made sacred in the administration of federal justice which Congress cannot transgress or ignore. In the Constitution as originally adopted not much federal protection was afforded against state action infringing individual liberty of the individual except that the states were forbidden to pass laws impairing the obligations of a contract; but, as a result of the Civil War, the desire to protect the negro in his new freedom led to the adoption of the thirteenth, fourteenth and fifteenth amendments, by which many individual rights were put under federal protection as against a violation of them by the state executives, legislatures and courts. The Federal Constitution today, therefore, guards a man in the enjoyment of his personal liberty, his property and his pursuit of happiness, whether violated by the Federal or State Government.

Thus are preserved to the individual that liberty of action and that equality of opportunity which it took a thousand years of struggle to secure from monarchy and aristocracy. The judicial branch of the Federal Government is vested with the final duty and power of making effective this protection of the individual in his right against the sovereign people.

The last feature of our Constitutional Government which we need notice is the machinery for its amendment. To change it, two-thirds of each House of Congress, and the legislatures of three-fourths of the states must concur. This is not a referendum to the people. It is a referendum to the people's representatives. We may reasonably infer that the framers of the Constitution did not intend to have our fundamental law amended by any temporary wave of popular frenzy.

When the Constitution was adopted, the proportion of the electorate to the whole population was much smaller than it is now. "We the people," who ordained and established the Constitution, were not more than 150,000 voters in the thirteen states which had then a population of four million, including men, women and children. This was due to the required qualifications for voting which, in many states, included not only the ownership of property but also religious conformity, and excluded women, children and slaves. The steady trend since that day has been toward an enlargement of the electorate, so that today we are a much more popular government than we were under Washington. Property and religious qualifications have all disappeared. The greater the number of the governed who can take part in the Government, the juster it is likely to be to each group or class, and so the stronger and more permanent it will become, assuming that all are sufficiently intelligent to know what their interests are. A small ratio of voters to the population does not necessarily, however, make an aristocracy. It was not true, for instance, that in the past women had no voice in the Government. They did have. They were represented by the men of their family and were willing to be so represented. Their identity with their husbands, fathers and brothers in the interest of the family unit was such that they felt that their interest was protected by their male voters. But the spread of education and knowledge of affairs among them, the increase of those who had no male voters to act for them, and the pressure on them to earn a separate livelihood, were circumstances giving many of them a consciousness of misrepresentation which led to the demand that has been heard. Minors are not allowed to vote because their immaturity unfits them to vote discreetly and wisely, and the identity of their interest with that of their parents secures them protection in the franchise of their parents. Alien residents are not allowed to vote because their allegiance to another country deprives them of that abiding loyalty to this which should be present as a controlling influence upon every voter.

By the fifteenth and nineteenth amendments we have so increased the ratio of those entitled to vote to the whole population that it is now two-fifths of all instead of one twenty-fifth as it was when the Constitution was adopted. The fifteenth amendment has been nullified in eleven Southern states so that at least a million colored voters do not vote, and in all parts of the country many of all colors and sexes who can vote do not exercise the privilege. Probably a fourth of the population now vote in a Presidential election. This leaves three-fourths of those who are governed who do not take voting part in the Government. Yet we have the widest franchise possible. It is well to bear this in mind when we are discussing practical government. We must understand that the purest democracy with the widest possible franchise must still be a representative government in the sense that one-fourth must always speak for three-fourths of the governed in determining the course of that government. Moreover, we must know that even under the most liberal franchise, a majority and more of the governed have to obey laws they take no part in making and the minority have to obey laws they oppose. The theory that in self-government men need obey only the laws they make is unsound in fact and vicious in its justification for lawlessness. There is no form of government the successful operation of which needs so much implicit obedience to law, whether agreeable or not, as a democracy.

Even with the expansion of the electorate from the one twenty-fifth to one-fourth of the people, the Federal Constitution is still substantially intact and works smoothly and effectively to accomplish the purpose of its framers and to defend us all against the danger of sudden gusts of popular passion and to secure for us the delay and deliberation in political changes essential to secure considered action by the people.

Ours is the oldest popular government in the world, and is today the strongest and most conservative. It is not an oligarchy or an aristocracy under the guise of Republican forms, and it never was. The people do rule and always have ruled in the United States. They have their will but they have it after a wholesome delay and deliberation which they have wisely forced themselves to take under the restrictions of a Constitution which, adopted by however small popular vote, they have fully approved by more than one hundred and thirty years of acquiescence. It is this voluntary self-restraint that has made their Government permanent and strong. It is a fundamental error to seek quick action in making needed changes of policy or in redressing wrong. Nations live a long time, and a year or five years are a short period in that life.

Most wrongs can be endured for a time without catastrophe. Reforms that are abiding are achieved step by step. It is better to endure wrongs than to effect disastrous changes in which the proposed remedy may be worse than the evil. Often things denounced as wrongs are not so. It needs attention and deliberation to decide first that a wrong exists, and second, what is the right remedy. A popular constituency may be misled by vigorous misrepresentation and denunciation. The shorter the time the people have to think, the better for the demagogue. One of the great difficulties in carrying on popular government is in getting into the heads of the intelligent voters what the real facts are and what reasonable deductions should be made from them. Any reasonable suspension of popular action until calm public consideration of reliable evidence can be secured is in the interest of a wise decision. That at least was what our forefathers thought in making our Federal Government and the result has vindicated them.

Many contrast our system with the Parliamentary Government to the disparagement of ours. I venture to think that sober-minded people in countries with responsible governments, as they are called, are beginning to note in these days of dangerous and demoralizing class consciousness the advantage of our system by which changes in government are delayed to respond to the real voice of the sober majority over one in which the tenure of a ministry in power is temporary and insecure, and in which changes of ministry follow in rapid succession. Such quick changes do not make for steady steering of the ship of state and create a doubt as to the future.

The effect of the War has been to shake dynasties to ruin. Those which have fallen deserved to fall. The Central European rulers merited what has come to them because they plotted to fasten upon the world the tyranny of military control. The Russian autocracy fell because the War gave the oppressed Russian people in all their suffering the chance to rid themselves of an abominably unjust rule. Yet in the ruins of these empires we have lost the equilibrium of obedience to law. It could not be otherwise. In the slow transition to well-ordered governments which shall succeed them, enemies of society, plotters of anarchy, destroyers of the bases upon which modern civilization has been built, have seized opportunity to array the lowest, the most ignorant, the most ill-conditioned against the intelligent, and the responsible. These latter are the saving part of all society and the hope of the world's progress. Yet it is sought to take away their beneficent leadership and influence, to end personal liberty and the right of property, and to establish a bloody tyranny of the proletariat under the control of a few misguided and cruel zealots. The Bolshevists in Russia have established themselves in power, have spread their propaganda aggressively in other countries and seek to concentrate into a moving and destructive force the unrest and dissatisfaction that the necessary upset of economic conditions and its accompanying hardships have created nearly everywhere. By dint of blatant lying, the utter failure of the Bolshevist rule to bring comfort or contentment to the masses of the people has been concealed somewhat from the discontented elsewhere, but it will out. Still, danger from the spirit which gave Bolshevism birth and life, continues throughout the world. We have it here but in less dangerous force than anywhere else. It is noisy here. It needs watching. It should be restrained. It may break out injuriously because modern lethal instruments give one man or a small group of men much greater power of local destruction than ever before, but the solid patriotism, conservatism and adherence to our system of government will make such attacks only futile waves against a stone wall. It is at such a time that the valuable rigidity of our changes in administration and our intervening representative agency, interpreting and enforcing the popular will, have their greatest value.

Our Constitution has been called too individualistic. It rests on personal liberty and the right of property. In the last analysis, personal liberty includes the right of property as it includes the right of contract and the right of labor. Our primary conception of a free man is one who can enjoy what he earns, who can spend it for his comfort or pleasure if he would, who can save it and keep it for his future use and benefit if he has the foresight and self-restraint to do so. This is the right of property. Upon this right rests the motive of the individual which makes the world materially to progress. Destroy it and material progress ceases. Until human nature becomes far more exalted in moral character and self-sacrifice than it is today, the motive of gain is the only one which will be constant to induce industry, saving, invention and organization, which will effect an increase in production greater than the increase in population. Indeed without it, production will decrease and so will the population, because starvation and disease will reduce it. With material progress, advance is possible in education and intelligence, in art, in morality and religion, in the spiritual. To such advance we must look for the antidote for the poison of crass materialism, of the selfish and cruel pursuit of wealth, of the ignoble lassitude of luxury and the evils of plutocracy. But these evils must not blind us, as they do blind many well-intentioned, dreamy reformers, to the fact that personal liberty and the right of property are indispensable to any possible useful progress of society.

The experiment which the Bolsheviki have been making in Russia has been hard upon the poor Russian people; but as a lesson to the world on the futility of communism, and of the destruction of property rights as a means of promoting better social conditions and greater comfort among the proletariat, it is very valuable. It is not being lost upon our workingmen. It is gratifying to find Mr. Gompers denouncing Bolshevism.

Our Government, our politics, and our society are not perfect, and abuses in one form or another persist that need abolition. In the period of enormous expansion of our country's prosperity during the closing twenty years of the last century, the politics of the country bade fair to pass into corporate control. The railroads then defied attempts to regulate them. Presidential campaigns were largely conducted on contributions from great corporations. Congress, legislatures, city councils and local authorities were under strong suspicion of yielding unduly to corporate influence. The situation called for a movement to drive corporations out of politics. Such a movement was undertaken and was successful. Accompanying it, however, was a demand for a change in our governmental system to prevent a recurrence of the evil. Direct and purer democracy, it was said, would be a permanent cure. It was urged that the representative system was at fault. The people as a mass must be given freedom to act at once and directly upon any evil in government. This was to be done by the Referendum, the Initiative, and the Recall. Through these, any one could initiate reform legislation and the people could pass it without trusting to the sense of duty of a legislature or a council. Through these, the people might end the official authority and life of an unsatisfactory public official. Moreover, the courts were to be subjected to direct supervision of the people, who might, after an unsatisfactory decision by a court, reverse the judgment by vote and in the same manner remove the judge from office. Nearly related to these new plans for popular government was the general primary, by which the representative system was abolished in party organization for the selection of party candidates and they were to be chosen by the votes of the people in a preliminary election.

After a decade or more of trial and test by actual experience, this adoption of so-called "purer" democracy has not been a success. It has been enormously expensive. The number of those voting on proposed statutes has been so much less than those voting for candidates at the same elections and, when the submission has been at a special election, the total vote has been so small as to show that voters do not think themselves fitted to express an opinion on legislation which should be discussed and adopted by men elected for the purpose to a legislative body. The Recall has not been much used and has only served to rob officials subject to it of that courage of action needed to do good work. Recall of judicial decisions and of judges has not been used at all.

This reform died "a-borning." The general primary has had a wide trial, but no one intimate with its working and results can be enthusiastic over it. Legislatures filled with men who have noted its effect would like to repeal the general primary laws and restore the party convention, but they do not dare to do so lest their opponents make political capital out of it. They know that it has vastly increased the expense of elections. It has made two necessary. It has not only cost the public a heavy outlay; but, what is worse, it has made impossible as a candidate for an elective office every one who is not the choice of the machine or is not independently wealthy. No one can afford to be a candidate unless he can count upon the support of the regular party organization or unless he can create a personal organization, and that costs much money. It has not destroyed, it has strengthened the control of the machine; but it has taken from it an obligation of responsibility. In this state, you have an informal extra-legal preliminary convention to avoid some of the abuses of the general primary. It is to be hoped that this masqueraded means of neutralizing the primary may yield to a courageous repeal of the law. There is no reason why the convention and the selection of delegates to it may not be surrounded with the same safeguards against corruption as a primary. We shall then have restored the opportunity for discussion and deliberation in the selection of party candidates.

The greatest evil the primary has done is the destruction of party responsibility for the fitness of candidates and of party discipline. In many states, men who are not loyal members of the party are enabled to take part in the primary and to seek to become candidates on the party ticket. Democratic voters in a Republican primary have not infrequently been able to foist on to the Republican party ticket a weak candidate whom the strong Democratic candidate can easily defeat, and *vice versa*. Factions who are not regular party supporters at all have put their own men on the regular party ticket and destroyed party solidarity. These things are impossible in a convention system. Moreover, the convention is needed to declare party principles. To have them declared by the candidates, as is often done under the primary system, is to put a premium on trimming and still further to impair the responsibility and utility of parties.

In my college days, I was wont to think of parties and partisanship as a necessary evil and something which ought to be abolished, if possible, and of the man who held himself aloof from party as the model to be followed. Washington, in his farewell address, deplores party and faction, and evidently hoped for a fading out of party in the carrying on of the Government. I am satisfied, after considerable opportunity for observation, that two great parties are the greatest aids to the successful administration of popular government. With-out them, the proper interpretation of the popular will into effective gov-ernmental action becomes very difficult. The division of voters into small groups with no majority control by any one paralyzes a government into doing nothing, into weak compromises, into a hand-to-mouth life. Division into groups means parties based on class and faction. It means the willing-ness of each to sacrifice the general interest of the country to the achieve-ment of a particular object. Parties based on class cleavage are inimical to broadly patriotic government for the benefit of all the people. Two great par-ties mean a cleavage down through all the strata of society, the wealthy, the educated, the moderate circumstanced, the business men, the workingmen, and the farmers. The group system tends to parties with a horizontal cleavage of the strata of society and we find the farmers in one party, the workingmen in another, the business men in another, the manufacturers in another, each contending for its special interest and ignoring the welfare of society as a whole. Normal party feeling in one of two great parties tends to neutralize this class and selfish spirit, and prompts a consideration of the interest of all classes of the people represented in the party. One great party makes the other better by its criticism and opposition. Each puts the other on its good behavior; but when there are many small groups, each for itself and its self-ish object, there is no considerable stimulus to good behavior on the part of any group. The group system is the opportunity of the socialist, the radical, the communist. It is the hope of the crank extremist. In every district where, though small in number, a group can exercise a balance of power, it bends the legislator to its will by threats. With no sense of responsibility as to gen-eral policies and the common good, it pushes its purpose. It thus sometimes happens that legislation is secured which the majority of the people would not favor on its merits but for which a comparatively small minority is will-ing to sacrifice everything.

I do not wish to deprecate the course of those broad-minded citizens of intelligent discrimination and patriotic purpose who, on grounds of general welfare, sometimes support one party and sometimes the other. They are es-sential in our system. They throw the election one way or the other as they vote. They do not exercise influence within the party but they have a most wholesome influence from without. But experience has shown that in nor-mal times, under natural impulses, many men attach themselves to one or the other of the great parties. That is, for the reason stated, a good thing. A great party is of necessity broad in its view of the country's welfare and from selfish motives somewhat careful in meeting its responsibility. Those who make up its rank and file insensibly acquire the same point of view. One of the essential aids to successful popular government is great leaders, and confidence in them is stimulated by the existence of parties.

I concede the evils which arise from hidebound partisanship at times. I am not blind to the motives of fancied political expediency which lead such parties into promotion of measures which are not best adapted to the needs of the country. They often put men in power who are neither the ablest nor the highest-minded of men available. They often trim when they should be courageous to meet an issue. But what I am pressing on you is that, constituted as they are of all sorts and conditions of men, they are much more likely to be American in their view and purpose, much more likely to be considerate of the whole country, and much less likely to be narrowly moved by the ambition of a selfish faction than the small "one-idea'd" group of whose dangerous purposes I have spoken.

Allegiance to a party should never lead one consciously to countenance wrong or injury to the public weal; but as we note the live dangers to our Republic, we are forced to admit that excessive partisanship is not now one of them, and that the institution and maintenance of great parties is an antidote for class consciousness and selfish factional diversion of national funds and energy into class preferment and away from the general good. We are still healthy. Organized labor seeks political ends at times. Often it presses for useful legislation and secures it. Then it seeks to defeat legislators and others who have not bent the knee to its class demands. It is gratifying to note that the leaders do not control the labor vote and that many workingmen refuse when they enter the voting booth to bear a class label. They are Republicans or Democrats. They look at the election from a broad American standpoint and vote their judgment. The man who carries the labor vote in his pocket is a bogy. Nor will the women constitute themselves a political party. No party can live founded on sex alone, now that sex is eliminated as a basis for political discrimination. Women voters will now become Democrats or Republicans as they ought to be, and will be guided by general country-wide considerations in the casting of their ballots.

The welfare of the community has been emphasized in modern days, and the ruder Anglo-Saxon doctrine of individual independence and every man for himself has properly yielded to a sense of greater responsibility of the community for its members. With this has come a greater qualification of the enjoyment of individual rights of liberty and property in the interest of the community as a whole. There was always such a qualification recognized by the courts and enforced by the Government, but the change in our social and physical conditions of life has emphasized it and enlarged it to conform to that change. As population has grown and great masses of people are concentrated in small areas, greater health preservatives are necessary, more careful provision for feeding the people from long distances has to be made, and all the machinery for maintaining them in comfort becomes more complicated, and the preservation of free currents of this kind becomes more important and a matter of government responsibility.

The right of property and the right of labor, when used in great combinations, have furnished means of extortion, oppression, and obstruction which Congress has passed laws to restrain and punish, and the courts have sustained such laws.

Social groups in a great community become more interdependent. One member cannot be as independent of another as when they lived in a wilderness miles apart. Our constitutional system has been easily elastic in these regards, and courts have not failed to apply it to conform to the needs of the community. These changing conditions have led some reformers to condemn what they call the excessive individualism of the Constitution. I confess I do not follow them. The rights of personal liberty and of property as protected by the courts are not obstructive to any reasonable qualification of these rights in the interest of the community. Indeed we may well question whether the paternalistic enthusiasm of such reformers has not gone too far. The strength of the American in the past has been in his independence and self-reliance. He asked only an equal chance with others and was content to abide the results of his own efforts. It was this spirit which carried our country on to its present marvellous development. A weakening sense of dependence on the Government, on the one hand, and an excessive confidence that legislation can do anything, on the other, have had a dangerous tendency to minimize this independence and self-reliance and have produced tons of statutory laws under which public money is wasted in futile attempts at their execution, and respect for all laws is injured by the ineffectiveness of so many. This disease of excessive legislation has been rendered more epidemic by the outbreak for pure democracy in the form of the Referendum and the Initiative. Through them private citizens, who conceive a panacea, can, by securing the necessary subscribers to a petition, impose upon a suffering public the obligation and cost of passing on the ill-digested product of ignorant, impracticable, but active and enthusiastic minds. Legislators learn that their industry and public service are measured by the glorious objects recited in the titles of their bills rather than by the practical working of them as laws for good. Hence their fecundity in bills and their eagerness in pressing them into law. The amount of useless legislation in the states of this country is appalling and is one of the most distressing signs of the times.

The lesson must be learned, expensive as it is proving to be, that there is only a limited zone within which legislation and governments can accomplish good. We cannot regulate beyond that zone with success or benefit. Governments are not adapted to do business as are individuals prompted by their gain in economy and efficiency, and should not be so burdened. Failures in government ownership and operation of enterprises, normally and legitimately adapted to private conduct, confront us on every side and should teach us their lesson.

If we do not conform to human nature in legislation we shall fail. We can waste money in helping individuals to a habit of dependence that will weaken our citizenship. We can, by passing laws which cannot be enforced, destroy that respect for laws and habituated obedience to law which has been the strength of people of English descent everywhere.

We must stop attempting to reform people by wholesale. It is the individual upon whom our whole future progress depends. In giving and securing scope for his ambition, energy, and free action our constitutional system has its chief merit, whatever would-be reformers say.

It goes without saying that if the government of the people would save itself it must secure to the individual person the education indispensable to his exercise of wide and wise discretion as a constituent member of the government. Our public school system is one of the foundation rocks of our community and, in theory at least, has always been declared by us to be so. It is not possible to give every man and woman a university education or even a secondary education, but it is possible to give him a thorough primary or common school education upon which, in the university of his life experience, he can build, as many of our greatest men have builded before him. We have always prided ourselves on our public schools; but we had a great shock to that pride when we examined the statistics of illiteracy revealed by the rigid examination of men enlisted or drafted into the army for the late war. We found a most distressing number of men who could not read or write among the native whites, of our citizenship. It is notorious, too, that our teachers are not properly paid, and that, therefore, they are not properly prepared to teach. We have a heavy task before us but we must do it. Not only is there this large number of native whites but the negroes and the foreign born greatly increase the number needing especial attention. It is so great a work that the agency of the National Government must be invoked to help in some practical and unobstructing way. In the wealthier states such aid is unnecessary, but in the states where illiteracy is more prevalent, public funds are not so available from state resources, and national assistance may be properly extended. The standard of agriculture in this country has been distinctly raised by the work of the Federal Agricultural Department although the Federal government has no constitutional control of agriculture. Why may we not have the standard of thoroughness improved in the common school system by federal activity even though the Central Government has no direct authority in matters of education?

With the native born as well as with the foreign born we must inculcate Americanism in its true sense. The greatness of the country, the good it does its citizens, the freedom it secures them, the equality of opportunity evident in the success of the humblest born and the leadership of the self-made, must all be enforced as a basis of grateful love of the country. But more than all should be pressed into the mind and soul of each boy and each girl that he or she is the country and that as he or she shall pursue an honest independent industrious moral life, he or she will be making for a greater America.

The great war relieved the minds of many who had come to think that our great prosperity and our increase in wealth and the spread in all classes of creature comforts to the point of making former luxuries necessities, had sapped the foundations of love of country and the spirit of patriotic self-sacrifice in our youth. The great world struggle evoked the spirit of '76 and '61 from the young men and women of our country in a thrilling way and the selfishness and love of comfort disappeared in the triumphant energy and courage and effectiveness of Young America. Now we have had a reaction. Now the shallows are murmuring again. Now the pro-German and the Irish Extremist occupy the stage with "an other worldliness" seeking to disturb our friendly relations with our allies. Such manifestations are misleading as to the real sentiment of the country while the deeps remain dumb. The Reds are again making night hideous with their threats and their prognostications of evil, and their attempts to stir class feeling and injurious discontent. Therefore, it is that in our public education, class consciousness and "other worldliness" should be fought at every turn. The breaking down of the fancied class barriers by the energy, ability, and independence of the humblest should be the text of every homily. So, too, should be the welfare of the United States and its responsibility to its fellow members of the family of nations. The lesson of obedience to law and government and political self-restraint and discipline should be an easy one to teach in schools and to exemplify. Respect for authority can be lost by lack of discipline and can be strengthened by its exercise. Liberty, abiding for each person, is impossible unless it be ordered liberty. Without law and conformity to it, we shall have license and not law, and anarchy, inequality and tyranny, and not liberty. In no respect do the lovers of America feel more concern than in the outbursts of lawlessness, not so much in personal crime, but in the manifestation of the mob spirit and indifference to the enforcement of law. Why can we not surround our youth with the atmosphere of respect for, and obedience to, authority? That is self-government. Without it, popular government is a failure, and our constitutional system is a hollow mockery.

Not only is education necessary but even more essential is moral training—a sense of responsibility for what we do—a standard of action which satisfies conscience. It can hardly be separated from religion. It is unfortunate that we cannot well unite religion and moral training in the instruction in our public schools. Men may be moral and not be religious, but they are exceptions. Religion is the great stay of morality. It is the conscious study and feeling of responsibility to God. It is a dwelling on our relations and duties to God. As Matthew Arnold puts it, it is our relation to the Being, not ourselves, who makes for righteousness. Its corner stone is unselfishness. It is the antidote for class hatred. It makes for the love of human kind. It prompts patriotism. It lifts one out of the sordid view of things. It broadens our horizon. It reveals true Americanism. And it reconciles individual freedom and responsibility with respect for Divine Authority. That is why the anarchist and the Bolshevist will have nothing of religion. The churches of the community are the great and useful agencies for stimulating religion and its practices. They need encouragement. Every university should encourage its students to the worship of God. Look over the world's history and tell me the nations who deserved well of the human race for their progress, and you will find that religion was the moving cause of their effort, their sacrifice and their success. As long as the United States remains a religious nation, there is no danger of the corrosion of Bolshevism, Communism or any destructive and cruel cult. Christian civilization rests ultimately on the inspiration of the religious spirit. It is that which will render innocuous and neutralize the evil effect of the selfishness which is necessary to give energy and thrift and industry to material progress. It is that spirit which sweetens life with the love of family, of country, and of God. It is the preservation of this spirit of the fatherhood of God and the brotherhood of man upon which we most depend for the maintenance of useful constitutional government.

I have thus tried to follow the text of the donor of this Foundation. I have attempted to give the essence of our constitutional system and to describe how it uses democracy to attain the welfare of the people and the greatest good for the greatest number. I have pointed out the errors, as I conceive of them, of many earnest supporters of what they call pure democracy, chiefly in forgetting that democracy is but a means to an end, just as liberty is. The end is the happiness of all individuals. To be useful, democracy and liberty must be regulated to attain this end and not to defeat it. I have emphasized the dangers against which we must guard our noble state and civilization, and have urged improved education and stimulated religion as most important agencies in defending against those dangers.

I am an optimist. I believe profoundly in our constitutional system and its value to us, because I believe it is the expression, accurate and responsive, of our American people. As it has preserved our liberties and happiness in the past, so may it serve us in our greater difficulties and achievements of the future!

SELECTED SUPREME COURT
OPINIONS OF
CHIEF JUSTICE
WILLIAM HOWARD TAFT

The opinions that follow have been edited. The use of ellipses (. . .) indicates that words or sentences in a paragraph have been omitted, whereas the use of five asterisks (* * * * *) indicates that one or more paragraphs have been omitted. Textual citations to cases have frequently been eliminated or significantly reduced in length. Footnotes generally have been omitted. The Court begins its sessions on the first Monday of October. The October term generally ends in late June the following year. The number of volumes per term varies with the number of cases and the length of opinions. The bracketed page citations [124] are to the pages of the *United States Supreme Court Reports,* the official reporter of the decisions of the Supreme Court of the United States.

October Term, 1921

William Howard Taft, Chief Justice
Joseph McKenna
Oliver Wendell Holmes
William R. Day
Willis Van Devanter
Mahlon Pitney
James Clark McReynolds
Louis D. Brandeis
John H. Clarke

VOLUME 257

Hildreth v. Mastoras

In addition to the necessity of ensuring geographical representation on the Court, presidents until the 1930s needed also to be concerned that certain specialty areas of the law were represented on the Court. Patent and admiralty were two such areas. William Howard Taft regularly handled most of the patent decisions and a good number of the admiralty opinions rendered by the Court in the 1920s. Although neither of these issues are of much concern to scholars of the Court and generally have been omitted from this collection, *Hildreth* is included an as example of Taft's work in the area of patent law. Much less technical and complex than the bulk of patent cases that Taft handled, *Hildreth* involved the issue of patent infringement in the candy-making industry.

Hildreth v. Mastoras

Certiorari to the Circuit Court of Appeals for the Ninth Circuit

No. 51. Argued October 21, 1921—Decided November 7, 1921

257 U.S. 27 (1921)

[28]

MR. CHIEF JUSTICE TAFT delivered the opinion of the court.

This is a certiorari to the Circuit Court of Appeals for the Ninth Circuit bringing here for review a decree of that court, reversing one of the District Court of Oregon granting an injunction against infringement of a patent for a candy pulling machine. . . .

* * * * *

[35] We come now to the question of infringement. In the Langer patent, applied for in 1916 and issued in 1917, which the alleged infringement embodies, there is a so-called "floating puller," which is carried through a course of travel corresponding in form to the figure 8, and around fixed supporting pins arranged concentrically within the two circular portions of figure 8. The candy is pulled by the floating puller and alternately carried thereby around the fixed supporting pins. Instead of having Dickinson's single stationary pin and two other pins which move relatively to it and to one another, the machine of the Langer patent has two stationary pins and a third one which moves relatively to both of them in an actual and rigid figure 8.

Taking the first claim of Dickinson's patent as it reads, one can trace every element of it in the Langer machine. We find there a plurality of oppositely-disposed candy hooks or supports. The candy-puller is found in the movable pin of Langer, and a relative in-and-out motion in the pulling process is palpably present.

Both Dickinson and Langer in their specifications characterize the path of the candy under the operation of the hooks as being along a course of travel corresponding in form to the figure 8. The Circuit Court of Appeals found, however, that the in-and-out movement of the Langer patent was different from the in-and-out movement of the Dickinson patent, in that it was a true figure 8 in the former, whereas in the Dickinson patent the candy follows a path of a series of V's and not a true figure 8 path at all. We differ from the Court of Appeals in this view. The actual movement of the candy in the Langer patent, even though the movable pin follows a fixed path of figure 8, forms a succession of V's closely resembling the V's [36] of the Dickinson patent, so that in each the path of the candy is better described as an in-and-out movement than as a figure 8. The arrangement of the hooks by Langer is better than Dickinson's, but the principle of their operation is the same.

* * * * *

The Circuit Court of Appeals held that the issuing of the Langer patent, after the Dickinson patent, raised the presumption of a patentable difference between that patent and the Dickinson patent, and against infringement. It is not necessary for us, however, to discuss that question, for we think that whatever presumption against infringement may attach to the issuing of the second [37] patent, if any, the evidence here is quite sufficient to overcome it.

The decree of the Circuit Court of Appeals is reversed, and that of the District Court is affirmed.

American Steel Foundries v. Tri-City Central Trades Council

Among the critics of President Warren Harding's decision to nominate William Howard Taft to the center chair of the Supreme Court of the United States, none was more concerned, nor had more reason to be so, than organized labor. Accordingly, the decision in *Tri-City* was seen as an early indicator of what might be expected of the new chief. The case arose from a dispute that had occurred prior to American entry into World War I and before the enactment by Congress of the Clayton Act of 1914, sometimes referred to as the Magna Carta of organized labor.

Taft was hardly an admirer of this major piece of legislation, saying of it that "it was passed for political purposes to satisfy the demands of the leaders of the American Federation of Labor . . . [by] representatives who yield their own convictions as to how they should vote on such measures in fear of the organized power of unions."[1] Given this opinion and his general antipathy to labor leaders from Samuel Gompers to Eugene Debs, Taft's opinion in *Tri-City* must have surprised some of the naysayers, at least in its tone if not in its result.

Tri-City is also important as an early example of Taft's ability to "mass the Court" and to end, almost overnight, the destructive divisiveness that more and more had plagued the later years of the White Court (Edward Douglass White was nominated as an associate justice by President Grover Cleveland in 1894; President Taft promoted him to the post of chief justice in 1910. White retired in 1921).

In *Tri-City*, only the increasingly marginalized Justice John Hessin Clarke (1916–22) dissented, and he did so without an opinion.

At dispute was the scope of section 20 of the Clayton Act, designed by Congress to increase labor's leverage in bargaining with management by reining in the power of federal judges to issue injunctions against unions. Section 20 specifically sought to restrain judges from issuing injunctions deigned harmful to organizing activities. Section 20, however, made an exception when "necessary to prevent irreparable injury to property." Chief Justice Taft, speaking for an eight to one Court, made it clear that "persuasion" could not be prohibited, but that it must be "peaceable and lawful." Taft's success in corralling the support of Holmes and Brandeis seems to indicate that, despite his earlier misgivings about both jurists, he would be able to have the Court work as a team.

Note

1. "Justice and Freedom for Industry" (pamphlet), address before the National Association of Manufacturers, May 26, 1915, as quoted in Mason, *William Howard Taft*, 159.

American Steel Foundries v. Tri-City Central Trades Council et al.

Certiorari to the Circuit Court of Appeals for the Seventh Circuit

No. 2. Argued January 17, 1919; restored to docket for reargument June 1, 1920; reargued October 5, 1920; restored to docket for reargument June 6, 1921; reargued October 4, 5, 1921—Decided December 5, 1921

257 U.S. 184 (1921)

[193]

MR. CHIEF JUSTICE TAFT delivered the opinion of the court.

The American Steel Foundries . . . filed . . . to enjoin the defendants, the Tri-City Central Trades Council, and fourteen individual defendants . . . from carrying on a conspiracy to prevent complainant from retaining and obtaining skilled laborers to operate its plant. The bill charged that the conspiracy was being executed by organized picketing, accompanied by threats, intimidation and violence toward persons employed or seeking employment there. The defendants . . . admitted that the Central Trades Council had established a picket upon streets leading to the plant, with instructions to notify all persons entering it that a strike had been called because of reduction of wages, and to use all honorable means to persuade such persons not to take the places of the men on the strike; admitted the participation of individual defendants in the picketing, but denied threats of injury or violence or responsibility for the violence that admittedly had occurred. . . . A restraining order issued . . . "perpetually restrained and enjoined" [defendants] from in any way or manner whatsoever by use of *persuasion,* threats, or personal injury, intimidation, suggestion of danger or threats of violence of any kind, from interfering with, hindering, obstructing or stopping, any person engaged in the employ of the American Steel Foundries . . .

[194] *and from picketing or maintaining at or near the premises of the complainant, or on the streets leading to the premises of said complainant, any picket or pickets.* . . .

* * * * *

[195] The Circuit Court of Appeals modified the final decree by striking out the word "persuasion" in the four places in which it occurred, and by inserting after the clause restraining picketing the following: "in a threatening or intimidating manner" (238 Fed. 728).

* * * * *

[200] It is clear from the evidence that from the outset, violent methods were pursued from time to time in such a way as to characterize the attitude of the picketers as continuously threatening. A number of employees, sometimes fifteen or more, slept in the plant for a week during the trouble, because they could not safely go to their homes. The result of the campaign was to put employees and would-be employees in such fear that many abandoned work and this seriously interfered with the complainant in operating the plant until the issue of the restraining order.

[201] The first question in the case is whether § 20 of the Clayton Act, October 15, 1914, c. 323, 38 Stat. 738, is to be applied in this case.

* * * * *

[203] The prohibitions of § 20, material here, are those which forbid an injunction against, first, recommending, advising or persuading others by peaceful means to cease employment and labor; second, attending at any place where such person or persons may lawfully be for the purpose of peacefully obtaining or communicating information, or peacefully persuading any person to work or to abstain from working; third, peaceably assembling in a lawful manner and for lawful purposes. . . . It is clear that Congress wished to forbid the use by the federal courts of their equity arm to prevent

peaceable persuasion by employees, discharged or expectant, in promotion of their side of the dispute, and to secure them against judicial restraint in obtaining or communicating information in any place where they might lawfully be. . . .

The object and problem of Congress in § 20, and indeed of courts of equity before its enactment, was to reconcile the rights of the employer in his business and in the access of his employees to his place of business and egress therefrom without intimidation or obstruction, on the one hand, and the right of the employees, recent or expectant, to use peaceable and lawful means to induce present employees and would-be employees to join their ranks, on the other. If, in their attempts at persuasion or communication with those whom they would enlist with them, those of the labor side adopt methods which however lawful in their announced purpose inevitably lead to intimidation and obstruction, then it is the court's duty which the terms of § 20 do not modify, so to limit what [204] the propagandists do as to time, manner and place as shall prevent infractions of the law and violations of the right of the employees, and of the employer for whom they wish to work.

How far may men go in persuasion and communication and still not violate the right of those whom they would influence? In going to and from work, men have a right to as free a passage without obstruction as the streets afford, consistent with the right of others to enjoy the same privilege. We are a social people and the accosting by one of another in an inoffensive way and an offer by one to communicate and discuss information with a view to influencing the other's action are not regarded as aggression or a violation of that other's rights. If, however, the offer is declined, as it may rightfully be, then persistence, importunity, following and dogging become unjustifiable annoyance and obstruction which is likely soon to savor of intimidation. From all of this the person sought to be influenced has a right to be free and his employer has a right to have him free.

The nearer this importunate intercepting of employees or would-be employees is to the place of business, the greater the obstruction and interference with the business and especially with the property right of access of the employer. Attempted discussion and argument of this kind in such proximity is certain to attract attention and congregation of the curious, or, it may be, interested bystanders, and thus to increase the obstruction as well as the aspect of intimidation which the situation quickly assumes. In the present case the three or four groups of picketers, were made up of from four to twelve in a group. They constituted the picket lines. Each union interested, electricians, cranemen, machinists and blacksmiths, had several representatives on the picket line, and assaults and violence ensued. They began early and continued from time to time during the three weeks of the strike [205] after the picketing began. All information tendered, all arguments advanced and all persuasion used under such circumstances were intimidation. They could not be otherwise. It is idle to talk of peaceful communication in such a place and under such conditions. The numbers of the pickets in the groups constituted intimidation. The name "picket" indicated a militant purpose, inconsistent with peaceable persuasion. The crowds they drew made the passage of the employees to and from the place of work, one of running the gauntlet. Persuasion or communication attempted in such a presence and under such conditions was anything but peaceable and lawful. When one or more assaults or disturbances ensued, they characterized the whole campaign, which became effective because of its intimidating character, in spite of the admonitions given by the leaders to their followers as to lawful methods to be pursued, however sincere. Our conclusion is that picketing thus instituted is unlawful and can not be peaceable and may be properly enjoined by the specific term because its meaning is clearly understood in the sphere of the controversy by those who are parties to it.

* * * * *

[206] Regarding as primary the rights of the employees to work for whom they will, and, undisturbed by annoying importunity or intimidation of numbers, to go freely to and from their place of labor, and keeping in mind the right of the employer incident to his property and business to free access of such employees, what can be done to reconcile the conflicting interests?

Each case must turn on its own circumstances. It is a case for the flexible remedial power of a court of equity which may try one mode of restraint, and if it fails or proves to be too drastic, may change it. We think that the strikers and their sympathizers engaged in the economic struggle should be limited to one representative for each point of ingress and egress in the plant or place of business and that all others be enjoined from congregating or loitering at the plant or in the neighboring streets by which access is had to the plant, that such representatives should have the right of observation communication and persuasion but with special admonition that their [207] communication, arguments and appeals shall not be abusive, libelous or threatening, and that they shall not approach individuals together but singly, and shall not in their single efforts at communication or persuasion obstruct an unwilling listener by importunate following or dogging his steps. This is not laid down as a rigid rule, but only as one which should apply to this case under the circumstances disclosed by the evidence and which may be varied in other cases. . . .

With these views, it is apparent that we can not sustain the qualification of the order of the District Court which the Circuit Court of Appeals made. That court followed the case of *Iron Molders' Union v. Allis-Chalmers Co.,* 166 F. 45, and modified the order of the District Court which enjoins defendants "from picketing or maintaining at or near the premises of the complainant, or on the streets leading to the premises of said complainant, any picket or pickets" by adding the words "in a threatening or intimidating manner." This qualification seems to us to be inadequate. In actual result, it leaves compliance largely to the discretion of the pickets. It ignores the necessary element of intimidation in the presence of groups as pickets. It does not secure practically that which the court must secure and to which the complainant and his workmen are entitled. The phrase really recognizes as legal that which bears the sinister name of "picketing" which it is to be observed Congress carefully refrained from using in § 20.

There remains to consider, so far as defendants Churchill and Cook, the ex-employees, are concerned, the [208] part of the decree of the District Court which forbade them by persuasion to induce employees, or would-be employees to leave, or stay out of, complainant's employ. The effect of it is to enjoin persuasion by them at any time or place. This certainly conflicts with § 20 of the Clayton Act. The decree must be modified as to these two defendants by striking out the word "persuasion."

The second important question in the case is as to the form of decree against the Tri-City Trades Council and the other defendants. What has been said as to picketing applies to them, of course, as fully as to the ex-employees, but how as to the injunction against persuasion?

* * * * *

[209] Is interference of a labor organization by persuasion and appeal to induce a strike against low wages under such circumstances without lawful excuse and malicious? We think not. Labor unions are recognized by the Clayton Act as legal when instituted for mutual help and lawfully carrying out their legitimate objects. They have long been thus recognized by the courts. They were organized out of the necessities of the situation. A single employee was helpless in dealing with an employer. He was dependent ordinarily on his daily wage for the maintenance of himself and family. If the employer refused to pay him the wages that he thought fair, he was nevertheless unable to leave the employ and to resist arbitrary and unfair treat-

ment. Union was essential to give laborers opportunity to deal on equality with their employer. They united to exert influence upon him and to leave him in a body in order by this inconvenience to induce him to make better terms with them. They were withholding their labor of economic value to make him pay what they thought it was worth. The right to combine for such a lawful purpose has in many years not been denied by any court. The strike became a lawful instrument in a lawful economic struggle or competition between employer and employees as to the share or division between them of the joint product of labor and capital. To render this combination at all effective, employees must make their combination extend beyond one shop. It is helpful to have as many as may be in the same trade in the same community united, because in the competition between employers they are bound to be affected by the standard of wages of their trade in the neighborhood. Therefore, they may use all lawful propaganda to enlarge their membership and especially among those whose labor at lower wages will injure their whole guild. It is impossible to hold such persuasion and propaganda without more, to be without excuse and malicious. The principle of the unlawfulness of maliciously enticing laborers still remains and action may be maintained therefor in proper cases, [210] but to make it applicable to local labor unions, in such a case as this, seems to us to be unreasonable.

* * * * *

[212] The *Hitchman* case was cited in the *Duplex* case, but there is nothing in the *ratio decidendi* of either which limits our conclusion here or which requires us to hold that the members of a local labor union and the union itself do not have sufficient interest in the wages paid to the employees of any employer in the community to justify their use of lawful and peaceable persuasion to induce those employees to refuse to accept such reduced wages [213] and to quit their employment. For this reason, we think that the restraint from persuasion included within the injunction of the District Court was improper, and in that regard the decree must also be modified. In this we agree with the Circuit Court of Appeals.

The decree of the Circuit Court of Appeals is reversed in part and affirmed in part and the case is remanded to the District Court for modification of its decree in conformity with this opinion.

MR. JUSTICE BRANDEIS concurs in substance in the opinion and the judgment of the court.

MR. JUSTICE CLARKE dissents.

Truax v. Corrigan

Corrigan had been employed by Truax, the owner/operator of the English Kitchen. As part of the efforts of the striking Restaurant Workers Union, Corrigan and other union members maintained a picket line in front of Truax's restaurant, seeking, among other things, to discourage customers from entering the restaurant. This effort proved quite successful, with the receipts of the English Kitchen cut by more than one half. Truax sought relief in state court by asking for an injunction. Truax argued that Corrigan's conduct intimidated potential customers and that the charges in the pamphlets distributed by the union members were libelous. The Arizona courts refused to issue the injunction, citing a state statute that allowed injunctions in labor disputes only if "necessary to prevent irreparable injury to property or to a property right." The state supreme court also did not find any evidence of what it considered to be acts or threats of violence. The five-member United States Supreme Court opinion, however, read the facts very differently.

Taft, who as president had unsuccessfully sought legislation distinguishing between legal and illegal picketing, used his new position as chief justice to write into law—over the ringing dissents of Justices Oliver Wendell Holmes, Mahlon Pitney (with whom Justice John H. Clarke concurred), and Louis D. Brandeis—his view of where the proper line should be drawn between legal and illegal picketing. In doing this, Taft utilized the Fourteenth Amendment's guarantees of due process and equal protection to void the challenged state statute.

For critics of Harding's nomination of Taft to the Court, the *Truax* opinion confirmed their worst fears. Still, despite *Truax,* Taft's earlier opinion in *Tri-City* may be used to support Taft defenders' argument that what really motivated the chief was his desire to have national, rather than local, remedies for labor disputes. Taft, after all, was throughout his long public career a firm disciple of the two great early nationalists, Alexander Hamilton and John Marshall.

Truax et al., Copartners, Doing Business under the Firm Name and Style of William Truax, v. Corrigan et al.

Error to the Supreme Court of the State of Arizona

No. 13. Argued April 29, 30, 1920; restored to docket for reargument June 6, 1921; reargued October 5, 6, 1921—Decided December 19, 1921

257 U.S. 312 (1921)

[320]

MR. CHIEF JUSTICE TAFT delivered the opinion of the court.

The plaintiffs . . . own, maintain and operate, on Main Street, in the

City of Bisbee, Arizona, a restaurant, known as the "English Kitchen." The defendants are cooks and waiters formerly in the employ of the plaintiffs, together with the labor union and the trades assembly of which [321] they were members. . . .

The complaint set out the following case:

In April, 1916, a dispute arose between the plaintiffs and the defendants' union concerning the terms and conditions of employment of the members of the union. The plaintiffs refused to yield to the terms of the union, which thereupon ordered a strike of those of its members who were in plaintiffs' employ. To win the strike and to coerce and compel the plaintiffs to comply with the demands of the union, the defendants and others unknown to the plaintiffs entered into a conspiracy and boycott to injure plaintiffs in their restaurant and restaurant business, by inducing plaintiffs' customers and others theretofore well and favorably disposed, to cease to patronize or trade with the plaintiffs. The method of inducing was set out at length and included picketing, displaying banners, advertising the strike, denouncing plaintiffs as "unfair" to the union and appealing to customers to stay away from the "English Kitchen," and the circulation of handbills containing abusive and libelous charges against plaintiffs, their employees and their patrons and intimations of injury to future patrons.

* * * * *

[322] The complaint further averred that the defendants were relying for immunity on Paragraph 1464 of the Revised Statutes of Arizona, 1913, which is in part as follows:

"No restraining order or injunction shall be granted by any court of this state, or a judge or the judges thereof, in any case between an employer and employees, or between employers and employees, or between employees, or between persons employed and persons seeking employment, involving or growing out of a dispute concerning terms or conditions of employment, unless necessary to prevent irreparable injury to property or to a property right of the party making the application, for which injury there is no adequate remedy at law, and such property or property right must be described with particularity in the application, which must be in writing and sworn to by the applicant or by his agent or attorney."

* * * * *

The plaintiffs alleged that this paragraph if it made lawful defendants' acts contravened the Fourteenth Amendment to the Constitution of the United States by depriving plaintiffs of their property without due process of law, and by denying to plaintiffs the equal protection of the laws, and was, therefore, void and of no effect. Upon the case thus stated the plaintiffs asked a temporary, and a permanent, injunction.

* * * * *

[323] The Superior Court for Cochise County . . . dismissed the complaint, and this judgment was affirmed by the Supreme Court of Arizona.

* * * * *

[324] The effect of this ruling is that, under the statute, loss may be inflicted upon the plaintiffs' property and business by "picketing" in any form if violence be not used, and that, because no violence was shown or claimed, the campaign carried on, as described in the complaint and exhibits, did not unlawfully invade complainants' rights.

* * * * *

[327] Plaintiffs' business is a property right (*Duplex Printing Press Co. v. Deering*, 254 U.S. 443, 465) and free access for employees, owner and customers to his place of business is incident to such right. Intentional injury caused to either right or both by a conspiracy is a tort. Concert of action is a conspiracy if its object is unlawful or if the means used are unlawful. Intention to inflict the loss and the actual loss caused are clear. The real question here is, were the means used illegal? The above recital of what the defendants did, can leave no doubt of that. The libelous attacks upon the plaintiffs, their business, their employees, and their customers, and the abusive epithets applied to them were palpable wrongs. They were uttered in aid of the plan to induce plaintiffs' customers and would-be customers to refrain from patronizing the plaintiffs. The patrolling of defendants immediately in front of the restaurant on the main street and within five feet of plaintiffs' premises continuously during business hours, with the banners announcing plaintiffs' unfairness; the attendance by the picketers at the entrance to the restaurant and their insistent and loud appeals all day long, the constant circulation by them of the libels and epithets applied to employees, plaintiffs and customers, and the threats of injurious consequences to future customers, all linked together in a campaign, were an unlawful annoyance and a hurtful nuisance in respect of the free access to the plaintiff's place of business. It was not lawful persuasion or inducing. It was not a mere appeal to the sympathetic aid of would-be customers by a simple statement of the [328] fact of the strike and a request to withhold patronage. It was compelling every customer or would-be customer to run the gauntlet of most uncomfortable publicity, aggressive

and annoying importunity, libelous attacks and fear of injurious consequences, illegally inflicted, to his reputation and standing in the community. No wonder that a business of $50,000 was reduced to only one-fourth of its former extent. Violence could not have been more effective. It was moral coercion by illegal annoyance and obstruction and it thus was plainly a conspiracy.

* * * * *

[330] It is to be observed that this is not the mere case of a peaceful secondary boycott as to the illegality of which courts have differed and States have adopted different statutory provisions. A secondary boycott of this kind is where many combine to injure one in his business by coercing third persons against their will to cease patronizing him by threats of similar injury. In such a case the many have a legal right to withdraw their trade from the one, they have the legal right to withdraw their trade from third persons, and they have the right to advise third persons of their intention to do so when each act is considered singly. The question in such cases is whether the moral coercion exercised over a stranger to the original controversy by steps in themselves legal becomes a legal wrong. But here the illegality of the means used is without doubt and fundamental. The means used are the libelous and abusive attacks on the plaintiffs' reputation, like attacks on their employees and customers, threats of such attacks on would-be customers, picketing and patrolling of the entrance to their place of business, and the consequent obstruction of free access thereto—all with the purpose of depriving the plaintiffs of their business. To give operation to a statute whereby serious losses inflicted by such unlawful means are in effect made remediless, is, we think, to disregard fundamental rights of liberty and property and to deprive the person suffering the loss of due process of law.

If, however, contrary to the construction which we put on the opinion of the Supreme Court of Arizona, it does not withhold from the plaintiffs all remedy for the wrongs they suffered but only the equitable relief of injunction, there still remains the question whether they are thus denied the equal protection of the laws.

[331] This brings us to consider the effect in this case of that provision of the Fourteenth Amendment which forbids any State to deny to any person the equal protection of the laws. The clause is associated in the Amendment [332] with the due process clause and it is customary to consider them together. It may be that they overlap, that a violation of one may involve at times the violation of the other, but the spheres of the protection they offer

are not coterminous. The due process clause, brought down from Magna Charta, was found in the early state constitutions, and later in the Fifth Amendment to the Federal Constitution as a limitation upon the executive, legislative and judicial powers of the Federal Government, while the equality clause does not appear in the Fifth Amendment and so does not apply to congressional legislation. The due process clause requires that every man shall have the protection of his day in court, and the benefit of the general law, a law which hears before it condemns, which proceeds not arbitrarily or capriciously but upon inquiry, and renders judgment only after trial, so that every citizen shall hold his life, liberty, property and immunities under the protection of the general rules which govern society. *Hurtado v. California,* 110 U.S. 516, 535. It, of course, tends to secure equality of law in the sense that it makes a required minimum of protection for every one's right of life, liberty and property, which the Congress or the legislature may not withhold. Our whole system of law is predicated on the general, fundamental principle of equality of application of the law. "All men are equal before the law," "This is a government of laws and not of men," "No man is above the law," are all maxims showing the spirit in which legislatures, executives and courts are expected to make, execute and apply laws. But the framers and adopters of this Amendment were not content to depend on a mere minimum secured by the due process clause, or upon the spirit of equality which might not be insisted on by local public opinion. They therefore embodied that spirit in a specific guaranty.

The guaranty was aimed at undue favor and individual or class privilege, on the one hand, and at hostile [333] discrimination or the oppression of inequality, on the other. It sought an equality of treatment of all persons, even though all enjoyed the protection of due process. Mr. Justice Field, delivering the opinion of this court in *Barbier v. Connolly,* 113 U.S. 27, 32, of the equality clause, said, "Class legislation, discriminating against some and favoring others, is prohibited, but legislation which, in carrying out a public purpose, is limited in its application, if within the sphere of its operation it affects alike all persons similarly situated, is not within the amendment." In *Hayes v. Missouri,* 120 U.S. 68, the court speaking through the same Justice said the Fourteenth Amendment "does not prohibit legislation which is limited either in the objects to which it is directed, or by the territory within which it is to operate. It merely requires that all persons subjected to such legislation shall be treated alike, under like circumstances and conditions, both in the privileges conferred and in the liabilities imposed." Thus the guaranty was intended to secure equality of protection not only for all but against all similarly situated. Indeed, protection is not protection unless it does so. Immunity granted to a class, however limited, having the effect to deprive another class, however limited, of a personal or property right, is just as clearly a denial of equal protection of the laws to the latter class as if the immunity were in favor of, or the deprivation of right permitted worked against, a larger class.

Mr. Justice Matthews, in *Yick Wo v. Hopkins,* 118 U.S. 356, 369, speaking for the court of both the due process and the equality clause of the Fourteenth Amendment, said:

"These provisions are universal in their application, to all persons within the territorial jurisdiction, without regard to any differences of race, of color, or of nationality; *and the equal protection of the laws is a pledge of the protection of equal laws.*"

* * * * *

[340] It is urged that in holding Paragraph 1464 invalid, we are in effect holding invalid § 20 of the Clayton Act. Of course, we are not doing so. In the first place, the equality clause of the Fourteenth Amendment does not apply to congressional but only to state action. In the second place, § 20 of the Clayton Act never has been construed or applied as the Supreme Court of Arizona has construed and applied Paragraph 1464 in this case.

We have but recently considered the clauses of § 20 of the Clayton Act, sometimes erroneously called the "picketing" clauses. *American Steel Foundries v. Tri-City Central Trades Council,* ante, 184. They forbid an injunction in labor controversies prohibiting any person "from attending at any place where any such person or persons may lawfully be, for the purpose of peacefully obtaining or communicating information, or from peacefully persuading any person to work or to abstain from working; or from ceasing to patronize or to employ any party to such dispute, or from recommending, advising, or persuading others by peaceful and lawful means so to do."

We held that under these clauses picketing was unlawful, and that it might be enjoined as such, and that peaceful picketing was a contradiction in terms which the statute sedulously avoided, but that, subject to the primary right of the employer and his employees and would-be employees to free access to his premises without obstruction by violence, intimidation, annoyance, importunity or dogging, it was lawful for ex-employees on a strike and their fellows in a labor union to have a single representative at each entrance to the plant of the employer to announce the strike and peaceably to persuade the employees and would-be employees to join them in it. We held that these clauses were merely declaratory of what had always been the law and the best practice in equity, and we thus applied them. The construction put [341] upon the same words by the Arizona Supreme Court makes these clauses of Paragraph 1464 as far from those of § 20 of the Clayton Act in meaning as if they were in wholly different language.

We conclude that the demurrer in this case should have been overruled, the defendants required to answer, and that if the evidence sustained the averments of the complaint, an injunction should issue as prayed.

* * * * *

[342] *The judgment of the Supreme Court of Arizona is reversed and the case remanded for further proceedings not inconsistent with this opinion.*

Terral v. Burke Construction Co.

Neither the decisions of the Marshall Court asserting federal supremacy nor the victory of the Union forces in the Civil War entirely quieted the voices of States' rights. Arkansas had enacted a statute that provided that foreign corporations doing business in that state would forfeit their license to do business in Arkansas if they used federal courts to assert their rights. Taft quickly declared the statute unconstitutional, in the process overriding several Supreme Court precedents.

Terral, as Secretary of State of the State of Arkansas, v. Burke Construction Company

*Appeal from the District Court of the United States
for the Eastern District of Arkansas*

No. 93. Argued January 17, 1922—Decided February 27, 1922.

257 U.S. 529 (1922)

[530]
MR. CHIEF JUSTICE TAFT delivered the opinion of the court.

* * * * *

[531] The sole question presented on the record is whether a state law is unconstitutional which revokes a license to a foreign corporation to do busi-

ness within the State [532] because, while doing only a domestic business in the State, it resorts to the federal court sitting in the State.

The cases in this court in which the conflict between the power of a State to exclude a foreign corporation from doing business within its borders, and the federal constitutional right of such foreign corporation to resort to the federal courts has been considered, can not be reconciled. . . .

The principle established by the more recent decisions of this court is that a State may not, in imposing conditions upon the privilege of a foreign corporation's doing business in the State, exact from it a waiver of the exercise of its constitutional right to resort to the federal courts, or thereafter withdraw the privilege of doing business because of its exercise of such right, whether waived in advance or not. The principle does not depend for its application on the character of the business the corporation does, whether state or interstate, although that has been suggested as a distinction in some cases. It rests on the ground that the Federal Constitution confers upon citizens of one State the right to resort to federal courts in another, that state action, whether legislative or executive, necessarily calculated to curtail the free exercise of the right thus secured is void because the sovereign power of a State in excluding foreign corporations, as in the exercise of all others of its sovereign powers, is subject to the [533] limitations of the supreme fundamental law. It follows that the cases of *Doyle v. Continental Insurance Co.*, 94 U.S. 535, and *Security Mutual Life Insurance Co. v. Prewitt*, 202 U.S. 246, must be considered as overruled and that the views of the minority judges in those cases have become the law of this court. The appellant in proposing to comply with the statute in question and revoke the license was about to violate the constitutional right of the appellee. In enjoining him the District Court was right, and its decree is

Affirmed.

Wallace v. United States

Wallace provided Taft with his first opportunity to write an opinion on the nature of presidential power. Although *Myers v. United States*, 272 U.S. 52 (1926), would give Taft more scope to probe and explain the nature of presidential power, even in *Wallace* one can plainly see the outlines of Taft's preference for vesting the chief executive with total control over all members of the executive branch of government.

Wallace had sued the army, arguing that his dismissal was illegal, that he could be removed only pursuant to a court-martial. This restriction had been imposed on the presidency by the same Congress that was to pass the Tenure of Office Act of 1867. Unlike the later *Myers* decision, Taft did not opt to opine on the constitutionality of the restrictions on executive power adopted by Congress during the presidency of Andrew Johnson. He did, however, uphold the legality of Wallace's removal.

Wallace v. United States

Appeal from the Court of Claims

No. 118. Argued January 27, 1922—Decided February 27, 1922

257 U.S. 541 (1922)

[543]

MR. CHIEF JUSTICE TAFT, after stating the case, delivered the opinion of the court.

The President acted under the 118th Article of War, which provides in part (39 Stat. 619, 650, 669) that,

> "No officer shall be discharged or dismissed from the service except by order of the President or by sentence of a general court-martial; and in time of peace no officer shall be dismissed except in pursuance of the sentence of court-martial or in mitigation thereof."

* * * * *

[544] Appellant claims that by the failure to grant him a court-martial, his dismissal under § 1230 was rendered void *ab initio* and that he is still a Colonel.

* * * * *

Before the Civil War there was no restriction upon the President's power to remove an officer of the Army or Navy. The principle that the power of removal was incident to the power of appointment was early determined by the Senate to involve the conclusion that, at least in absence of restrictive legislation, the President, though he could not appoint without the consent of the Senate, could remove without such consent in the case of any officer whose tenure was not fixed by the Constitution. [545] The first legislative restriction upon this power was enacted March 3, 1865, by the very provision we are here considering (13 Stat. 489), which subsequently became § 1230, Rev. Stats. Thereafter, on July 13, 1866, Congress took away altogether the power of the President to dismiss an officer of the Army or Navy in time of peace, except in pursuance of a court-martial sentence or in commutation thereof (c. 176, 14 Stat. 92). After that, in the controversy between President Johnson and the Senate, the tenure of office act was passed which cut down the power of the President to remove civil officers. Act of March 2, 1867, c. 154, 14 Stat. 430. The validity of these acts has never been directly passed on by this court in any case. The question has been expressly saved. *Parsons v. United States,* 167 U.S. 324, 339.

While, thus, the validity and effect of statutory restrictions upon the power of the President alone to remove officers of the Army and Navy and civil officers have been the subject of doubt and discussion, it is settled, *McElrath v. United States,* 102 U.S. 426; *Blake v. United States,* 103 U.S. 227; *Keyes v. United States,* 109 U.S. 336; *Mullan v. United States,* 140 U.S. 240, that the President with the consent of the Senate may effect the removal of an officer of the Army or Navy by the appointment of another to his place, and that none of the limitations in the statutes affects his power of removal when exercised by and with the consent of the Senate. Indeed the same ruling has been made as to civil officers. *Parsons v. United States,* 167 U.S. 324.

The question here, then, is whether the Senate joined the President in his removal of the appellant. That the President intended to separate him from the Army is, of course, plain. What are we to infer from the Senate's action in confirming appointments by the President which filled the complement of officers of the rank of appellant allowed by law? . . . [546] We must presume, therefore, in the absence of any showing to the contrary, that the Senate was advised of the facts in respect to the nomination of Lieut. Colonel Smith and that it intended to supply the vacancy occasioned by the dismissal of appellant. Otherwise we must conclude that the Senate Committee was recommending, and the Senate was deliberately voting, confirmation of a nomination to a place for which there was no provision by law.

* * * * *

The judgment of the Court of Claims is

Affirmed.

Railroad Commission v. Chicago, Burlington & Quincy Railroad

In the *Shreveport Rate Cases,* 234 U.S. 342 (1914), Associate Justice Charles Evans Hughes, writing for a seven-member majority, held that the Interstate Commerce

Commission could consider intrastate rates in rendering its judgments on appropriate rates. Specifically, the Court held that the ICC could order intrastate rates raised because of their impact on interstate commerce. The Taft Court, as a consequence, found itself on numerous occasions required to apply the *Shreveport* decision to issues involving intrastate railroad rates.

The issue was exacerbated by the passage of the Transportation Act of 1920, which sought, among other things, to ensure the health of the nation's railroad industry. Frequently, this entailed ordering railroads to increase their rates for intrastate travel. This brought the federal government into conflict with state agencies that wanted, quite naturally, to hold rates down for their citizens.

The Wisconsin Railroad Commission had refused to allow the railroads to increase their rates for intrastate passengers over the maximum of two cents per mile provided by Wisconsin law. This was in violation of the findings of the Interstate Commerce Commission. The United States District Court had enjoined the action of the Wisconsin authorities. The Supreme Court affirmed the decision of the lower federal court.

Railroad Commission of Wisconsin et al. v. Chicago, Burlington & Quincy Railroad Company

Appeal from the District Court of the United States for the Eastern District of Wisconsin

No. 206. Argued March 11, 14, 15, 1921; restored to docket for reargument October 24, 1921; reargued December 5, 6, 7, 1921—Decided February 27, 1922

257 U.S. 563 (1922)

[578]

MR. CHIEF JUSTICE TAFT, after stating the case, delivered the opinion of the court.

The Commission's order, interference with which was enjoined by the District Court, effects the removal of the unjust discrimination found to exist against persons in interstate commerce, and against interstate commerce, by fixing a minimum for intrastate passenger fares in Wisconsin at 3.6 cents per mile per passenger. This is done under paragraph 4 of § 13 of the Interstate Commerce Act as amended by the Transportation Act of 1920. . . .

* * * * *

[582] The Interstate Commerce Act of 1887, 24 St. 379, was enacted by Congress to prevent interstate railroad carriers from charging unreasonable rates and from unjustly discriminating between persons and localities. The

railroads availed themselves of the weakness and cumbrous machinery of the original law to defeat its purpose, and this led to various amendments culminating in the amending Act of 1910, 36 Stat. 539, in which the authority of the Commission in dealing with the carriers was made summary and effectively complete. Whatever the causes, the fact was that the carrying capacity of the railroads did not thereafter develop proportionately with the growth of the country, and it became difficult for them [583] to secure additional investment of capital on feasible terms. When the extraordinary demand for transportation arose in 1917, the Congress and the President concluded to take over all the railroads into the management of the Federal Government, and by joint use of facilities, which the Anti-Trust Law was thought to forbid under private management, and by use of Government credit, to increase their effectiveness. This was done by appropriate legislation and executive action under the war power. From January 1, 1918, until March 1, 1920, when the Transportation Act went into effect, the common carriers by steam railroad of the country were operated by the Federal Government. Due to the rapid rise in the [584] prices of material and labor in 1918 and 1919, the expense of their operation had enormously increased by the time it was proposed to return the railroads to their owners. The owners insisted that their properties could not be turned back to them by the Government for useful operation without provision to aid them to meet a situation in which they were likely to face a demoralizing lack of credit and income. Congress acquiesced in this view. The Transportation Act of 1920 was the result. It was adopted after elaborate investigations by the Interstate Commerce Committees of the two Houses.

* * * * *

[585] It is manifest from this very condensed recital that the act made a new departure. Theretofore the control which Congress through the Interstate Commerce Commission exercised was primarily for the purpose of preventing injustice by unreasonable or discriminatory rates against persons and localities, and the only provisions of the law that inured to the benefit of the carriers were the requirement that the rates should be reasonable in the sense of furnishing an adequate compensation for the particular service rendered and the abolition of rebates. The new measure imposed an affirmative duty on the Interstate Commerce Commission to fix rates and to take other important steps to maintain an adequate railway service for the people of the United States. This is expressly declared in § 15a to be one of the purposes of the bill.

Intrastate rates and the income from them must play a most important part in maintaining an adequate national railway system. Twenty per cent.

of the gross freight receipts of the railroads of the country are from intrastate traffic, and fifty per cent. of the passenger receipts. The ratio of the gross intrastate revenue to the [586] interstate revenue is a little less than one to three. If the rates, on which such receipts are based, are to be fixed at a substantially lower level than in interstate traffic, the share which the intrastate traffic will contribute will be proportionately less. If the railways are to earn a fixed net percentage of income, the lower the intrastate rates, the higher the interstate rates may have to be. The effective operation of the act will reasonably and justly require that intrastate traffic should pay a fair proportionate share of the cost of maintaining an adequate railway system. . . .

* * * * *

[588] It is objected here, as it was in the *Shreveport Case,* that orders of the Commission which raise the intrastate rates to a level of the interstate structure violate the specific proviso of the original Interstate Commerce Act repeated in the amending acts, that the Commission is not to regulate traffic wholly within a State. To this, the same answer must be made as was made in the *Shreveport Case* (234 U.S. 342, 358), that such orders as to intrastate traffic are merely incidental to the regulation of interstate commerce and necessary to its efficiency. Effective control of the one must embrace some control over the other in view of the blending of both in actual operation. The same rails and the same cars carry both. The same men conduct them. Commerce is a unit and does not regard state lines, and while, under the Constitution, interstate and intrastate commerce are ordinarily subject to regulation by different sovereignties, yet when they are so mingled together that the supreme authority, the Nation, cannot exercise complete effective control over interstate commerce without incidental regulation of intrastate commerce, such incidental regulation is not an invasion of state authority or a violation of the proviso.

* * * * *

[590] In *Minnesota Rate Cases,* 230 U.S. 352, where relevant cases were carefully reviewed, it was said, p. 399: "The authority of Congress extends to every part of interstate commerce, and to every instrumentality or agency by which it is carried on; and the full control by Congress of the subjects committed to its regulation is not to be denied or thwarted by the commingling of interstate and intrastate operations. This is not to say that the Nation may deal with the internal concerns of the State, as such, but that the execution by Congress of its constitutional power to regulate interstate commerce is not limited by the fact that intrastate transactions may have become so interwoven therewith that the effective government of the former incidentally

controls the latter. This conclusion necessarily results from the supremacy of the national power within its appointed sphere."

It is said that our conclusion gives the Commission unified control of interstate and intrastate commerce. It is only unified to the extent of maintaining efficient regulation of interstate commerce under the paramount power of Congress. It does not involve general regulation of intrastate commerce. Action of the Interstate Commerce Commission in this regard should be directed to substantial disparity which operates as a real discrimination [591] against, and obstruction to, interstate commerce, and must leave appropriate discretion to the state authorities to deal with intrastate rates as between themselves on the general level which the Interstate Commerce Commission has found to be fair to interstate commerce.

It may well turn out that the effect of a general order in increasing all rates, like the one at bar, will, in particular localities, reduce income instead of increasing it, by discouraging patronage. Such cases would be within the saving clause of the order herein, and make proper an application to the Interstate Commerce Commission for appropriate exception. So, too, in practice, when the state commissions shall recognize their obligation to maintain a proportionate and equitable share of the income of the carriers from intrastate rates, conference between the Interstate Commerce Commission and the state commissions may dispense with the necessity for any rigid federal order as to the intrastate rates, and leave to the state commissions power to deal with them and increase them or reduce them in their discretion.

The order of the District Court granting the interlocutory injunction is

Affirmed.

New York v. United States

New York v. United States involved the same issues as the case of *Railroad Commission of Wisconsin,* 257 U.S. 563 (1922). The Interstate Commerce Commission had directed that interstate rail carriers increase their intrastate rates to 3.6 cents per mile.

State of New York et al. v. United States, Clark et al., Constituting the Interstate Commerce Commission, and (Intervening) Lehigh Valley Railroad Company, et al.

*Appeal from the District Court of the United States for the
Northern District of New York*

No. 283. Argued October 19, 20, 1921—Decided February 27, 1922

257 U.S. 591 (1922)

[597]

MR. CHIEF JUSTICE TAFT delivered the opinion of the court.

This was a bill in equity against the United States and the Interstate Commerce Commission and others brought by the State of New York and its Attorney General to annul and enjoin the enforcement of an order of the Interstate Commerce Commission requiring the interstate railroads operating in intrastate commerce in the State of New York to charge in such commerce 3.6 cents a mile for all passengers. . . .

[598] . . . As soon as the order in *Ex parte 74* was made, the railroads concerned applied to the Public Service Commission of the State of New York for similar increases in intrastate rates. That commission granted the increase in freight rates, but denied it as to milk rates and passenger fares. The passenger intrastate fares were 3 cents a mile under the order of the President during the war control, but, when that should become ineffective, a statute of New York fixing passenger fares on the New York Central Railroad from Albany to Buffalo at two [599] cents a mile would come into force and operation. As soon as the state commission made its ruling, the railroads applied to the Interstate Commerce Commission under § 13 of the act, of which proceeding notice was given to the State of New York, the Attorney General and the Public Service Commission, all of whom appeared, for an order directing the railroads to put intrastate passenger fares, excess baggage charges, sleeping car surtaxes and milk rates on the same level with interstate rates. Proof was offered by the railways to show that conditions of operation in state and interstate passenger traffic were alike and there was no showing otherwise. The record in *Ex parte 74* was put in evidence. There was evidence also to show that at Buffalo and other border points the difference between the interstate and intrastate fares would divert business from the interstate lines between New York City and Buffalo to the New York Central lines, and that the same difference would break up interstate journeys to the west into intrastate journeys to Buffalo from New York and an interstate journey beyond, thus reducing interstate travel and discriminating against passengers carried therein. . . .

* * * * *

[601] The main objections to the order are the same as those presented, considered and overruled in the *Wisconsin Rate* case, just decided. The evidence in this case shows that, if the passenger and other rates here in controversy were to continue in force as ruled by the Public Service Commission of New York, the annual gross revenues of the interstate railroads operating in the State of New York from both interstate and intrastate passenger and milk business would be less by nearly twelve millions of dollars than those revenues if the intrastate fares and rates were on the same level as the interstate rates as fixed by the Interstate Commerce Commission. If the lower level of intrastate fares and rates is to be maintained, it will discriminate against interstate commerce, in that it will require higher fares and rates in the interstate commerce of [602] the State to secure the income for which the Interstate Commerce Commission must attempt to provide by fixing rates under § 15a of the Interstate Commerce Act, as amended by § 422 of the Transportation Act of 1920, 41 Stat. 456, 488, in carrying out the declared congressional purpose "to provide the people of the United States with adequate transportation." As we have just held in the *Wisconsin Rate* case, this constitutes "undue, unreasonable, or unjust discrimination against interstate . . . commerce," which is declared to be unlawful and prohibited by § 13, par. 4, of the Interstate Commerce Act, as amended by § 416 of the Transportation Act of 1920, 41 Stat. 456, 484, and which the Interstate Commerce Commission is authorized therein to remove by fixing intrastate rates for the purpose. We need not repeat our reasons for our ruling. Nor need we consider and give again the grounds upon which we hold § 13, par. 4 as thus construed to be valid under the Constitution of the United States.

The decree of the District Court dismissing the bill of complaint is

Affirmed.

Omitted Taft Opinions

Yazoo & Mississippi Valley Railroad Company v. Clarksdale, 257 U.S. 10 (1921)—tax dispute.

United States v. M. Rice & Company, 257 U.S. 536 (1922)—interpretation of Tariff Act of 1913.

United States v. Cook, 257 U.S. 523 (1922)—contract dispute.

Missouri Pacific Railroad Company v. Clarendon Boat Oar Company, 257 U.S. 533 (1922)—state corporation law.

Commissioners of Road Improvement v. St. Louis Southwestern Railway Company, 257 U.S. 547 (1922)—assessments.

Smietanka v. First Trust & Savings Bank, 257 U.S. 602 (1922)—legislative interpretation of Income Tax Act of 1913.

VOLUME 258

Howat v. Kansas

The Court dismissed an appeal from the Kansas Supreme Court that challenged that state's establishment of a court of industrial relations. The Court found that the challenge failed to raise any issues pertaining to the United States Constitution. *Howat* is an example of a case that would not have reached the Court after the passage in 1925 of the Judges' Act, which gave the Court greater discretion as to the cases it would take.

Howat et al. v. State of Kansas

Error to the Supreme Court of the State of Kansas

Nos. 154 and 491. Argued February 27, 28, 1922—Decided March 13, 1922

258 U.S. 181 (1922)

[182]

MR. CHIEF JUSTICE TAFT delivered the opinion of the court.

These are two writs of error to the Supreme Court of Kansas sued out (§ 237, Judicial Code) with the hope and purpose of testing the validity, under the Federal Constitution, [183] of the act of the Legislature of Kansas creating a Court of Industrial Relations. C. 29, Special Session, Laws of Kansas of 1920.

* * * * *

We are of opinion that in neither case is the Kansas Industrial Relations Act presented in such way as to permit us to pass upon those features which are attacked by the plaintiffs in error as violative of the Constitution of the United States.

* * * * *

[190] As the matter was disposed of in the state courts on principles of general, and not federal law, we have no choice but to dismiss the writ of error as in No. 154.

Writs of error dismissed.

United States v. Balint

Less than two months before the Court would hand down its famous decision in the *Child Labor Tax Case (Bailey v. Drexel Furniture Company)*, 259 U.S. 20 (1922), a unanimous Court upheld a conviction brought under the Harrison Narcotic Act of 1914, which, like the facts that would be brought out in the *Child Labor Tax Case,* used the taxing power to prohibit a particular type of behavior—manufacturing using child labor—that Congress wished to suppress. In *Balint,* however, the Court did not touch on the scope of Congress's taxing power, but rather addressed the issue of whether the Narcotic Act's not requiring *scienter* (knowledge) raised a constitutional issue.

United States v. Balint et al.

Error to the District Court of the United States for the
Southern District of New York

No. 480. Argued March 7, 1922—Decided March 27, 1922

258 U.S. 250 (1922)

[251]

MR. CHIEF JUSTICE TAFT delivered the opinion of the court.

This is a writ of error to the District Court under the Criminal Appeals Act of March 2, 1907, c. 2564, 34 Stat. 1246. Defendants in error were indicted for a violation of the Narcotic Act of December 17, 1914, c. 1, 38 Stat. 785. The indictment charged them with unlawfully selling to another a certain amount of a derivative of opium and a certain amount of a derivative of coca leaves, not in pursuance of any written order on a form issued in blank for that purpose by the Commissioner of Internal Revenue, contrary to the provisions of § 2 of the act. The defendants demurred to the indictment on the ground that it failed to charge that they had sold the inhibited drugs knowing them to be such. The statute does not make such knowledge an element of the offense. The District Court sustained the demurrer and quashed the indictment. The correctness of this ruling is the question before us.

While the general rule at common law was that the *scienter* was a necessary element in the indictment and proof of every crime, and this was followed in regard to statutory crimes even where the statutory definition did [252] not in terms include it (*Reg. v. Sleep*, 8 Cox C. C. 472), there has been a modification of this view in respect to prosecutions under statutes the purpose of which would be obstructed by such a requirement. It is a question of legislative intent to be construed by the court. . . .

[253] The question before us, therefore, is one of the construction of the statute and of inference of the intent of Congress. The Narcotic Act has been held by this court to be a taxing act with the incidental purpose of minimizing the spread of addiction to the use of poisonous and demoralizing drugs. *United States v. Doremus*, 249 U.S. 86, 94; *United States v. Jin Fuey Moy*, 241 U.S. 394, 402.

Section 2 of the Narcotic Act, 38 Stat. 786, we give in part in the margin. It is very evident from a reading of [254] it that the emphasis of the section is in securing a close supervision of the business of dealing in these dangerous drugs by the taxing officers of the Government and that it merely uses a criminal penalty to secure recorded evidence of the disposition of such drugs as a means of taxing and restraining the traffic. Its manifest purpose is to require every person dealing in drugs to ascertain at his peril whether that which he sells comes within the inhibition of the statute, and if he sells the inhibited drug in ignorance of its character, to penalize him. Congress weighed the possible injustice of subjecting an innocent seller to a penalty against the evil of exposing innocent purchasers to danger from the drug, and concluded that the latter was the result preferably to be avoided. Doubtless considerations as to the opportunity of the seller to find out the fact and the difficulty of proof of knowledge contributed to this conclusion. We think the demurrer to the indictment should have been overruled.

Judgment reversed.

MR. JUSTICE CLARKE took no part in this decision.

Ponzi v. Fessenden

The famous 1920s scam artist who has been memorialized in the term "Ponzi scheme" challenged the right of the federal government to move him from the federal prison cell to which he had been sentenced to a state court in Massachusetts for a state trial. Taft upheld the right of the federal government, a sovereign power, to move Ponzi to the jurisdiction of another sovereign power, the Commonwealth of Massachusetts.

Ponzi v. Fessenden et al.

On Certificate from the Circuit Court of Appeals for the First Circuit

No. 631. Argued March 8, 9, 1922—Decided March 27, 1922

258 U.S. 254 (1922)

[259]

MR. CHIEF JUSTICE TAFT, after stating the case as above, delivered the opinion of the court.

We live in the jurisdiction of two sovereignties, each having its own system of courts to declare and enforce its laws in common territory. It would be impossible for such courts to fulfil their respective functions without embarrassing conflict unless rules were adopted by them to avoid it. The people for whose benefit these two systems are maintained are deeply interested that each system shall be effective and unhindered in its vindication of its laws. The situation requires, therefore, not only definite rules fixing the powers of the courts in cases of jurisdiction over the same persons and things in actual litigation, but also a spirit of reciprocal comity and mutual assistance to promote due and orderly procedure.

[260] One accused of crime has a right to a full and fair trial according to the law of the government whose sovereignty he is alleged to have offended, but he has no more than that. He should not be permitted to use the machinery of one sovereignty to obstruct his trial in the courts of the other, unless the necessary operation of such machinery prevents his having a fair trial. He may not complain if one sovereignty waives its strict right to exclusive custody of him for vindication of its laws in order that the other may also subject him to conviction of crime against it. *In re Andrews*, 236 F. 300; *United States v. Marrin*, 227 F. 314. Such a waiver is a matter that addresses itself solely to the discretion of the sovereignty making it and of its representatives with power to grant it.

One accused of crime, of course, can not be in two places at the same time. He is entitled to be present at every stage of the trial of himself in each jurisdiction with full opportunity for defense. *Frank v. Mangum*, 237 U.S. 309, 341; *Lewis v. United States*, 146 U.S. 370. If that is accorded him, he can not complain. The fact that he may have committed two crimes gives him no immunity from prosecution of either.

* * * * *

United Zinc & Chemical Co. v. Britt

Taft's tenure as chief justice is remembered, among other things, for the great effort he expended in suppressing dissents. Accordingly, rarely was Taft himself found in dissent. *United Zinc & Chemical* was an exception to this policy. It involved the issue of an "attractive nuisance." Two young children climbed over a fence and went for a swim in the appellant company's pond. The water poisoned them, and they died. They children's families prevailed in the lower court, but the Supreme Court, speaking through Justice Oliver Wendell Holmes, Jr., reversed, finding the company not responsible for the deaths. Taft, along with Justice William R. Day, joined in a dissent written by Justice John H. Clarke.[1]

Note

1. David H. Burton labels this decision by Holmes as evidence that the Boston Brahmin was in fact a "closet conservative" (*Oliver Wendell Holmes, Jr.: What Manner of Liberal?* [Huntington, N.Y.: Robert E. Krieger Publishing Company, 1979], 89).

United Zinc & Chemical Company v. Britt et al.

Certiorari to the Circuit Court of Appeals for the Eighth Circuit

No. 164. Submitted March 13, 1922—Decided March 27, 1922

258 U.S. 268 (1922)

* * * * *

[274]

MR. JUSTICE HOLMES delivered the opinion of the court.

This is a suit brought by the respondents against the petitioner to recover for the death of two children, sons of the respondents. The facts that for the purposes of decision we shall assume to have been proved are these. The petitioner owned a tract of about twenty acres in the outskirts of the town of Iola, Kansas. Formerly it had there a plant for the making of sulphuric acid and zinc spelter. In 1910 it tore the building down but left a basement and cellar, in which in July, 1916, water was accumulated, clear in appearance but in fact dangerously poisoned by sulphuric acid and zinc sulphate that had come in one way or another from the petitioner's works, as the petitioner knew. The respondents had been travelling and encamped at some distance from this place. A travelled way passed within 120 or 100 feet of it. On July 27, 1916, the children, who were eight and eleven years old, came upon the petitioner's land, went into the water, were poisoned and died. . . .

* * * * *

[275] In the case at bar it is at least doubtful whether the water could be seen from any place where the children lawfully [276] were and there is no evidence that it was what led them to enter the land. But that is necessary to start the supposed duty. There can be no general duty on the part of a landowner to keep his land safe for children, or even free from hidden dangers, if he has not directly or by implication invited or licensed them to come there. . . .

The decision is very far from establishing that the petitioner is liable for poisoned water not bordering a road, not shown to have been the inducement that led the children to trespass, if in any event the law would deem it sufficient to excuse their going there, and not shown to have been the indirect inducement because known to the children to be frequented by others. It is suggested that the roads across the place were invitations. A road is not an invitation to leave it elsewhere than at its end.

Judgment reversed.

MR. JUSTICE CLARKE, with whom concurred THE CHIEF JUSTICE and MR. JUSTICE DAY, dissenting.

The courts of our country have sharply divided as to the principles of law applicable to "attractive nuisance" cases, of which this one is typical.

* * * * *

[278] The case was given to the jury in a clear and comprehensive charge, and the judgment of the District Court upon the verdict was affirmed by the Circuit Court of [279] Appeals. The court charged the jury that if the water in the pool was not poisonous and if the boys were simply drowned there could be no recovery, but that if it was found, that the defendant knew or in the exercise of ordinary care should have known, that the water was impregnated with poison, that children were likely to go to its vicinity, that it was in appearance clear and pure and attractive to young children as a place for bathing, and that the death of the children was caused by its alluring appearance and

by its poisonous character, and because no protection or warning was given against it, the case came within the principle of the "attractive nuisance" or "turntable" cases and recovery would be allowed.

This was as favorable a view of the federal law, as it has been until today, as the petitioner deserved. . . .

The facts, as stated, make it very clear that in the view most unfavorable to the plaintiffs below there might be a difference of opinion between candid men as to, whether the pool was so located that the owners of the land should have anticipated that children might frequent its vicinity, whether its appearance and character rendered it attractive to childish instincts so as to make it a temptation to children of tender years, and whether, therefore, it was culpable negligence to maintain it in that location, unprotected and without warning as to its poisonous condition. This being true, the case would seem to be one clearly for a jury, under the ruling in the *Stout Case, supra.*

Believing as I do that the doctrine of the *Stout* and *McDonald* cases, giving weight to, and making allowance, as they do, for, the instincts and habitual conduct of children of tender years, is a sound doctrine, calculated to [280] make men more reasonably considerate of the safety of the children of their neighbors, than will the harsh rule which makes trespassers of little children which the court is now substituting for it; I cannot share in setting aside the verdict of the jury in this case, approved by the judgments of two courts, upon what is plainly a disputed question of fact and in thereby overruling two decisions which have been accepted as leading authorities for half a century, and I therefore dissent from the judgment and opinion of the court.

Balzac v. Porto Rico

Jesus Balzac, a newspaper editor, was convicted of libel. His appeal sought to raise both First Amendment issues of freedom of the press and the Sixth Amendment issue of right to a jury trial. Taft concluded that it was for Congress to determine how far the guarantees of the Bill of Rights extended to persons living in the territories acquired in the aftermath of the Spanish-American War.

Taft found that the Foraker Act specifically declined to extend the right to a jury trial to the Territory of Porto Rico (Puerto Rico) and that the guarantee of freedom of the press, which did apply, did not protect what Balzac had printed.

Balzac v. People of Porto Rico

Error to the Supreme Court of Porto Rico

Nos. 178, 179. Argued March 20, 1922—Decided April 10, 1922

258 U.S. 298 (1922)

[300]

MR. CHIEF JUSTICE TAFT delivered the opinion of the court.

These are two prosecutions for criminal libel brought against the same defendant, Jesus M. Balzac, on informations filed in the District Court for Arecibo, Porto Rico, by the District Attorney for that District. Balzac was the editor of a daily paper published in Arecibo, known as "El Baluarte," and the articles upon which the charges of libel were based were published on April 16 and April 23, 1918, respectively. In each case the defendant demanded a jury. The code of criminal procedure of Porto Rico grants a jury trial in cases of felony but not in misdemeanors. The defendant, nevertheless, contended that he was entitled to a jury in such a case, under the Sixth Amendment to the Constitution, and that the language of the alleged libels was only fair comment and their publication was protected by the First Amendment. His contentions were overruled, he was tried by the court and was convicted in both cases and sentenced to five months' imprisonment in the district jail in the first, and to four months in the second, and to the payment of the costs in each. The defendant appealed to the Supreme Court of Porto Rico. That court affirmed both judgments. . . .

* * * * *

[304] We have . . . to inquire whether that part of the Sixth Amendment to the Constitution, which requires that, in all criminal prosecutions, the accused shall enjoy the right to a speedy and public trial, by an impartial jury of the State and district wherein the crime shall have been committed, which district shall have been previously ascertained by law, applies to Porto Rico. Another provision on the subject is in Article III of the Constitution providing that the trial of all crimes, except in cases of impeachment, shall be by jury; and such trial shall be held in the State where the said crimes shall have been committed; but, when not committed within any State, the trial shall be at such place or places as the Congress may by law have directed. The Seventh Amendment of the Constitution provides that in suits at common law, where the value in controversy shall exceed twenty dollars, the

right of trial by jury shall be preserved. It is well settled that these provisions for jury trial in criminal and civil cases apply to the Territories of the United States. *Webster v. Reid*, 11 How. 437, 460; *Reynolds v. United States*, 98 U.S. 145, 167; *Callan v. Wilson*, 127 U.S. 540, 556; *American Publishing Co. v. Fisher*, 166 U.S. 464; *Thompson v. Utah*, 170 U.S. 343, 347; *Capital Traction Co. v. Hof*, 174 U.S. 1; *Black v. Jackson*, 177 U.S. 349; *Rassmussen v. United States*, 197 U.S. 516, 528; *Gurvich v. United States*, 198 U.S. 581. But it is just as clearly settled that they do not apply to territory belonging to the [305] United States which has not been incorporated into the Union. *Hawaii v. Mankichi*, 190 U.S. 197; *Dorr v. United States*, 195 U.S. 138, 145. It was further settled in *Downes v. Bidwell*, 182 U.S. 244, and confirmed by *Dorr v. United States*, 195 U.S. 138, that neither the Philippines nor Porto Rico was territory which had been incorporated in the Union or become a part of the United States, as distinguished from merely belonging to it; and that the acts giving temporary governments to the Philippines, 32 Stat. 691, and to Porto Rico, 31 Stat. 77, had no such effect. The *Insular Cases* revealed much diversity of opinion in this court as to the constitutional status of the territory acquired by the Treaty of Paris ending the Spanish War, but the *Dorr* case shows that the opinion of Mr. Justice White of the majority, in *Downes v. Bidwell*, has become the settled law of the court. The conclusion of this court in the *Dorr* case, p. 149, was as follows:

"We conclude that the power to govern territory, implied in the right to acquire it, and given to Congress in the Constitution in Article IV, § 3, to whatever other limitations it may be subject, the extent of which must be decided as questions arise, does not require that body to enact for ceded territory, not made a part of the United States by Congressional action, a system of laws which shall include the right of trial by jury, and that the Constitution does not, without legislation and of its own force, carry such right to territory so situated."

The question before us, therefore, is: Has Congress, since the Foraker Act of April 12, 1900, c. 191, 31 Stat. 77, enacted legislation incorporating Porto Rico into the Union? . . .

[306] The act is entitled "An Act To provide a civil government for Porto Rico, and for other purposes." It does not indicate by its title that it has a purpose to incorporate the Island into the Union. It does not contain any clause which declares such purpose or effect. While this is not conclusive, it strongly tends to show that Congress did not have such an intention. Few questions have been the subject of such discussion and dispute in our country as the status of our territory acquired from Spain in 1899. The division between the political parties in respect to it, the diversity of the views of the

members of this court in regard to its constitutional aspects, and the constant recurrence of the subject in the Houses of Congress, fixed the attention of all on the future relation of this acquired territory to the United States. Had Congress intended to take the important step of changing the treaty status of Porto Rico by incorporating it into the Union, it is reasonable to suppose that it would have done so by the plain declaration, and would not have left it to mere inference. Before the question became acute at the close of the Spanish War, the distinction between acquisition and incorporation was not regarded as important, or at least it was not fully understood and had not aroused great controversy. Before that, the purpose of Congress might well be a matter of mere inference from various legislative acts; but in these latter days, incorporation is not to be assumed without express declaration, or an implication so strong as to exclude any other view.

Again, the second section of the act is called a "Bill of Rights," and included therein is substantially every one of the guaranties of the Federal Constitution, except those relating to indictment by a grand jury in the case of infamous crimes and the right of trial by jury in civil and criminal cases. If it was intended to incorporate Porto Rico into the Union by this act, which would *ex proprio vigore* make applicable the whole Bill of Rights [307] of the Constitution to the Island, why was it thought necessary to create for it a Bill of Rights and carefully exclude trial by jury? In the very forefront of the act is this substitute for incorporation and application of the Bill of Rights of the Constitution. This seems to us a conclusive argument against the contention of counsel for the plaintiff in error.

* * * * *

[310] The jury system needs citizens trained to the exercise of the responsibilities of jurors. In common-law countries centuries of tradition have prepared a conception of the impartial attitude jurors must assume. The jury system postulates a conscious duty of participation in the machinery of justice which it is hard for people not brought up in fundamentally popular government at once to acquire. One of its greatest benefits is in the security it gives the people that they, as jurors actual or possible, being part of the judicial system of the country can prevent its arbitrary use or abuse. Congress has thought that a people like the Filipinos or the Porto Ricans, trained to a complete judicial system which knows no juries, living in compact and ancient communities, with definitely formed customs and political conceptions, should be permitted themselves to determine how far they wish to adopt this institution of Anglo-Saxon origin, and when. Hence the care with which from the time when Mr. McKinley wrote his historic letter to Mr. Root in April of 1900, Public Laws, Philippine Commission, pp. 6–9—Act

of July 1, 1902, c. 1369, 32 Stat. 691, 692, concerning the character of government to be set up for the Philippines by the Philippine Commission, until the Act [311] of 1917, giving a new Organic Act to Porto Rico, the United States has been liberal in granting to the Islands acquired by the Treaty of Paris most of the American constitutional guaranties, but has been sedulous to avoid forcing a jury system on a Spanish and civil-law country until it desired it. We can not find any intention to depart from this policy in making Porto Ricans American citizens, explained as this is by the desire to put them as individuals on an exact equality with citizens from the American homeland, to secure them more certain protection against the world, and to give them an opportunity, should they desire, to move into the United States proper and there without naturalization to enjoy all political and other rights.

* * * * *

[314] A second assignment of error is based on the claim that the alleged libels here did not pass the bounds of legitimate comment on the conduct of the Governor of the Island against whom they were directed, and that their prosecution is a violation of the First Amendment to the Constitution securing free speech and a free press. A reading of the two articles removes the slightest doubt that they go far beyond the "exuberant expressions of meridional speech," to use the expression of this court in a similar case in *Gandia v. Pettingill*, 222 U.S. 452, 458. Indeed they are so excessive and outrageous in their character that they suggest the query whether their superlative vilification has not overleapt itself and become unconsciously humorous. But this is not a defence.

The judgments of the Supreme Court of Porto Rico are

Affirmed.

MR. JUSTICE HOLMES concurs in the result.

Stafford v. Wallace

The precedents of *Munn v. Illinois*, 94 U.S. 113 (1877), and *Swift & Company v. United States*, 196 U.S. 375 (1905), gave the federal government in exercising its power under I-8-3 (the Commerce Clause) a broad right "to regulate Commerce . . . among the several States." In contrast, *E. C. Knight Co. v. United States*, 156 U.S. 1 (1895), took a much narrower view of the power of Congress to use the commerce clause to regulate local activities. For the Taft Court and the subsequent Hughes Court (1930–41), the question in cases dealing with I-8-3 was whether the Court would adopt the narrow interpretation of federal powers enunciated in *E. C. Knight* or take the broader view as represented by *Swift & Company.*

Did the regulations in the Packers and Stockyards Act of 1921 resemble the local activities held to be outside the reach of the federal government in *Knight*, or were they part of the flow of commerce that the Court in *Swift & Company* found to be subject to federal control? Taft mustered seven justices to hold that the act was similar to the facts in *Swift.* Only Justice James C. McReynolds dissented.

Stafford et al., Copartners, Doing Business as Stafford Brothers, et al. v. Wallace, Secretary of Agriculture, et al.

Burton et al. v. Clyne, United States District Attorney for the Northern District of Illinois

Appeals from the District Court of the United States for the Northern District of Illinois

Nos. 687, 691. Argued March 20, 21, 1922—Decided May 1, 1922

258 U.S. 495 (1922)

[512]

MR. CHIEF JUSTICE TAFT . . . delivered the opinion of the court.

[513] The Packers and Stockyards Act of 1921 seeks to regulate the business of the packers done in interstate commerce and forbids them to engage in unfair, discriminatory or deceptive practices in such commerce, or to subject any person to unreasonable prejudice therein, or to do any of a number of acts to control prices or establish a monopoly in the business. It constitutes the Secretary of Agriculture a tribunal to hear complaints and make findings thereon, and to order the packers to cease any forbidden practice. . . .

* * * * *

[514] The object to be secured by the act is the free and unburdened flow of live stock from the ranges and farms of the West and the Southwest through the great stockyards and slaughtering centers on the borders of that region, and thence in the form of meat products to the consuming cities of the country in the Middle West and East, or, still as live stock, to the feeding places and fattening farms in the Middle West or East for further preparation for the market.

The chief evil feared is the monopoly of the packers, enabling them unduly and arbitrarily to lower prices to [515] the shipper who sells, and unduly and arbitrarily to increase the price to the consumer who buys. Congress thought that the power to maintain this monopoly was aided by control of the stockyards. Another evil which it sought to provide against by the act, was exorbitant charges, duplication of commissions, deceptive practices in respect of prices, in the passage of the live stock through the stockyards, all made possible by collusion between the stockyards management and the commission men, on the one hand, and the packers and dealers on the other. . . .

The stockyards are not a place of rest or final destination. Thousands of head of live stock arrive daily by [516] carload and trainload lots, and must be promptly sold and disposed of and moved out to give place to the constantly flowing traffic that presses behind. The stockyards are but a throat through which the current flows, and the transactions which occur therein are only incident to this current from the West to the East, and from one State to another. Such transactions can not be separated from the movement to which they contribute and necessarily take on its character. The commission men are essential in making the sales without which the flow of the current would be obstructed, and this, whether they are made to packers or dealers. The dealers are essential to the sales to the stock farmers and feeders. The sales are not in this aspect merely local transactions. They create a local change of title, it is true, but they do not stop the flow; they merely change the private interests in the subject of the current, not interfering with, but, on the contrary, being indispensable to its continuity. . . .

The act, therefore, treats the various stockyards of the country as great national public utilities to promote the flow of commerce from the ranges and farms of the West to the consumers in the East. It assumes that they conduct a business affected by a public use of a national character and subject to national regulation. That it is a business within the power of regulation by legislative action needs no discussion. That has been settled since the case of *Munn v. Illinois,* 94 U.S. 113. . . . A similar [517] question has been before this court and had great consideration in *Swift & Co. v. United States,* 196 U.S. 375. The judgment in that case gives a clear and comprehensive exposition which leaves to us in this case little but the obvious application of the principles there declared.

The *Swift Case* presented to this court the sufficiency of a bill in equity brought against substantially the same packing firms as those against whom this legislation is chiefly directed, charging them as a combination of a dominant proportion of the dealers in fresh meat throughout the United States not to bid against each other in the live stock markets of the different States, to bid up prices for a few days in order to induce the cattle men to send their stock to the stockyards, to fix prices at which they would sell, and to that end to restrict shipments of meat. . . .

* * * * *

[518] The application of the commerce clause of the Constitution in the *Swift Case* was the result of the natural development of interstate commerce under modern conditions. It was the inevitable recognition of the great [519] central fact that such streams of commerce from one part of the country to another which are ever flowing are in their very essence the commerce among the States and with foreign nations which historically it was one of the chief purposes of the Constitution to bring under national protection and control. This court declined to defeat this purpose in respect of such a stream and take it out of complete national regulation by a nice and technical inquiry into the non-interstate character of some of its necessary incidents and facilities when considered alone and without reference to their association with the movement of which they were an essential but subordinate part.

The principles of the *Swift Case* have become a fixed rule of this court in the construction and application of the commerce clause. Its latest expression on the subject is found in *Lemke v. Farmers Grain Co., ante,* 50. . . .

* * * * *

[523] Counsel for appellants cite cases to show that transactions like those of the commission men or dealers here are not interstate commerce or within the power of Congress to regulate. The chief of these are *Hopkins v.* [524] *United States,* 171 U.S. 578, and *Anderson v. United States,* 171 U.S. 604. These cases were considered in the *Swift Case* and disposed of. . . .

* * * * *

[528] The orders of the District Court refusing the interlocutory injunctions are

Affirmed.

MR. JUSTICE MCREYNOLDS dissents.

MR. JUSTICE DAY did not sit in these cases and took no part in their decision.

Omitted Taft Opinions

Irwin v. Wright County Treasurer, 258 U.S. 219 (1922)—effect of death on suit against state officer.

Wallace v. United States, 255 U.S. 296 (1922)—further appeal in earlier case of same name (257 U.S. 541 [1922]).

Sloan Shipyards v. United States Shipping Board Emergency Fleet Corp., 258 U.S. 549 (1922)—dissent by Taft in bankruptcy case.

VOLUME 259

British Columbia Mills Tug & Barge Co. v. Mylroie

As noted earlier, admiralty cases still made up a significant portion of the Court's docket in the 1920s, as exemplified by the following case, one of little note. In affirming the lower court decision, Taft seized upon the concept of "reasonable assistance" as central to whether or not there was in fact any liability in the action of the tug. Taft agreed that the tugboat company was responsible for the damages to the barge.

British Columbia Mills Tug & Barge Company v. Mylroie

Certiorari to the Circuit Court of Appeals for the Ninth Circuit

No. 190. Argued March 23, 24, 1922—Decided May 15, 1922

259 U.S. 1 (1922)

[2]

MR. CHIEF JUSTICE TAFT delivered the opinion of the court.

This case was begun by a libel *in rem* filed by A. W. Mylroie, the respondent herein, as owner of the American barge "Bangor," and lawful bailee of its cargo, against the British tug "Commodore," in the District Court of Alaska. . . .

[3] The petitioner joined issue upon these allegations by denying negligence, lack of skill and unseaworthiness, and charged the stranding of the barge, with the consequent loss, to the unseaworthiness of the shackle which had been furnished by the barge owner. The tug owner further set up the defense against recovery that he was exempted from liability for negligence because of a clause of the towing contract.

* * * * *

[4] We have read the voluminous evidence in this retort and have compared with care the findings of the two courts. After giving due weight to the findings of the court which heard the witnesses, the examination satisfies us that the District Court was influenced too much by the mere preponderance in number of the witnesses for the tug owner, and that it did not sufficiently consider the significance of certain conceded facts in sustaining the evidence of the fewer witnesses for the barge owner.

* * * * *

[11] This brings us to the question how far the tug is exculpated from liability for negligence by the contract. The clause of the contract relied on by the tug owner is as follows:

> "3. That the Tug will render to the said Barge 'Bangor' reasonable assistance from time to time in any emergency which might arise, and while discharging at Anchorage the Tug is to be within call of the Barge at all times to render such reasonable assistance in case of any emergency which might arise. The Tug Company is not to be held liable for any damage which might happen to the said barge 'Bangor' or its cargo while in tow or at anchor."

* * * * *

[12] Dealing with the clause in this case in the same way, we must read it to mean that the tug was not to be held liable for any damage which might happen to the barge or its cargo, while in tow, unless the tug should not render reasonable assistance to the tow in an emergency. As our view of the evidence results in the conclusion that the negligence of the tug in not providing a proper lookout created the emergency and that the tug did not render proper assistance to the tow in the emergency so created, the tug is clearly liable for the loss. This makes it unnecessary for us to consider the contention on behalf of the barge that the exemption clause is void.

The Circuit Court of Appeals directed a decree for the owner of the tow and sent the case back for a more satisfactory assessment of damages. We brought the decree here by certiorari under § 240 of the Judicial Code. We now affirm the decree and remand the case to the District Court for assessment of damages in conformity to the mandate of the Circuit Court of Appeals.

Affirmed.

Atherton Mills v. Johnston

Gaining fame by having one's name attached to a major precedent is almost like winning a lottery. Ernesto Miranda had the "luck"—he was later retried and convicted on other evidence—not only of having his confession thrown out, but of having his name put on the lead case that established the so-called Miranda rule, 384 U.S. 436 (1966). The same fate could have attached itself to the Johnstons, who challenged the constitutionality of the Child Labor Tax Act. Unfortunately for their place in history, the Court found the fact that the Johnston boy was no longer a minor by the time the case reached the Supreme Court rendered the controversy "moot."

Atherton Mills v. Johnston et al.

*Appeal from the District Court of the United States for the
Western District of North Carolina*

No. 16. Argued December 10, 1919; restored to docket for reargument June 6,
1921; reargued March 7, 8, 1922—Decided May 15, 1922

259 U.S. 13 (1922)

[13]

MR. CHIEF JUSTICE TAFT delivered the opinion of the court.

The two Johnstons, father and son, citizens of North Carolina, the former in his own right, and as the authorized next friend of his son, filed their bill of complaint [14] April 15, 1919, against the Atherton Mills, a corporation of the same State. The bill averred that Johnston, the son, was a minor between the ages of fourteen and sixteen years, that Johnston, the father, supporting his son, was entitled to his earnings until he attained his majority, that the son was in the employ of the defendant, that by the terms of the so-called Child Labor Tax Act, approved February 24, 1919, c. 18, § 1200, 40 Stat. 1057, 1138, the defendant was subjected to a tax of one-tenth of its annual profits if it employed a child within the ages of fourteen and sixteen for more than eight hours a day, six days a week, or before the hour of 6 A. M. or after the hour of 7 P. M.; that the defendant was unwilling to arrange a schedule of working hours to comply with this requirement for the minor complainant, and was about to discharge him because of the act, thus depriving the son and father of all of the son's earnings. On the ground that the act was invalid because beyond the powers of Congress, and that the discharge would injure both complainants by a serious deprivation of earnings, which but for the law they would enjoy, and that the granting of an injunction would prevent a multiplicity of suits, they prayed for an injunction against the defendant from discharging the complainant son or in any manner curtailing his employment to eight hours a day or otherwise.

* * * * *

[15] The lapse of time since the case was heard and decided in the District Court has brought the minor, whose employment was the subject matter of the suit, to an age which is not within the ages affected by the act. The act, even if valid, can not affect him further. The case for an injunction has, therefore, become moot and we can [16] not consider it.

* * * * *

Reversed.

Bailey v. George

Another case involving "Tax on Employment of Child Labor," this case focused on whether or not a person challenging the constitutionality of a tax had the right not to pay the tax. The Court ruled that this was not the case. The tax must be paid and then action taken to recover the money paid.

Bailey, Collector of Internal Revenue, et al. v. George, Trading and Doing Business as Vivian Cotton Mills, et al.

Appeal from the District Court of the United States for the Western District of North Carolina

No. 500. Argued March 7, 3, 1922—Decided May 15, 1922

259 U.S. 16 (1922)

[19]

MR. CHIEF JUSTICE TAFT delivered the opinion of the court.

* * * * *

[20] . . . Section 3224, Rev. Stats., provides that "No suit for the purpose of restraining the assessment or collection of any tax shall be maintained in any court." The averment that a taxing statute is unconstitutional does not take this case out of the section. There must be some extraordinary and exceptional circumstance not here averred or shown to make the provisions of the section inapplicable.

* * * * *

The decree of the District Court is reversed and the cause remanded with directions to dismiss the bill.

Reversed.

Bailey v. Drexel Furniture Co.
(Child Labor Tax Case)

The Child Labor Tax of 1919 was adopted by Congress by overwhelming majorities in both houses. Congressmen were still smarting from the Supreme Court's vote in *Hammer v. Dagenhart,* 247 U.S. 251 (1918), voiding the Keating-Owen Child Labor Act of 1916. This statute had relied on the Commerce Clause (I-8-3) to outlaw what most Americans of the time saw as the barbaric practice of child labor. Unlike the sharply divided Court (5–4) that had found the Keating-Owen Act unconstitutional, the decision in the Child Labor Tax Case was almost unanimous. Only Justice John H. Clarke dissented, and he did not write an opinion.

Although many historians of the Court see the *Bailey* opinion as further evidence of the conservatism of Chief Justice Taft and of the Taft Court in general—and explain the fact that Justices Holmes and Brandeis joined the opinion in terms of tactical considerations on their parts—Taft's overriding concern with protecting the power and prestige of the Court may have been equally relevant to the case's outcome. Had the Court upheld the Child Labor Tax only four years after the brethren had struck down Keating-Owen, many might have seen the decision as a surrender on the part of the Court to the greater power of the Congress and president. A similar rationale was put forth in the unusual—indeed almost unprecedented—joint opinion of Justices Anthony Kennedy, David Souter, and Sandra Day O'Connor in the abortion decision, *Planned Parenthood v. Casey*, 505 U.S. 833 (1992).

For Taft, the most difficult task in the *Child Labor Tax Case* was to distinguish the circumstances of this law from the various well-known precedents in which the Court had upheld a liberal interpretation of the scope of Congress's power to tax. One such example was the opinion by then Associate Justice William Douglass White in the case of *McCray v. United States*, 195 U.S. 27 (1904), in which White upheld a tax on colored oleomargarine that clearly had the intent of making the product noncompetitive with butter by raising margarine's price. Like the Narcotic Act, discussed in *United States v. Balint*, 258 U.S. 250 (1922), the tax statute clearly acted as a regulatory and not as a revenue-raising measure.

How successful Taft was in drawing a meaningful distinction in *Bailey* between the two types of legislation remains for the reader to determine. Let it be said, though, that even the post-1937 "Modern Court" continues to be much more reluctant to uphold the use of the taxing power to regulate in contrast to the much more latitudian position the Court, at least until the Rehnquist Court, has adopted regarding the Commerce Clause.

Bailey v. Drexel Furniture Company

Error to the District Court of the United States for the
Western District of North Carolina

No. 657. Argued March 7, 8, 1922—Decided May 15, 1922

259 U.S. 20 (1922)

[34]

MR. CHIEF JUSTICE TAFT delivered the opinion of the court.

This case presents the question of the constitutional validity of the Child Labor Tax Law. The plaintiff below, the Drexel Furniture Company, is engaged in the manufacture of furniture in the Western District of North Carolina.

* * * * *

[36] The law is attacked on the ground that it is a regulation of the employment of child labor in the States—an exclusively state function under the Federal Constitution and within the reservations of the Tenth Amendment. It is defended on the ground that it is a mere excise tax levied by the

Congress of the United States under its broad power of taxation conferred by § 8, Article I, of the Federal Constitution. We must construe the law and interpret the intent and meaning of Congress from the language of the act. The words are to be given their ordinary meaning unless the context shows that they are differently used. Does this law impose a tax with only that incidental restraint and regulation which a tax must inevitably involve? Or does it regulate by the use of the so-called tax as a penalty? If a tax, it is clearly an excise. If it were an excise on a commodity or other thing of value we might not be permitted under previous decisions of this court to infer solely from its heavy burden that the act intends a prohibition instead of a tax. But this act is more. It provides a heavy exaction for a departure from a detailed and specified course of conduct in business. That course of business is that employers shall employ in mines and quarries, children of an age greater than sixteen years; in mills and factories, children of an age greater than fourteen years, and shall prevent children of less than sixteen years in mills and factories from working more than eight hours a day or six days in the week. If an employer departs from this prescribed course of business, he is to pay to the Government one-tenth of his entire net income in the business for a full year. The amount is not to be proportioned in any degree to the extent or frequency of the departures, but is to be paid by the employer in full measure whether he employs five hundred children for a year, or employs only one for a day. Moreover, if he does not know the child is within the named age limit, he is not to pay; [37] that is to say, it is only where he knowingly departs from the prescribed course that payment is to be exacted. Scienter is associated with penalties not with taxes. The employer's factory is to be subject to inspection at any time not only by the taxing officers of the Treasury, the Department normally charged with the collection of taxes, but also by the Secretary of Labor and his subordinates whose normal function is the advancement and protection of the welfare of the workers. In the light of these features of the act, a court must be blind not to see that the so-called tax is imposed to stop the employment of children within the age limits prescribed. Its prohibitory and regulatory effect and purpose are palpable. All others can see and understand this. How can we properly shut our minds to it?

It is the high duty and function of this court in cases regularly brought to its bar to decline to recognize or enforce seeming laws of Congress, dealing with subjects not entrusted to Congress but left or committed by the supreme law of the land to the control of the States. We can not avoid the duty even though it require us to refuse to give effect to legislation designed to promote the highest good. The good sought in unconstitutional legislation is an insidious feature because it leads citizens and legislators of good purpose to promote it without thought of the serious breach it will make in the ark of our covenant or the harm which will come from breaking down recognized standards. In the maintenance of local self government, on the one hand, and the national power, on the other, our country has been able to endure and prosper for near a century and a half.

Out of a proper respect for the acts of a coordinate branch of the Government, this court has gone far to sustain taxing acts as such, even though there has been ground for suspecting from the weight of the tax it was intended to destroy its subject. But, in the act before [38] us, the presumption of validity cannot prevail, because the proof of the contrary is found on the very face of its provisions. Grant the validity of this law, and all that Congress would need to do, hereafter, in seeking to take over to its control any one of the great number of subjects of public interest, jurisdiction of which the States have never parted with, and which are reserved to them by the Tenth Amendment, would be to enact a detailed measure of complete regulation of the subject and enforce it by a so-called tax upon departures from it. To give such magic to the word "tax" would be to break down all constitutional limitation of the powers of Congress and completely wipe out the sovereignty of the States.

The difference between a tax and a penalty is sometimes difficult to define and yet the consequences of the distinction in the required method of their collection often are important. Where the sovereign enacting the law has power to impose both tax and penalty the difference between revenue production and mere regulation may be immaterial, but not so when one sovereign can impose a tax only, and the power of regulation rests in another. Taxes are occasionally imposed in the discretion of the legislature on proper subjects with the primary motive of obtaining revenue from them and with the incidental motive of discouraging them by making their continuance onerous. They do not lose their character as taxes because of the incidental motive. But there comes a time in the extension of the penalizing features of the so-called tax when it loses its character as such and becomes a mere penalty with the characteristics of regulation and punishment. Such is the case in the law before us. Although Congress does not invalidate the contract of employment or expressly declare that the employment within the mentioned ages is illegal, it does exhibit its intent practically to achieve the latter result by adopting the criteria of wrongdoing and imposing its principal consequence on those who transgress its standard.

[39] The case before us can not be distinguished from that of *Hammer v. Dagenhart,* 247 U.S. 251. Congress there enacted a law to prohibit transportation

in interstate commerce of goods made at a factory in which there was employment of children within the same ages and for the same number of hours a day and days in a week as are penalized by the act in this case. This court held the law in that case to be void. It said:

> "In our view the necessary effect of this act is, by means of a prohibition against the movement in interstate commerce of ordinary commercial commodities, to regulate the hours of labor of children in factories and mines within the States, a purely state authority."

In the case at the bar, Congress in the name of a tax which on the face of the act is a penalty seeks to do the same thing, and the effort must be equally futile.

The analogy of the *Dagenhart Case* is clear. The congressional power over interstate commerce is, within its proper scope, just as complete and unlimited as the congressional power to tax, and the legislative motive in its exercise is just as free from judicial suspicion and inquiry. Yet when Congress threatened to stop interstate commerce in ordinary and necessary commodities, unobjectionable as subjects of transportation, and to deny the same to the people of a State in order to coerce them into compliance with Congress's regulation of state concerns, the court said this was not in fact regulation of interstate commerce, but rather that of State concerns and was invalid. So here the so-called tax is a penalty to coerce people of a State to act as Congress wishes them to act in respect of a matter completely the business of the state government under the Federal Constitution. This case requires as did the *Dagenhart Case* the application of the principle announced by Chief Justice Marshall in *McCulloch v. Maryland,* 4 Wheat. 316, 423, in a much quoted passage:

> [40] "Should Congress, in the execution of its powers, adopt measures which are prohibited by the Constitution; or should Congress, under the pretext of executing its powers, pass laws for the accomplishment of objects not entrusted to the government; it would become the painful duty of this tribunal should a case requiring such a decision come before it, to say, that such an act was not the law of the land."

But it is pressed upon us that this court has gone so far in sustaining taxing measures the effect or tendency of which was to accomplish purposes not directly within congressional power that we are bound by authority to maintain this law.

The first of these is *Veazie Bank v. Fenno,* 8 Wall. 533.

* * * * *

[41] It will be observed that the sole objection to the tax there was its excessive character. Nothing else appeared on the face of the act. It was an increase of a tax admittedly legal to a higher rate and that was all.

* * * * *

[42] The next case is that of *McCray v. United States,* 195 U.S. 27. That, like the *Veazie Bank Case,* was the increase of an excise tax upon a subject properly taxable in which the taxpayers claimed that the tax had become invalid because the increase was excessive. It was a tax on oleomargarine, a substitute for butter. The tax on the white oleomargarine was one-quarter of a cent a pound, and on the yellow oleomargarine was first two cents and was then by the act in question increased to ten cents per pound. This court held that the discretion of Congress in the exercise of its constitutional powers to levy excise taxes could not be controlled or limited by the courts because the latter might deem the incidence of the tax oppressive or even destructive. It was the same principle as that applied in the *Veazie Bank Case.* This was that Congress in selecting its subjects for taxation might impose the burden where and as it would and that a motive disclosed in its selection to discourage sale or manufacture of an article by a higher tax than on some other did not invalidate the tax. In neither of these cases did the law objected to show on its face as does the law before us the detailed specifications of a regulation of a state concern and business with a heavy exaction to promote the efficacy of such regulation.

[43] . . . The [next] case is *United States v. Doremus,* 249 U.S. 86. That involved the validity of the Narcotic Drug Act, 38 Stat. 785, which imposed a special tax on the manufacture, importation and sale or gift of opium or coca leaves or their compounds or derivatives. It required every person subject to the special tax to register with the Collector of Internal Revenue his name and place of business and forbade him to sell except upon the written order of the person to whom the sale was made on a form prescribed by the Commissioner of Internal Revenue. . . . The validity of a special tax in the nature of an excise tax on the manufacture, importation and sale of such drugs was, of course, unquestioned. The provisions for subjecting the sale and distribution of the drugs to official supervision and inspection were held to have a reasonable relation to the enforcement of the tax and were therefore held valid.

* * * * *

[44] For the reasons given, we must hold the Child Labor Tax Law invalid and the judgment of the District Court is

Affirmed.

Mr. Justice Clarke dissents.

Hill v. Wallace

The issue in this case was almost identical to that in the *Child Labor Tax Case,* 259 U.S. 20 (1922). Congress had adopted the Future Trading Act, which imposed a tax on future contracts. The purpose clearly was regulatory; it was not intended to raise revenue. Relying on its taxing power and not its commerce power, Congress sought to use the tax as a means by which the secretary of agriculture, working through the Chicago Board of Trade, could regulate the contact market in commodities futures.

The constitutionality of the federal Future Trading Act posed particular problems for the Court and for Chief Justice Taft. According to Mason, several votes were taken by the justices before they reached the result announced to the public. "At one point the Court voted 5 to 4 against sustaining the . . . Act as a regulation of interstate commerce. Later, by a vote of 5 to 3, Justice Brandeis not voting, its validity was upheld."[1] When the decision finally came down, the Court was unanimous, but the decision rested on an unconstitutional use of the taxing power similar to the Court's reasoning in the *Child Labor Tax Case,* handed down on the same day as *Hill.* According to Mason, Brandeis was influential in bringing about this switch, persuading his colleagues to find the statute to represent an unconstitutional use of Congress's taxing power. This left the Commerce Clause intact as a possible basis for future exercises of federal power.

Note

1. Mason, *William Howard Taft,* 207.

Hill, Jr., et al. v. Wallace, Secretary of Agriculture, et al.

*Appeal from the District Court of the United States for the
Northern District of Illinois*

No. 616. Argued January 11, 12, 1922—Decided May 15, 1922

259 U.S. 44 (1922)

[60]

MR. CHIEF JUSTICE TAFT delivered the opinion of the court.

The first question for our consideration is whether, assuming the act to be invalid, the complainants on the face of their bill state sufficient equitable grounds to justify granting the relief they ask. . . .

The bill shows that the act, if enforced, will seriously injure the value of the Board of Trade to its members, and the pecuniary value of their memberships. If the law be unconstitutional, then it was the duty of the Board of Directors to bring an action to resist its enforcement. . . .

* * * * *

[63] The act whose constitutionality is attacked is entitled "An Act Taxing contracts for the sale of grain for future delivery, and options for such contracts, and *providing for the regulation of boards of trade,* and for other purposes." (Italics ours.)

Section 4 imposes a tax, in addition to any imposed by law, of 20 cents a bushel involved in every contract of sale of grain for future delivery, with two exceptions. The first exception is where the seller holds and owns the grain at the time of sale, or is the owner or renter of land on which the grain is to be grown, or is an association made of such owners or renters. The second exception is where such contracts are made by or through a member of the Board of Trade designated by the Secretary of Agriculture as a contract market. . . .

* * * * *

[66] It is impossible to escape the conviction, from a full reading of this law, that it was enacted for the purpose of regulating the conduct of business of boards of trade through supervision of the Secretary of Agriculture and the use of an administrative tribunal consisting of that Secretary, the Secretary of Commerce, and the Attorney General. Indeed the title of the act recites that one of its purposes is the regulation of boards of trade. As the bill shows, the imposition of 20 cents a bushel on the various grains affected by the tax is most burdensome. The tax upon contracts for sales for future delivery under the Revenue Act is only 2 cents upon $100 of value, whereas this tax varies according to the price and character of the grain from 15 per cent. of its value to 50 per cent. The manifest purpose of the tax is to compel boards of trade to comply with regulations, many of which can have no relevancy to the collection of the tax at all. . . .

[67] Our decision, just announced, in the *Child Labor Tax Case, ante,* 20, involving the constitutional validity of the Child Labor Tax Law, completely covers this case. We there distinguish between cases like *Veazie Bank v. Fenno,* 8 Wall. 533, and *McCray v. United States,* 195 U.S. 27, in which it was held that this court could not limit the discretion of Congress in the exercise of its constitutional powers to levy excise taxes because the court might deem the incidence of the tax oppressive or even destructive. It was pointed out that in none of those cases did the law objected to show on its face, as did the Child Labor Tax Law, detailed regulation of a concern or business wholly within the police power of the State, with a heavy exaction to promote the efficacy of such regulation. . . .

* * * * *

[68] We come to the question then, Can these regulations of boards of trade by Congress be sustained under the commerce clause of the Constitution? Such regulations are held to be within the police powers of the State. *House v. Mayes,* 219 U.S. 270; *Brodnax v. Missouri,* 219 U.S. 285. There is not a word in the act from which it can be gathered that it is confined in its operation to interstate commerce. The words "interstate commerce" are not to be found in any part of the act from the title to the closing section. The transactions upon which the tax is to be imposed, the bill avers, are sales made between members of the Board of Trade in the City of Chicago for future delivery of grain, which will be settled by the process of offsetting purchases or by a delivery of warehouse receipts of grain stored in Chicago. Looked at in this aspect and without any limitation of the application of the tax to interstate commerce, or to that which the Congress may deem from evidence before it to be an obstruction to interstate commerce, we do not find it possible to sustain the validity of the regulations as they are set forth in this act. A reading of the act makes it quite clear that Congress sought to use the taxing power to give validity to the act. It did not have the exercise of its power under the commerce clause in mind and so did not [69] introduce into the act the limitations which certainly would accompany and mark an exercise of the power under the latter clause.

* * * * *

[72] The injunction against the Board of Trade and its officers, and the injunction against the Collector of Internal Revenue and the District Attorney, should be granted, so far as § 4 is concerned and the regulations of the act interwoven within it. The court below acquired no personal jurisdiction of the Secretary of Agriculture and the Commissioner of Internal Revenue by proper service and the dismissal as to them was right.

The decree of the District Court is reversed, and the cause is remanded for further proceedings in conformity to this opinion.

MR. JUSTICE BRANDEIS, concurring.

I agree that the Future Trading Act is unconstitutional; but I doubt whether the plaintiffs are in a position to require the court to pass upon the constitutional question in this case. It seems proper to state the reasons for my doubt.

* * * * *

[74] If, after the corporation has become a "contract market" its directors and managing officers should seek to subject the plaintiffs, as members,

to unauthorized restrictions or should attempt to deprive them of vested rights, [75] relief may, of course, be had in a proper proceeding. And likewise if the plaintiffs now have, as individuals, rights entitled to protection, there are appropriate remedies. But this is not such a suit. Here members of a corporation seek to enforce alleged derivative rights; and I doubt whether they have shown that they are in a position to do so.

United Mine Workers v. Coronado Co.

From the outset of his chief justiceship, Taft was determined to "mass" the Court. Few cases were less likely candidates for "massing" than the Coronado case. The issue had been before the White Court, which had decided by a divided vote that the UMWA was liable under the Sherman Act.

The case arose from an effort by a receiver in bankruptcy to reorganize coal mines in Arkansas, a highly unionized state, and to operate the mines on a nonunion basis. Taft was to refer to the receiver as a "hugger-mugger of . . . numerous corporations."[1] The unions resisted and engaged in a variety of tactics designed to frustrate the receiver's efforts to run the mines on a nonunion basis.

As a result, the Coronado Coal Company sought damages against the coal miners' unions for violation of federal antitrust legislation. Although the Court's narrow interpretation of the power of Congress to regulate commerce in cases such as *E. C. Knight*, 156 U.S. 1 (1895), and *Hammer v. Dagenhart*, 247 U.S. 251 (1918), produced results that satisfied defenders of property rights, this was not always the case. In this case, a similarly narrow view of commerce benefited the union, at least immediately, by exempting its local activities from the scope of the federal legislation. Coal mining was a local activity, just like manufacturing.

Although this particular case represented a victory for the union, the overall effect of the decision was very much against trade unionism. Unions were found to be suable, in the future, under the Sherman Act if it could be established that the national union had had any role in the illegal local activities.

Note

1. Pringle, *Life and Times,* 2:1040.

United Mine Workers of America et al. v. Coronado Coal Company et al.

Error to the Circuit Court of Appeals for the Eighth Circuit

No. 31. Argued October 15, 1920; restored to docket for reargument January 3, 1922; reargued March 22, 23, 1922—Decided June 5, 1922

259 U.S. 344 (1922)

[381]

MR. CHIEF JUSTICE TAFT, after stating the case, delivered the opinion of the court.

There are five principal questions pressed by the plaintiffs in error here, the defendants below. . . .

* * * * *

[383] Second. Were the unincorporated associations, the International Union, District No. 21, and the local unions suable in their names?

* * * * *

[385] The membership of the union has reached 450,000. The dues received from them for the national and district organizations make a very large annual total, and the obligations assumed in travelling expenses, holding of conventions, and general overhead cost, but most of all in strikes, are so heavy that an extensive financial business is carried on, money is borrowed, notes are given to banks, and in every way the union acts as a business entity, distinct from its members. No organized corporation has greater unity of action, and in none is more power centered in the governing executive bodies.

Undoubtedly at common law, an unincorporated association of persons was not recognized as having any other character than a partnership in whatever was done, and it could only sue or be sued in the names of its members, and their liability had to be enforced against each member. *Pickett v. Walsh,* 192 Mass. 572; *Karges Furniture Co. v. Amalgamated Woodworkers Local Union,* 165 Ind. 421; *Baskins v. United Mine Workers o f America,* 234 S. W. 464. But the growth and necessities of these great labor organizations have brought affirmative legal recognition of their [386] existence and usefulness and provisions for their protection, which their members have found necessary. Their right to maintain strikes, when they do not violate law or the rights of others, has been declared. The embezzlement of funds by their officers has been especially denounced as a crime. The so-called union label, which is a quasi trademark to indicate the origin of manufactured product in union labor, has been protected against pirating and deceptive use by the statutes of most of the States, and in many States authority to sue to enjoin its use has been conferred on unions.

* * * * *

[388] . . . It would be unfortunate if an organization with as great power as this International Union has in the raising of large funds and in directing the conduct of four hundred thousand members in carrying on, in a wide territory, industrial controversies and strikes, out of which so much unlawful injury to private rights is [389] possible, could assemble its assets to be used therein free from liability for injuries by torts committed in course of such strikes. To remand persons injured to a suit against each of the 400,000 members to recover damages and to levy on his share of the strike fund, would be to leave them remediless.

* * * * *

[392] Our conclusion as to the suability of the defendants is confirmed in the case at bar by the words of §§ 7 and 8 of the Anti-Trust Law. The persons who may be sued under § 7 include "corporations and associations existing under or authorized by the laws of either the United States, the laws of any of the Territories, the laws of any State, or the laws of any foreign country" [§ 8]. This language is very broad, and the words given their natural signification certainly include labor unions like these. . . .

* * * * *

[393] Third. The next question is whether the International Union was shown by any substantial evidence to have initiated, participated in or ratified the interference with plaintiffs' business which began April 6, 1914, and continued at intervals until July 17, when the matter culminated in a battle and the destruction of the Bache-Denman properties. The strike was a local strike declared by the president and officers of the District Organization No. 21, embracing Arkansas, Oklahoma and Texas. By Art. XVI of the International constitution, as we have seen, it could not thus engage in a strike if it involved all or a major part of its district members without sanction of the International Board. There is nothing to show that the International Board ever authorized it, took any part in preparation for it or in its maintenance. Nor did they or their organization ratify it by paying any of the expenses. It came exactly within the definition of a local strike in the constitutions of both the National and the District organizations. . . .

* * * * *

[395] But it is said that the District was doing the work of the International and carrying out its policies and this circumstance makes the former an agent. We can not agree to this in the face of the specific stipulation between them that in such a case unless the International expressly assumed responsibility,

the District must meet it alone. The subsequent events showing that the District did meet [396] the responsibility with its own funds confirm our reliance upon the constitution of the two bodies.

We conclude that the motions of the International Union, the United Mine Workers of America, and of its president and its other officers, that the jury be directed to return a verdict for them, should have been granted.

Fourth. The next question is twofold: (a) Whether the District No. 21 and the individual defendants participated in a plot unlawfully to deprive the plaintiffs of their employees by intimidation and violence and in the course of it destroyed their properties, and, (b), whether they did these things in pursuance of a conspiracy to restrain and monopolize interstate commerce.

* * * * *

[407] Coal mining is not interstate commerce, and the power of Congress does not extend to its regulation as such. In [408] *Hammer v. Dagenhart,* 247 U.S. 251, 272, we said: "The making of goods and the mining of coal are not commerce, nor does the fact that these things are to be afterwards shipped or used in interstate commerce, make their production a part thereof. *Delaware, Lackawanna & Western R. R. Co. v. Yurkonis,* 238 U.S. 439." Obstruction to coal mining is not a direct obstruction to interstate commerce in coal, although it, of course, may affect it by reducing the amount of coal to be carried in that commerce. We have had occasion to consider the principles governing the validity of congressional restraint of such indirect obstructions to interstate commerce in *Swift & Co. v. United States,* 196 U.S. 375; *United States v. Patten,* 226 U.S. 525; *United States v. Ferger,* 250 U.S. 199; *Railroad Commission of Wisconsin v. Chicago, Burlington & Quincy R. R. Co.,* 257 U.S. 563; and *Stafford v. Wallace,* 258 U.S. 495. It is clear from these cases that if Congress deems certain recurring practices, though not really part of interstate commerce, likely to obstruct, restrain or burden it, it has the power to subject them to national supervision and restraint. Again, it has the power to punish conspiracies in which such practices are part of the plan, to hinder, restrain or monopolize interstate commerce. But in the latter case, the intent to injure, obstruct or restrain interstate commerce must appear as an obvious consequence of what is to be done, or be shown by direct evidence or other circumstances.

* * * * *

[411] In the case at bar, there is nothing in the circumstances or the declarations of the parties to indicate that Stewart, the president of District No. 21, or Hull, its secretary-treasurer, or any of their accomplices had in mind interference with interstate commerce or competition when they entered

upon their unlawful combination to break up Bache's plan to carry on his mines with non-union men. The circumstances were ample to supply a full local motive for the conspiracy. Stewart said: "We are not going to let them dig coal—the scabs." His attention and that of his men was fastened on the presence of non-union-men in the mines in that local community.

* * * * *

Bache's breach of his contract with the District No. 21 in employing non-union men three months before it expired, his attempt to evade his obligation by a manipulation of his numerous corporations, his advertised anticipation of trespass and violence by warning notices, by enclosing his mining premises with a cable and stationing guards with guns to defend them, all these in the heart of a territory that had been completely unionized for years, were calculated to arouse a bitterness of spirit entirely local among the union miners against a policy that brought in strangers and excluded themselves or their union colleagues from the houses they had occupied and [412] the wages they had enjoyed. In the letter which Bache dictated in favor of operating the mines on a non-union basis, he said, "To do this means a bitter fight but in my opinion it can be accomplished by proper organization." Bache also testified that he was entering into a matter he knew was perilous and dangerous to his companies because in that section there was only one other mine running on a non-union basis. Nothing of this is recited to justify in the slightest the lawlessness and outrages committed, but only to point out that as it was a local strike within the meaning of the International and District constitutions, so it was in fact a local strike, local in its origin and motive, local in its waging, and local in its felonious and murderous ending.

But it is said that these District officers and their lieutenants among the miners must be charged with an intention to do what would be the natural result of their own acts, that they must have known that obstruction to mining coal in the Bache-Denman mines would keep 75 per cent. of their output from being shipped out of the State into interstate competition, and to that extent would help union operators in their competition for business. In a national production of from ten to fifteen million tons a week, or in a production in District No. 21 of 150,000 tons a week, 5,000 tons a week which the Bache-Denman mines in most prosperous times could not exceed, would have no appreciable effect upon the price of coal or non-union competition. The saving in the price per ton of coal under non-union conditions was said by plaintiffs' witnesses to be from seventeen to twenty cents, but surely no one would say that such saving on 5,000 tons would have a substantial effect on prices of coal in interstate commerce. Nor could it be inferred that Bache intended to cut the price of coal. His purpose was probably to pocket the profit that such a reduction made possible. . . .

[413] The result of our consideration of the entire record is that there was no evidence submitted to the jury upon which they properly could find that the outrages, felonies and murders of District No. 21 and its companions in crime were committed by them in a conspiracy to restrain or monopolize interstate commerce. The motion to direct the jury to return a verdict for the defendants should have been granted.

* * * * *

The judgment is reversed, and the case remanded to the District Court for further proceedings in conformity to this opinion.

Omitted Taft Opinion

Continental Insurance Company v. United States, 259 U.S. 156 (1922)—role of the Court in supervising the breakup of a railroad company.

October Term, 1922

VOLUME 260

Lederer v. Stockton

A trust had been established with the provision that at the death of all the annuitants the entire residue would go to a charity, the Pennsylvania Hospital. The Internal Revenue Service assessed taxes on the income. The trustee successfully challenged this action in the lower courts. Chief Justice Taft affirmed the lower court rulings, concluding that this was in accord with the purpose of Congress in "exempting from tax 'income received' by a charity."

Lederer, Collector of Internal Revenue for the First District of Pennsylvania, v. Stockton, Sole Surviving Trustee of Derbyshire, Deceased

Certiorari to the Circuit Court of Appeals for the Third Circuit

No. 16. Argued October 5, 1922—Decided October 16, 1922

260 U.S. 3 (1922)

[6]

MR. CHIEF JUSTICE TAFT delivered the opinion of the Court.

The question in this case is whether the Income Tax Law of September 8, 1916, c. 463, 39 Stat. 756, as amended by the Act of October 3, 1917, c. 63, 40 Stat. 300, requires the Contributors to the Pennsylvania Hospital, a corporation of Pennsylvania, created for charitable uses and purposes, no part of whose net income is for the benefit of any private stockholder or individual, to pay a tax on the income of a residuary estate devised to it by the will of Alexander J. Derbyshire in 1879 and inuring to its benefit under the following circumstances. The devise was subject to the payment of certain annuities. All of the annuitants are dead save one. The Supreme Court of that State decided that the income could not be paid outright to the Hospital until the death of all the annuitants and until then, must remain in control of the trustee appointed under the will. *Derbyshire's Estate,* 239 Pa. St. 389. The trustee transferred the whole residuary [7] fund as a loan for fifteen years to the Hospital, and secured himself by mortgage on property of the Hospital. Under the terms of the loan and mortgage, the Hospital only pays interest enough to satisfy the administrative charges and the annuity. It uses the remainder of the income from the fund for its expenses. It is thus actually receiving the full benefit of the income of $15,000 from the residuary fund, reduced only by the annuity of $800.

* * * * *

This residuary fund was vested in the Hospital. The death of the annuitant would completely end the trust. For this reason, the trustee was able safely to make the arrangement by which the Hospital has really received the benefit of the income subject to the annuity. As the Hospital is admitted to be a corporation, whose income when received is exempted from taxation under § 11 (a), we see no reason why the exemption should not be given effect under the circumstances. To allow the technical formality of the trust, which does not prevent the Hospital from really enjoying the income, would be to defeat the beneficent purpose of Congress.

The judgment of the Circuit Court of Appeals is

Affirmed.

Chicago & Northwestern Railway Co. v. Nye Schneider Fowler Co.

State regulation of railroads was an issue that almost invariably attracted the concern of the Supreme Court. It raised not only the issue of whether state regulations affected areas clearly "occupied" by the federal government in exercising its power under Article I-8–3 (the Commerce Clause) "to regulate Commerce . . . among the several States," but also questions concerning the Fourteenth Amendment's restrictions on the states' "depriv[ing] any person of . . . property, without due process of law; nor deny[ing] to any person . . . the equal protection of the laws." Farming states, such as Nebraska, were perhaps most suspect, given the years of tension between railroads and farmers over fair treatment. Although the Taft opinion upheld part of the decision of the Nebraska state supreme court against the railroad, it found that the provision regarding attorney's fees was biased against the railroad and struck it down.

Chicago & Northwestern Railway Company v. Nye Schneider Fowler Company

Error to the Supreme Court of the State of Nebraska

No. 24. Argued April 18, 1922—Decided November 13, 1922

260 U.S. 35 (1922)

[36]

MR. CHIEF JUSTICE TAFT delivered the opinion of the Court.

In this case, the constitutional validity of two statutes of Nebraska is questioned, the first subjecting the initial railroad of two connecting roads, receiving freight, to liability for safe delivery by the other, and the second making every common carrier liable for a reasonable attorney's fee in the court of first instance and on appeal, for collection from it of every claim for damage or loss to property shipped, not adjusted within 60 days, for intrastate shipments.

* * * * *

[37] . . . The questions made involved separate statutes and we shall take them up in order.

First. Section 6058 of the Revised Statutes of Nebraska, 1913, provides as follows:

"Any railroad company receiving freight for transportation shall be entitled to the same rights and be subject to the same liabilities as common carriers. Whenever two or more railroads are connected together, the company owning either of such roads receiving freight to be transported to any place on the line of either of the roads so connected shall be liable as common carriers for the delivery of such freight, to the consignee of the freight, in the same order in which such freight was shipped."

It is objected that this imposes on one railroad liability for the default of another without providing reimbursement by that other and so deprives the one of its property [38] without due process of law. But the Supreme Court of Nebraska has declared in this case that, in such a case under the statute, the initial carrier has a right of reimbursement under the general principle of subrogation. . . .

Second. Authority for taxing of attorney's fees as part of the costs in such cases is founded in c. 134, Laws of Nebraska, 1919, amending § 6063, Revised Statutes, 1913. . . .

* * * * *

[43] The general rule . . . is, that common carriers engaged in the public business of transportation may be grouped in a special class to secure the proper discharge of their functions, and to meet their liability for injuries inflicted upon the property of members of the public in their performance; that the seasonable payment of just claims against them for faulty performance of their functions is a part of their duty, and that a reasonable penalty may be imposed on them for failure promptly to consider and [44] pay such claims, in order to discourage delays by them. This penalty or stimulus may be in the form of attorney's fees. But it is also apparent from these cases that such penalties or fees must be moderate and reasonably sufficient to accomplish their legitimate object and that the imposition of penalties or conditions that are plainly arbitrary and oppressive and "violate the rudiments of fair play" insisted on in the Fourteenth Amendment, will be held to infringe it. . . .

* * * * *

[46] The evident theory of the amendment of § 6063, as thus interpreted, is that the burden of the litigation, both in the trial and appellate court, could be avoided by reasonable assiduity of the defendant carrier in availing itself of its peculiar sources of knowledge, ascertaining the actual damage and making a genuine tender of what it believes to be due, and, if the ultimate recovery is not more than the tender, that the claimant shall have neither interest nor attorney's fee. Under the circumstances, does the statute thus construed work a

fair result? Here is an excessive claim of $2,000 reduced to $800 by a trial in one court, with an attorney's fee fixed at $600, and then an appeal by which the claim is reduced to $600, and the fee to $200. . . .

* * * * *

[47] . . . Thus what we have here is a requirement that the carrier shall pay the attorneys of the claimant full compensation for their labors in resisting its successful effort on appeal to reduce an unjust and excessive claim against it. This we do not think is fair play. Penalties imposed on one party for the privilege of appeal to the courts, deterring him from vindication of his rights, have been held invalid under the Fourteenth Amendment. *Missouri Pacific Ry. Co. v. Tucker*, 230 U.S. 340. While the present case does not involve any such penalties as were there imposed, we think the principle applies to the facts of this case. We hold that so much of the statute as imposed an attorney's [48] fee upon the carrier in this case in the Supreme Court was invalid. The judgment of the Supreme Court is to this extent reversed and in other respects affirmed. The costs in this court will be taxed one-third to the defendant in error, and two-thirds to the plaintiff in error.

Reversed in part and

Affirmed in part.

Wichita Railroad & Light Co. v. Public Utilities Commission of Kansas

Kansas's public utilities commission allowed a supplier of electricity to the Wichita Railroad & Light Company to increase its rates based on the supplier's arguments that it would lose money if it were forced to continue supplying electricity at the agreed-upon rates. In addition to a dispute over whether the federal courts had jurisdiction that Taft settled in favor of asserting jurisdiction, the case involved what limits courts could impose on the rate-making power of a utility commission. Taft's opinion found that the utility commission had exceeded its powers by rendering a decision without an appropriate finding and that the rates charged were "unjust, unreasonable, unjustly discriminatory, or unusually preferential." Taft further found that the commission's failure to follow such procedures violated the constitutional proscription against the delegation of legislative power to regulatory agencies.

Wichita Railroad & Light Company v. Public Utilities Commission of the State of Kansas et al.

Appeal from the Circuit Court of Appeals for the Eighth Circuit

No. 27. Argued April 24, 1922—Decided November 13, 1922

260 U.S. 48 (1922)

[53]

MR. CHIEF JUSTICE TAFT, after stating the case as above, delivered the opinion of the Court.

The appellees urge that the concession of the appellant that contracts in respect to the rates to be charged by a public utility are subject to suspension or abrogation by the police power of the State validly exercised through an administrative agency takes out of this case any federal question, because the issue then is only a state question, to wit, whether, under the state statute, the police power was validly exercised. Upon this ground they insist that the bill should have been, and must be now, dismissed for want of jurisdiction and without an inquiry into the other issues of law and fact. . . .

[54] The jurisdiction of the District Court was not limited to federal questions presented by the bill, but extended to the entire suit and every question, whether federal or state, involved in its determination.

The appellant assigns for error that the Circuit Court of Appeals, by directing a dismissal of the bill, refused it a hearing on the truth of the averments of the answer as to the validity of the order, and also on the issue made by the bill and answer as to whether the rates, as fixed by the Commission, deprived it of its property without due process of law and denied it the equal protection of the laws. In this ruling we think there was error.

* * * * *

[58] The proceeding we are considering is governed by § 13. That is the general section of the act comprehensively describing the duty of the Commission, vesting it with power to fix and order substituted new rates for existing rates. The power is expressly made to depend on the condition that after full hearing and investigation the Commission shall find existing rates to be unjust, unreasonable, unjustly discriminatory or unduly preferential. We conclude that a valid order of the Commission under the act must contain a finding of fact after hearing and investigation, upon which the order is founded, and that for lack of such a finding, the order in this case was void.

This conclusion accords with the construction put upon similar statutes in other States. *Public Utilities Commission v. Springfield Gas & Electric Co.,* 291 Ill. 209; *Public Utilities Commission v. Baltimore & Ohio Southwestern R. R. Co.,* 281 Ill. 405. Moreover, it accords with general principles of constitutional government. The maxim that a legislature may not delegate legislative power has some qualifications, as in the creation of municipalities, and also in the creation of administrative [59] boards to apply to the myriad details of rate schedules the regulatory police power of the State. The latter qualification is made necessary in order that the legislative power may be effectively exercised. In creating such an administrative agency the legislature, to prevent its being a pure delegation of legislative power, must enjoin upon it a certain course of procedure and certain rules of decision in the performance of its function. It is a wholesome and necessary principle that such an agency must pursue the procedure and rules enjoined and show a substantial compliance therewith to give validity to its action. When, therefore, such an administrative agency is required as a condition precedent to an order, to make a finding of facts, the validity of the order must rest upon the needed finding. If it is lacking, the order is ineffective.

It is pressed on us that the lack of an express finding may be supplied by implication and by reference to the averments of the petition invoking the action of the Commission. We can not agree to this. It is doubtful whether the facts averred in the petition were sufficient to justify a finding that the contract rates were unreasonably low; but we do not find it necessary to answer this question. We rest our decision on the principle that an express finding of unreasonableness by the Commission was indispensable under the statutes of the State.

We think the motion for judgment on the pleadings should have been granted.

The decree of the Circuit Court of Appeals is reversed and that of the District Court is affirmed.

Freund v. United States

The United States Court of Claims had ruled that the United States Post Office owed a contractor money in excess of what was provided for by a contract to move mail in the city of St. Louis. Both parties disagreed with this decision and both appealed to the Supreme Court. The latter found that justice required a higher payment to the contractor, given the additional costs he had incurred because of changes in the delivery routes.

Freund et al. v. United States
United States v. Freund et al.

Appeals from the Court of Claims

Nos. 29, 37. Argued October 5, 6, 1922—Decided November 13, 1922

260 U.S. 60 (1922)

[61]

MR. CHIEF JUSTICE TAFT delivered the opinion of the Court.

This is a suit against the Government to recover $34,012.90 as the remainder unpaid of an amount earned by 16 months' service in carrying the mails by wagons in the City of St. Louis. . . .

[62] The contractors' claim was that the substitution of the new route for the one they bid on was not within the terms of the contract, but was unconscionable, and that they were entitled to recover for the work done on the new route on a *quantum meruit*. The Court of Claims held that it was not necessary to determine whether the new route was properly substituted for the old, because the contractors had acquiesced in this view by their performance, but that the Government had not, in adapting the mileage rate of the original route under the contract to the new route, done justice to the contractors in the number of miles allowed, and on this basis gave judgment for $7,346.66. From this the contractors appealed. The Government brings a cross appeal, claiming that, as the contractors accepted full pay under the contract as construed and expressed by the Department, they should recover nothing.

It is, of course, wise and necessary that government agents in binding their principal in contracts for construction or service should make provision for alterations in the plans, or changes in the service, within the four corners of the contract, and thus avoid the presentation of unreasonable claims for extras. This court has recognized that necessity and enforced various provisions to which it has given rise. But sometimes such contract provisions have been interpreted and enforced by executive officials as if they enabled those officers to remould the contract at will. The temptation of the bureau to adopt such clauses arises out of the fact that they avoid the necessity of labor, foresight and care in definitely drafting the contract, and reserve power in the bureau. This does [63] not make for justice; it promotes the possibility of official favoritism as between contractors, and results in enlarged expenditures, because it increases the prices which contractors, in view of the added risk, incorporate in their bids for government contracts. These considerations, especially the first, have made this Court properly attentive to any language or phrase of these enlarging provisions which may be properly held to limit their application to what should be regarded as having been fairly and reasonably within the contemplation of the parties when the contract was entered into.

* * * * *

[70] . . . We can not ignore the suggestion of duress there was in the situation or the questionable fairness of the conduct of the Government, aside from the illegality of the construction of the contract insisted on. . . .

We think that the contractors are entitled to recover the reasonable value of their services for the 16 months including a fair profit.

This relieves us of considering the conclusion reached by the Court of Claims.

The judgment is reversed, the cross appeal of the United States is dismissed, and the case is remanded to the Court of Claims, with directions to find the value of the services rendered by appellants on the substituted or restated route including a fair profit, and to enter judgment for the balance found due.

Reversed.

National Union Fire Insurance Co. v. Wanberg

One of the familiar accusations made against the "Old Court"—the pre-1937 Court, which saw its role as primarily that of protector of private property—was that it was inclined too often to substitute its view of wise social policy for that of the legislature. Advocates of self-restraint such as Oliver Wendell Holmes, Jr., rejected this stance as illegitimate. As Holmes had noted in his famous dissent in the case of *Lochner v. New York*, "A Constitution is not intended to embody a particular economic theory. It is made for people of fundamentally differing views" (198 U.S. 45, 74 [1905]). In rejecting a challenge to a North Dakota regulation that provided that insurance companies must reject policies within twenty-four hours of their being authorized by their local agent, Taft sounded an almost Holmsian note, allowing that "whether it is wise legislation is not for us to consider."

National Union Fire Insurance Company v. Wanberg

Error to the Supreme Court of the State of North Dakota

No. 32. Submitted October 6, 1922—Decided November 13, 1922

260 U.S. 71 (1922)

[72]

MR. CHIEF JUSTICE TAFT delivered the opinion of the Court.

This is a writ of error to the Supreme Court of North Dakota, brought to reverse its judgment affirming one of the District Court of William County of that State for $1,254.25, with interest and costs, upon a contract of hail insurance, against the National Union Fire Insurance Company, a corporation of Pennsylvania. The judgment rests for its validity on § 4902 of the Compiled Laws of North Dakota, 1913, as follows:

"Every insurance company engaged in the business of insuring against loss by hail in this State, shall be bound, and the insurance shall take effect from and after twenty-four hours from the day and hour the application for such insurance has been taken by the authorized local agent of said company, and if the company shall decline to write the insurance upon receipt of the application, it shall forthwith notify the applicant and agent who took the application, by telegram, and in that event, the insurance shall not become effective. Provided, that nothing in this article shall prevent the company from issuing a policy on such an application and putting the insurance in force prior to the expiration of said twenty-four hours."

* * * * *

[73] The only error we can consider which was duly reserved is that § 4902 as applied to this case violates the Fourteenth Amendment in that it operates to deprive the company of liberty of contract, and therefore of its property, without due process of law, and of the equal protection of the laws.

* * * * *

[75] The legislature was evidently convinced that it would help the public interest if farmers could be induced generally to take out hail insurance and "temper the wind" so injurious to the agriculture of the State, and that they would be more likely to avail themselves of this protection if they could effect the insurance promptly and on the eve of the danger. The legislature said, therefore, to companies intending to engage in hail insurance, "To accomplish our purpose we forbid you to engage in this kind of business un-

less you agree to close your contracts within twenty-four hours after application is made. You must so extend the scope of the authority of your local agents, or must so speed communication between them and your representatives who have authority, as to enable an applicant to know within the limits of a day whether he is protected, so that, if not, he may at once go to [76] another company to secure what he seeks. If, therefore, you engage in this exigent business, and allow an application to pend more than twenty-four hours, you will be held to have made the contract of insurance for which the farmer has applied."

This does not force a contract on the company. It need not accept an application at all or it can make its arrangements to reject one within twenty-four hours. It is urged that no company, to be safe and to make the business reasonably profitable, can afford to place more than a certain number of risks within a particular section or township, and that what is called "mapping" must be done to prevent too many risks in one locality and to distribute them so that the company may not suffer too heavily from the same storm. Applications are often received by agents in different towns for the crops in the same section or township, so that, if local agents were given authority finally to accept applications, this "mapping," essential to the security of the company in doing the business at all, would be impossible. It seems to us that this is a difficulty easily overcome by appointing agents with larger territorial authority and sub-agents near them, or by the greater use of the telegraph or telephone in consulting the home office or more trusted local agencies. While the time allowed is short, we can not say that it is unreasonable in view of the legitimate purpose of the legislation and the possibilities of modern business methods.

There is nothing in the statute under discussion which requires a company to receive applications or prevents it from insisting on the payment of a premium in advance before receiving them, or from reserving the usual right on the part of the insurer at any time to cancel the contract of insurance on service of due notice with a return of a proper proportion of the premium. Not infrequently companies in their own interest in some kinds of insurance, entrust to local insurance agents authority to bind [77] their principals temporarily until the application can be examined and approved by the head office. The statute here in question has been in force since 1913, and it does not seem to have driven companies out of the hail insurance business, an indication that they are able profitably and safely to adjust themselves and their methods to its requirements. Whether it is wise legislation is not for us to consider. All we have to decide, and that we do decide, is that it is not so arbitrary or unreasonable as to deprive those whom it affects of their property or liberty without due process of law.

* * * * *

The judgment of the Supreme Court of North Dakota is

Affirmed.

Brewer-Elliott Oil & Gas Co. v. United States

In disputes pitting the United States government against a state, Chief Justice Taft was a committed disciple of Chief Justice John Marshall in upholding federal rights. In the instant case, the lower federal courts had both ruled in favor of the United States. Taft affirmed their decisions, noting that state courts could not be relied upon to decide issues that involved federal land.

Brewer-Elliott Oil & Gas Company et al.
v. United States et al.

Appeal from the Circuit Court of Appeals for the Eighth Circuit

No. 52. Argued October 12, 13, 1922—Decided November 13, 1922

260 U.S. 77 (1922)

[79]

MR. CHIEF JUSTICE TAFT delivered the opinion of the Court.

This is an appeal from a decree of the Circuit Court of Appeals of the Eighth Circuit affirming that of the District Court for Western Oklahoma. The bill in equity was filed by the United States for itself and as trustee for the Osage Tribe of Indians, against the Brewer-Elliott Oil & Gas Company, and five other such companies, lessees, under oil and gas leases granted by the State of Oklahoma, of portions of the bed of the Arkansas River, opposite the Osage Reservation in that State. It averred that the river bed thus leased belonged to the Osages, and not to Oklahoma, and that the leases were void, that the defendants were prospecting for, and drilling for, oil in the leased lots in the river bed, and were erecting oil derricks and other structures therein, and prayed for the canceling of the leases, the enjoining of defendants from further operations under their leases, and a quieting of the title to the premises in the United States as trustee.

The State of Oklahoma intervened by leave of court and in its answer denied that the Osage Tribe or the United States as its trustee owned the river bed of which these lots were a part, but averred that it was owned by the State in fee. The other defendants adopted the answer of the State.

After a full hearing and voluminous evidence, the District Court found that at the place in question the Arkansas River was, and always had been, a non-navigable [80] stream, that by the express grant of the Government, made before Oklahoma came into the Union, the Osage Tribe of Indians took title in the river bed to the main channel and still had it. It entered a decree as prayed in the bill. The Circuit Court of Appeals held that, whether the river was navigable or non-navigable, the United States, as the owner of the territory through which the Arkansas flowed before statehood, had the right to dispose of the river bed, and had done so, to the Osages.

* * * * *

[87] . . . If the Arkansas River is not navigable, then the title of the Osages as granted certainly included the bed of the river as far as the main channel, because the words of the grant expressly carry the title to that line.

But it is said that the navigability of the Arkansas River is a local question to be settled by the legislature and the courts of Oklahoma, and that the Supreme Court of the State has held that at the very point here in dispute, the river is navigable. . . . In such a case as this the navigability of the stream is not a local question for the state tribunals to settle. The question here is what title, if any, the Osages took in the river bed in 1872 when this grant was made, and that was thirty-five years before Oklahoma was taken into the Union and before there were any local tribunals to decide any such questions. As to such a grant, the judgment of the state court does not bind us, for the validity and effect of an act done by the United States is necessarily a federal question. The title of the Indians grows out of a federal grant when the Federal Government had complete sovereignty over the territory in question. Oklahoma when she came into the Union took sovereignty over the public lands in the condition of ownership as they were then, and, if the bed of a non-navigable stream had then become the property [88] of the Osages, there was nothing in the admission of Oklahoma into a constitutional equality of power with other States which required or permitted a divesting of the title. It is not for a State by courts or legislature, in dealing with the general subject of beds of streams, to adopt a retroactive rule for determining navigability which would destroy a title already accrued under federal law and grant or would enlarge what actually passed to the State, at the time of her admission, under the constitutional rule of equality here invoked.

* * * * *

[89] *The decree of the Circuit Court of Appeals is affirmed.*

Ryan v. United States

Ryan was a customs inspector in New York who claimed that he was owed a higher salary for performing his duties. His claim was rejected by the Court of Claims and he appealed to the Supreme Court. Taft interpreted the statute as allowing the treasury secretary to give a supplemental increase in salary, but not mandating it.

Ryan v. United States

Appeal from the Court of Claims

No. 64. Argued October 16, 1922—Decided November 13, 1922

260 U.S. 90 (1922)

[90]

MR. CHIEF JUSTICE TAFT delivered the opinion of the Court.

Ryan, the claimant and appellant, by his amended petition in the Court of Claims, sought to recover from the United States $3,465, being $1.00 per diem from April 16, 1910, to and including October 10, 1919. He was during that period a customs inspector at New York, and received $4.00 per day. He says that by law he was entitled to $5.00 per day, and he brings suit to recover the difference. The Court of Claims gave judgment for the Government. The question for our decision is what was [91] Ryan's lawful compensation during this period of nine and a half years.

* * * * *

[92] By Act of December 16, 1902, c. 2, 32 Stat. 753, the Secretary was authorized to increase the compensation of inspectors of customs at the port of New York as he might think advisable and proper by adding to their then compensation a sum not exceeding $1.00 per day, such additional compensation to be for work performed at unusual hours for which no compensation was then allowed, and as reimbursement of expenses for meals and trans-

portation while in the performance of official duties. Under the foregoing, in 1903, the Secretary increased the pay of inspectors then in office in New York to $5.00 per day, Class 4. The Act of 1902 is wholly permissive in its language. It does not require an increase of $1.00 a day or any part of it to inspectors in New York. It only authorizes it.

*****

[93] It would be straining provisions of a deficiency act applying to special instances to hold that it was intended to change a plainly permissive statute into a mandatory one. The much more natural interpretation of the language used is that Congress thought that the pay of these inspectors which had been increased to $5.00 a day under the Act of 1902 by the Secretary, had thus become fixed by law and so that the Secretary had no power to reduce them. This fully satisfies the words relied on without amending the statute or making it mean what it plainly does not mean.

*****

[94] *Affirmed.*

United States v. Bowman

This case involved a prosecution of four individuals for fraud against the United States government for actions committed outside the United States. The U.S. District Court for the Southern District of New York had thrown out the indictments, concluding that the criminal code did not specifically provide that acts committed outside the United States were covered. Chief Justice Taft's opinion reversed the lower court decision, reinstating the indictments and concluding that Congress had "in mind that a wide field for such frauds upon the Government" was in fact "on the high seas and in foreign ports."

United States v. Bowman

*Error to the District Court of the United States
for the Southern District of New York*

No. 69. Argued October 17, 1922—Decided November 13, 1922

260 U.S. 94 (1922)

[95]

MR. CHIEF JUSTICE TAFT delivered the opinion of the Court.

This is a writ of error under the Criminal Appeals Act (c. 2564, 34 Stat. 1246) to review the ruling of the District Court sustaining a demurrer of one of the defendants to an indictment for a conspiracy to defraud a corporation in which the United States was and is a stockholder, under § 35 of the Criminal Code, as amended October 23, 1918, c. 194, 40 Stat. 1015.

* * * * *

[97] We have in this case a question of statutory construction. The necessary locus, when not specially defined, depends upon the purpose of Congress as evinced by the description and nature of the crime and upon the territorial limitations upon the power and jurisdiction of a [98] government to punish crime under the law of nations. Crimes against private individuals or their property, like assaults, murder, burglary, larceny, robbery, arson, embezzlement and frauds of all kinds, which affect the peace and good order of the community, must of course be committed within the territorial jurisdiction of the government where it may properly exercise it. If punishment of them is to be extended to include those committed outside of the strict territorial jurisdiction, it is natural for Congress to say so in the statute, and failure to do so will negative the purpose of Congress in this regard. . . .

But the same rule of interpretation should not be applied to criminal statutes which are, as a class, not logically dependent on their locality for the Government's jurisdiction, but are enacted because of the right of the Government to defend itself against obstruction, or fraud wherever perpetrated, especially if committed by its own citizens, officers or agents. . . .

* * * * *

[101] [The statute] is directed generally against whoever presents a false claim against the United States, knowing it to be such, to any officer of the civil, military or naval service or to any department thereof, or any corporation in which the United States is a stockholder, or whoever connives at the same by the use of any cheating device, or whoever enters a conspiracy to do these things. The section was amended in 1918 to include a corporation in which the United States owns stock. This was evidently intended to protect the Emergency Fleet Corporation in which the [102] United States was the sole stockholder, from fraud of this character. That Corporation was expected to engage in, and did engage in, a most extensive ocean transportation business and its ships were seen in every great port of the world open during the war. The same section of the statute protects the arms, ammuni-

tion, stores and property of the army and navy from fraudulent devices of a similar character. We can not suppose that when Congress enacted the statute or amended it, it did not have in mind that a wide field for such frauds upon the Government was in private and public vessels of the United States on the high seas and in foreign ports and beyond the land jurisdiction of the United States, and therefore intend to include them in the section.

* * * * *

Section 41 of the Judicial Code provides that "the trial of all offenses committed upon the high seas, or elsewhere out of the jurisdiction of any particular State or district, shall be in the district where the offender is found, or into which he is first brought." The three defendants who were found in New York were citizens of the United States and were certainly subject to such laws as it might pass to protect itself and its property. Clearly it is no offense to the dignity or right of sovereignty of Brazil to hold them for this crime against the government to which they owe allegiance. The other defendant is a subject of Great Britain. He has never been apprehended, and it will be time enough to consider what, if any, jurisdiction the District [103] Court below has to punish him when he is brought to trial.

The judgment of the District Court is reversed, with directions to overrule the demurrer and for further proceedings.

Reversed.

Cumberland Telephone & Telegraph Co. v. Louisiana Public Service Commission

The Louisiana Public Service Commission, represented before the bar of the Supreme Court by future Louisiana governor Huey P. Long, sought to have a district court order enjoining the commission from reducing the phone company's rates set aside. The issue before the Supreme Court was whether a single federal judge could issue such an order or whether this was prohibited by section 266 of the Judicial Code.

Cumberland Telephone & Telegraph Company v. Louisiana Public Service Commission et al.

*Appeal from the District Court of the United States for the
Eastern District of Louisiana*

No. 650. Argued on return to rule to show cause why supersedeas and
injunction should not be set aside and injunction dissolved, November 13,
1922—Decided November 20, 1922

260 U.S. 212 (1922)

[214]

MR. CHIEF JUSTICE TAFT delivered the opinion of the Court.

This is a motion by the appellees to set aside the supersedeas and injunction granted by District Judge Foster at the time he allowed an appeal
from an order of three judges, Circuit Judge Bryan, District Judge Clayton,
and himself, denying an application for an interlocutory injunction under §
266 of the Judicial Code.

* * * * *

[216] Section 266 of the Judicial Code is a codification of § 17 of the
Act of June 18, 1910, c. 309, 36 Stat. 557, amended by the Act of March 3,
1913, c. 160, 37 Stat. 1013. The legislation was enacted for the manifest purpose of taking away the power of a single United States Judge, whether District Judge, Circuit Judge or Circuit Justice holding a District Court of the
United States, to issue an interlocutory injunction against the execution of
a state statute by a state officer or of an order of an administrative board of
the State pursuant to a state statute, on the ground of the federal unconstitutionality of the statute. Pending the application for an interlocutory injunction, a single judge may grant a restraining order to be in force until
the hearing of the application, but thereafter, so far as enjoining the state
officers, his power is exhausted. The wording of the section leaves no doubt
that Congress was by provisions *ex industria* seeking to make interference
by interlocutory injunction from a federal court with the enforcement of
state legislation, regularly enacted and in course of execution, a matter of
the adequate hearing and the full deliberation which the presence of three
judges, one of whom should be a Circuit Justice or Judge, was likely to secure. It was to prevent the improvident granting of such injunctions by a
single judge, and the possible unnecessary conflict between federal and
state authority always to be deprecated.

* * * * *

[220] The orders in this Court will be two:

First. The motion of appellees is granted and the order of injunction granted by Judge Foster when allowing the appeal is set aside as without jurisdiction.

Second. The application to this Court for an injunction maintaining the status quo is referred to the District Court constituted of three judges for its determination.

The costs on this motion will be taxed to the appellant.

Liberty Oil Co. v. Condon National Bank

In this case, the Supreme Court reversed the Court of Appeals for the Eighth Circuit, concluding that it had misread the particular case, which was one not of law but of equity.

Liberty Oil Company v. Condon National Bank et al.

Certiorari to the Circuit Court of Appeals for the Eighth Circuit

No. 98. Argued November 15, 16, 1922—Decided November 27, 1922

260 U.S. 235 (1922)

[240]

MR. CHIEF JUSTICE TAFT, after stating the case, delivered the opinion of the Court.

We differ with the Circuit Court of Appeals in its holding that, as brought in review before it, this cause was an action at law. We think the cause was then equitable and the proper review was by appeal. The case began as an action at law for money had and received. When the defendant bank claimed to be only a stakeholder of the deposit, disclaimed interest therein and offered to pay it into court, and asked that the other claimants of the fund be made parties, its answer and cross petition became an equitable defense and a prayer for affirmative equitable relief in the nature of a bill for interpleader.

* * * * *

[245] *Reversed.*

City of Boston v. Jackson

The Boston Elevated Railway Company was a private company that operated trolley and subway cars in Boston and adjacent suburbs. Plagued with financial problems, it turned to the legislature. The state legislature entered into an agreement that guaranteed that the company's stockholders would continue to receive a return on their investments and that service would be improved. To do this, the legislature imposed assessments on the communities served by the Boston Elevated. The City of Boston sued, arguing that the arrangement deprived it of property without due process of law. Specifically, the city argued that it had built the subways used by the Boston Elevated cars and had been paid by the company for their use. As a result of the act of the state legislature, the rents due for use of the subways would be considered costs of the company, and any resulting deficits made up by the assessments on Boston and the suburbs. Chief Justice Taft rejected the city's complaints and affirmed in its entirety the decision of the Supreme Judicial Court, the highest Massachusetts court.

City of Boston v. Jackson, Treasurer and Receiver General of the Commonwealth of Massachusetts, et al.

Error to the Supreme Judicial Court of the State of Massachusetts

No. 141. Motion to dismiss or affirm submitted
November 13, 1922—Decided December 4, 1922

260 U.S. 309 (1922)

[311]

MR. CHIEF JUSTICE TAFT delivered the opinion of the Court.

* * * * *

[314] The plaintiff in error comes to this Court because, as it says, the statute of 1918 of the Commonwealth, by which the trustees took over and are now operating the railway, impairs the obligation of the contract of lease of its property in the tunnels and subways to the railway company, and so violates the contract clause of the Federal Constitution. It further contends that the imposition of a tax merely to aid a private corporation, as in the Act of 1918 complained of, is not for a public purpose, and taxes collected therefor from it is taking its property without due process of law. Thirdly, it avers that vesting power in the trustees to fix the deficit in operation of the railway and to assess the city for a large part thereof is also taking its property without due process of law.

We are relieved from full or detailed consideration of these grounds urged for reversal by the satisfactory opinion of the Supreme Judicial Court in this case. *Boston v. Treasurer and Receiver General,* 237 Mass. 403.

What the Commonwealth did was to help the people of the towns which the railway served when the railway's finances threatened its collapse, by taking over the lease of the railway company for a valuable consideration.

* * * * *

[315] In disposing of this objection we have in effect disposed of those objections to the Act of 1918 based on the [316] Fourteenth Amendment. If the constitution and laws of Massachusetts authorize the Commonwealth to operate a railway company for the public benefit, there is nothing in the Fourteenth Amendment to prevent. Nor is there anything in it preventing the State from using the trustees as agents to operate the railway and in such operation to determine the needed expenditures to comply with the obligations of the lease or the requirements of adequate public service. This is delegating to proper agents the decision of a proper administrative policy in the management of a state enterprise and the ascertainment of facts peculiarly within their field of authorized action.

* * * * *

Decree affirmed.

Champlain Realty Co. v. Brattleboro

The Town of Brattleboro, Vermont, assessed taxes of $484.50 on pulpwood logs that were floating in the West River on April 1, 1919. The Champlain Realty Company paid the taxes under protest and sued. The county court found for the realty company, but the town successfully appealed to the Vermont Supreme Court, which upheld the tax. Chief Justice Taft reversed, finding that the logs were in interstate commerce and, thus, not subject to local taxation.

Champlain Realty Company v. Town of Brattleboro

Certiorari to the Supreme Court of the State of Vermont

No. 128. Argued November 27, 28, 1922—Decided December 11, 1922

260 U.S. 366 (1922)

[371]

MR. CHIEF JUSTICE TAFT, after stating the case, delivered the opinion of the Court.

The Vermont Supreme Court depended for its conclusions chiefly upon *Coe v. Errol,* 116 U.S. 517, which is the leading case on this subject. There logs had been cut on Wentworth's Location in New Hampshire during the winter, and had been drawn down to Errol in the same State, and placed in Clear Stream and on the banks thereof on lands of John Akers and part on land of George C. Demerritt in said town, to be from thence floated down the Androscoggin River to the State of Maine (p. 518).

It is not clear how long they had lain there, but certainly for part of one winter season. This Court, speaking by Mr. Justice Bradley, sought to fix the time when [372] such logs, in the course of their being taken from New Hampshire to Maine, ceased to be part of the mass of property of New Hampshire and passed into the immunity from state taxation as things actually in interstate commerce. The learned Justice states the rule to be "that such goods do not cease to be part of the general mass of property in the State, subject, as such, to its jurisdiction, and to taxation in the usual way, until they have been shipped, or entered with a common carrier for transportation to another State, or have been started upon such transportation in a continuous route or journey." (P. 527.)

* * * * *

[373]   The question here then is, Where did the interstate shipment begin? When the wood was placed in the waters of the West River in the towns of Jamaica, Stratton, Londonderry and Winhall, or at the boom in Brattleboro? The whole drive was ten thousand cords. Six thousand cords of that, shipped from these towns after the third of April, went through directly to Hinsdale, New Hampshire, without stopping. Certainly that was a continuous passage and the wood when floating in the West River was as much in interstate commerce as when on the Connecticut. Why was it any more in interstate commerce than that which had been shipped before April 3rd from the same towns for the same destination by the same natural carrying agency, to wit, the flowing water of the West and Connecticut Rivers? Did the fact that before April 3rd the waters of the Connecticut were frozen, or so high as to prevent the logs reaching Hinsdale, requiring a temporary halting at the mouth of the West River, break the real continuity of the interstate journey? We think not. The preparation for the interstate journey had all been completed at the towns on the West River where the wood had been put in the stream. The boom at the mouth of the West River did not

constitute an entrepot or depot for the gathering of logs preparatory for the final journey. It was only a safety appliance in the course of the journey. It was a harbor of refuge from danger to a shipment on its way. It was not used by the owner for any beneficial purpose of his own except to facilitate the safe delivery of the wood at Hinsdale on their final journey already begun. The logs were not detained to be classified, measured, counted [374] or in any way dealt with by the owner for his benefit, except to save them from destruction in the course of their journey that but for natural causes, over which he could exercise no control, would have been actually continuous. This was not the case in *Coe v. Errol.*

* * * * *

[376] The interstate commerce clause of the Constitution does not give immunity to movable property from local taxation which is not discriminative, unless it is in actual continuous transit in interstate commerce. When it is shipped by a common carrier from one State to another, in the course of such an uninterrupted journey it is clearly immune. The doubt arises when there are interruptions in the journey and when the property in its transportation is under the complete control of the owner during the passage. If the interruptions are only to promote the safe or convenient transit, then the continuity of the interstate trip is not broken.

* * * * *

[377] *Reversed and remanded for further proceedings not inconsistent with this opinion.*

United States v. Lanza

Vito Lanza was convicted under a statute of the state of Washington for a liquor violation and was then subsequently indicted under the terms of the federal Volstead Act. Lanza challenged the latter indictment, asserting that it violated his Fifth Amendment right against double jeopardy. In a unanimous decision, the Court, *per* Chief Justice Taft, upheld the right of the federal government to bring the second set of charges for the same act for which Lanza had been prosecuted by the state.

Although the Warren Court applied the right against double jeopardy to the states through the due process clause of the Fourteenth Amendment, *Benton v. Maryland,* 395 U.S. 784 (1969), the Warren Court and its successor Courts have continued to adhere to the position put forth by Taft in *Lanza*. Double jeopardy does not mean that the federal government cannot prosecute you for the same act for which a state has already prosecuted you, and the reverse is also true, cf., *Heath v. Alabama*, 474 U.S. 82 (1985).

United States v. Lanza et al.

260 U.S. 377 (1922)

[378]

MR. CHIEF JUSTICE TAFT delivered the opinion of the Court.

* * * * *

[379] The Eighteenth Amendment is as follows:

"Section 1. After one year from the ratification of this article the manufacture, sale, or transportation of intoxicating liquors within, the importation thereof into, or the exportation thereof from the United States and all territory subject to the jurisdiction thereof for beverage purposes is hereby prohibited.

"Sec. 2. The Congress and the several States shall have concurrent power to enforce this article by appropriate legislation."

The defendants insist that two punishments for the same act, one under the National Prohibition Act and the other under a state law, constitute double jeopardy under the Fifth Amendment; and in support of this position it is argued that both laws derive their force from the same [380] authority—the second section of the Amendment—and therefore that in principle it is as if both punishments were in prosecutions by the United States in its courts.

* * * * *

[381] The Amendment was adopted for the purpose of establishing prohibition as a national policy reaching every part of the United States and affecting transactions which are essentially local or intrastate, as well as those pertaining to interstate or foreign commerce. The second section means that power to take legislative measures to make the policy effective shall exist in Congress in respect of the territorial limits of the United States and at the same time the like power of the several States within their territorial limits shall not cease to exist. Each State, as also Congress, may exercise an inde-

pendent judgment in selecting and shaping measures to enforce prohibition. Such as are adopted by Congress become laws of the United States and such as are adopted by a State become laws of that State. They may vary in many particulars, including the penalties prescribed, but this is an inseparable incident of independent legislative action in distinct jurisdictions.

To regard the Amendment as the source of the power of the States to adopt and enforce prohibition measures is to take a partial and erroneous view of the matter. Save for some restrictions arising out of the Federal Constitution, chiefly the commerce clause, each State possessed that power in full measure prior to the Amendment, and the probable purpose of declaring a concurrent power to be in the States was to negative any possible inference that in vesting the National Government with the power of country-wide prohibition, state power would be excluded. . . .

[382] We have here two sovereignties, deriving power from different sources, capable of dealing with the same subject-matter within the same territory. Each may, without interference by the other, enact laws to secure prohibition, with the limitation that no legislation can give validity to acts prohibited by the Amendment. Each government in determining what shall be an offense against its peace and dignity is exercising its own sovereignty, not that of the other.

It follows that an act denounced as a crime by both national and state sovereignties is an offense against the peace and dignity of both and may be punished by each. The Fifth Amendment, like all the other guaranties in the first eight amendments, applies only to proceedings by the Federal Government, *Barron v. Baltimore,* 7 Pet. 243, and the double jeopardy therein forbidden is a second prosecution under authority of the Federal Government after a first trial for the same offense under the same authority. Here the same act was an offense against the State of Washington, because a violation of its law, and also an offense against the United States under the National Prohibition Act. The defendants thus committed two different offenses by the same act, and a conviction by a court of Washington of the offense against that State is not a conviction of the different offense against the United States and so is not double jeopardy.

* * * * *

[385] If Congress sees fit to bar prosecution by the federal courts for any act when punishment for violation of state prohibition has been imposed, it can, of course, do so by proper legislative provision; but it has not done so. If a State were to punish the manufacture, transportation and sale

of intoxicating liquor by small or nominal fines, the race of offenders to the courts of that State to plead guilty and secure immunity from federal prosecution for such acts would not make for respect for the federal statute or for its deterrent effect. But it is not for us to discuss the wisdom of legislation, it is enough for us to hold that, in the absence of special provision by Congress, conviction and punishment in a state court under a state law for making, transporting and selling intoxicating liquors is not a bar to a prosecution in a court of the United States under the federal law for the same acts.

Judgment reversed with direction to sustain the demurrer to the special plea in bar of the defendants and for further proceedings in conformity with this opinion.

Heitler v. United States

These cases all arose from prosecutions for violations of Prohibition, a staple of the Taft Court.

Heitler v. United States
Perlman v. United States
Greenberg v. United States
McCann v. United States
Quinn v. United States

Error to the District Court of the United States for the Northern District of Illinois

Nos. 185–189. Motion to transfer to Circuit Court of Appeals submitted December 11, 1922—Decided January 2, 1923

260 U.S. 438 (1923)

[439]

MR. CHIEF JUSTICE TAFT delivered the opinion of the Court.

These were writs of error issued directly to the District Court under § 238 of the Judicial Code to review sentences of fine and imprisonment on the ground that they were cases in which the constitutionality of the National Prohibition Act, under which the convictions were had, was drawn in question. In addition to the constitutionality of the Prohibition Act, the assignments of error raised many questions as to the admissions of evidence and the charge of the court. We held that in view of our previous decision affirming the validity of the National Prohibition Act (*National Prohibition Cases,* 253 U.S. 350), the plaintiffs in error were precluded from raising the question again and basing thereon a claim of jurisdiction for a writ of error under § 238, that the question made was, therefore, not substantial but frivolous, and that the writ should be dismissed for want of jurisdiction on the authority of *Sugarman v. United States,* 249 U.S. 182, 184, and cases cited. *Heitler v. United States, post,* 703. This conclusion made it impossible for us to consider the other errors assigned.

The plaintiffs in error now invite our attention to an Act of Congress approved September 14, 1922, c. 305, 42 Stat. 837, adding § 238 (a) to the Judicial Code, which provides that " . . . if an appeal or writ or error has been or shall be taken to, or issued out of, the Supreme Court in a case wherein such appeal or writ of error should have been taken to, or issued out of, a circuit court of appeals, such appeal or writ of error shall not for such reason be dismissed, but shall be transferred to the proper court, which shall thereupon be possessed of the same and shall proceed to the determination thereof, with the same force [440] and effect as if such appeal or writ of error had been duly taken to, or issued out of, the court to which it is so transferred."

This is a remedial statute and should be construed liberally to carry out the evident purpose of Congress. The fact that the opportunity therein given to litigants in the Circuit Courts of Appeals where they have mistakenly sought a review in this Court may at times be abused and unduly prolong the litigation and delay the successful party below, is no reason why when the case comes clearly within the language of the statute the transfer should not be made. The successful party below may avoid undue delay by a prompt motion to dismiss in this Court in such cases.

The cases before us are clearly within the remedy of the statute. Based on the assumption of the presence of a real constitutional question in the case, plaintiffs in error sought review here not only of that question but of the numerous other errors assigned in the record. *Williamson v. United States,* 207 U.S. 425, 432, 434; *Goldman v. United States,* 245 U.S. 474, 476. We find that there is no constitutional question of sufficient substance to give us jurisdiction to consider these other errors. In other words, we find that to have such alleged errors considered and reviewed, the writ of error herein should have issued out of the Circuit Court of Appeals of the proper circuit. Accordingly we hold that these several cases should be transferred to the Circuit Court of Appeals, of the Seventh Circuit at the costs of the respective plaintiffs in error, that that court be thereupon possessed of the jurisdiction of the same and proceed to the determination of said writs of error as if such writs had issued out of such court.

And it is so ordered.

Sioux City Bridge Co. v. Dakota County

The Sioux City Bridge Company appealed an assessment of its bridge that it considered excessive. The Nebraska supreme court upheld the assessment. The Supreme Court, speaking through Taft, found it a violation of the Fourteenth Amendment's equal protection guarantee.

Sioux City Bridge Company v. Dakota County, Nebraska

Certiorari to the Supreme Court of the State of Nebraska

No. 105. Argued November 20, 1922—Decided January 2, 1923

260 U.S. 441 (1923)

[441]

MR. CHIEF JUSTICE TAFT delivered the opinion of the Court.

* * * * *

[445] The charge made by the Bridge Company in this case was that the State, through its duly constituted agents, to wit, the county assessor and the County Board of Equalization, improperly executed the constitution and taxing laws of the State and intentionally and arbitrarily assessed the Bridge Company's property at 100 per cent. of its true value and all the other real estate and its improvements in the county at 55 per cent.

The Supreme Court does not make it clear whether it thinks the discrimination charged was proved or not, but assuming the discrimination, it holds that the Bridge Company has no remedy except "to have the property [446] assessed below its true value raised, rather than to have property assessed at its true value reduced." The dilemma presented by a case where one or a few of a class of taxpayers are assessed at 100 per cent. of the value of their property in accord with a constitutional or statutory requirement, and the rest of the class are intentionally assessed at a much lower percentage in violation of the law, has been often dealt with by courts and there has been a conflict of view as to what should be done. There is no doubt, however, of the view taken of such cases by the federal courts in the enforcement of the uniformity clauses of state statutes and constitutions and of the equal protection clause of the Fourteenth Amendment. . . . The conclusion . . . is that such a result as that reached by the Supreme Court of Nebraska is to deny the injured taxpayer any remedy at all because it is utterly impossible for him by any judicial proceeding to secure an increase in the assessment of the great mass of under-assessed property in the taxing district. This Court holds that the right of the taxpayer whose property alone is taxed at 100 per cent. of its true value is to have his assessment reduced to the percentage of that value at which others are taxed even though this is a departure from the requirement of statute. The conclusion is based on the principle that where it is impossible to secure both the standard of the true value, and the uniformity and equality required by law, the latter requirement is to be preferred as the just and ultimate purpose of the law. . . .

[447] *The judgment of the Supreme Court of Nebraska is reversed and the case is remanded for further proceedings not inconsistent with this opinion.*

Walker v. Gish

A District of Columbia regulation, dating back to the presidency of George Washington, was challenged as a deprivation of property without due process as guaranteed by the Fifth Amendment. Taft's opinion examined the legal lineage of the regulation requiring adjacent lot owners to share the cost of constructing a common or party wall, and concluded that "the questions . . . raised might justify discussion," but that the issue was settled by reason of the fact that the plaintiff, Walker, had used the party wall.

Walker v. Gish

Error to the Court of Appeals of the District of Columbia

No. 135. Argued November 28, 29, 1922—Decided January 2, 1923

260 U.S. 447 (1923)

[448]

MR. CHIEF JUSTICE TAFT delivered the opinion of the Court.

* * * * *

[449] The history of the law of party walls in Washington is interesting. Its application is not free from difficulty in that part of the present Washington which was not included within the original Federal City. The original proprietors of the land in the Federal City conveyed it in trust to certain named persons to be laid out in such streets, squares and lots as the President of the United States should approve. Under the trust provisions, the lots to be sold or distributed were to be subject to such terms and conditions as might be thought reasonable by the President for regulating the materials and manner of the buildings and improvements. President Washington issued regulations, one of which is in force today. They provided that a person appointed to superintend buildings might enter on the land of any person to set out the foundation and regulate the walls to be built between party and party, as to the breadth and thickness thereof, that the foundations were to be laid equally upon each lot and to be of the breadth and thickness thought proper by the superintendent, that the first builder was to be reimbursed one-half of the cost of the wall, or so much thereof as the next builder might use, but that such use could not begin till he had paid the amount fixed by the superintendent.

* * * * *

[452] The questions thus raised might justify discussion if the plaintiff in error were in a position to urge them, and had not used the original party wall of which he complains. His contention below was that he had not used the wall of his neighbor, that he had built a new wall at the side of the original party wall as high as the original wall and then had widened it to 13 inches so as to extend over the original wall without resting on it. The jury found against him on this issue. If he did use the original wall, then he must pay for the value of the use. *Fowler v. Saks,* 7 Mackey, 570, 581; *Fowler v. Koehler,* 43 App. D. C. 349, 360. In using it, he waived the right to object to the regulations with which he complied without objection, until he was called upon to pay his share of that which he had taken and used.

The judgment is affirmed.

Federal Trade Commission v. Curtis Publishing Co.

The United States Court of Appeals for the Third Circuit had set aside a decision of the FTC against the Curtis Publishing Company, publisher of the *Saturday*

Evening Post and several other magazines. In doing so, the appeals court had made certain findings of fact. The question before the Court was whether this was in violation of federal law, since Congress had vested in the FTC the sole responsibility of making findings of fact.

Justice James C. McReynolds wrote the opinion of the Court. According to Taft biographer Alpheus Thomas Mason, Taft viewed McReynolds as a "major obstacle to judicial teamwork" and "never held the former Attorney General in high regard."[1] Perhaps this is what led Chief Justice Taft to break his rule about going along with the opinion of the Court. Interestingly, Taft's opinion is not labeled as a concurring opinion (in which a justice agrees with a decision but bases his or her conclusion on different arguments or a different view of the case), but rather as a "doubting opinion." Very likely, it is the only example of such a variant. The fact that Associate Justice Louis Brandeis joined Taft is also interesting, given McReynolds's widely known and widely expressed anti-Semitism.

Note

1. Mason, *William Howard Taft*, 215.

Federal Trade Commission v. Curtis Publishing Company

Certiorari to the Circuit Court of Appeals for the Third Circuit

No. 86. Argued November 17, 1922—Decided January 8, 1923

261 U.S. 541 (1923)

[582]

MR. CHIEF JUSTICE TAFT, doubting.

The sentence in the majority opinion, which makes me express doubt, is that discussing the duty of the court in reviewing the action of the Federal Trade Commission when it finds that there are material facts not reported by the Commission. The opinion says:

> "If there be substantial evidence relating to such facts from which different conclusions reasonably may be drawn, the matter may be and ordinarily, we think, should [583] be remanded to the Commission—the primary fact-finding body—with direction to make additional findings, but if from all the circumstances it clearly appears that in the interest of justice the controversy should be decided without further delay the court has full power under the statute so to do."

If this means that where it clearly appears that there is no substantial evidence to support additional findings necessary to justify the order of the Commission complained of, the court need not remand the case for further findings, I concur in it. It is because it may bear the construction that the court has discretion to sum up the evidence *pro* and *con* on issues undecided by the Commission and make itself the fact-finding body, that I venture with deference to question its wisdom and correctness. I agree that in the further discussion of the evidence, the reasoning of the opinion of the Court would seem to justify the view that it does not find the evidence sufficient to support additional findings by the Commission justifying its order. I only register this doubt because I think it of high importance that we should scrupulously comply with the evident intention of Congress that the Federal Commission be made the fact-finding body and that the Court should in its rulings preserve the Board's character as such and not interject its views of the facts where there is any conflict in the evidence.

I am authorized to say that MR. JUSTICE BRANDEIS concurs with me in this.

Omitted Taft Opinions

American Mills Company v. American Surety Company of New York, 260 U.S. 360 (1922)—fraud.
Blamberg Brothers v. United States, 260 U.S. 452 (1923)—admiralty case.

VOLUME 261

Charles Nelson Co. v. United States

American involvement in World War I led to an unparalleled level of government involvement in the economy and extraordinary expenditures of money. This resulted in a series of cases coming to the Court in the early 1920s involving contract disputes between private contractors and the United States government. *Nelson* is one such case.

Charles Nelson Company v. United States

Appeal from the Court of Claims

No. 287. Argued January 25, 26, 1923—Decided February 19, 1923

261 U.S. 17 (1923)

[17]

MR. CHIEF JUSTICE TAFT delivered the opinion of the Court.

* * * * *

[23] The Court of Claims further found that "no protest against furnishing more than 1,675,000 feet of lumber under the contract was ever made by the plaintiff company itself or any of its officers," and the VII finding was as follows;

> "The plaintiff company furnished to the defendant on orders placed by the defendant under contract 28942, 3,688,259 feet of lumber, for which it was paid at the contract price, and it did not at the time of any payment make to the United States any protest against payment at that price, and so far as the United States was informed such payments were accepted as in full.
>
> "The amount of lumber furnished over and above 1,675,000 feet was worth at market price, delivered at the navy yard, $18,310.21 more than the plaintiff was paid therefor at contract price."

On these findings we can see no escape for the plaintiff from acquiescence by its conduct in the price bid for the whole amount of lumber delivered.

The plaintiff relies on the opinion of this Court in *Freund v. United States,* 260 U.S. 60. The facts of that case are very different from this. They involved conduct on the part of the representatives of the Government of questionable fairness toward the contractors and showed no such acquiescence and absence of protest as here appear.

It may be as counsel suggest that the plaintiff's course was influenced by a patriotic wish to help the Government when it was engaged in war. If so, it was to be commended. But this can not change the legal effect of its evident acquiescence seen in its letter of June 18th [24] and its failure to protest thereafter and to put the Government on notice that it intended to claim a recovery on a *quantum valebat* when it was delivering the extra two million feet of lumber and receiving the payments therefor from the Government at the prices named in the bid. The judgment of the Court of Claims is

Affirmed.

Pennsylvania Railroad Co. v. United States Railroad Labor Board

The Transportation Act was adopted by Congress in 1920 in order to stabilize the railroad industry after World War I. The Railroad Labor Board was established under Title III of the act. Its task was to hear disputes involving unfair labor practices. It had no enforcement powers, but could publicize its findings. The Pennsylvania Railroad Company was found by the board to have engaged in unfair practices. The company challenged the board's right to do so. A United States District Court agreed and issued an injunction. The injunction was overturned by the United States Court of Appeals for the Seventh Circuit, and the Supreme Court, speaking through Chief Justice Taft, unanimously affirmed the appeals court decision.

Pennsylvania Railroad Company v. United States Railroad Labor Board et al.

Appeal from and Certiorari to the Circuit Court of Appeals for the Seventh Circuit

No. 585. Argued January 11, 1923—Decided February 19, 1923

261 U.S. 72 (1923)

[79]

MR. CHIEF JUSTICE TAFT . . . delivered the opinion of the Court.

It is evident from a review of Title III of the Transportation Act of 1920 that Congress deems it of the highest public interest to prevent the interruption of interstate commerce by labor disputes and strikes, and that its plan is to encourage settlement without strikes, first by conference between the parties; failing that, by reference to adjustment boards of the parties' own choosing, and if this is ineffective, by a full hearing before a National Board appointed by the President, upon which are an equal number of representatives of the Carrier Group, the Labor Group, and the Public. The decisions of the Labor Board are not to be enforced by process. The only sanction of its decision is to be the force of public opinion invoked by the fairness of a full hearing, the intrinsic justice of the conclusion, strengthened by the official prestige of the Board, and the full publication of the violation of such decision by any party to the proceeding. The evident thought of Congress in these provisions is that the economic interest of every member of the Public in the undisturbed flow of interstate commerce and the acute inconvenience to which all must be subjected by an interruption caused by a serious and widespread labor dispute, fastens public attention closely on all the circumstances [80] of the controversy and arouses public criticism of the side thought to be at fault. The function of the Labor Board is to direct that public criticism against the party who, it thinks, justly deserves it.

* * * * *

Counsel of the Railroad Company insist that the Board had no jurisdiction to make an order or to take up the controversies between the Government Railroad Administration and the National Labor Unions; that when the railroads [81] were turned back to their owners each company had the right to make its own rules and conditions and to deal with its own employees under § 301, and that the jurisdiction of the Board did not attach until a dispute as to such rules and conditions between the company and its employees had thereafter arisen.

We are not called upon to pass upon the propriety or legality of what the Labor Board did in continuing the existing rules and labor conditions which had come over from the Railroad Administration, or in hearing an argument as to their amendment by its decision. It suffices for our decision that the Labor Board at the instance of the carriers finally referred the whole question of rules and labor conditions to each company and its employees to be settled by conference under § 301; that such conferences were attempted in this case, and that thereafter the matter was brought before the Board by Federation No. 90 of Shop Crafts of the Pennsylvania System under § 307. It is the alleged invalidity of this proceeding, thus initiated, which is really the basis of the bill of complaint of the Company herein, and it is this only which we need consider.

First, Did Federation No. 90 have the right under § 307 to institute the hearing of the dispute? Section 307 says that this may be invoked on the application of the chief executive of any organization of employees whose members are directly interested in the dispute. Its name indicates, and the record shows, that the Federation is an association of employees of the Pennsylvania Company directly interested in the dispute. The only question between the Company and the Federation is whether the membership of the latter includes a majority of the Company's employees who are interested. But it is said that the Federation is a labor union affiliated with the American Federation of Labor and that the phrase "organization [82] of employees" used in the act was not intended by Congress to include labor unions. We find nothing in the act to impose any such limitation if the organization in other respects fulfills the description of the act. Congress has frequently recognized the legality of labor unions, *United Mine Workers v. Coronado Coal Co.*, 259 U.S. 344, and no reason suggests itself why such an association, if its membership is properly inclusive, may not be regarded as among the organizations of employees referred to in this legislation.

The next objection made by the Company to the jurisdiction of the Board to entertain the proceeding initiated by the Federation is that it did not involve the kind of dispute of which the Board could take cognizance under the act. The result of the conferences between the Pennsylvania Railroad Company and its employees under § 301 appears in the statement of the case. By a vote of 3,000 out of more than 30,000 employees, a representative committee was appointed with which the officers of the Company made an agreement as to rules and working conditions. Federation No. 90 for its members objected to the settlement on the ground that it had not been made by properly chosen representatives of the employees and brought this dispute before the Labor Board. The Pennsylvania Company was summoned and appeared before the Board and the issue was heard.

It is urged that the question who may represent the employees as to grievances, rules and working conditions under § 301 is not within the jurisdiction of the Labor Board to decide; that these representatives must be determined before the conferences are held under that section; that the jurisdiction of the Labor Board does not begin until after these conferences are held, and that the representatives who can make application under § 307 to the Board are representatives engaged in the conference under § 301. Such a construction would give either side [83] an easy opportunity to defeat the operation of the act and to prevent the Labor Board from considering any dispute. It would tend to make the act unworkable. If the Board has jurisdiction to hear representatives of the employees, it must of necessity have the power to determine who are proper representatives of the employees. . . .

* * * * *

... The purpose of Congress to promote harmonious relations between the managers of railways and their employees is seen in every section of this act, and the importance attached by Congress to conferences between them for this purpose is equally obvious. Congress must have intended, therefore, to include the procedure for determining representatives of employees as a proper subject matter of dispute to be considered by the Board under § 307. The act is to be liberally construed to effect the manifest effort of Congress to compose differences between railroad companies and their employees, and it would not help this effort, to exclude from the lawful consideration of the Labor Board a question which has so often seriously affected the relations between the companies and their employees in the past and is often encountered on the very threshold of controversies between them.

The second objection is that the Labor Board in Decision 119 and Principles 5 and 15, and in Decision 218, [84] compels the Railroad Company to recognize labor unions as factors in the conduct of its business. The counsel for the Company insist that the right to deal with individual representatives of its employees as to rules and working conditions is an inherent right which can not be constitutionally taken from it. The employees, or at least those who are members of the labor unions, contend that they have a lawful right to select their own representatives, and that it is not within the right of the Company to restrict them in their selection to employees of the Company or to forbid selection of officers of their labor unions qualified to deal with and protect their interests. This statute certainly does not deprive either side of the rights claimed.

But Title III was not enacted to provide a tribunal to determine what were the legal rights and obligations of railway employers and employees or to enforce or protect them. Courts can do that. The Labor Board was created to decide how the parties ought to exercise their legal rights so as to enable them to cooperate in running the railroad. It was to reach a fair compromise between the parties without regard to the legal rights upon which each side might insist in a court of law. The Board is to act as a Board of Arbitration. It is to give expression to its view of the moral obligation of each side as members of society to agree upon a basis for cooperation in the work of running the railroad in the public interest. The only limitation upon the Board's decisions is that they should establish a standard of conditions, which, in its opinion, is just and reasonable. The jurisdiction of the Board to direct the parties to do what it deems they should do is not to be limited by their constitutional or legal right to refuse to do it. Under the act there is no constraint upon them to do what the Board decides they should do except the moral constraint, already mentioned, of publication of its decision.

[85] . . . [W]e think that the District Court was wrong in enjoining the Labor Board from proceeding to entertain further jurisdiction and from publishing its [86] opinions, and that the Court of Appeals was right in reversing the District Court and in directing a dismissal of the bill. . . .

Decree affirmed.

Work v. Mosier

This case involved the question of the amount of discretion possessed by the secretary of the interior in determining payments to Native Americans out of trust funds administered by the United States government. The payments—to the Osage Indians—came from royalties for gas and oil leases. As a result of discoveries of significant oil and gas deposits, the previously insignificant royalties increased greatly. The secretary of the interior consequently imposed regulations that had to be met before individual members of the tribe received payments for minors in their custody. The Court disallowed this discretion, but allowed that the secretary could require an accounting of how the monies were spent.

Work, Secretary of the Interior, v. United States ex rel. Mosier et al.

Error to the Court of Appeals of the District of Columbia

No. 25. Argued April 20, 1922; restored to docket for reargument May 29, 1922; reargued February 27, 28, 1923—Decided March 19, 1923

261 U.S. 352 (1923)

[353]

Statement of the Case.

This writ of error brings in review a judgment of the Court of Appeals of the District of Columbia, affirming a judgment of mandamus against the Secretary of the Interior commanding him to pay to the relators all the moneys due their minor children, members of the Tribe of Osage Indians of Oklahoma, by reason of the distributions made under the Act of June 28, 1906, 34 Stat. 539, including their respective shares of bonus moneys paid the Secretary for oil leases made by the Tribal Council.

The relators are W. T. Mosier and Louisa Mosier, members of the Osage Tribe of Indians and enrolled as such under the Act of Congress of June 28, 1906, 34 Stat. 539, and are parents of John T. Mosier, Edwin P. Mosier, Luther C. Mosier and Agnes C. Mosier, also enrolled members of the same tribe, who are minors and in the care and keeping of the relators.

* * * * *

[356] . . . While it was admitted that many of the Osages are idle, wasteful, extravagant and improvident, it was also admitted that the relators were not so. . . .

[357] MR. CHIEF JUSTICE TAFT, after stating the case as above, delivered the opinion of the Court.

The questions presented are, first, the proper classification of bonuses under the statute, second, the validity of the conditions imposed by the Secretary on the payment of the minors' incomes to the parents, and third, the propriety of mandamus as a remedy in this case.

The bonus which was the result of bidding for desirable and profitable oil and gas leases secured for the members of the Osage Tribe the just value of the use of their property which the fixing of royalties in advance by the President was not adapted to give them. It was in effect a supplement to the royalties already determined. It was really part of the royalty or rental in a lump sum or down [358] payment. We do not see how it can be classified as anything else. It was income from the use of the mineral resources of the land. . . .

Nor is the settlement of this question a matter of discretionary construction by the Secretary. The Act of June 28, 1906, 34 Stat. 539, was enacted to make a definite disposition of the Osage Indians' resources. . . .

[359] Having thus determined that the duty of the Secretary to pay this income to the adult members of the tribe is ministerial, we come now to the question how much discretion the statute gives him in withholding payment from minors. . . .

With respect to the payment of income from United States bonds, mineral leases, sale of extra lands and grazing rents, belonging to minors, Congress . . . did vest in the Commissioner of Indian Affairs, subject to the supervision of the Secretary of the Interior, discretion to see that its confidence in the natural parental feeling as a motive for care of the minors' interest in such income should not be abused, and whenever he found misuse or squandering by the parents of the income, he was given authority to withhold payment.

The record shows that the Secretary enlarged this discretion vested in him and his subordinate into a power to lay down regulations, limiting in advance the amount to be paid to the parents to a certain monthly rate, and declaring that no use of the funds would be permitted which [360] did not inure to the separate benefit of the minor. He was led to take this action, which was a departure from the previous practice of the Department during the decade immediately following the passage of the act, because of the sudden increase in the income of the minors resulting from the bonuses given for mineral leases. However desirable such regulations were, in view of the changed circumstances, we think they were in the nature of legislation beyond the power of the Secretary. Congress has since met the need by an amendment to the Act of 1906 by the Act of March 3, 1921, 41 Stat. 1249.

. . . Congress evidently intended that the Commissioner should through his agents keep track of the conduct of parents in the use of the income of their children and necessarily vested him and the Secretary with power to require an account of how the income was being used; but this was not a regulatory function to be exercised in advance of payment which is positively enjoined. The proviso imposes on the Commissioner the duty of supervising each case and determining from the circumstances whether there has been, in cases of payments made, misuse or squandering, and if so, of withholding further payment on account of it. . . .

* * * * *

[363] *Reversed.*

Hallanan v. Eureka Pipe Line Co.

An earlier Supreme Court decision had invalidated a state tax on the shipment of oil among states. The Taft opinion stated that it was up to state courts to determine whether the state's tax on intrastate shipments was still legal or whether the United States Supreme Court's invalidation of the tax on interstate shipment rendered the entire West Virginia statute void.

Hallanan, State Tax Commissioner, et al. v. Eureka Pipe Line Company

*On Petition for a Writ of Certiorari and in Error to the Supreme Court of
Appeals of the State of West Virginia*

Nos. 569 and 885. Motion to dismiss or affirm, etc., submitted March 12, 1923—
Decided April 9, 1923

261 U.S. 393 (1923)

[394]

MR. CHIEF JUSTICE TAFT delivered the opinion of the Court. . . .

. . . It is contended by the state authorities seeking review here that the
Supreme Court of Appeals did not enter the judgment required by our
mandate and that we should in some appropriate way direct that court
specifically what judgment it should enter.

* * * * *

[397] . . . This Court gave no consideration to the question whether
the invalidity of part of the tax rendered the whole law void because indi-
visible, as the Circuit Court had held it to be. That was peculiarly a state
question and when we reversed the case for the reason that oil in transport
which the Supreme Court of Appeals held to be intrastate and so taxable
was interstate and immune, and remanded the case for further proceedings, it was entirely within the power and duty of that court to decide what
under the state law would be the effect of the invalidity of part of the tax
levied by the law as adjudged by this Court upon the validity of the whole
tax law. The Supreme Court of Appeals evidently reached the conclusion
that the Circuit Court had been right in deciding that if so much of the tax
was invalid, it could [398] not infer that the Legislature would have enacted the law at all. Accordingly it affirmed the decree of that court as it
had full power to do.

*The application for the writ of certiorari is denied and the writ of error is
dismissed.*

Keller v. Potomac Electric Power Co.

Keller involved an issue of separation of powers. By federal law, the supreme court
of the District was empowered not only to decide legal questions, but to change
the rates and evaluations as determined by the Public Utilities Commission. The

latter is clearly a legislative function. The Court, however, found that the supreme court of the District was an Article I and not an Article III court.

Keller et al., Constituting the Public Utilities Commission of the District of Columbia, v. Potomac Electric Power Company et al.

Appeal from the Court of Appeals of the District of Columbia

No. 260. Argued February 26, 27, 1923—Decided April 9, 1923

261 U.S. 428 (1923)

[436]

MR. CHIEF JUSTICE TAFT delivered the opinion of the Court.

* * * * *

[438] The Public Utilities Law is a very comprehensive one. It applies to all public utilities in the District, except steam railways and steamboat lines. It creates a Commission to supervise and regulate them in the matter of rates, tolls, charges, service, joint rates, and other matters of interest to the public. It directs investigation into the financial history and affairs of each utility and its valuation at a fair value as of the time of valuation. It requires a public hearing on this subject. It also provides that while the utility may fix a schedule of rates, not exceeding the lawful rates at the passage of the act, which it must publish, the Commission may of its own initiative, or upon the complaint of another, or indeed of the utility itself, investigate the reasonableness, lawfulness and adequacy of the rate or service and may change the same. The utility must then adopt the change and publish its schedules accordingly. The law further provides that in such proceedings, the utility shall have notice and a hearing, that a stenographic record of the proceedings shall be kept and produced by the Commission in any court proceeding thereafter instituted to question the validity, reasonableness or adequacy of the action of the Commission.

The relevant part of paragraph 64 is given in full in the margin. In short, it enables the Commission by action [439] in equity to invoke the advice of the District Supreme Court upon the elements in value to be by it considered in arriving at a true valuation of the property of a utility. It further grants to any utility or any person or corporate interest dissatisfied with any valuation, rate or rates or regulation or requirement, act, service or other thing fixed by the Commission the right to begin a proceeding in equity in the Supreme Court, to vacate, set aside or modify the order on the ground that the valuation, rate, regulation, or requirement is unlawful, inadequate or unreasonable. . . .

[440] What is the nature of the power thus conferred on the District Supreme Court? Is it judicial or is it legislative? Is the court to pass solely on questions of law, and look to the facts only to decide what are the questions of law really arising, or to consider whether there was any showing of facts before the Commission upon which, as a matter of law, its finding can be justified? Or has it the power, in this equitable proceeding to review the exercise of discretion by the Commission and itself raise or lower valuations, rates, or restrict or expand orders as to service? Has it the power to make the order the Commission should have made? If it has, then the court is to exercise legislative power in that it will be laying down new rules, to change present conditions and to guide future action and is not confined to definition and protection of existing rights. . . .

* * * * *

[441] Counsel seek to establish an analogy between the jurisdiction of the District Supreme Court to review the action of the Commission, and that conferred on, and exercised by, the Federal District Courts in respect of the orders of the Interstate Commerce Commission. We think, however, that the analogy fails. The act for the creation of the Commerce Court provided (Judicial Code, § 207) that it should have the jurisdiction of the then Circuit Courts of all cases brought to enjoin, set aside or annul or suspend in whole or in part any order of the Commission. When the Commerce Court was abolished by the [442] Act of October 22, 1913, 38 Stat. 219, this jurisdiction was conferred on the several District Courts of the United States. This permits these Courts to consider all relevant questions of constitutional power or right and all pertinent questions whether the administrative order is within the statutory authority, or is an attempted exercise of it so unreasonable as not to be within it; but these are questions of law only, *Interstate Commerce Commission v. Illinois Central R. R. Co.*, 215 U.S. 452, 470. Of course the consideration and decision of questions of law may involve a consideration of controverted facts to determine what the question of law is, but it is settled that any finding of fact by the Commission if supported by evidence is final and conclusive on the courts. . . .

Can the Congress vest such jurisdiction in the courts of the District of Columbia? By the Constitution, clause 17, § 8, Article I, Congress is given power "To exercise exclusive legislation in all cases whatsoever, over" the District of Columbia. This means that as to the District Congress possesses not only the power which belongs to it in respect of territory within a State but the power of [443] the State as well. In other words, it possesses a dual authority over the District and may clothe the courts of the District not only with the jurisdiction and powers of federal courts in the several States but with such authority as a State may confer on her courts. . . .

Subject to the guaranties of personal liberty in the amendments and in the original Constitution, Congress has as much power to vest courts of the District with a variety of jurisdiction and powers as a state legislature has in conferring jurisdiction on its courts. . . .

It follows that the provisions in the law for a review of the Commission's proceedings by the Supreme Court of the District and for an appeal to the District Court of Appeals are valid. A different question arises, however, when we come to consider the validity of the provision for appeal to this Court. It is contained in the following sentence in paragraph 64:

> "Any party, including said commission, may appeal from the order or decree of said court to the Court of Appeals of the District of Columbia, and therefrom to the Supreme Court of the United States, which shall thereupon have and take jurisdiction in every such appeal."

* * * * *

[444] Such legislative or administrative jurisdiction, it is well settled can not be conferred on this Court either directly or by appeal. The latest and fullest authority upon this point is to be found in the opinion of Mr. Justice Day, speaking for the Court in *Muskrat v. United States,* 219 U.S. 346. The principle there recognized and enforced on reason and authority is that the jurisdiction of this Court and of the inferior courts of the United States ordained and established by Congress under and by virtue of the third article of the Constitution is limited to cases and controversies in such form that the judicial power is capable of acting on them and does not extend to an issue of constitutional law framed by Congress for the purpose of invoking the advice of this Court without real parties or a real case, or to administrative or legislative issues or controversies. *Hayburn's Case,* 2 Dall. 410, note; *United States v. Ferreira,* 13 How. 40, 52; *Ex parte Siebold,* 100 U.S. 371, 398; *Gordon v. United States,* 117 U.S. 697; *Baltimore & Ohio R. R. Co. v. Interstate Commerce Commission,* 215 U.S. 216.

The fact that the appeal to this Court is invalid does not, however, render paragraph 64 invalid as a whole.

* * * * *

[445] *Appeal dismissed.*

Adkins v. Children's Hospital

In 1918, Congress passed the Minimum Wage Act, which provided for a minimum wage for women in the District of Columbia. Children's Hospital challenged the statute, arguing that it was in violation of the liberty of contract protected by the due process clause of the Fifth Amendment. A five-member majority struck the law. Justice George Sutherland wrote the opinion of the Court, which found that "freedom of contract is . . . the general rule and restraint the exception," and that the Nineteenth Amendment required that there be no differences between labor practices pertaining to women and those applicable to men.

In response, Taft wrote one of his rare dissenting opinions. So uncomfortable was Taft, who as chief had labored tirelessly to persuade others not to dissent, in the position of dissenter that he spent numerous paragraphs giving the reasons that he felt required him to break ranks with the majority. Taft also sought to explain fully the differences between his stance and the one taken by Justice Holmes in a separate dissent. The latter used his dissent to inveigh against the invidious tendency of the Court to expand "that innocuous generality [depriving any person of liberty or property without due process of law] into the dogma, Liberty of Contract."

Adkins et al., Constituting the Minimum Wage Board of the District of Columbia, v. Children's Hospital of the District of Columbia

Same v. Lyons

Appeals from the Court of Appeals of the District of Columbia

Nos. 795, 796. Argued March 14, 1923—Decided April 9, 1923

261 U.S. 525 (1923)

[562]

MR. CHIEF JUSTICE TAFT, dissenting.

I regret much to differ from the Court in these cases.

The boundary of the police power beyond which its exercise becomes an invasion of the guaranty of liberty under the Fifth and Fourteenth Amendments to the Constitution is not easy to mark. Our Court has been laboriously engaged in pricking out a line in successive cases. We must be careful, it seems to me, to follow that line as well as we can and not to depart from it by suggesting a distinction that is formal rather than real.

Legislatures in limiting freedom of contract between employee and employer by a minimum wage proceed on the assumption that employees, in the class receiving least pay, are not upon a full level of equality of choice with their employer and in their necessitous circumstances are prone to accept pretty much anything that is offered. They are peculiarly subject to the overreaching of the harsh and greedy employer. The evils of the sweating system and of the long hours and low wages which are characteristic of it are well known. Now, I agree that it is a disputable question in the field of political economy how far a statutory requirement of maximum hours or minimum wages may be a useful remedy for these evils, and whether it may not make the case of the oppressed employee worse than it was before. But it is not the function of this Court to hold congressional acts invalid simply because they are passed to carry out economic views which the Court believes to be unwise or unsound.

[563] Legislatures which adopt a requirement of maximum hours or minimum wages may be presumed to believe that when sweating employers are prevented from paying unduly low wages by positive law they will continue their business; abating that part of their profits, which were wrung from the necessities of their employees, and will concede the better terms required by the law; and that while in Individual cases hardship may result, the restriction will enure to the benefit of the general class of employees in whose interest the law is passed and so to that of the community at large.

The right of the legislature under the Fifth and Fourteenth Amendments to limit the hours of employment on the score of the health of the employee, it seems to me, has been firmly established. As to that, one would think, the line had been pricked out so that it has become a well formulated rule. In *Holden v. Hardy,* 169 U.S. 366, it was applied to miners and rested on the unfavorable environment of employment in mining and smelting. In *Lochner v. New York,* 198 U.S. 45, it was held that restricting those employed in bakeries to ten hours a day was an arbitrary and invalid interference with the liberty of contract secured by the Fourteenth Amendment. Then followed a number of cases beginning with *Muller v. Oregon,* 208 U.S. 412, sustaining the validity of a limit on maximum hours of labor for women to which I shall hereafter allude, and following these cases came *Bunting v.*

Oregon, 243 U.S. 426. In that case, this Court sustained a law limiting the hours of labor of any person, whether man or woman, working in any mill, factory or manufacturing establishment to ten hours a day with a proviso as to further hours to which I shall hereafter advert. The law covered the whole field of industrial employment and certainly covered the case of persons employed in bakeries. Yet the opinion in the *Bunting* case does not mention the *Lochner* case. No one can [564] suggest any constitutional distinction between employment in a bakery and one in any other kind of a manufacturing establishment which should make a limit of hours in the one invalid, and the same limit in the other permissible. It is impossible for me to reconcile the *Bunting* case and the *Lochner* case and I have always supposed that the *Lochner* case was thus overruled *sub silentio.* Yet the opinion of the Court herein in support of its conclusion quotes from the opinion in the *Lochner* case as one which has been sometimes distinguished but never overruled. Certainly there was no attempt to distinguish it in the *Bunting* case.

However, the opinion herein does not overrule the *Bunting* case in express terms, and therefore I assume that the conclusion in this case rests on the distinction between a minimum of wages and a maximum of hours in the limiting of liberty to contract. I regret to be at variance with the Court as to the substance of this distinction. In absolute freedom of contract the one term is as important as the other, for both enter equally into the consideration given and received, a restriction as to one is not any greater in essence than the other, and is of the same kind. One is the multiplier and the other the multiplicand.

If it be said that long hours of labor have a more direct effect upon the health of the employee than the low wage, there is very respectable authority from close observers, disclosed in the record and in the literature on the subject quoted at length in the briefs, that they are equally harmful in this regard. Congress took this view and we can not say it was not warranted in so doing.

With deference to the very able opinion of the Court and my brethren who concur in it, it appears to me to exaggerate the importance of the wage term of the contract of employment as more inviolate than its other terms. Its conclusion seems influenced by the fear that the [565] concession of the power to impose a minimum wage must carry with it a concession of the power to fix a maximum wage. This, I submit, is a *non sequitur.* A line of distinction like the one under discussion in this case is, as the opinion elsewhere admits, a matter of degree and practical experience and not of pure logic. Certainly the wide difference between prescribing a minimum wage and a maximum wage could as a matter of degree and experience be easily affirmed.

Moreover, there are decisions by this Court which have sustained legislative limitations in respect to the wage term in contracts of employment. . . .

[566] I do not feel, therefore, that either on the basis of reason, experience or authority, the boundary of the police power should be drawn to include maximum hours and exclude a minimum wage.

Without, however, expressing an opinion that a minimum wage limitation can be enacted for adult men, it is enough to say that the case before us involves only the application of the minimum wage to women. If I am right in thinking that the legislature can find as much support in experience for the view that a sweating wage has as great and as direct a tendency to bring about an injury to the health and morals of workers, as for the view that long hours injure their health, then I respectfully submit that *Muller v. Oregon,* 208 U.S. 412, controls this case. The law which was there sustained forbade the employment of any female in any mechanical establishment or factory or laundry for more than ten hours. This covered a pretty wide field in women's work and it would not seem that any sound distinction between that case and this can be built up on the fact that the law before us applies to all occupations of women with power in the board to make certain exceptions. Mr. Justice Brewer, who spoke for the Court in *Muller v. Oregon,* based its conclusion on the natural limit to women's physical strength and the likelihood that long hours would therefore injure her health, and we have had since a series of cases which may be said to have established a rule of decision. *Riley v. Massachusetts,* 232 U.S. 671; *Miller v. Wilson,* 236 U.S. 373; *Bosley v. McLaughlin,* 236 U.S. 385. The cases covered restrictions in wide and varying fields of employment and in the later cases it will be found that the objection to the particular law was based not on the ground that it had general application but because it left out some employments.

[567] I am not sure from a reading of the opinion whether the Court thinks the authority of *Muller v. Oregon* is shaken by the adoption of the Nineteenth Amendment. The Nineteenth Amendment did not change the physical strength or limitations of women upon which the decision in *Muller v. Oregon* rests. The Amendment did give women political power and makes more certain that legislative provisions for their protection will be in accord with their interests as they see them. But I don't think we are warranted in varying constitutional construction based on physical differences between men and women, because of the Amendment.

But for my inability to agree with some general observations in the forcible opinion of MR. JUSTICE HOLMES who follows me, I should be silent and merely record my concurrence in what he says. It is perhaps wiser for me, however, in a case of this importance, separately to give my reasons for dissenting.

I am authorized to say that MR. JUSTICE SANFORD concurs in this opinion.

Omitted Taft Opinions

Gorham Manufacturing Company v. Wendell, 261 U.S. 1 (1923)—substitution of parties to a suit.

Vandenburgh v. Truscon Steel Company, 261 U.S. 6 (1923)—patent case.

Concrete Steel Company v. Vandenbergh, 261 U.S. 16 (1923)—patent case.

Crown Die & Tool Company v. Nye Tool & Machine Works, 261 U.S. 24 (1923)—patent case.

Eibel Process Company v. Minnesota & Ontario Paper Company, 261 U.S. 45 (1923)—patent case.

Pothier v. Rodman, 261 U.S. 307 (1923)—lack of jurisdiction.

City of New York v. New York Telephone Company, 261 U.S. 312 (1923)—issue of standing in regards to the City of New York.

United States v. Rider, 261 U.S. 363 (1923)—salary dispute involving military personnel.

Layne & Bowler Corporation v. Western Well Works, Inc., et al., 261 U.S. 387 (1923)—patent case.

Hallanan v. United Fuel Gas Company, 261 U.S. 398 (1923)—denial of writ of *certiorari.*

Toledo Scale Company v. Computing Scale Company, 261 U.S. 399 (1923)—patent and fraud case.

VOLUME 262

Board of Trade v. Olsen

Questioned during his presidency as to which of the founders he most admired, Taft replied that is was John Marshall.[1] This identification with Marshall might help to explain those Taft decisions that do not fit the portrait of Taft most frequently painted by American historians. Like any well-versed student of constitutional law, Taft saw the great Chief Justice's opinions in *McCulloch v. Maryland,* 4 Wheat. (17 U.S.) 316 (1819), and *Gibbons v. Ogden,* 9 Wheat. (22 U.S.) 1 (1824), as providing the essential foundation stones upon which the great commercial republic of the United States rested. Although his view of the scope of the Commerce Clause might not have been as broad as that of Brandeis, Taft's interpretative approach to I-8–3 was worlds apart from the narrowness that would characterize the jurisprudence of the Hughes Court's "Four Horsemen" and of the Hughes Court prior to "the switch in time that saved nine."

The *Olsen* case is in many ways a replay of child labor legislation that the Court had earlier struck down, but in reverse and with a very different outcome. Congress, having failed to gain control over speculative practices in grain trading by using the taxing power—held unconstitutional in *Hill v. Wallace*, 259 U.S. 44 (1922), decided on the same day as *Bailey v. Drexel Furniture Company*—turned to the Commerce Clause and adopted the Grain Futures Act of 1922. In challenging the measure, the Chicago Board of Trade emphasized the fact that the regulated activities were local, did not burden interstate commerce, ran counter to such precedents as *Hammer v. Dagenhart,* and constituted a taking of property. Although these arguments persuaded Justices McReynolds and Sutherland, two of the future "Four Horsemen," they did not persuade Marshall admirer Taft.

Note

1. Archibald Butt, *Taft and Roosevelt* (Garden City, N.J.: Doubleday, 1930), 1:293–94.

Board of Trade of the City of Chicago et al. v. Olsen, United States Attorney for the Northern District of Illinois, et al.

Appeal from the District Court of the United States for the Northern District of Illinois

No. 701. Argued February 26, 1923—Decided April 16, 1923

262 U.S. 1 (1923)

[31]

MR. CHIEF JUSTICE TAFT . . . delivered the opinion of the Court.

Appellants contend that the decision of this Court in *Hill v. Wallace,* 259 U.S. 44, is conclusive against the constitutionality of the Grain Futures Act. Indeed in their bill they pleaded the judgment in that case as *res judicata* in this, as to its invalidity. The act whose constitutionality was in question in *Hill v. Wallace* was the Futures Trading Act (c. *86, 42* Stat. 187). It was an effort by Congress, through taxing at a prohibitive rate sales of grain for future delivery, to regulate such sales on boards of trade by exempting them from the tax if they would comply with the congressional regulations. It was [32] held that sales for future delivery where the parties were present in Chicago, to be settled by offsetting purchases or by delivery, to take place there, were not interstate commerce and that Congress could not use its taxing power in this indirect way to regulate business not within federal control. . . .

* * * * *

The Grain Futures Act which is now before us differs from the Future Trading Act in having the very features the absence of which we held . . . prevented our sustaining the Future Trading Act. As we have seen in the statement of the case, the act only purports to regulate interstate commerce and sales of grain for future delivery on boards of trade because it finds that by manipulation they have become a constantly recurring burden and obstruction to that commerce. Instead, [33] therefore, of being an authority against the validity of the Grain Futures Act, it is an authority in its favor.

The Chicago Board of Trade is the greatest grain market in the world. *Chicago Board of Trade v. United States*, 246 U.S. 231, 235. Its report for 1922 shows that on that market in that year were made cash sales for some three hundred and fifty millions of bushels of grain, most of which was shipped from States west and north of Illinois into Chicago, and was either stored temporarily in Chicago or was retained in cars and after sale was shipped in large part to eastern States and foreign countries. . . .

The fact that the grain shipped from the west and taken from the cars may have been stored in warehouses and mixed with other grain, so that the owner receives other grain when presenting his receipt for [34] continuing the shipment, does not take away from the interstate character of the through shipment any more than a mixture of the oil or gas in the pipe lines of the oil and gas companies in West Virginia, with the right in the owners to withdraw their shares before crossing state lines, prevented the great bulk of the oil and gas which did thereafter cross state lines from being a stream or current of interstate commerce. *Eureka Pipe Line Co. v. Hallanan*, 257 U.S. 265, 272; *United Fuel Gas Co. v. Hallanan*, 257 U S. 277, 281.

It is impossible to distinguish the case at bar, so far as it concerns the cash grain, the sales to arrive, and the grain actually delivered in fulfillment of future contracts, from the current of stock shipments declared to be interstate commerce in *Stafford v. Wallace*, 258 U.S. 495. That case presented the question whether sales and purchases of cattle made in Chicago at the stockyards by commission men and dealers and traders under the rules of the stockyards corporation could be brought by Congress under the supervision of the Secretary of Agriculture to prevent abuses of the commission men and dealers in exorbitant charges and other ways, and in their relations with packers prone to monopolize trade and depress and increase prices thereby. . . .

* * * * *

[35] This case was but the necessary consequence of the conclusions reached in the case of *Swift & Co. v. United States,* 196 U.S. 375. That case was a milestone in the interpretation of the commerce clause of the Constitution. It recognized the great changes and development in the business of this vast country and drew again the dividing line between interstate and intrastate commerce where the Constitution intended it to be. It refused to permit local incidents of great interstate movement, which taken alone were intrastate, to characterize the movement as such. The *Swift* case merely fitted the commerce clause to the real and practical essence of modern business growth. It applies to the case before us just as it did in *Stafford v. Wallace.*

The distinction that the exchange of the Chicago Board of Trade building is not within the same enclosure as the railroad yards and warehouses in which the grain is received and stored on its way from the West to the East as it is being sold on the exchange, while the stockyards exchange and the actual receipt and shipment of cattle are within the same fence, surely can make no difference in the application of the principle. The sales on the Chicago Board of Trade are just as indispensable to the continuity of the flow of wheat, from the West to the mills and distributing points of the East and Europe, as are the Chicago sales of cattle to the flow of stock toward the feeding places and slaughter and packing houses of the East.

* * * * *

[40] The Board of Trade conducts a business which is affected with a public interest and is, therefore, subject to [41] reasonable regulation in the public interest. The Supreme Court of Illinois has so decided in respect to its publication of market quotations. *New York & Chicago Grain Exchange v. Chicago Board of Trade,* 127 Ill. 153. In view of the actual interstate dealings in cash sales of grain on the exchange, and the effect of the conduct of the sales of futures upon interstate commerce, we find no difficulty under *Munn v. Illinois,* 94 U.S. 113, 133, and *Stafford v. Wallace, supra,* in concluding that the Chicago Board of Trade is engaged in a business affected with a public national interest and is subject to national regulation as such. Congress may, therefore, reasonably limit the rules governing its conduct with a view to preventing abuses and securing freedom from undue discrimination in its operations. The incidental effect which such reasonable rules may have, if any, in lowering the value of memberships does not constitute a taking, but is only a reasonable regulation in the exercise of the police power of the National Government. Congress evidently deems it helpful in the preservation of the vital function which such a board of trade exercises in interstate com-

merce in grain that producers and shippers should be given an opportunity to take part in the transactions in this world market through a chosen representative. . . .

*   *   *   *   *

[43] For the reasons given the decree of the District Court is

Affirmed.

MR. JUSTICE MCREYNOLDS and MR. JUSTICE SUTHERLAND dissent.

Ex parte Fuller

The Old Court, the pre-1937 Court, tended to be far more interested in protecting the rights of property than in what we today refer to as issues of civil rights and liberties. The Taft Court, however, in many ways was a transitional Court. It was the Taft Court, for instance, that in *Gitlow v. New York*, 268 U.S. 652 (1925), would apply the First Amendment's protection of freedom of speech to the states. In the *Fuller* case, a bankruptcy case, the Court was forced to explore the Fourth and Fifth Amendment rights of a bankrupt against "unreasonable searches and seizures" and self-incrimination.

Ex Parte: In the Matter of Fuller et al., Individually and as Copartners under the Name of E. M. Fuller & Company, Petitioners

Application for a Stay of Orders of District Court Pending Appeal

No.— Motion for stay submitted April 27, 1923—Decided April 30, 1923

262 U.S. 91 (1923)

[92]

MR. CHIEF JUSTICE TAFT delivered the opinion of the Court.

On June 26, 1922, a petition in involuntary bankruptcy was filed against Fuller and McGee, individually and as partners, in the name of E. M. Fuller & Company, in the District Court for the Southern District of New York. Thereafter Strasbourger was appointed Receiver and at once demanded of the bankrupts the books of accounts, records, documents, both of themselves individually and of the firm. The bankrupts claimed that the books would tend to incriminate them and refused to turn them over unless the Receiver agreed that they were to be used in connection with the civil administration of bankrupts' estate only. . . .

[93] . . . On April 21st, the District Attorney of New York County had subpoenaed the Trustee to produce the books and papers of the bankrupts he then had in his custody and on the 24th of April offered them in evidence in the Court of General Sessions of New York as evidence against E. M. Fuller under an indictment arising out of the business of the bankrupts. On the 25th of April Judge Mack granted an application for a stay pending proceedings for appeal to this Court and an application for a stay here; and Judge Nott presiding in the state court adjourned the trial there until April 30th.

Proceedings for appeal to this Court have now been begun under the authority of *Perlman v. United States,* 247 U.S. 7, and the application for a stay of Judge Mack's two orders has now been made.

A man who becomes a bankrupt or who is brought into a bankruptcy court has no right to delay the legal transfer of the possession and title of any of his property to the officers appointed by law for its custody or for its disposition, on the ground that the transfer of such property will carry with it incriminating evidence against him. His property and its possession pass from him by operation and due proceedings of law, and when control and possession have passed from him, he has no constitutional right to prevent its use for any legitimate purpose. His privilege secured to him by the Fourth and Fifth Amendments to the Constitution is that of refusing himself to produce, as incriminating evidence against him, anything which he owns or has in his possession and control, but his privilege in respect to what was his and in his custody [94] ceases on a transfer of the control and possession which takes place by legal proceedings and in pursuance of the rights of others, even though such transfer may bring the property into the ownership or control of one properly subject to subpoena *duces tecum.* . . .

* * * * *

The application is denied.

Dier v. Banton

Dier is a replay of the preceding *Fuller* case. It is interesting to note that Taft, while concluding that the bankruptcy proceeding vitiated the appellants' Fourth and Fifth Amendment rights, did not take the position that individuals do not have such rights against state authorities. It would be only during the Warren Court that the Supreme Court would explicitly incorporate these two guarantees onto the states.

Dier et al., Individually and as Copartners under the Firm Name of E. D. Dier & Company, et al., v. Banton, District Attorney of the County of New York, et al.

Appeal from the District Court of the United States for the Southern District of New York

No. 330. Argued April 17, 1923—Decided May 7, 1923

262 U.S. 147 (1923)

[148]

MR. CHIEF JUSTICE TAFT delivered the opinion of the Court.

This appeal is from an order of the District Court for the Southern District of New York discharging a rule *nisi* and [149] refusing an injunction. On January 14, 1922, a petition in involuntary bankruptcy was filed against Elmore D. Dier and others, partners, as E. D. Dier & Company. Two days after the filing of the petition, Manfred W. Ehrich was appointed Receiver of the estate of the alleged bankrupt and they and their servants were directed to turn over all their property, assets, account books and records and were restrained from suing out of any other court any process to impound or take possession of them. The order was complied with and the Receiver took possession of the books and papers of the alleged bankrupts and of the firm. On February 16th, Dier informed the court that the District Attorney of New York County had applied to the Receiver for the production of these books and papers before the Grand Jury, and asked for the rule *nisi* against the Receiver and the District Attorney, and upon a hearing thereof an injunction to prevent the use of such books and papers against him before the Grand Jury, on the ground that they would incriminate him and that his right to refuse to testify against himself under the Fourth and Fifth Amendments would thus be violated by the process of the Federal District Court. Judge Learned Hand, sitting in bankruptcy, discharged the rule and refused to enjoin the proposed use of the books. Judge Hand's action was based on the ruling of this Court in *Johnson v. United States,* 228 U.S. 457. He quoted the language used in the *Johnson* case, "A party is privileged from producing the evidence but not from its production." He alluded to the circumstance that in the *Johnson* case there were both title and possession in the Trustee, whereas in this case, the books and papers were in the hands of the Receiver who has no title but that, he said, made no difference. We agree with this view and hold that the right of the alleged bankrupt to protest against the use of his books and papers relating to his business as evidence against him ceases as soon as his [150] possession and control over them pass from him by the order directing their delivery into the hands of the Receiver and into the custody of the court. This change of possession and control is for the purpose of properly carrying on the investigation into the affairs of the alleged bankrupt and the preservation of his assets pending such investigation, the adjudication of bankruptcy *vel non*, and if bankruptcy is adjudged, the proper distribution of the estate. It may be that the allegation of bankruptcy will not be sustained, and in that case, the alleged bankrupt will be entitled to a return of his property including his books and papers; and when they are returned, he may refuse to produce them and stand on his constitutional rights. But while they are, in the due course of the bankruptcy proceedings, taken out of his possession and control, his immunity from producing them, secured him under the Fourth and Fifth Amendments, does not enure to his protection. He has lost any right to object to their use as evidence because, not for purpose of evidence, but in the due investigation of his alleged bankruptcy and the preservation of his estate pending such investigation, the control and possession of his books and papers relating to his business were lawfully taken from him.

* * * * *

[151] Of course, where such books and papers are in the custody of the Bankruptcy Court, they can not be taken therefrom by subpoena of a state court except upon consent of the federal court. In granting or withholding that consent the latter exercises a judicial discretion dependent on the circumstances, and having due regard to the comity which should be observed toward state courts exercising jurisdiction within the same territory. *Ponzi v. Fessenden,* 258 U.S. 254, 259. All we hold here is that the court below having exercised discretion to allow the use of the books and papers in the custody of its officer upon subpoena by another court, the alleged bankrupt's rights under the Fourth and Fifth Amendments have not been violated.

Order affirmed.

Essgee Co. v. United States

The two companies were charged by federal authorities with fraud and were required to produce their books. The Taft opinion dealt with the nature of "unreasonable searches and seizures" that was raised by the defendants.

Essgee Company of China et al. v. United States
Hanclaire Trading Corporation et al. v. United States

*Error to and Appeal from the District Court of the United States
for the Southern District of New York*

Nos. 706 and 707. Submitted April 25, 1923—Decided May 7, 1923

262 U.S. 151 (1923)

[152]

MR. CHIEF JUSTICE TAFT delivered the opinion of the Court.

These are appeals and writs of error to review the action of the District Court in denying petitions of the two companies, the Essgee Company of China and the Hanclaire Trading Corporation, praying that the books and papers produced by an officer of the two companies, in response to a *duces tecum* issued to them by order of the Federal Grand Jury, be returned to the petitioners, on the ground that the process issued and the detention of the books by the Government were and are in violation of their rights under the Fourth and Fifth Amendments to the Federal Constitution.

* * * * *

[153] The Hanclaire Trading Corporation and the Essgee Company of China were organized under the laws of New York and were doing an importing business in New York City. Schratter was an officer in both companies and Kramer was an officer of one and attorney for both. The Federal Grand Jury in the Southern District of New York was investigating charges of frauds in importations by these two companies whose interests and transactions were intermingled. On October 14, 1921, a subpoena *duces tecum* was served upon each of the corporations by personal service upon Schratter as a chief officer thereof. Schratter then directed Kramer to gather together the [154] books and papers called for and produce them at the Federal Court House. The subpoena was served by the U.S. Marshal for the District. . . .

Kramer and Schratter brought the records and papers called for by the sub-poena to a room in the Court House and deposited them on a table where the District Attorney found them and took charge of them. Neither Schrat-ter nor Kramer was then called before the Grand Jury, but they were both at once arrested upon warrants for violation of the importing laws. . . .

* * * * *

[155] The books and papers brought before the Grand Jury and the court in this case were the books, records and papers of corporations of the State of New York. Such corporations do not enjoy the same immunity that individu-als have, under the Fourth and Fifth Amendments, from being compelled by due and lawful process to produce them for examination by the state or Fed-eral Government. Referring to the books and papers of a corporation, Mr. Justice Hughes speaking for this Court in *Wilson v. United States,* 221 U.S. 361, 382, said:

> "They have reference to business transacted for the benefit of the group of individuals whose association has the advantage of corporate organi-zation. But the corporate form of business activity, with its charter privi-leges, raises a distinction when the authority of government demands the examination of books. That demand, expressed in lawful process, confining its requirements within the limits which reason imposes in the circumstances of the case, the corporation has no privilege to refuse. It cannot resist production upon the ground of self-incrimination. Al-though the object of the inquiry may be to detect the abuses it has com-mitted, to discover its violations of law and to inflict punishment by forfeiture of franchises or otherwise; it must submit its books and pa-pers to duly constituted authority when demand is suitably made. This is involved in the reservation of the visitatorial power of the State, and in the [156] authority of the National Government where the corporate activities are in the domain subject to the powers of Congress." . . .

Counsel for appellants rely upon *Silverthorne Lumber Co. v. United States,* 251 U.S. 385, but it has no application to the case before us. The *Sil-verthorne* case was a writ of error to reverse a judgment for contempt against a corporation for refusal to obey an order of the court to produce books and documents of the company to be used to show violation of law by the offic-ers of the company. This Court found that without a shadow of authority and under color of an invalid writ, the marshal and other government offic-ers had made a clean sweep of all the books, papers and documents in the office of the company while its officers were under arrest. These documents were copied and photographed and then the court ordered their return to the company. A subpoena was then issued to compel the production of the originals. The company refused to obey the subpoena. The court made an order requiring obedience and refusal to obey the order was the contempt alleged. This Court held that the Government could not, while in form repudiating the illegal seizure, maintain its right to avail itself of the knowledge obtained by that means which otherwise it would not have had. In other words, we held that the search thus made was an unreasonable one against which the corporation was protected by the Fourth Amendment and which vitiated all the subsequent proceedings to compel production. . . .

[157] In the case before us the demand was suitably made by duly constituted authority. In the *Silverthorne* case, it was not. Here it was expressed in lawful process, confining its requirements to certain described documents and papers easily distinguished and clearly described. Their relevancy to the subject of investigation was not denied. . . .

* * * * *

[158] Appellants cite the cases of *Boyd v. United States*; 116 U.S. 616; *Weeks v. United States*, 232 U.S. 383, and *Gouled v. United States*, 255 U.S. 298, to support their contention that the proceedings complained of herein violate their rights under the Fourth and Fifth Amendments. Those cases were all unreasonable searches of documents and records belonging to individuals. The distinction between the cases before us and those cases lies in the more limited application of the Amendments to the compulsory production of corporate documents and papers as shown in the *Henkel, Wilson* and *Wheeler* cases.

The order of the District Court is affirmed.

Work v. McAlester-Edwards Co.

The Court in *McAlester-Edwards Company* was called upon to rule on the degree of discretion given the secretary of interior. As in the earlier case of *Mosier*, 261 U.S. 352, the Court found that the appropriate federal legislation vested no discretion in the secretary of the interior.

Work, Secretary of the Interior, Johnson, Governor of the Chickasaw Nation, et al. v. United States Ex Rel. McAlester-Edwards Company

Appeal from the Court of Appeals of the District of Columbia

No. 258. Argued April 12, 1923—Decided May 21, 1923

262 U.S. 200 (1923)

[205]

MR. CHIEF JUSTICE TAFT, after stating the case as above, delivered the opinion of the Court.

Two questions are to be decided in this case. The first is under what appraisement the preferential right conferred on the relator by the second section of the Act of 1918 to purchase the surface previously reserved to it by the Secretary of the Interior, was to be exercised. Should it have been under that of the Act of 1912, or under that ordered by the Secretary after the Act of 1918? The second question is whether the construction necessary to determine the first question is vested by the statute in [206] the legal discretion of the Secretary which it is not within the power of the Supreme Court of the District by mandamus to control.

* * * * *

[207] There is nothing in the Act of 1918 expressly or impliedly authorizing the Secretary to order a [208] reappraisement of the surface land. There is no appropriation for the purpose.

If by the words quoted from § 4 of the act it was intended to authorize a new appraisement of the surface reservations, the language would not have been "*the*" appraisement but "*an*" appraisement. The use of the definite article means an appraisement specifically provided for. Such an appraisement of the minerals was provided for in the Act of 1918 and this is mentioned in the same sentence in which "*the* appraisement" of the surface land is referred to. Construing the Acts of 1912 and 1918 together, the appraisement can only refer to that so elaborately provided for in 1912.

Second. We think that the preferential right of relator conferred by § 4 of the Act of 1918 was not to be left to the legal discretion of the Secretary in the construction of that act. There are no words to qualify that which the lessee has as a right granted by the statute, or to vest in the Secretary the final discretion to determine or define that right.

* * * * *

[209] The decree of the Court of Appeals of the District of Columbia is

Affirmed.

Sonneborn Brothers v. Cureton

Brown v. Maryland, 12 Wheat. (25 U.S.) 419 (1827), was one of only a handful of Marshall Court decisions that was not unanimous. In it, Chief Justice John Marshall established the so-called "original package" doctrine. So long as goods in interstate commerce remained in their "original packages," they were not subject to state taxation. The Taft Court was confronted, as earlier courts had been, with numerous cases that required it to determine whether or not the original package had been broken and, as a result, the goods were no longer in interstate commerce. In this case, Taft found that the circumstances were such that the Court could uphold the Texas taxes as valid.

Sonneborn Brothers v. Cureton, Attorney General of the State of Texas, et al.

Appeal from the District Court of the United States for the Western District of Texas

No. 20. Argued March 24, 1922; restored to docket for reargument May 29, 1922; reargued October 5, 1922—Decided June 11, 1923

262 U.S. 506 (1923)

[507]

MR. CHIEF JUSTICE TAFT delivered the opinion of the Court.

This is an appeal from a decree of a United States District Court under § 238, Judicial Code, in a case in which a law of Texas is claimed to be in contravention of the Constitution of the United States. The law in question is Art. 7377 of the Revised Civil Statutes of Texas, approved May 16, 1907, Acts of 1907, p. 479. It provides that every individual, firm or corporation, foreign or domestic, engaging as a wholesale dealer in coal oil or other oils refined from petroleum, shall make a quarterly report to the State Comptroller, showing the gross amount collected and uncollected from any and all sales made within the State during the quarter next preceding, and that an occupation tax shall be paid by such dealer equal to two per cent. of the gross amount of such sales collected or uncollected.

From an agreed statement of facts, the following appears:

Sonneborn Brothers is a firm of non-resident merchants selling petroleum products, with its principal place of business in New York City. In January, 1910, it opened an office in Dallas, Texas, and since that time has maintained it and connecting warerooms and has rented space in a public warehouse at San Antonio, Texas. From January, 1910, until April 11, 1919, receipts from its total [508] sales, made through orders received at the Dallas office, have amounted to $860,801.50. This sum included:

1. Those from the sale of oil which, when sold, was not in Texas.

3. Those from sales of oil to be delivered from Texas out of the State.

5. Those arising from the sale of oil shipped into Texas and afterwards sold from the storerooms in unbroken original packages.

7. Those from sales in Texas from broken packages.

The receipts from the first two classes amounted to $643,622.40 and the state authorities made no effort to tax them. The receipts from (4) amounted in the period named to $16,549.84, and appellants do not deny their liability for the tax thereon. The sales made under (3) of unbroken packages, after their arrival in Texas, and after storage in the warerooms or warehouse of appellants, amounted to $217,179.10, and the tax on this amounting to $4,674.58 is the subject of the contest here.

* * * * *

Our conclusion must depend on the answer to the question: Is this a regulation of, or a burden upon, interstate commerce? We think it is neither. The oil had come to a state of rest in the warehouse of the appellants and had become a part of their stock with which they proposed to do business as wholesale dealers in the State. The interstate transportation was at an end, and whether in the original packages or not, a state tax upon the oil [509] as property or upon its sale in the State, if the state law levied the same tax on all oil or all sales of it, without regard to origin, would be neither a regulation nor a burden of the interstate commerce of which this oil had been the subject.

* * * * *

But the argument is that for articles in original packages, the sale is a final step in the interstate commerce, and that the owner may not be taxed upon such sale because this is a direct burden on that step. The reasoning is based on the supposed analogy of the immunity from state taxation of imports from foreign countries which lasts until the article imported has been sold, or has been taken from its original packages of importation and added to the mass of merchandise of the State. This immunity of imports was established by this Court in *Brown v. Maryland,* 12 Wheat. 419, 446, 447, and was declared in obedience to the prohibition of the Constitution contained in § 10, Article I, par. 2, providing that:

"No State shall, without the consent of the Congress, lay any imposts or duties on imports or exports, except what may be absolutely necessary for executing its inspection laws."

The holding was that the sale was part of the importation. It is the article itself to which the immunity attaches and whether it is in transit or is at rest, so long as it is in the form and package in which imported and in the custody and ownership of the importer, the State may not tax it. This immunity has been enforced as against [510] a license or occupation tax on the importer in *Brown v. Maryland,* 12 Wheat. 419, as against a personal property tax on a stock of wines of a wine dealer to the extent to which the stock included imported wines in the original packages, *Low v. Austin,* 13 Wall. 29, and as against an occupation tax on an auctioneer measured by his commissions on the sales of such imports, *Cook v. Pennsylvania,* 97 U.S. 566. When, however, the article imported is sold or is taken from the original packages and exposed for sale, the immunity is gone. *Waring v. The Mayor,* 8 Wall. 110; *May v. New Orleans,* 178 U.S. 496.

Cases subsequent to *Brown v. Maryland* show that the analogy between imports and articles in original packages in interstate commerce in respect of immunity from taxation fails. The distinction is that the immunity attaches to the import itself before sale, while the immunity in case of an article because of its relation to interstate commerce depends on the question whether the tax challenged regulates or burdens interstate commerce.

The first of the cases making this distinction is *Woodruff v. Parham,* 8 Wall. 123. In that case, Woodruff, an auctioneer in Mobile, received, in the course of his general business for himself and as consignee and agent for others, merchandise from Alabama and from other States and sold it in unbroken packages. The City of Mobile under its charter levied a uniform tax on real and personal property, on sales at auction, on sales of merchandise, and on capital employed in the business in the city. Woodruff objected to paying any tax on the auction sales of merchandise from other States in original packages. The question most considered by the Court was whether merchandise exported from one State to another was an export which a State was forbidden to tax by Article I, § 10, par. 2, of the Federal Constitution, above quoted. It was held that it was not, and that the words "imports and exports" as there used referred to, and included only [511] merchandise brought in from, or transported to foreign countries. The Court (p. 140) further held that such a tax which did not discriminate against the sales of goods from other States, but was imposed upon sales of all merchandise, whether its origin was in Alabama or in any other State, was not "an attempt to fetter commerce among the States."

At the close of the opinion in *Brown v. Maryland,* Chief Justice Marshall made the remark "that we suppose the principles laid down in this case apply equally to importations from a sister State." This was pronounced in *Woodruff v. Parham* not to be a judicial decision of the question but an *obiter dictum.*

While the opinion by Mr. Justice Miller in *Woodruff v. Parham is* chiefly devoted to showing that exports are limited to goods sent out of the country, the decision on the interstate commerce phase of the issue was most fully considered. The adverse view was pressed with all the learning and force of argument of John A. Campbell, formerly a Justice of this Court.

* * * * *

[512] The case of *Woodruff v. Parham* has never been overruled but has often been approved and followed as the cases above cited show. As an authority it controls the case before us and shows conclusively that the tax in question is valid.

* * * * *

[521] The decree of the District Court is

Affirmed.

MR. JUSTICE MCREYNOLDS, concurring.

I am unable to concur in all said to support the conclusion adopted by the Court. To me the result seems out of harmony with the theory upon which recent opinions proceed. There is unfortunate confusion concerning the general subject and certainly some pronouncement that can abide is desirable.

Apparently no great harm, and possibly some good, will follow a flat declaration that irrespective of analogies and [522] for purposes of taxation we will hold interstate commerce ends when an original package reaches the consignee and comes to rest within a State, although intended for sale there in unbroken form. It may be said that the effect on interstate commerce is not substantial and too remote, notwithstanding the rather clear logic of *Brown v. Maryland,* 12 Wheat. 419, to the contrary and the much discussed theory respecting freedom of interstate commerce from interference by the States, announced and developed long after *Woodruff v. Parham* (1868), 8 Wall. 123. Logic and taxation are not always the best of friends.

Wolff v. Court of Industrial Relations

Coming just two months after Taft's generally surprising dissent in *Adkins*, 261 U.S. 525 (1923), *Wolff* is frequently cited as being more representative of Taft's conservatism and, particularly, his reverence for private property and the "liberty of contract."[1] University of Minnesota historian Paul Murphy, for example, charges that "the ruling [in *Wolff*] negated a half century of legal development since *Munn v. Illinois* (1877) by putting the majority of businesses outside the reach of state regulation."[2]

Be that as it may, Taft's opinion in *Wolff* was for a unanimous Court, carrying with it the votes of both Justice Holmes and Justice Brandeis, somewhat surprising given the fact that the Taft opinion was as far reaching as Murphy and the others have alleged.

Notes

1. E.g., David H. Burton, *William Howard Taft: In the Public Service* (Malabar, Fla.: Krieger Publishing, 1986), 136–37; Mason, *William Howard Taft*, 251–53.
2. Paul L. Murphy, "Wolff Packing Company v. Court of Industrial Relations," in *The Oxford Companion to the Supreme Court of the United States*, ed. Kermit L. Hall, James W. Ely, Joel B. Grossman, and William M. Wiecek (New York: Oxford University Press, 1992), 936.

Chas. Wolff Packing Company v. Court of Industrial Relations of the State of Kansas

Error to the Supreme Court of the State of Kansas

No. 739. Argued April 27, 1923—Decided June 11, 1923

262 U.S. 522 (1923)

[533]

MR. CHIEF JUSTICE TAFT. . . delivered the opinion of the Court.

The necessary postulate of the Industrial Court Act is that the State, representing the people, is so much interested in their peace, health and comfort that it may compel those engaged in the manufacture of food, and clothing, and the production of fuel, whether owners or [534] workers, to continue in their business and employment on terms fixed by an agency of the State if they can not agree. Under the construction adopted by the State Supreme Court the act gives the Industrial Court authority to permit the owner or employer to go out of the business, if he shows that he can only continue on the terms fixed at such heavy loss that collapse will follow; but this privilege under the circumstances is generally illusory. *Block v. Hirsh,* 256 U.S. 135, 157. A laborer dissatisfied with his wages is permitted to quit, but he may not agree with his fellows to quit or combine with others to induce them to quit.

These qualifications do not change the essence of the act. It curtails the right of the employer on the one hand, and of the employee on the other, to contract about his affairs. This is part of the liberty of the individual protected by the guaranty of the due process clause of the Fourteenth Amendment. *Meyer v. Nebraska, ante,* 390. While there is no such thing as absolute freedom of contract and it is subject to a variety of restraints, they must not be arbitrary or unreasonable. Freedom is the general rule, and restraint the exception. The legislative authority to abridge can be justified only by exceptional circumstances. *Adkins v. Children's Hospital,* 261 U.S. 525.

It is argued for the State that such exceptional circumstances exist in the present case and that the act is neither arbitrary nor unreasonable. Counsel maintain:

First. The act declares that the preparation of human food is affected by a public interest and the power of the legislature so to declare and then to regulate the business is established in *Munn v. Illinois,* 94 U.S. 113. . . .

[535] Second. The power to regulate a business affected with a public interest extends to fixing wages and terms of employment to secure continuity of operation. *Wilson v. New,* 243 U.S. 332, 352, 353.

* * * * *

[536] In a sense, the public is concerned about all lawful business because it contributes to the prosperity and well being of the people. The public may suffer from high prices or strikes in many trades, but the expression clothed with a public interest, as applied to a business, means more than that the public welfare is affected by continuity or by the price at which a commodity is sold or a service rendered. The circumstances which clothe a particular kind of business with a public interest, in the sense of *Munn v. Illinois* and the other cases, must be such as to create a peculiarly close relation between the public and those engaged in it, and raise implications of an affirmative obligation on their part to be reasonable in dealing with the public.

It is urged upon us that the declaration of the legislature that the business of food preparation is affected with a public interest and devoted to a public use should be most persuasive with the Court and that nothing but the clearest reason to the contrary will prevail with the Court to hold otherwise. . . .

* * * * *

[537] It has never been supposed, since the adoption of the Constitution, that the business of the butcher, or the baker, the tailor, the wood chopper, the mining operator or the miner was clothed with such a public interest that the price of his product or his wages could be fixed by State regulation. It is true that in the days of the early common law an omnipotent Parliament did regulate prices and wages as it chose, and occasionally a Colonial legislature sought to exercise the same power; but nowadays one does not devote one's property or business to the public use or clothe it with a public interest merely because one makes commodities for, and sells to, the public in the common callings of which those above mentioned are instances.

An ordinary producer, manufacturer or shopkeeeper may sell or not sell as he likes. . . .

* * * * *

[538] . . . Food is now produced in greater volume and variety than ever before. Given uninterrupted interstate commerce, the sources of the food supply in Kansas are countrywide, a short supply is not likely, and the danger from local monopolistic control less than ever.

It is very difficult under the cases to lay down a working rule by which readily to determine when a business has become "clothed with a public interest." All business is subject to some kinds of public regulation; but when the public becomes so peculiarly dependent upon a particular business that one engaging therein subjects [539] himself to a more intimate public regulation is only to be determined by the process of exclusion and inclusion and to gradual establishment of a line of distinction. We are relieved from considering and deciding definitely whether preparation of food should be put in the third class of quasi-public businesses, noted above, because even so, the valid regulation to which it might be subjected as such, could not include what this act attempts.

To say that a business is clothed with a public interest, is not to determine what regulation may be permissible in view of the private rights of the owner. The extent to which an inn or a cab system may be regulated may differ widely from that allowable as to a railroad or other common carrier. It is not a matter of legislative discretion solely. It depends on the nature of the business, on the feature which touches the public, and on the abuses reasonably to be feared. To say that a business is clothed with a public interest is not to import that the public may take over its entire management and run it at the expense of the owner. The extent to which regulation may reasonably go varies with different kinds of business. The regulation of rates to avoid monopoly is one thing. The regulation of wages is another. A business may be of such character that only the first is permissible, while another may involve such a possible danger of monopoly on the one hand, and such disaster from stoppage on the other, that both come within the public concern and power of regulation.

If, as, in effect, contended by counsel for the State, the common callings are clothed with a public interest by a mere legislative declaration, which necessarily authorizes full and comprehensive regulation within legislative discretion, there must be a revolution in the relation of government to general business. This will be running the public interest argument into the ground, to use a phrase of Mr. Justice Bradley when characterizing a similarly [540] extreme contention. *Civil Rights Cases,* 109 U.S. 3, 24. It will be impossible to reconcile such result with the freedom of contract and of labor secured by the Fourteenth Amendment.

* * * * *

[541] Justification for such regulation is said to be found in *Wilson v. New,* 243 U.S. 332. It was there held that in a nationwide dispute over wages between railroad companies and their train operatives, with a general strike, commercial paralysis and grave loss and suffering [542] overhanging the country, Congress had power to prescribe wages not confiscatory, but obligatory on both for a reasonable time to enable them to agree. The Court said that the business of common carriers by rail was in one aspect a public business because of the interest of society in its continued operation and rightful conduct and that this gave rise to a public right of regulation to the full extent necessary to secure and protect it; that viewed as an act fixing wages it was an essential regulation for protection of public right, that it did not invade the private right of the carriers because their property and business were subject to the power of government to insure fit relief by appropriate means and it did not invade private rights of employees since their right to demand wages and to leave the employment individually or in concert was subject to limitation by Congress because in a public business which Congress might regulate under the commerce power.

It is urged that, under this act, the exercise of the power of compulsory arbitration rests upon the existence of a temporary emergency as in *Wilson v. New.* If that is a real factor here as in *Wilson v. New,* and in *Block v. Hirsh,* 256 U.S. 135, 157 (see *Pennsylvania Coal Co. v. Mahon,* 260 U.S. 393), it is enough to say that the great temporary public exigencies recognized by all and declared by Congress, were very different from that upon which the control under this act is asserted. Here it is said to be the danger that a strike in one establishment may spread to all the other similar establishments of the State and country and thence to all the national sources of food supply so as to produce a shortage. Whether such danger exists has not been determined by the legislature but is determined under the law by a subordinate agency and on its findings and prophecy, owners and employers are to be deprived of freedom of contract and workers of a most important element of their freedom of labor. [543] The small extent of the injury to the food supply of Kansas to be inflicted by a strike and suspension of this packing company's plant is shown in the language of the Kansas Supreme Court in this case (*Court of Industrial Relations v. Packing Co.*, 111 Kans. 501):

> "The defendant's plant is a small one, and it may be admitted that, if it should cease to operate, the effect on the supply of meat and food in this State would not greatly inconvenience the people of Kansas; yet the plant manufactures food products and supplies meat to a part of the people of this State, and, if it should cease to operate, that source of supply would be cut off."

* * * * *

. . . The power of a legislature to compel continuity in a business can only arise where the obligation of continued service by the owner and its employees is direct and is assumed when the business is entered upon. A common carrier which accepts a railroad franchise is not free to withdraw the use of that which it has granted to the public. . . .

The minutely detailed government supervision, including that of their relations to their employees, to which the railroads of the country have been gradually subjected by Congress through its power over interstate commerce, furnishes no precedent for regulation of the business of [544] the plaintiff in error whose classification as public is at the best doubtful. It is not too much to say that the ruling in *Wilson v. New* went to the border line, although it concerned an interstate common carrier in the presence of a nationwide emergency and the possibility of great disaster. Certainly there is nothing to justify extending the drastic regulation sustained in that exceptional case to the one before us.

We think the Industrial Court Act, in so far as it permits the fixing of wages in plaintiff in error's packing house, is in conflict with the Fourteenth Amendment and deprives it of its property and liberty of contract without due process of law.

The judgment of the court below must be

Reversed.

Omitted Taft Opinions

Magnum Import Company, Inc. v. Coty, 262 U.S. 159 (1923)—jurisdiction of the Supreme
    Court over the federal appeals courts.

American Steel Foundries v. Robertson, 262 U.S. 209 (1923)—trade mark violation.

Curtis, Collins & Holbrook Company v. United States, 262 U.S. 215 (1923)—contract dis-
    pute.

Wagner Electric Manufacturing Company v. Lyndon, 262 U.S. 226 (1923)—patent case.

Graham v. duPont, 262 U.S. 234 (1923)—tax dispute.

October Term, 1923

William Howard Taft, Chief Justice
Joseph McKenna
Oliver Wendell Holmes
Willis Van Devanter
James Clark McReynolds
Louis D. Brandeis
George Sutherland
Pierce Butler
Edward T. Sanford

VOLUME 263

Director General of Railroads v. Kastenbaum

Kastenbaum had been arrested by railroad detectives, who suspected him of stealing butter from a freight car. The issue before the Court was whether an officer of the United States government could be sued for false arrest. The Court concluded that he could be sued, since under federal law the government was operating "as if it were a railway corporation."

Director General of Railroads v. Kastenbaum

Certiorari to the Supreme Court of the State of New York

No. 39. Argued October 3, 4, 1923—Decided November 12, 1923

263 U.S. 25 (1923)

[25]

MR. CHIEF JUSTICE TAFT delivered the opinion of the Court.

* * * * *

[26] Does an action for false arrest lie against the petitioner, an officer of the United States Government, under the provisions of § 10 of the Act of Congress of March 21, 1918, c. 25, 40 Stat. 451, providing for federal control of carriers?

Twenty-one tubs of butter were taken from a freight car of the Lehigh Valley Railroad in Buffalo. A trolley car of that city, late at night, collided with a horse and wagon and, in the wreck which followed, the stolen tubs of butter were discovered. Two men who had been driving the wagon escaped. The detective force of the railway company sought to discover the owner of the horse and thought they had traced the ownership to Kastenbaum, who was a huckster. The railroad detective notified the police authorities of the city, who detailed two policemen to accompany him to Kastenbaum's house, where they arrested him without warrant. They took him to a police station and kept him there over night and until he was released the next day on bail. He was brought to a hearing before an examining magistrate on a charge of grand larceny and burglary. After four or five adjournments, at the instance of the prosecution, the magistrate discharged Kastenbaum. His horse proved to be one of another color. Under the charge of the court [27] the jury were permitted to return only compensatory damages.

* * * * *

[28] The Government under § 10, in a case of false imprisonment, stands exactly as if it were a railway corporation operating as a common carrier. Such a corporation would clearly be responsible for an arrest of the kind here shown, if without probable cause and made by one of its detectives employed to protect the property entrusted to its care as a common carrier. It is within the scope of the agency of such an employee to discover the perpetrators of crime against the property in order to recover it and to procure the arrest of supposed offenders and their prosecution and conviction in order to deter others from further depredations. If, in the field of such employment, the agent acts without probable cause and an illegal arrest without judicial warrant is made, the corporation [29] is liable as for any other act of its agents within the scope of their employment in carrying on the business of a common carrier. *Philadelphia, Wilmington & Baltimore R. R. Co. v. Quigley*, 21 How. 202, 210; *Genga v. Director General of Railroads*, 243 Mass. 101.

We have not before us the question whether the Director General might be held for exemplary damages in a case like this, under the restrictions of Order No. 50, as construed in the *Ault* case, because, as already said, the court limited the recovery to compensatory damages.

Affirmed.

Craig v. Hecht

Craig was found guilty of contempt. He appealed to Judge Martin Manton for a writ of *habeas corpus* and the appeals court judge issued it. Justice McReynolds wrote for the Court, finding Manton's action *ultra vires*. Taft wrote one of his infrequent concurring opinions, discussing the necessity of judges to protect themselves and the independence of the judiciary.

Craig v. Hecht, United States Marshal for the Southern District of New York

Certiorari to the Circuit Court of Appeals for the Second Circuit

No. 82. Argued October 17, 1923—Decided November 19, 1923

263 U.S. 255 (1923)

[268]

MR. JUSTICE MCREYNOLDS delivered the opinion of the Court.

The opinions below are reported in 266 F. 230; 274 F. 177; 279 F. 900; 282 F. 138.

In October, 1919, petitioner Craig, Comptroller of New York City, wrote and published a letter to Public Service Commissioner Nixon, wherein he assailed United States District Judge Mayer because of certain action taken in receivership proceedings then pending. The United States District Attorney filed an information charging him with criminal contempt under § 268, Judicial Code.

[269] Having heard the evidence, given the matter prolonged consideration and offered the accused opportunity to retract, on February 24, 1921—some fifteen months after the offense—Judge Mayer, holding the District Court, sentenced petitioner to jail for sixty days and committed him to the

custody of the United States Marshal. Immediately, without making any effort to appeal, Craig presented his verified petition, addressed "To the Honorable Martin T. Manton, Circuit Judge of the United States," asking for a writ of *habeas corpus* and final discharge. The record of all evidence and proceedings before the District Court was annexed to or, by reference, made part of the petition. The judge promptly signed and issued the following writing, which bore neither seal of court nor clerk's attestation. . . .

* * * * *

[273] As Circuit Judges have no authority to issue writs of *habeas corpus,* Judge Manton acted unlawfully unless the proceeding was before him either as District Judge or as the District Court. . . .

* * * * *

[278] *Affirmed.*

MR. JUSTICE SUTHERLAND took no part in the consideration or decision of this cause.

MR. CHIEF JUSTICE TAFT, concurring.

I concur fully in the opinion of the Court.

It is of primary importance that the right freely to comment on and criticise the action, opinions and judgments of courts and judges should be preserved inviolate; but it is also essential that courts and judges should not be impeded in the conduct of judicial business by publications having the direct tendency and effect of obstructing the enforcement of their orders and judgments, or of impairing the justice and impartiality of verdicts.

If the publication criticises the judge or court after the matter with which the criticism has to do has been finally adjudicated and the proceedings are ended so that the carrying out of the court's judgment can not be thereby obstructed, the publication is not contempt and can not be summarily punished by the court however false, malicious or unjust it may be. The remedy of the judge as an individual is by action or prosecution for libel. If, however, the publication is intended and calculated to obstruct and embarrass the court in a pending proceeding in the matter of the rendition of an impartial verdict, or in the carrying out of its orders and judgment, the court may, and it is its duty to protect the administration of justice by punishment of the offender for contempt.

The federal statute concerning contempts as construed by this Court in prior cases vests in the trial judge the jurisdiction to decide whether a publication is obstructive [279] or defamatory only. The delicacy there is in the judge's deciding whether an attack upon his own judicial action is mere criticism or real obstruction, and the possibility that impulse may incline his view to personal vindication, are manifest. But the law gives the person convicted of contempt in such a case the right to have the whole question on facts and law reviewed by three judges of the Circuit Court of Appeals who have had no part in the proceedings, and if not successful in that court, to apply to this Court for an opportunity for a similar review here.

The petitioner and his counsel have made such a review impossible. Instead of pursuing this plain remedy for injustice that may have been done by the trial judge and securing by an appellate court a review of this very serious question on the merits, they sought by applying to a single judge of only coordinate authority for a writ of *habeas corpus* to release the petitioner on the ground that the trial judge was without jurisdiction to make the decision he did. This raised the sole issue whether the trial judge had authority to decide the question, not whether he had rightly decided it.

Relying on a decision of this Court made years ago when the statutory provisions were different from those which now apply, the petitioner and his counsel thought that if they could secure a decision from a single circuit judge releasing the petitioner, no appeal would lie from his decision and that thus resort to the appellate courts could be avoided. The single judge to whom they applied released the prisoner. They were, however, mistaken in supposing that no appeal lay from the judge's decision on the question of the trial court's jurisdiction. The Government prosecuted its appeal and the only issue presented in that review is the matter of the trial court's jurisdiction which the Circuit Court of Appeals and we uphold. In this way, the petitioner and his counsel threw [280] away opportunity for a review of the case on its merits in the Circuit Court of Appeals and in this Court in their purpose to make a short cut and secure final release through the act of a single judge. This is the situation the petitioner finds himself in and we are without power to relieve him.

MR. JUSTICE HOLMES, dissenting.

I think that the petitioner's resort to *habeas corpus* in this case was right and was the only proper course.

[281] I think that the sentence from which the petitioner seeks relief was more than an abuse of power. I think it should be held wholly void. I think

in the first place that there was no matter pending before the Court in the sense that it must be to make this kind of contempt possible. It is not enough that somebody may hereafter move to have something done. There was nothing then awaiting decision when the petitioner's letter was published. . . . Unless a judge while sitting can lay hold of any one who ventures to publish anything that tends to make him unpopular or to belittle him I cannot see what power Judge Mayer had to touch Mr. Craig. Even if feeling was tense there is no such thing as what Keating, J., in *Metzler v. Gounod* calls contingent contempt. A man cannot be summarily laid by the heels because his words may make public feeling more unfavorable in case the judge should be asked to act at some [282] later date, any more than he can for exciting public feeling against a judge for what he already has done.

MR. JUSTICE BRANDEIS concurs in this opinion.

Dayton–Goose Creek Railway Co. v. Interstate Commerce Commission

Among other things, the Transportation Act of 1920 provided that a certain portion of railroads' profits would be held by the government and used to make loans to support less profitable railroads. The Dayton–Goose Creek Railway Company challenged this as depriving it of property without due process of law as guaranteed by the Fifth Amendment.

Dayton–Goose Creek Railway Company v. United States, Interstate Commerce Commission et al.

Appeal from the District Court of the United States for the Eastern District of Texas

No. 330. Argued November 16, 19, 1923—Decided January 7, 1924

263 U.S. 456 (1924)

[474]

MR. CHIEF JUSTICE TAFT delivered the opinion of the Court.

The main question in this case is whether the so-called "recapture" paragraphs of the Transportation Act of 1920, c. 91, § 422, § 15a, paragraphs 5–17, 41 Stat. 456, 489–491, are constitutional.

The Dayton–Goose Creek Railway Company is a corporation of Texas, engaged in intrastate, interstate and foreign commerce. Its volume of intrastate traffic exceeds that of its interstate and foreign traffic. . . .

* * * * *

[479] If Congress may build railroads under the commerce clause, it may certainly exert affirmative control over privately owned railroads, to see that such railroads are equipped to perform, and do perform, the requisite public service.

Title IV of the Transportation Act, embracing §§ 418 and 422, is carefully framed to achieve its expressly declared objects. Uniform rates enjoined for all shippers will tend to divide the business in proper proportion so that, when the burden is great, the railroad of each carrier will be used to its capacity. If the weaker roads were permitted to charge higher rates than their competitors, the business would seek the stronger roads with the lower rates, and congestion would follow. The directions given to the Commission in fixing uniform rates will tend to put them on a scale enabling a railroad of average efficiency among all the carriers of the section to earn the prescribed maximum return. Those who earn more must hold one-half of the excess primarily to preserve their sound economic condition and avoid wasteful expenditures and [480] unwise dividends. Those who earn less are to be given help by credit secured through a fund made up of the other half of the excess. By the recapture clauses Congress is enabled to maintain uniform rates for all shippers and yet keep the net returns of railways, whether strong or weak, to the varying percentages which are fair respectively for them. The recapture clauses are thus the key provision of the whole plan.

Having regard to the property rights of the carriers and the interest of the shipping public, the validity of the plan depends on two propositions. First. Rates which as a body enable all the railroads necessary to do the business of a rate territory or section, to enjoy not more than a fair net operating income on the aggregate value of their properties therein economically and efficiently operated, are reasonable from the standpoint of the individual shipper in that section. . . .

* * * * *

[481] Second. The carrier owning and operating a railroad, however strong financially, however economical in its facilities, or favorably situated as to traffic, is not entitled as of constitutional right to more than a fair net operating income upon the value of its properties which are being devoted

to transportation. By investment in a business dedicated to the public service the owner must recognize that, as compared with investment in private business, he can not expect either high or speculative dividends but that his obligation limits him to only fair or reasonable profit. . . .

* * * * *

[484] We have been greatly pressed with the argument that the cutting down of income actually received by the carrier for its service to a so-called fair return is a plain appropriation of its property without any compensation, that the income it receives for the use of its property is as much protected by the Fifth Amendment as the property itself. The statute declares the carrier to be only a trustee for the excess over a fair return received by it. Though in its possession, the excess never becomes its property and it accepts custody of the product of all the rates with this understanding. It is clear, therefore, that the carrier never has such a title to the excess as to render the recapture of it by the Government a taking without due process.

It is then objected that the Government has no right to retain one-half of the excess, since, if it does not belong to the carrier, it belongs to the shippers and should be returned to them. If it were valid, it is an objection which the carrier can not be heard to make. It would be soon enough to consider such a claim when made by the shipper. But it is not valid. The rates are reasonable from the standpoint of the shipper, as we have shown, though their net product furnishes more than a fair return for the carrier. The excess caused by the discrepancy between the standard of reasonableness for the shipper and that for the carrier due to the necessity of maintaining uniform rates to be charged the shippers, may properly be appropriated by the Government for public uses because the appropriation takes away nothing which equitably belongs either to the shipper or to the carrier. . . .

[485] The third question for our consideration is whether the recapture clause, by reducing the net income from intrastate rates, invades the reserved power of the States and is in conflict with the Tenth Amendment. In solving the problem of maintaining the efficiency of an interstate commerce railway system which serves both the States and the Nation, Congress is dealing with a unit in which state and interstate operations are often inextricably commingled. When the adequate maintenance of interstate commerce involves and makes necessary on this account the incidental and partial con-

trol of intrastate commerce, the power of Congress to exercise such control has been clearly established. . . .

* * * * *

[487] *The decree of the District Court is affirmed.*

First National Bank v. Missouri

McCulloch v. Maryland, 4 Wheat. (17 U.S.) 316 (1819), is rightly hailed as one of the great nationalizing decisions of Chief Justice John Marshall. In that decision, Marshall not only found that the "necessary and proper" clause gave to Congress the power to establish a national bank, but further held that a state tax on the operation of such a bank must fall under the supremacy clause.

The action of the state of Missouri requiring a nationally chartered bank to comply with a state requirement prohibiting branch banks was challenged in the *First National Bank in St. Louis* case. A six-member majority upheld the statute. Chief Justice Taft disagreed and joined in a dissent written "with great deference" by Justice Van Devanter.

First National Bank in St. Louis v. State of Missouri at the Information of Barrett, Attorney General

Error to the Supreme Court of the State of Missouri

No. 252. Argued May 7, 1923; restored to docket for reargument May 21, 1923; reargued November 21, 22, 1923—Decided January 28, 1924

263 U.S. 640 (1924)

[654]

MR. JUSTICE SUTHERLAND delivered the opinion of the Court.

The State of Missouri brought this proceeding in the nature of *quo warranto* in the State Supreme Court against the plaintiff in error to determine its authority to establish and conduct a branch bank in the City of St. Louis. . . .

* * * * *

... The Missouri statute (§ 11737, R. S. Mo., 1919) provides "that no bank shall maintain in this state a branch bank or receive deposits or pay checks except in its own banking house." ...

* * * * *

[656] National banks are brought into existence under federal legislation, are instrumentalities of the Federal Government and are necessarily subject to the paramount authority of the United States. Nevertheless, national banks are subject to the laws of a State in respect of their affairs unless such laws interfere with the purposes of their creation, tend to impair or destroy their efficiency as federal agencies or conflict with the paramount law of the United States. ...

* * * * *

[660] ... It is insisted with great earnestness that the United States alone may inquire by *quo warranto* whether a national bank is acting in excess of its charter powers, and that the State is wholly without authority to do so. This contention will be conceded since it is plainly correct, but the attempt to apply it here proceeds upon a complete misconception of what the State is seeking to do, a misconception which arises from confounding the relief sought with the circumstances relied upon to justify it. The State is neither seeking to enforce a law of the United States nor endeavoring to call the bank to account for an act in excess of its charter powers. What the State is seeking to do is to vindicate and enforce its own law, and the ultimate inquiry which it propounds is whether the bank is violating that law, not whether it is complying with the charter or law of its creation. ...

* * * * *

[661] The judgment of the Supreme Court of Missouri is therefore

Affirmed.

[662] MR. JUSTICE VAN DEVANTER, dissenting.

I am constrained to dissent from the opinion and judgment just announced.

National banks are corporate instrumentalities of the United States created under its laws for public purposes essentially national in character and scope. Their powers are derived from the United States, are to be exercised under its supervision and can be neither enlarged nor restricted by state laws. The decisions uniformly have been to this effect and have proceeded on principles which were settled a century ago in the days of the Bank of the United States.

In *McCulloch v. Maryland,* 4 Wheat. 316, where the status of that bank was drawn in question and elaborately discussed, this Court reached the conclusion that the Constitution invests the United States with authority to provide, independently of state laws, for the creation of banking institutions, and their maintenance at suitable points within the States, as a means of carrying into execution its fiscal and other powers. Chief Justice Marshall there dealt with the respective relations of the United States and the States to such an instrumentality in a very plain and convincing way. Among the other things, he said:

> (p. 424) "After the most deliberate consideration, it is the unanimous and decided opinion of this court, that the act to incorporate the Bank of the United States is a law made in pursuance of the constitution, and is a part of the supreme law of the land."
>
> (p. 427) "It is of the very essence of supremacy to remove all obstacles to its action within its own sphere, and so to modify every power vested in subordinate governments, as to exempt its operations from their influence. This effect need not be stated in terms. It is so involved in the declaration of supremacy, so necessarily implied in it, that the expression of it could not make it more certain."
>
> [663] (p. 429) "The sovereignty of a State extends to everything which exists by its own authority, or is introduced by its permission; but does it extend to those means which are employed by Congress to carry into execution powers conferred on that body by the people of the United States? We think it demonstrable that it does not. Those powers are not given by the people of a single State. They are given by the people of the United States, to a government whose laws, made in pursuance of the constitution, are declared to be supreme."

In *Osborn v. Bank of the United States,* 9 Wheat. 738, there was drawn in question the validity of a state statute which, after reciting that the bank had been pursuing its operations contrary to a law of the State, provided that if the operations were continued the bank should be liable to specified exactions, called a tax. The statute was held invalid. . . .

* * * * *

[665] It must be admitted that, in so far as the legislation of Congress does not provide otherwise, the general laws of a State have the same application to the ordinary transactions of a national bank, such as incurring and discharging obligations to depositors, presenting drafts for acceptance or payment and

giving notice of their dishonor, taking pledges for the repayment of money loaned, and receiving or making conveyances of real property, that they have to like transactions of others. But not so of questions of corporate power. . . .

* * * * *

[666] The proceeding now before us is an information in the nature of *quo warranto* brought in the Supreme Court of Missouri, whereby that State challenges the power of a national bank in the City of St. Louis to conduct a branch bank established by it in that city and asks that the bank be ousted from that privilege on the grounds, first, that establishing and conducting the branch is a violation of the bank's charter powers, and, secondly, that it is prohibited by a law of the State.

It is not claimed that the laws of the United States contain any provision whereby the privilege asserted by the bank is made to depend on the will or legislative policy of the State; nor do they in fact contain any such provision. Whether the bank has the privilege which it asserts is therefore in no way dependent on or affected by the state law, but turns exclusively on the laws of the United States. If they grant the privilege, expressly or by fair implication, no law of the State can abridge it or take it away. And if they do not grant it, they in effect prohibit it, and no law of the State can strengthen or weaken the prohibition. In either event nothing can turn on the state law. It simply has no bearing on the solution of the question.

* * * * *

[668] With great deference, I think the judgment below should be reversed on the ground that the State is without capacity to bring or maintain this proceeding, and the court below without authority to entertain it.

THE CHIEF JUSTICE and MR. JUSTICE BUTLER authorize me to say that they concur in this dissent.

Omitted Taft Opinions

Denby v. Berry, 263 U.S. 29 (1923)—change of naval officer from active to inactive duty.
McConaughey v. Morrow, 263 U.S. 39 (1923)—salary dispute by federal employee.
Woodbridge v. United States, 263 U.S. 50 (1923)—patent case.
Myers v. International Trust Company, 263 U.S. 64 (1923)—bankruptcy case.
Brown v. United States, 263 U.S. 78 (1923)—federal land condemnation.
North Dakota v. Minnesota, 263 U.S. 365 (1923)—original jurisdiction, water rights.
Brady v. Work, 263 U.S. 436 (1924)—jurisdiction.

McMillan Contracting Company v. Abernathy, 263 U.S. 438 (1924)—jurisdiction.

Tidal Oil Company v. Flanagan, 263 U.S. 444 (1924)—nature of appellate jurisdiction.

North Dakota v. Minnesota, 263 U.S. 583 (1924)—apportionment of costs in original jurisdiction cases.

United States v. New York Coffee and Sugar Exchange, Inc., 263 U.S. 611 (1924)—contract dispute.

VOLUME 264

Puget Sound Power & Light Co. v. County of King

The Puget Sound Power & Light Company challenged taxes on a street railway that it owned in the city of Seattle. The company claimed that the tax violated the state constitution's requirement of equality in taxation and that its failure to prevail on this issue in state courts violated the Fourteenth Amendment's due process clause. Taft affirmed the decision of the Washington state supreme court, allowing that equality in taxation was in fact "unattainable" and "that the Fourteenth Amendment was not intended, and is not to be construed, as having any such object as these stiff and unyielding requirements of equality in state constitutions."

Puget Sound Power & Light Company et al.
v. County of King et al.

Error to the Supreme Court of the State of Washington

No. 138. Motion to dismiss or affirm submitted January 2, 1924—Decided February 18, 1924

264 U.S. 22 (1924)

[23]

MR. CHIEF JUSTICE TAFT delivered the opinion of the Court.

The Puget Sound Power and Light Company owned a street railway, part of which was in Seattle. This part it sold to the City in 1919. In the contract of purchase it was agreed that if when the deed was delivered any lien should have attached to the property for the taxes of 1919, it should not constitute a breach of warranty, and the tax should be paid in amounts proportioned to the parts of the year during which the parties were respectively in possession. The deed was delivered March 31, 1919, and possession then taken. On March 15, 1919, an assessment had been made by the Tax Commissioner of the State on the operating property of the street railway, including that part then contracted to be sold to the city. The Power Company brought this suit in the Superior Court of King County, Washington, against the County and its taxing authorities, the State Tax Commissioner, and the City of Seattle to restrain the collection of taxes under the assessment as illegal. The Superior Court dismissed the complaint. Its action was affirmed by the Supreme Court of the State and this is a writ of error to that court. The case comes before us on a motion to dismiss or affirm.

* * * * *

[27] We are considering this case only from the standpoint of the Fourteenth Amendment to the Federal Constitution. The objections based on the state constitution of Washington have been settled adversely and conclusively for us by the decision herein of the State Supreme Court. Counsel cite us cases which have little relation to the federal question before us. *Johnson v. Wells Fargo & Co.,* 239 U.S. 234; *Ewert v. Taylor,* 38 S. D. 124; *State ex rel. Owen v. Donald,* 161 Wisc. 188, and like cases involved the application of somewhat stringent provisions of state constitutions as to equality of taxation on [28] all kinds of property which left but little room for classification. Such restrictions have much embarrassed state legislatures because actual equality of taxation is unattainable. The theoretical operation of a tax is often very different from its practical incidence, due to the weakness of human nature and anxiety to escape tax burdens. This justifies the legislature, where the Constitution does not forbid, in adopting variant provisions as to the rate, the assessment and the collection for different kinds of property. The reports of this Court are full of cases which demonstrate that the Fourteenth Amendment was not intended, and is not to be construed, as having any such object as these stiff and unyielding requirements of equality in state constitutions. . . .

* * * * *

[29] Clearly there is nothing of an unusual character in the method adopted in this case for the assessment and collection of taxes upon street railways. The general practice of providing special methods of estimating the burden of taxation which this peculiar kind of property should bear is well known and proves that it justifies a separate classification.

The judgment of the Supreme Court of Washington is

Affirmed.

Mahler v. Eby

Mahler, an alien, had been convicted under the Espionage and Selective Draft Acts, adopted during World War I. Based on these convictions, the Department of Labor, as authorized by the Alien Act of 1920, sought to have him deported as an "undesirable resident." The Court found that by giving this power to the Department of Labor, Congress had not violated the prohibition against delegating legislative power to the executive and "that the same constitutional restrictions [do not] apply to an alien deportation act as to a law punishing crime."

Mahler et al. v. Eby, Inspector in Charge Immigration Service, U.S. Department of Labor, at Chicago, Illinois

Appeal from the District Court of the United States for the Northern District of Illinois

No. 184. Argued January 24, 25, 1924—Decided February 18, 1924

264 U.S. 32 (1924)

[38]

MR. CHIEF JUSTICE TAFT . . . delivered the opinion of the Court.

The theory of the draftsman of the petition for the writ and of the assignment of errors was that the same [39] constitutional restrictions apply to an alien deportation act as to a law punishing crime. It is well settled that deportation, while it may be burdensome and severe for the alien, is not a punishment. *Fong Yue Ting v. United States,* 149 U.S. 698, 730; *Bugajewitz v. Adams,* 228 U.S. 585, 591. The right to expel aliens is a sovereign power necessary to the safety of the country and only limited by treaty obligations in respect thereto entered into with other governments. *Fong Yue Ting v. United States, supra.* The inhibition against the passage of an *ex post facto* law by Congress in § 9 of Article I of the Constitution applies only to criminal laws. *Calder v. Bull,* 3 Dall. 386; *Johannessen v. United States,* 225 U.S. 227, 242; and not to a deportation act like this, *Bugajewitz v. Adams,* 228 U.S. 585, 591. Congress by the Act of 1920 was not increasing the punishment for the crimes of which petitioners had been convicted, by requiring their deportation if found undesirable residents. It was, in the exercise of its unquestioned right, only seeking to rid the country of persons who had shown by their career that their continued presence here would not make for the safety or welfare of society. . . .

The brief for appellants insists that as the laws under which the appellants were convicted have been repealed, the fact of their conviction can not be made the basis for deportation. It was their past conviction that put them in the class of persons liable to be deported as undesirable citizens. That record for such a purpose was not affected by the repeal of the laws which they had violated and under which they had suffered punishment. The repeal [40] did not take the convicted persons out of the enumerated classes or take from the convictions any probative force rightly belonging to them.

Nor is the act invalid in delegating legislative power to the Secretary of Labor. The sovereign power to expel aliens is political and is vested in the political departments of the Government. Even if the executive may not exercise it without congressional authority, Congress can not exercise it effectively save through the executive. It can not, in the nature of things, designate all the persons to be excluded. It must accomplish its purpose by classification and by conferring power of selection within classes upon an executive agency. *Tiaco v. Forbes,* 228 U.S. 549, 557. That is what it has done here. . . .

We do not think that the discretion vested in the Secretary under such circumstances is any more vague or [41] uncertain or any less defined than that exercised in deciding whether aliens are likely to become a public charge, a discretion vested in the immigration executives for half a century and never questioned. . . .

* * * * *

[46] Accordingly, the judgment of the District Court is reversed with directions not to discharge the petitioners until the Secretary of Labor shall have reasonable time in which to correct and perfect his finding on the evidence produced at the original hearing, if he finds it adequate, or to initiate another proceeding against them.

Reversed.

Omitted Taft Opinions

Board of Trade of the City of Chicago v. Johnson, 264 U.S. 1 (1924)—bankruptcy.
Barnett v. Kunkel, 264 U.S. 16 (1924)—jurisdiction of district courts.

Fleming v. Fleming, 264 U.S. 29 (1924)—impairment of contract.

YMCA v. Davis, 264 U.S. 47 (1924)—estate tax involved in charitable contribution.

Keller v. Adams-Campbell Company, Inc., 264 U.S. 314 (1924)—patent case.

John E. Thropp's Sons Company v. Seiberling, 264 U.S. 320 (1924)—patent case.

Railroad Commissions of the State of California v. Southern Pacific Company, 264 U.S. 331 (1924)—power of Interstate Commerce Commission to set rules.

Oklahoma v. Texas, 264 U.S. 565 (1924)—original jurisdiction, boundary dispute.

VOLUME 265

Hammerschmidt v. United States

Hammerschmidt and twelve other persons had been convicted of violating section 37 of the Penal Code by conspiring to defraud the United States government. Specifically, they had sought to discourage men from registering for military service as required by the Selective Service Act of 1917. This case was decided by the Supreme Court five years after Justice Holmes's famous opinion in *Schenck v. United States,* 249 U.S. 47 (1919), in which he put forth the famous "clear and present danger" test (*Schenck,* 52). Applying the new test to the facts of the *Schenck* case, Holmes upheld the conviction for obstructing the draft under the Espionage Act.

In *Hammerschmidt,* Taft did not address the First Amendment issue that Holmes had confronted in *Schenck.* Instead, Taft based his decision on whether the federal government could define the word "defraud" in such a broad fashion as to be able to punish Hammerschmidt and his antiwar colleagues. Taft concluded that the government could not and set aside the indictments. By contrast, Holmes's opinion concluded that Schenck's speech was not protected and upheld the latter's conviction.

Hammerschmidt et al. v. United States

Certiorari to the Circuit Court of Appeals for the Sixth Circuit

No. 254. Argued April 29, 30, 1924—Decided May 26, 1924

265 U.S. 182 (1924)

[183]

The Selective Service Act, among other things, required that all male citizens between the ages of twenty-one and thirty should register for service in the military and naval forces of the United States.

In the face of this statute petitioners caused to be printed, with the idea of distributing to the public at large, several thousand handbills attacking the Draft Act and counseling or commanding to "refuse to register for conscription." The indictment avers that a number of them were distributed. The conduct of petitioners constituted a conspiracy to defraud the United States in that the intention and necessary effect of their agreement and acts was to obstruct and defeat the purpose of a measure enacted by Congress for the preservation of the Government. Such conduct was not within the criminal provisions of the Selective Service Act (§§ 5 and 6), and at the time of the offense the Espionage Act had not been enacted.

* * * * *

[185] MR. CHIEF JUSTICE TAFT delivered the opinion of the Court.

This is a review by certiorari of the conviction of thirteen persons charged in one indictment with the crime of violating § 37 of the Penal Code. The charge was that the petitioners wilfully and unlawfully conspired to defraud the United States by impairing, obstructing and defeating a lawful function of its government, to wit: that of registering for military service all male persons between the ages of twenty-one and thirty as required by the Selective Service Act of May 18, 1917, c. 15, 40 Stat. 76, through the printing, publishing and circulating of handbills, dodgers and other matter intended and designed to counsel, advise and procure persons subject to the Selective Act to refuse to obey it. . . .

* * * * *

[188] To conspire to defraud the United States means primarily to cheat the Government out of property or money, but it also means to interfere with or obstruct one of its lawful governmental functions by deceit, craft or trickery, or at least by means that are dishonest. It is not necessary that the Government shall be subjected to property or pecuniary loss by the fraud, but only that its legitimate official action and purpose shall be defeated by misrepresentation, chicane or the overreaching of those charged with carrying out the governmental intention. It is true that the words "to defraud" as used in some statutes have been given a wide meaning, wider than their ordinary scope. They usually signify the deprivation of something of value by trick, deceit, chicane or overreaching. They do not extend to theft by violence. They refer rather to wronging one in his property rights by dishonest

methods or schemes. One would not class robbery or burglary among frauds. In *Horman v. United States*, 116 F. 350, § 5480, Rev. Stats., as amended March 2, 1889, c. 393, 25 Stat. 873, making it a crime to devise any scheme or artifice to defraud by use of the mails and opening correspondence with any person, and to mail a letter in execution thereof, was held to be violated by the sending of a letter threatening to blacken the character of another unless that other paid the blackmailer money. It was held that the word "scheme" in that section was of broader meaning and did not necessarily involve trickery or cunning in the scheme, if use of the mails was part of it; that intent to defraud in such a statute was satisfied by the wrongful purpose of injuring one in his property rights. The question had much consideration. The decision, however, went to the verge and should be [189] confined to pecuniary or property injury inflicted by a scheme to use the mails for the purpose. Section 5480 has since been again amended to make its scope clearer. Its construction in the *Horman* case can not be used as authority to include within the legal definition of a conspiracy to defraud the United States a mere open defiance of the governmental purpose to enforce a law by urging persons subject to it to disobey it.

We think the demurrer to the indictment in this case should have been sustained and the indictment quashed.

Judgment reversed.

Hetrick v. Village of Lindsey

The Village of Lindsey, Ohio, had imposed special assessments for street improvement, but had not provided individual notices to those assessed. Hetrick alleged that this failure was a violation of the guarantees of due process provided under the Fourteenth Amendment. Taft found that prior notice was not necessary since Hetrick had other avenues by which he could, subsequently, challenge the assessment in court.

Hetrick v. Village of Lindsey et al.

Error to the Supreme Court of the State of Ohio

No. 231. Argued April 23, 1924—Decided June 2, 1924

265 U.S. 384 (1924)

[384]

MR. CHIEF JUSTICE TAFT delivered the opinion of the Court.

* * * * *

[386] The decisions of fact by the state Court of Appeals that the assessment did not exceed the benefit of the property and that it did not exceed one-third of the value of the property after the improvement was completed, are not questioned here. The only point of contention made is that the Ohio statutes relating to special assessments for street improvements do not require a notice to, and a hearing on behalf of, the owner of the property assessed by the village council and therefore permit the owner to be deprived of his property without due process of law.

* * * * *

[387] Under this section the plaintiff had two full hearings in two courts upon the merits of the assessments, that is, upon the question whether the special benefits conferred were greater than the value of the property, and second, whether the assessment exceeded one-third of the value of the property. This is in accord with the previous decisions of the Supreme Court of Ohio in reference to the power of the state courts in passing on the validity of assessments either in a suit to collect the same or in a suit by the assessment payer to enjoin them. *Walsh v. Sims,* 65 Oh. St. 211; *Griswold v. Pelton,* 34 Oh. St. 482. It thus appears that the plaintiff in this case had had opportunity by contesting the assessment in court to review all the questions of law and fact as to the validity and fairness of the assessment under the statutes of Ohio, that these facts were passed upon by the court and that the plaintiff had secured from that court a reduction of the assessment. In such a case it has been frequently decided that the judicial procedure constitutes due process of law and supplies every requirement for due notice and hearing. . . .

Decree affirmed.

United Leather Workers Union
v. Herkert & Meisel Trunk Co.

For Taft, the issue in *United Leather Workers* was identical to that in the more famous case of *United Mine Workers v. Coronado Co.,* 259 U.S. 344. Like the Coronado Company, the employer had argued that the leather workers union action violated federal antitrust legislation. Taft, speaking for himself and five other justices, found that the activities were totally local and did not directly burden interstate commerce and, therefore, that there was no violation of antitrust legislation.

United Leather Workers International Union, Local Lodge or Union No. 66, et al. v. Herkert & Meisel Trunk Company et al.

Appeal from the Circuit Court of Appeals for the Eighth Circuit

No. 233. Argued April 24, 25, 1924—Decided June 9, 1924

265 U.S. 457 (1924)

[461]

MR. CHIEF JUSTICE TAFT delivered the opinion of the Court.

* * * * *

[463] The evidence adduced before the District Court showed that the defendant, the Local Union No. 66 of the United Leather Workers, having declared a strike against the complainants and withdrawn its members from their employ, instituted an illegal picketing campaign of intimidation against their employees who were willing to remain and against others willing to take the places of the striking employees, that the effect of this campaign was to prevent the complainants from continuing to manufacture their goods needed to fill the orders they had received from regular customers and would-be purchasers in other States, that such orders covered ninety per cent. of all goods manufactured by complainants, that the character of their business was known to the defendants, and that the illegal strike campaign of defendants thus interfered with and obstructed complainants' interstate commerce business to their great loss. There was no evidence whatever to show that complainants were obstructed by the strike or the strikers in shipping to other States the products they had ready to ship or in their receipt of materials from other States needed to make their goods. While the bill averred that defendants had instituted a boycott against complainants and were prosecuting the same by illegal methods, there was no evidence whatever that any attempt was made to boycott the sale of the complainants' products in other States or anywhere or to interfere with their interstate shipments of goods ready to ship.

* * * * *

[464] The sole question here is whether a strike against manufacturers by their employees, intended by the strikers to prevent, through illegal picketing and intimidation, continued manufacture, and having such effect, was a conspiracy to restrain interstate commerce under the Anti-Trust Act because such products when made were, to the knowledge of the strikers, to be shipped in interstate commerce to fill orders given and accepted by would-be purchasers in other States, in the absence of evidence that the strikers interfered or attempted to interfere with the free transport and delivery of the products when manufactured from the factories to their destination in other States, or with their sale in those States.

We think that this question has already been answered in the negative by this Court. In *United Mine Workers v. Coronado Co.*, 259 U.S. 344, a coal mining company in Arkansas changed its arrangement with its employees from a closed shop to an open shop.

* * * * *

[471] This review of the cases makes it clear that the mere reduction in the supply of an article to be shipped in interstate commerce, by the illegal or tortious prevention of its manufacture, is ordinarily an indirect and remote obstruction to that commerce. It is only when the intent or necessary effect upon such commerce in the article is to enable those preventing the manufacture to monopolize the supply, control its price or discriminate as between its would-be purchasers, that the unlawful interference with its manufacture can be said directly to burden interstate commerce.

The record is entirely without evidence or circumstances to show that the defendants in their conspiracy to deprive the complainants of their workers were thus directing their scheme against interstate commerce. It is true that they were, in this labor controversy, hoping that the loss of business in selling goods would furnish a motive to the complainants to yield to demands in respect to the terms of employment; but they did nothing which in any way directly interfered with the interstate transportation or sales of the complainants' product.

We concur with the dissenting Judge in the Circuit Court of Appeals when, in speaking of the conclusion of the majority, he said: "The natural, logical and inevitable result will be that every strike in any industry or even in any single factory will be within the Sherman Act and subject to federal jurisdiction provided any appreciable amount of its product enters into interstate commerce" (284 F. 446, 464).

[472] We can not think that Congress intended any such result in the enactment of the Anti-Trust Act or that the decisions of this Court warrant such construction.

Decree reversed.

MR. JUSTICE MCKENNA, MR. JUSTICE VAN DEVANTER, and MR. JUSTICE BUTLER, dissent.

Omitted Taft Opinions

Cunningham v. Brown, 265 U.S. 1 (1924)—bankruptcy.

Newton v. Consolidated Gas Company, 265 U.S. 78 (1924)—limits on appeals in federal courts.

Ex parte: In the matter of Skinner & Eddy Corporation, 265 U.S. 86 (1924)—procedural rules.

United States v. Ferris, 265 U.S. 165 (1924)—military salary dispute.

Baldwin Co. v. Robertson, 265 U.S. 168 (1924)—trade mark.

United States v. Supplee-Biddle Hardware Company, 265 U.S. 189 (1924)—income tax.

Pacific Telephone & Telegraph Company v. Kuykendall, 265 U.S. 196 (1924)—rate case.

Home Telephone & Telegraph Company of Spokane v. Kuykendall, 265 U.S. 206 (1924)—rate case, identical to *Pacific Telephone.*

United States & Cuban Allied Works Engineering Corporation v. Lloyds, 265 U.S. 454 (1924)—jurisdiction.

October Term, 1924

VOLUME 266

Chicago Great Western Railway Co. v. Kendall

The railroads challenged the fact that their property was taxed at a different rate than that for farmlands. Taft affirmed the decision of the United States District Court, which had upheld the tax, noting that the right to tax was a sovereign power possessed by both the states and the federal government.

Chicago Great Western Railway Company v. Kendall, Governor of the State of Iowa, et al.

Chicago, Rock Island & Pacific Railway Company v. Kendall, Governor of the State of Iowa, et al.

Appeals from the District Court of the United States for the Southern District of Iowa

Nos. 22 and 23. Argued October 7, 1924—Decided November 17, 1924

266 U.S. 94 (1924)

[95]

MR. CHIEF JUSTICE TAFT delivered the opinion of the Court.

. . . The injunction was sought [by the railroads] on the ground that although, under the laws and constitution of Iowa, all property, real and personal, including railways, must be assessed at its actual value, there was an intentional discrimination by the Executive Council against complainants, in that farm lands in the State were assessed at slightly over 38 [96] per cent. of their actual value, while the railway of the Great Western Railway Company in the State was intentionally assessed at 111.5 per cent. of its actual value, and that of the Rock Island at 75 per cent. . . .

* * * * *

[97] In the cases before us, we are relieved from considering and deciding the alleged infringement of the Federal Constitution, because in view of the basis for jurisdiction of the District Court, the cases can be disposed of as a question of state law.

* * * * *

[100] . . . The three judges in the District Court found that the Executive Council might reasonably and without arbitrary or intentional discrimination reach the conclusion that the properties of the two companies in Iowa, tangible and intangible, were not assessed by the Executive Council in proportion to their actual value substantially more than the 61 per cent. imposed on farm lands. The court pointed out that railroad values were very difficult to fix and there was a wide range within which reasonable men might differ, and after an examination of the evidence, concluded they could not find that there was any arbitrary and unconscionable difference between the values assessed upon the two kinds of property. . . .

It would take a very clear case upon the record to justify this Court in setting aside the conclusion of a court of three judges under § 266 upon what is solely a [101] question of fact and an exercise of sound judicial discretion as to the just balance of convenience in granting or withholding a temporary suspension of the operation of a state law in the collection of taxes. This Court must respect in the fullest degree the sensitiveness of Congress in hedging about the sovereign power of taxation by the States and precluding temporary federal judicial interference with it save in clear cases. The present cases are not of that character.

Affirmed.

Tod v. Waldman

The immigration service had denied the Waldmans admission to the United States based on its belief that they would not be able to find gainful employment because of language and physical disabilities. Although agreeing with the appeals court that the Waldmans should have an opportunity to disprove these claims, Taft reversed the appeals court decision to release them from the custody of the immigration authorities pending that determination.

Tod, Commissioner of Immigration, v. Waldman et al.

Certiorari to the Circuit Court of Appeals for the Second Circuit

No. 95. Argued October 20, 21, 1924—Decided November 17, 1924

266 U.S. 113 (1924)

[118]

MR. CHIEF JUSTICE TAFT . . . delivered the opinion of the Court.

We think that the complaint of the Government is well founded. The petitioners in the writ of *habeas corpus* were aliens who had not been legally admitted to the country—that is, neither the immigration authorities nor the court had held that they were entitled to admission. The immigration authorities had ordered their deportation. The Circuit Court of Appeals merely found that in the course of the examination by the immigration authorities the relators had not been given a fair opportunity to appeal to the Secretary of Labor as provided by the statute. This denial of appeal did not give to them a right to admission to the country. In the due and orderly disposition of the writ of *habeas corpus,* relators should not have been discharged and their bail released, but the order should have been framed so as to secure the benefit of the appeal to the relators, to which the court by its decision had held them entitled. To discharge them was to take them out of the proper custody of the government authorities pending their admission or exclusion, was to entail upon the Government the affirmative and initial duty of rearresting them and was improperly discharging the security for their response to any lawful order of the immigration authorities. . . .

* * * * *

[120] We see no reason, therefore, why upon the appeal which it is now decided the Secretary of Labor must afford the relators, he should not consider and make a definite finding on the issues made by the petition, to wit, first, whether the relators are not relieved from the test as to language because they are refugees from religious persecution; second, whether, if it be necessary, a proper test as to the reading knowledge of Yiddish only, which Mrs. Waldman had, was sufficient to meet the requirements of the statute, and, if not, to order another; and, third, whether the lameness of Zenia Waldman is likely to affect her ability to earn her living or to make her a public charge. The order of the Circuit Court of Appeals is reversed and modified in accordance with this opinion, with instructions to remand the petitioners to the custody of the immigration authorities to await the hearing on the appeal before the Secretary of Labor. Failing the granting and hearing of the appeal within thirty days after the coming down of the mandate herein, the [121] relators and their bail are to be discharged. *Mahler v. Eby,* 264 U.S. 32, 46.

Reversed and remanded to the District Court for further proceedings in conformity with this opinion.

Panama Railroad Co. v. Rock

As mentioned earlier, Taft was most reluctant to dissent from the majority. In this particular case, the Court was called upon to determine whether the common law or the civil code of Panama applied to a wrongful death suit. Under the common law, the widower was not entitled to recover, but under the Code Napoleon he could. Taft's agreeing with the Holmes opinion that would have applied the civil code remedy may have been a product of his experience in the Philippines, where he had been governor.

Panama Railroad Company v. Rock

Error to the Circuit Court of Appeals for the Fifth Circuit

No. 4. Submitted October 6, 1924—Decided November 17, 1924

266 U.S. 209 (1924)

[210]

MR. JUSTICE SUTHERLAND delivered the opinion of the Court.

This is an action brought in the District Court for the Canal Zone by James Rock to recover damages for the death of his wife, alleged to have resulted in 1918 from the negligence of the railroad company, while she was being transported as a passenger. . . .

* * * * *

[215] . . . Under the principles of the common law, it has required specific statutes to fix civil liability for death by wrongful act; and it is this requirement, rather than the construction put upon the statute in civil law countries, that the inhabitants of the Canal Zone are presumed to be familiar with, and which affords the rule by which the meaning and scope of the statute in question are to be determined.

Judgment reversed.

MR. JUSTICE HOLMES, dissenting.

There is no dispute that the language of the Civil Code of Panama, Art. 2341, which has been quoted, is broad enough on its face to give an action for negligently causing the death of the plaintiff's wife. Taken literally it gives such an action in terms. The article of the Code Napoleon from which it is said to have been copied is construed by the French Courts in accord with its literal meaning. *La Bourgogne,* 210 U.S. 95, 138, 139. It would seem natural and proper to accept the interpretation given to the article at its source, and by the more authoritative jurists who have had occasion to deal with it, irrespective of whether that local interpretation was before or after its adoption by Spanish States, so long as nothing seriously to the contrary is shown. The only thing that I know of to the contrary is the tradition of the later common law. The common law view of the responsibility of a master for his servant was allowed to help in the interpretation of an ambiguous statute in

[216] *Panama R. R. Co. v. Bosse*, 249 U.S. 41, 45, for reasons there stated. But those reasons have far less application here, even if we refer to the common law apart from statute, and in any case are not enough to override the plain meaning of statutory words.

The common law as to master and servant, whatever may be thought of it, embodied a policy that has not disappeared from life. But it seems to me that courts in dealing with statutes sometimes have been too slow to recognize that statutes even when in terms covering only particular cases may imply a policy different from that of the common law, and therefore may exclude a reference to the common law for the purpose of limiting their scope. *Johnson v. United States*, 163 F. 30, 32. Without going into the reasons for the notion that an action (other than an appeal) does not lie for causing the death of a human being, it is enough to say that they have disappeared. The policy that forbade such an action, if it was more profound than the absence of a remedy when a man's body was hanged and his goods confiscated for the felony, has been shown not to be the policy of present law by statutes of the United States and of most if not all of the States. In such circumstances it seems to me that we should not be astute to deprive the words of the Panama Code of their natural effect.

The decision in the *Hubgh Case*, 6 La. Ann. 495, stands on nothing better than the classic tradition that the life of a free human being (it was otherwise with regard to slaves) did not admit of valuation, which no longer is true sentimentally, as is shown by the statutes, and which economically is false.

I think that the judgment should be affirmed.

THE CHIEF JUSTICE, MR. JUSTICE MCKENNA and MR. JUSTICE BRANDEIS concur in this opinion.

Omitted Taft Opinions

Nassau Smelting & Refining Works v. United States, 266 U.S. 101 (1924)—claim against United States government for payment.
Shewan & Sons v. United States, 266 U.S. 108 (1924)—admiralty case.
Mellon v. Orinoco Iron Company, 266 U.S. 121 (1924)—tax case.
Westinghouse Electric & Manufacturing Company v. Formica Insulation Company, 266 U.S. 342 (1924)—patent case.
Tod v. Waldman, 266 U.S. 547 (1925)—petition for rehearing.

VOLUME 267

Swiss National Insurance Co. v. Miller

Judicial review, the power of the Court to determine the constitutionality of legislation and to declare void that legislation that violates the Constitution, is generally seen as the greatest source of judicial power. Statutory interpretation, sometimes overlooked, is, however, also a source of judicial power. In this case, Chief Justice Taft for the majority and Justice McReynolds in solo dissent came to very different conclusions as to what the Trading with the Enemy Act meant and whether the word "person" was meant to include corporations. Taft held that it did not.

Swiss National Insurance Company, Limited, v. Thomas W. Miller, as Alien Property Custodian, and Frank White, as Treasurer of the United States

Appeal from the Court of Appeals of the District of Columbia

No. 132. Argued November 18, 1924—Decided February 2, 1925

267 U.S. 42 (1925)

[43]

MR. CHIEF JUSTICE TAFT delivered the opinion of the Court.

This is an appeal from the Court of Appeals of the District of Columbia under Section 250 of the Judicial Code.

The Swiss National Insurance Company filed a bill in equity against the Alien Property Custodian and the Treasurer of the United States in the Supreme Court of the District to recover securities to the value of about one million dollars. These it had before the War deposited in the various state treasuries because required by the state laws as a condition of doing insurance therein. The Alien Property Custodian had seized them in November, 1918, as property of an enemy, under the definition of Section 2, par. (a) of the Trading with the Enemy Act. . . .

* * * * *

[45] The . . . argument of the appellant is . . . directed to the question whether the appellant comes within the classes of enemies given the right to recover their property from the Alien Property Custodian by the 1920 amend-

ment. Section 9, paragraph a, of that amendment provides for a return by order of the President to a person not an enemy claiming an interest in property seized by the Custodian, and, failing such order, allows a suit in equity to recover the property or money due.

* * * * *

[46] It is urged for appellant that it is a citizen of Switzerland and is thus included with those favored in the first class. Section 2 of the original Trading with the Enemy Act approved October 6, 1917, c. 106, 40 Stat. 411, and unrepealed provides that: "The word 'person' as used herein shall be deemed to mean an individual, partnership, association, company or other unincorporated body of individuals, or corporation or body politic" and the word "enemy" is declared to be equally inclusive. But there is in the Act and its amendments no such definition of the words citizen or subject. The term citizen or subject may be broad enough to include corporations of the country whose citizens are in question. *Paul v. Virginia,* 8 Wall. 168; *Selover v. Walsh,* 226 U.S. 112; *Western Turf Association v. Greensburg,* 204 U.S. 359. Whether it is so inclusive in any particular instance depends upon the intent to be gathered from the context and the general purpose of the whole legislation in which it occurs. . . .

* * * * *

[47] . . . [T]he strongest and to us the convincing argument that the language of clause 1 of par. b was not intended to include corporations is the especial mention of partnerships, associations and corporations in clause 6 as a different class from that of clause 1 of the same section. . . .

* * * * *

[49] Much has been said in respect to the intent of Congress to be liberal in this series of acts as shown by the correspondence of the Attorney General and his subordinates with the Congressional Committees, but nothing has been called to our attention that seems to us to have real significance in respect to the exact point in this discussion.

In order to supply some reason or occasion for clause 6, if clause 1 is to be held to include corporations as citizens or subjects, it is suggested for appellants that the clause was intended to cover German and Austrian corporations entirely owned by citizens of the United States or of other countries than Germany or Austria. We think this a far fetched argument to explain the very general words of this clause when such a purpose might have been easily attained by specific provision for such exceptional instances. Under the appellant's construction of clause 6, the improbable overlapping duplication of clause 1 and clause 6 is so manifest that we think the construction must be rejected. We concur, therefore, with the conclusion of the Court of Appeals, and the District Supreme Court.

Affirmed.

MR. JUSTICE McKENNA participated in the consideration of this case and concurred in the opinion prior to his resignation.

The separate [dissenting] opinion of MR. JUSTICE McREYNOLDS.

* * * * *

[75] That the construction asked by appellees is neither natural nor necessary and would lead to the unfortunate conclusion that seized property of a neutral corporation must be retained because a German owns one share out of many thousand. Without doing violence to any part of the Act and by giving effect to every word therein, citizens of neutrals may secure just relief and the United States escape the serious charge of oppressive and unfriendly action.

In view of all these things, I am unable to accept the view which appellees urge upon us. It seems sufficiently plain that the court below fell into error; and to affirm the challenged decree would leave our Government in a most unenviable position. "There is no debt with so much prejudice put off as that of justice."

Ex Parte Grossman

Article II delegates to the president the power "to grant Reprieves and Pardons for Offences against the United States, except in Cases of Impeachment." President Calvin Coolidge had commuted the sentence of Philip Grossman, who had been convicted of violating the Volstead (Prohibition) Act, but required that Grossman pay the fine. Normally, that would have been done with it. There was a twist in the circumstances, however, that caused the case eventually to come to the Court and allowed Chief Justice Taft to issue a lengthy, heavily historical disquisition on the nature of the presidential pardoning power.

Grossman had ignored a restraining order prohibiting him from liquor sales. For that he had been sent to jail for contempt of court. Two federal judges in Chicago interpreted Coolidge's commutation as "a slur on the judiciary. 'The power to punish for contempt,' they ruled, 'is inherent in and essential to the very existence of the judiciary.'"[1] Accordingly, Taft, in rendering this decision, was called upon to decide between the power of the executive and the power of the judiciary. Taft found in favor of the executive, determining that the only restrictions on the power of the president to pardon were to be found in cases of impeachment and state offenses.

Note

1. Alpheus Thomas Mason, *Harlan Fiske Stone: Pillar of the Law* (New York: The Viking Press, 1956), 167.

Ex Parte in the Matter of Philip Grossman, Petitioner

Error to the District Court of the United States for the Northern District of Illinois

No. 24, Original. Argued December 1, 1924—Decided March 2, 1925

267 U.S. 87 (1925)

[107]

MR. CHIEF JUSTICE TAFT delivered the opinion of the Court.

This is an original petition in this Court for a writ of *habeas corpus* by Philip Grossman against Ritchie V. Graham, Superintendent of the Chicago House of Correction, Cook County, Illinois. . . .

. . . In December, 1923, the President issued a pardon in which he commuted the sentence of Grossman to the fine of $1,000 on condition that the fine be paid. The pardon was accepted, the fine was paid and the defendant was released. In May, 1924, however, the District Court committed Grossman to the Chicago House of Correction to serve the sentence notwithstanding the pardon. 1 Fed. (2d) 941. The only [108] question raised by the pleadings herein is that of the power of the President to grant the pardon.

Special counsel, employed by the Department of Justice, appear for the respondent to uphold the legality of the detention. The Attorney General of the United States, as *amicus curiae*, maintains the validity and effectiveness of the President's action. The petitioner, by his counsel, urges his discharge from imprisonment.

Article II, Section 2, clause one, of the Constitution, dealing with the powers and duties of the President, closes with these words:

" . . . and he shall have power to grant Reprieves and Pardons for Offences against the United States, except in Cases of Impeachment."

The argument for the respondent is that the President's power extends only to offenses against the United States and a contempt of Court is not such an offense, that offenses against the United States are not common law offenses but can only be created by legislative act, that the President's pardoning power is more limited than that of the King of England at common law, which was a broad prerogative and included contempts against his courts chiefly because the judges thereof were his agents and acted in his name; that the context of the Constitution shows that the word "offences" is used in that instrument only to include crimes and misdemeanors triable by jury and not contempts of the dignity and authority of the federal courts, and that to construe the pardon clause to include contempts of court would be to violate the fundamental principle of the Constitution in the division of powers between the Legislative, Executive and Judicial branches, and to take from the federal courts their independence and the essential means of protecting their dignity and authority.

The language of the Constitution cannot be interpreted safely except by reference to the common law and to [109] British institutions as they were when the instrument was framed and adopted. The statesmen and lawyers of the Convention who submitted it to the ratification of the Conventions of the thirteen States, were born and brought up in the atmosphere of the common law, and thought and spoke in its vocabulary. . . .

* * * * *

In *Ex parte William Wells*, 18 Howard, 307, 311, the question was whether the President under his power to pardon could commute a death sentence to life imprisonment by granting a pardon of the capital punishment on condition that the convict be imprisoned during his natural life. This Court, speaking through Mr. Justice Wayne, after quoting the above language of the Chief Justice, said:

> "We still think so, and that the language used in the Constitution, conferring the power to grant reprieves and pardons, must be construed with reference to its meaning [110] at the time of its adoption. At the time of our separation from Great Britain, that power had been exercised by the King, as the chief executive. Prior to the Revolution, the Colonies, being in effect under the laws of England, were accustomed to the exercise of it in the various forms, as they may be found in the English law books. They were, of course, to be applied as occasions occurred, and they constituted a part of the jurisprudence of Anglo-America. At the time of the adoption of the Constitution, American statesmen were conversant with the laws of England and familiar with the prerogatives exercised by the

crown. Hence, when the words to grant pardons were used in the Constitution, they conveyed to the mind the authority as exercised by the English crown, or by its representatives in the colonies. . . .

The King of England before our Revolution, in the exercise of his prerogative, had always exercised the power to pardon contempts of court, just as he did ordinary crimes and misdemeanors and as he has done to the present day. In the mind of a common law lawyer of the eighteenth century the word pardon included within its scope the ending by the King's grace of the punishment of such derelictions, whether it was imposed by the court without a jury or upon indictment, for both forms of trial for contempts were had. . . .

* * * * *

[112] With this authoritative background of the common law and English history before the American Revolution to show that criminal contempts were within the understood scope of the pardoning power of the Executive, we come now to the history of the clause in the Constitutional Convention of 1787. . . .

As referred to the Committee on Style, the clause read (II Farrand, 575) : "He shall have power to grant reprieves and pardons except in cases of impeachment." The Committee on Style reported this clause as it now is: "and he shall have power to grant reprieves and pardons for offences against the United States except in cases of impeachment." There seems to have been no discussion over the substance of the clause save that a motion to except cases of treason was referred to the Committee on Style, September 10th (II Farrand, 564), was not approved by the Committee and after discussion was defeated in the Convention September 15th (II Farrand, 626, 627).

[113] We have given the history of the clause to show that the words "for offences against the United States" were inserted by a Committee on Style, presumably to make clear that the pardon of the President was to operate upon offenses against the United States as distinguished from offenses against the States. It can not be supposed that the Committee on Revision by adding these words, or the Convention by accepting them, intended *sub silentio* to narrow the scope of a pardon from one at common law or to confer any different power in this regard on our Executive from that which the members of the Convention had seen exercised before the Revolution.

. . . The framers of our Constitution had in mind no necessity for curtailing this feature of the King's prerogative in transplanting it into the American governmental structures, save by excepting cases of impeachment;

and even in that regard, as already pointed out, the common law forbade the pleading a pardon in bar to an impeachment. The suggestion that the President's power of pardon should be regarded as necessarily less than that of the King was pressed upon this Court and was agreed to by Mr. Justice McLean, one of the dissenting Judges, in *Ex parte William Wells,* 18 Howard, 307, 321, but it did not prevail with the majority.

* * * * *

[118] . . . [C]riminal contempts of a federal court have been pardoned for eighty-five years. In that time the power has been exercised twenty-seven times. . . .

[119] . . . [I]t is [however] urged that criminal contempts should not be held within the pardoning power because it will tend to destroy the independence of the judiciary and violate the primary constitutional principle of a separation of the legislative, executive and judicial powers. This argument influenced the two district judges below. . . .

The Federal Constitution nowhere expressly declares that the three branches of the Government shall be kept separate and independent. All legislative powers are vested in a Congress. The executive power is vested in a President. The judicial power is vested in one Supreme Court and in such inferior courts as Congress may from time to time establish. The Judges are given life tenure and a compensation that may not be diminished during their continuance in office, with the evident purpose of securing them and their courts an independence of Congress and the Executive. Complete independence and separation between the three branches, however, are not attained, or intended, as other provisions of the Constitution and the normal operation of government under it [120] easily demonstrate. By affirmative action through the veto power, the Executive and one more than one-third of either House may defeat all legislation. One-half of the House and two-thirds of the Senate may impeach and remove the members of the Judiciary. The Executive can reprieve or pardon all offenses after their commission, either before trial, during trial or after trial, by individuals, or by classes, conditionally or absolutely, and this without modification or regulation by Congress. *Ex parte Garland,* 4 Wall. 333, 380. Negatively, one House of Congress can withhold all appropriations and stop the operations of Government. The Senate can hold up all appointments, confirmation of which either the Constitution or a statute requires, and thus deprive the President of the necessary agents with which he is to take care that the laws be faithfully executed.

These are some instances of positive and negative restraints possibly available under the Constitution to each branch of the government in defeat of the action of the other. They show that the independence of each of the others is qualified and is so subject to exception as not to constitute a broadly positive injunction or a necessarily controlling rule of construction. The fact is that the Judiciary, quite as much as Congress and the Executive, is dependent on the cooperation of the other two, that government may go on. Indeed, while the Constitution has made the Judiciary as independent of the other branches as is practicable, it is, as often remarked, the weakest of the three. It must look for a continuity of necessary cooperation, in the possible reluctance of either of the other branches, to the force of public opinion.

Executive clemency exists to afford relief from undue harshness or evident mistake in the operation or enforcement of the criminal law. The administration of justice by the courts is not necessarily always wise or certainly considerate of circumstances which may properly mitigate [121] guilt. To afford a remedy, it has always been thought essential in popular governments, as well as in monarchies, to vest in some other authority than the courts power to ameliorate or avoid particular criminal judgments. It is a check entrusted to the executive for special cases. To exercise it to the extent of destroying the deterrent effect of judicial punishment would be to pervert it; but whoever is to make it useful must have full discretion to exercise it. Our Constitution confers this discretion on the highest officer in the nation in confidence that he will not abuse it. An abuse in pardoning contempts would certainly embarrass courts, but it is questionable how much more it would lessen their effectiveness than a wholesale pardon of other offenses. If we could conjure up in our minds a President willing to paralyze courts by pardoning all criminal contempts, why not a President ordering a general jail delivery? A pardon can only be granted for a contempt fully completed. Neither in this country nor in England can it interfere with the use of coercive measures to enforce a suitor's right. The detrimental effect of excessive pardons of completed contempts would be in the loss of the deterrent influence upon future contempts. It is of the same character as that of the excessive pardons of other offenses. The difference does not justify our reading criminal contempts out of the pardon clause by departing from its ordinary meaning confirmed by its common law origin and long years of practice and acquiescence.

If it be said that the President, by successive pardons of constantly recurring contempts in particular litigation, might deprive a court of power to enforce its orders in a recalcitrant neighborhood, it is enough to observe that such a course is so improbable as to furnish but little basis for argument. Exceptional cases like this, if to be imagined at all, would suggest a resort to impeachment rather than to a narrow and strained construction of the general powers of the President.

[122] The power of a court to protect itself and its usefulness by punishing contemnors is of course necessary, but it is one exercised without the restraining influence of a jury and without many of the guaranties which the bill of rights offers to protect the individual against unjust conviction. Is it unreasonable to provide for the possibility that the personal element may sometimes enter into a summary judgment pronounced by a judge who thinks his authority is flouted or denied? May it not be fairly said that in order to avoid possible mistake, undue prejudice or needless severity, the chance of pardon should exist at least as much in favor of a person convicted by a judge without a jury as in favor of one convicted in a jury trial? The pardoning by the President of criminal contempts has been practiced more than three-quarters of a century, and no abuses during all that time developed sufficiently to invoke a test in the federal courts of its validity.

It goes without saying that nowhere is there a more earnest will to maintain the independence of federal courts and the preservation of every legitimate safeguard of their effectiveness afforded by the Constitution than in this Court. But the qualified independence which they fortunately enjoy is not likely to be permanently strengthened by ignoring precedent and practice and minimizing the importance of the coordinating checks and balances of the Constitution.

The rule is made absolute and the petitioner is discharged.

Carroll v. United States

William Howard Taft's legendary love for the law may be exemplified best in the way he dealt with the many cases coming to the High Court as a result of Prohibition.[1] Although Alpheus Thomas Mason surmised that Taft's worship of the law was often a façade behind which Taft hid his other love, respect for private property rights,[2] the "noble experiment" did not at all please Taft.[3] Nevertheless, despite his earlier opposition to a constitutional amendment on the subject and his belief that the matter, if legislated on at all, should be the subject of state action, Taft, both on and off the bench, urged adherence to the law. He also regularly took upon himself the less than popular task of writing many of the Court's opinions on the topic.[4]

Two of his Prohibition-related decisions remain among the most cited of Taft's opinions. However, unlike the wire tapping case of *Olmstead v. United States*, 277 U.S. 438 (1928), which was swept aside by the Warren Court's decision in *Katz v. United States*, 389 U.S. 347 (1967) (*Katz* read into the Fourth Amendment the concept of "expectation of privacy"), *Carroll* remains good law. Indeed, it can still be dubbed a leading case, which is quite rare for a decision by the pre-1937 "Old Court."[5] In fact, the so-called "automobile exception" created by Taft in *Carroll* not only continues as precedent but has been considerably expanded by the current Rehnquist Court (1986–present).[6]

The national prohibition act of 1921 (the Volstead Act) specifically required the use of a search warrant in enforcing the statute and further provided that failure by a federal officer to secure a warrant constituted a misdemeanor. In *Carroll* Taft found the challenged search to have been reasonable, distinguishing between searches of automobiles and those of private dwellings. Taft apparently was very proud of this particular decision and wrote his brother that he had had his way "after a great fight."[7] Justices Sutherland and McReynolds, though, were not won over and held that the search violated the Fourth Amendment.

Notes

1. Pringle, *Life and Times*, 2:981–91.
2. Mason, *William Howard Taft*, 264.
3. Pringle, *Life and Times*, 2:981.
4. Ragan, *Chief Justice Taft*, 90–91. Taft himself was a total abstainer. See, for example, Pringle, *Life and Times*, 2:1072.
5. O'Brien, *Constitutional Law*, 2:815.
6. Ibid., 2:815–21.
7. Pringle, *Life and Times*, 2:988.

Carroll et al. v. United States

*Error to the District Court of the United States
for the Western District of Michigan*

No. 15. Argued December 4, 1923; restored to docket for reargument January 28, 1924; reargued March 14, 1924—Decided March 2, 1925

267 U.S. 132 (1925)

[143]

MR. CHIEF JUSTICE TAFT . . . delivered the opinion of the Court.

The constitutional and statutory provisions involved in this case include the Fourth Amendment and the National Prohibition Act.

The Fourth Amendment is in part as follows:

"The right of the people to be secure in their persons, houses, papers, and effects, against unreasonable searches and seizures, shall not be violated, and no Warrants shall issue, but upon probable cause, supported by Oath or affirmation, and particularly describing the place to be searched, and the person, or things to be seized."

Section 25, Title II, of the National Prohibition Act, c. 85, 41 Stat. 305, 315, passed to enforce the Eighteenth Amendment, makes it unlawful to have or possess any liquor intended for use in violating the Act, or which has been so used, and provides that no property rights shall exist in such liquor. A search warrant may issue and such liquor, with the containers thereof, may be seized under the warrant and be ultimately destroyed. The section further provides:

"No search warrant shall issue to search any private dwelling occupied as such unless it is being used for the unlawful sale of intoxicating liquor, or unless it is in part used for some business purpose such as a store, shop, saloon, restaurant, hotel, or boarding house. The term 'private dwelling' shall be construed to include the room or rooms used and occupied not transiently but solely as [144] a residence in an apartment house, hotel, or boarding house."

Section 26, Title II, under which the seizure herein was made, provides in part as follows:

"When the commissioner, his assistants, inspectors, or any officer of the law shall discover any person in the act of transporting in violation of the law, intoxicating liquors in any wagon, buggy, automobile, water or air craft, or other vehicle, it shall be his duty to seize any and all intoxicating liquors found therein being transported contrary to law. Whenever intoxicating liquors transported or possessed illegally shall be seized by an officer he shall take possession of the vehicle and team or automobile, boat, air or water craft, or any other conveyance, and shall arrest any person in charge thereof."

* * * * *

By Section 6 of an Act supplemental to the National Prohibition Act, c. 134, 42 Stat. 222, 223, it is provided that if any officer or agent or employee of the United States engaged in the enforcement of the Prohibition Act or this Amendment, "shall search any private dwelling," as defined in that Act, "without a warrant directing such search," or "shall without a search warrant maliciously and without reasonable cause search any other building or property," he shall be guilty of a misdemeanor and subject to fine or imprisonment or both.

In the passage of the supplemental Act through the Senate, Amendment No. 32, known as the Stanley Amendment, was adopted, the relevant part of which was as follows:

> "Section 6. That any officer, agent or employee of the United States engaged in the enforcement of this Act or [145] the National Prohibition Act, or any other law of the United States, who shall search or attempt to search the property or premises of any person without previously securing a search warrant, as provided by law, shall be guilty of a misdemeanor and upon conviction thereof shall be fined not to exceed $1000, or imprisoned not to exceed one year, or both so fined and imprisoned in the discretion of the Court."

This Amendment was objected to in the House, and the Judiciary Committee. . . .

* * * * *

[146] The conference report resulted, so far as the difference between the two Houses was concerned, in providing for the punishment of any officer, agent or employee of the Government who searches a "private dwelling" without a warrant, and for the punishment of any such officer, [147] etc., who searches any "other building or property" where, and only where, he makes the search without a warrant "maliciously and without probable cause." In other words, it left the way open for searching an automobile, or vehicle of transportation, without a warrant, if the search was not malicious or without probable cause.

The intent of Congress to make a distinction between the necessity for a search warrant in the searching of private dwellings and in that of automobiles and other road vehicles is the enforcement of the Prohibition Act is thus clearly established by the legislative history of the Stanley Amendment. Is such a distinction consistent with the Fourth Amendment? We think that it is. The Fourth Amendment does not denounce all searches or seizures, but only such as are unreasonable.

The leading case on the subject of search and seizure is *Boyd v. United States*, 116 U.S. 616. An Act of Congress of June 22, 1874, authorized a court of the United States, in revenue cases, on motion of the government attorney, to require the defendant to produce in court, his private books, invoices and papers on pain in case of refusal of having the allegations of the attorney in his motion taken as confessed. This was held to be unconstitutional and void as applied to suits for penalties or to establish a forfeiture of goods, on the ground that under the Fourth Amendment the compulsory production of invoices to furnish evidence for forfeiture of goods constituted an unreasonable search even where made upon a search warrant, and that it was also a violation of the Fifth Amendment, in that it compelled the defendant in a criminal case to produce evidence against himself or be in the attitude of confessing his guilt.

In *Weeks v. United States*, 232 U.S. 383, it was held that a court in a criminal prosecution could not retain letters of the accused seized in his house, in his absence and without his authority, by a United States marshal [148] holding no warrant for his arrest and none for the search of his premises, to be used as evidence against him, the accused having made timely application to the court for an order for the return of the letters.

In *Silverthorne Lumber Company v. United States*, 251 U.S. 385, a writ of error was brought to reverse a judgment of contempt of the District Court, fining the company and imprisoning one Silverthorne, its president, until he should purge himself of contempt in not producing books and documents of the company before the grand jury to prove violation of the statutes of the United States by the company and Silverthorne. Silverthorne had been arrested and while under arrest the marshal had gone to the office of the company without a warrant and made a clean sweep of all books, papers and documents found there and had taken copies and photographs of the papers. The District Court ordered the return of the originals, but impounded the photographs and copies. This was held to be an unreasonable search of the property and possessions of the corporation and a violation of the Fourth Amendment and the judgment for contempt was reversed.

* * * * *

[149] In *Boyd v. United States*, 116 U.S. 616, as already said, the decision did not turn on whether a reasonable search might be made without a warrant; but for the purpose of showing the principle on which the Fourth Amendment proceeds, and to avoid any misapprehension of what was decided, the Court, speaking through Mr. Justice Bradley, used language

which is of particular significance and applicability here. It was there said (page 623):

> "The search for and seizure of stolen or forfeited goods, or goods liable to duties and concealed to avoid the payment thereof, are totally different things from a search for and seizure of a man's private books and papers for the purpose of obtaining information therein contained, or of using them as evidence against him. The two things differ *toto coelo*. In the one case, the government is entitled to the possession of the property; in the other it is not. The seizure of stolen goods is authorized by the [150] common law; and the seizure of goods forfeited for a breach of the revenue laws, or concealed to avoid the duties payable on them, has been authorized by English statutes for at least two centuries past; and the like seizures have been authorized by our own revenue acts from the commencement of the government. The first statute passed by Congress to regulate the collection of duties, the act of July 31, 1789, 1 Stat. 29, 43, contains provisions to this effect. As this act was passed by the same Congress which proposed for adoption the original amendments to the Constitution, it is clear that the members of that body did not regard searches and seizures of this kind as 'unreasonable,' and they are not embraced within the prohibition of the amendment. . . .

* * * * *

[151] Thus contemporaneously with the adoption of the Fourth Amendment we find in the first Congress, and in the following Second and Fourth Congresses, a difference made as to the necessity for a search warrant between goods subject to forfeiture, when concealed in a dwelling house or similar place, and like goods in course of transportation and concealed in a movable vessel where they readily could be put out of reach of a search warrant. . . .

* * * * *

[153] We have made a somewhat extended reference to these statutes to show that the guaranty of freedom from unreasonable searches and seizures by the Fourth Amendment has been construed, practically since the beginning of the Government, as recognizing a necessary difference between a search of a store, dwelling house or other structure in respect of which a proper official warrant readily may be obtained, and a search of a ship, motor boat, wagon or automobile, for contraband goods, where it is not practicable to secure a warrant because the vehicle can be quickly

moved out of the locality or jurisdiction in which the warrant must be sought.

Having thus established that contraband goods concealed and illegally transported in an automobile or other vehicle may be searched for without a warrant, we come now to consider under what circumstances such search may be made. It would be intolerable and unreasonable [154] if a prohibition agent were authorized to stop every automobile on the chance of finding liquor and thus subject all persons lawfully using the highways to the inconvenience and indignity of such a search. Travellers may be so stopped in crossing an international boundary because of national self protection reasonably requiring one entering the country to identify himself as entitled to come in, and his belongings as effects which may be lawfully brought in. But those lawfully within the country, entitled to use the public highways, have a right to free passage without interruption or search unless there is known to a competent official authorized to search, probable cause for believing that their vehicles are carrying contraband or illegal merchandise. . . .

* * * * *

[156] We here find the line of distinction between legal and illegal seizures of liquor in transport in vehicles. It is certainly a reasonable distinction. It gives the owner of an automobile or other vehicle seized under Section 26, in absence of probable cause, a right to have restored to him the automobile, it protects him under the *Weeks* and *Amos* cases from use of the liquor as evidence against him, and it subjects the officer making the seizures to damages. On the other hand, in a case showing probable cause, the Government and its officials are given the opportunity which they should have, to make the investigation necessary to trace reasonably suspected contraband goods and to seize them.

Such a rule fulfills the guaranty of the Fourth Amendment. In cases where the securing of a warrant is reasonably practicable, it must be used, and when properly supported by affidavit and issued after judicial approval protects the seizing officer against a suit for damages. In cases where seizure is impossible except without warrant, the seizing officer acts unlawfully and at his peril unless he can show the court probable cause. *United States v. Kaplan,* 286 Fed. 963, 972.

But we are pressed with the argument that if the search of the automobile discloses the presence of liquor and leads under the statute to the arrest of the person in charge of the automobile, the right of seizure should be limited by the common law rule as to the circumstances justifying an arrest without warrant for a misdemeanor. The usual rule is that a police officer may arrest without warrant one believed by the officer upon reasonable cause to have been guilty of a felony, and that he may only arrest without a warrant one guilty of a misdemeanor if committed [157] in his presence. . . .

* * * * *

[158] We do not think such a nice distinction is applicable in the present case. When a man is legally arrested for an offense, whatever is found upon his person or in his control which it is unlawful for him to have and which may be used to prove the offense may be seized and held as evidence in the prosecution. *Weeks v. United States*, 232 U.S. 383, 392; *Dillon v. O'Brien and Davis*, 16 Cox. C. C. 245; *Getchell v. Page*, 103 Me. 387; *Kneeland v. Connally*, 70 Ga. 424; 1 Bishop, Criminal Procedure, Sec. 211; 1 Wharton, Criminal Procedure (10th edition), Sec. 97. The argument of defendants is based on the theory that the seizure in this case can only be thus justified. If their theory were sound, their conclusion would be. The validity of the seizure then would turn wholly on the validity of the arrest without a seizure. But the theory is unsound. The right to search and the validity of the seizure are not dependent on the right to arrest. They are dependent on the reasonable cause the seizing officer [159] has for belief that the contents of the automobile offend against the law. The seizure in such a proceeding comes before the arrest as Section 26 indicates. . . .

* * * * *

Finally, was there probable cause? In *The Apollon*, 9 Wheat. 362, the question was whether the seizure of a French vessel at a particular place was upon probable cause that she was there for the purpose of smuggling. In this discussion Mr. Justice Story, who delivered the judgment of the Court, said (page 374):

> "It has been very justly observed at the bar, that the Court is bound to take notice of public facts and [160] geographical positions; and that this remote part of the country has been infested, at different periods, by smugglers, is a matter of general notoriety, and may be gathered from the public documents of the government."

* * * * *

[162] In the light of these authorities, and what is shown by this record, it is clear the officers here had justification for the search and seizure. This is to say that the facts and circumstances within their knowledge and of which

they had reasonably trustworthy information were sufficient in themselves to warrant a man of reasonable caution in the belief that intoxicating liquor was being transported in the automobile which they stopped and searched.

* * * * *

The judgment is

Affirmed.

[163]

MR. JUSTICE MCKENNA, before his retirement, concurred in this opinion.

The separate opinion of MR. JUSTICE MCREYNOLDS concurred in by MR. JUSTICE SUTHERLAND.

1. The damnable character of the "bootlegger's" business should not close our eyes to the mischief which will surely follow any attempt to destroy it by unwarranted methods. "To press forward to a great principle by breaking through every other great principle that stands in the way of its establishment; . . . in short, to procure an eminent good by means that are unlawful, is as little consonant to private morality as to public justice." Sir William Scott, *The Louis,* 2 Dodson 210, 257.

While quietly driving an ordinary automobile along a much frequented public road, plaintiffs in error were arrested by Federal officers without a warrant and upon mere suspicion—ill founded, as I think. The officers then searched the machine and discovered carefully secreted whisky, which was seized and thereafter used as evidence against plaintiffs in error when on trial for transporting intoxicating liquor contrary to the Volstead Act (c. 85, 41 Stat. 305). They maintain that both arrest and seizure were unlawful and that use of the liquor as evidence violated their constitutional rights.

[164] Whether the officers are shielded from prosecution or action by Rev. Stat. Sec. 970 is not important. That section does not undertake to deprive the citizen of any constitutional right or to permit the use of evidence unlawfully obtained. It does, however, indicate the clear understanding of Congress that probable cause is not always enough to justify a seizure.

Samuels v. McCurdy

Samuels sued to recover a quantity of alcohol that had been seized pursuant to a valid warrant. Samuels had purchased the alcohol prior to the adoption of Prohibition and used it only for private consumption. The state did not dispute either of these claims.

Although mentioned by neither the Taft opinion nor the typically brief dissent of Justice Butler, *Wynehamer v. People,* 13 N.Y. 358 (1856), involved exactly the same issue. Raoul Berger labels *Wynehamer* as the *locus classicus* of substantive due process.[1] Essentially, substantive due process is the doctrine that allows the Court to invalidate laws that are procedurally flawless and violate no specific guarantee of the Constitution, but are found by the Court to violate what it determines to be fundamental rights. Liberty of contract is the classic example of such a right. More recently, the right of privacy as delineated in *Griswold v. Connecticut,* 381 U.S. 479 (1965) (striking down a Connecticut statute prohibiting the use of contraceptives), and *Roe v. Wade,* 410 U.S. 113 (1973) (invalidating state restrictions on abortion), has been viewed by critics of these two decisions as an example of the contemporary Court using the Fourteenth Amendment to impose its view of right and wrong on society.

Despite his distaste for government efforts to restrict alcohol, Taft in this case rejected the siren call of substantive due process and upheld the seizure. Justice Butler's dissent did not. For Butler, the law was both "oppressive and arbitrary."

Note

1. Berger, *Government by Judiciary: The Transformation of the Fourteenth Amendment* (Cambridge: Harvard University Press, 1977), 254–55.

Samuels v. McCurdy, Sheriff of Dekalb County, Georgia

Error to the Supreme Court of the State of Georgia

No. 225. Argued January 22, 1925—Decided March 2, 1925

267 U.S. 188 (1925)

[190]

MR. CHIEF JUSTICE TAFT delivered the opinion of the Court.

Sig Samuels, a resident of DeKalb County, Georgia, filed his petition in the Superior Court of that county against its sheriff, J. A. McCurdy, in which he prayed for the specific recovery of certain intoxicating liquors belonging to him which he averred had been seized on search warrant by the defendant. . . .

[191] The petition averred that Phillips, a deputy of the defendant, went to Samuels' residence and acting under a search warrant seized and carried

away a large quantity of whiskeys, wines, beer, cordials and liquors; that he stored these in the jail of the county; that it was the purpose of the defendant to destroy them, without any hearing of the petitioner; that the value of the liquors, at the scale of prices current before the prohibition laws, was approximately $400, but at the prices paid thereafter, if illegally sold, would be very much more; that the greater part of the liquors was bought by the petitioner and kept at his home prior to the year 1907; that the balance thereof was legally purchased by him in the State of Florida and legally shipped to him in interstate commerce prior to the year 1915; that, although a citizen of the United States and the State of Georgia, the petitioner was born in Europe where the use of such liquors had been common; that he had been accustomed to their use all his life; that he purchased them lawfully for the use of his family and friends at his own home, and not for any unlawful purpose.

* * * * *

[193] Three grounds are urged for reversal. First, the 1917 law under which liquor lawfully acquired can be seized and destroyed is an *ex post facto* law. Second, the law in punishing the owner for possessing liquor he had lawfully acquired before its enactment, deprives him of his property without due process. Third, it violates the due process requirement by the seizure and destruction of the liquor without giving the possessor his day in court.

First. This law is not an *ex post facto* law. It does not provide a punishment for a past offense. It does not fix a penalty for the owner for having become possessed of the liquor. The penalty it imposes is for continuing to possess the liquor after the enactment of the law. . . .

* * * * *

[194] Second. Does the seizure of this liquor and its destruction deprive the plaintiff in error of his property without due process of law, in violation of the Fourteenth Amendment?

In *Crane v. Campbell*, 245 U.S. 304, Crane was arrested for having in his possession a bottle of whiskey for his own use, and not for the purpose of giving away or selling the same to any person. This was under a provision of the statute of Idaho that it should be unlawful for any person to import, ship, sell, transport, deliver, receive or have in his possession any intoxicating liquors. It was held that the law was within the police power of the State.

* * * * *

The Court pointed out that as the State had the power to prohibit, it might adopt such measures as were reasonably appropriate or needful to render exercise of that power effective; and that considering the notorious difficulties always attendant upon efforts to suppress traffic in liquors, the Court was unable to say that the challenged inhibition of their possession was arbitrary and unreasonable or without proper relation to the legitimate legislative purpose, that the right to hold intoxicating liquor for personal use was not one of those fundamental [195] privileges of a citizen of the United States which no State could abridge, and that a contrary view would be incompatible with the undoubted power to prevent manufacture, gift, sale, purchase or transportation of such articles—the only feasible ways of getting them. It did not appear in that case when the liquor seized had been acquired, but presumably after the prohibitory act.

* * * * *

[197] The ultimate legislative object of prohibition is to prevent the drinking of intoxicating liquor by any one because of the demoralizing effect of drunkenness upon society. The state has the power to subject those members of society who might indulge in the use of such liquor without injury to themselves to a deprivation of access to liquor in order to remove temptation from those whom [198] its use would demoralize and to avoid the abuses which follow in its train. Accordingly laws have been enacted by the States, and sustained by this Court, by which it has been made illegal to manufacture liquor for one's own use or for another's, to transport it or to sell it or to give it away to others. The legislature has this power whether it affects liquor lawfully acquired before the prohibition or not. Without compensation it may thus seek to reduce the drinking of liquor. It is obvious that if men are permitted to maintain liquor in their possession, though only for their own consumption, there is danger of its becoming accessible to others. Legislation making possession unlawful is therefore within the police power of the States as a reasonable mode of reducing the evils of drunkenness, as we have seen in the *Crane* and *Barbour* cases. The only question which arises is whether for the shrunken opportunity of the possessor of liquor who acquired it before the law, to use it only for his own consumption, the State must make compensation. By valid laws, his property rights have been so far reduced that it would be difficult to measure their value. That which had the qualities of property has, by successive provisions of law in the interest of all, been losing its qualities as property. For many years, every one who has made or stored liquor has known that it was a kind of property which because of its possible vicious uses might be denied by the State the character and attributes as such; that legislation calculated to suppress its use in the interest of public health and morality was lawful and possible, and this without compensation. Why

should compensation be made now for the mere remnant of the original right if nothing was paid for the loss of the right to sell the liquor, give it away or transport it? The necessity for its destruction is claimed under the same police power to be for the public betterment as that which authorized its previous restrictions. It seems to us that this conclusion finds support [199] in the passage quoted above from the opinion in the *Mugler* case. . . .

Finally, it is said that the petitioner here has no day in court provided by the law, and therefore that in this respect the liquors have been taken from him without due process. The Supreme Court of Georgia has held in *Delaney v. Plunkett*, 146 Ga. 547, 565, that, under the 20th Section of the Act of November 17, 1915 (Georgia Laws, Extra. Session 1915, 77), quoted above, which declares that no property rights of any kind shall exist in prohibited liquors and beverages, no hearing need be given the possessor of unlawfully held liquors, but that they may be destroyed by order of the court. . . .

* * * * *

[200]

Judgment affirmed.

MR. JUSTICE BUTLER, dissenting.

I cannot agree with the opinion of the Court in this case. Plaintiff in error is a man of temperate habits, long accustomed to use alcoholic liquor as a beverage. He never sold or in any way illegally dealt with intoxicating liquors and has never been accused of so doing. His supply was lawfully acquired years before the passage of the [201] enactment in question (the Act of March 8, 1917) for the use of himself, his family and friends in his own home, and not for any unlawful purpose.

* * * * *

[203] Any suggestion that the destruction of such private supply lawfully acquired and held for the use of the owner in his own home is necessary for or has any relation to the suppression of sales or to the regulation of the liquor traffic or to the protection of the public from injury would be fanciful and without foundation. The facts in the case do not permit the application of the doctrine applied in *Purity Extract Co. v. Lynch*, 226 U.S. 192, 204.

To me it seems very plain that, as applied, the law is oppressive and arbitrary, and that the seizure deprived plaintiff in error of his property in violation of the due process clause of the Fourteenth Amendment. I would reverse the judgment of the state court.

Pennsylvania Railroad System v. Pennsylvania Railroad Co.

This case represented a continuation of the dispute seen earlier in the case of *Pennsylvania Railroad Company v. United States Labor Board,* 261 U.S. 72 (1923). In that case, the Court, *per* Chief Justice Taft, had upheld the power of the board to make public its findings against the railroad's unfair labor practices. In this 1925 case, the union sought to have the federal courts use their injunctive power to find the railroad in violation of section 19 of the criminal code for failing to comply with the labor board's earlier findings of unfair labor practices. The union contended that the railroad's behavior injured citizens' rights as guaranteed by law. Taft was as unsympathetic to the union's claims as he had previously been to the claims of the railroad. For Taft, it was plain what Congress had intended and what it had not intended.

Pennsylvania Railroad System and Allied Lines Federation No. 90 et al. v. Pennsylvania Railroad Company et al.

Appeal from the Circuit Court of Appeals for the Third Circuit

No. 661. Argued January 13, 1925—Decided March 2, 1925

267 U.S. 203 (1925)

[204]

MR. CHIEF JUSTICE TAFT delivered the opinion of the Court.

The Pennsylvania Railroad System and Allied Lines Federation No. 90, by its bill in equity herein against the Pennsylvania Company and its officers, continued the controversy which was considered in *Pennsylvania Railroad Company v. Labor Board,* 261 U.S. 72. . . .

The Pennsylvania Railroad System and Allied Lines Federation No. 90 is a trades union of 50,000 employees or more affiliated with the American Federation of Labor, and embracing those crafts which have to do with the mechanical part of railroad service. . . .

* * * * *

[210] The whole case for Federation No. 90 rests upon the contention that the conduct of the Company and its officers is a statutory offense in the nature of a conspiracy under the provisions of Section 19 of the Criminal Code, which provides that if two or more persons conspire to injure, oppress, threaten or intimidate any citizen in the free exercise, or enjoyment of any right or privilege secured to him by the laws of the United States, they shall be punished; and further that injunction will lie to restrain the means for promoting such conspiracy. . . .

* * * * *

[216] What the complainants here are seeking to do is to enforce by mandatory injunction a compliance with a decision of the Board, not based on the legal rights of the parties, but on its judgment as to what legal rights the disputants should surrender or abate in the public interest and in the interest of each other, to maintain harmonious relations between them necessary to the continuance of interstate commerce, and to avoid severing those relations as they would have the strict legal right to do. Such a remedy by injunction in a court, it was not the intention of Congress to provide.

The ultimate decision of the Board, it is conceded, is not compulsory, and no process is furnished to enforce it, [217] but it is urged that the preliminary steps are not the final decision, and it will make the Act meaningless and wholly ineffective if under the Act the parties may not be forced to a conference and to a contest before the Labor Board. This very point was considered by us in the *Labor Board* case and we held that the questions how the representatives of each side should be selected and whom the Board should recognize as accredited representatives were of primary importance affecting the working conditions of the railroad, and such decisions, therefore, must be regarded, although preliminary, as of the same class of decisions as those with respect to wages and ultimate working conditions. The same sanction, therefore, of publication and public opinion, exists for them and nothing else.

The Pennsylvania Company is using every endeavor to avoid compliance with the judgment and principles of the Labor Board as to the proper method of securing representatives of the whole body of its employees, it is seeking to control its employees by agreements free from the influence of an independent trade union, it is, so far as its dealings with its employees go, refusing to comply with the decisions of the Labor Board and is thus defeating the purpose of Congress. Appellants charge that the Company is attempting, by threats to discharge its employees, to secure their consent to the agreement of July 1, 1921, as to wages and working conditions agreed to by the representatives of its employees it declared elected. This is denied, though there is some evidence tending to support the charge. All these things it might do and remain within its strict legal rights after it came fully into control of its railroad property subsequent to September 1, 1920. We do not think Congress, while it would deprecate such action, intended to make it criminal or legally actionable. Therefore, the bill of complaint does not aver a conspiracy and without that, equitable relief can not be granted.

* * * * *

Decree affirmed.

Lancaster v. McCarty

McCarty sued to recover damages suffered to his property while it was being transported within the state of Texas. The issue for the Court was whether McCarty could recover damages under state law or under regulations promulgated by the Interstate Commerce Commission, the latter being more favorable to his interests. Taft, as usual in such cases, ruled in favor of federal supremacy, citing the *Shreveport* case, 234 U.S. 342 (1914), as furnishing the controlling precedent.

Lancaster et al., Receivers of the Texas & Pacific Railway, v. McCarty et al.

Error to the Court of Civil Appeals for the
Second Supreme Judicial District of the State of Texas

No. 148. Submitted December 11, 1924—Decided March 9, 1925

267 U.S. 427 (1925)

[428]

MR. CHIEF JUSTICE TAFT delivered the opinion of the Court.

This was a suit for damages in the County Court of Eastland County, Texas, by the defendants in error, partners as the Cisco Furniture Company, to recover from the plaintiffs in error, the Receivers of the Texas & Pacific Railway, $198 for injury to two rugs and to three chairs shipped by the Furniture Company from Fort Worth, Texas, over the Railway to Cisco, Texas, and $20 for attorney's fees exacted by a state statute for the delay of the Railway in allowing and paying the claim. The real issue here is whether the amount of the damages for the admitted injury should be measured by the statutory law of Texas or by the regulations of the Interstate Commerce

Commission with respect to the classification of traffic and fixing of rates, as directed by it in accordance with the decree by the Commerce Court of the United States, affirmed by this Court in *Houston & Texas Railway Co. v. United States,* 234 U.S. 342, known as the *Shreveport* case. . . .

* * * * *

[430] The *Shreveport* case began by an application of railway carriers running west from Shreveport across the Texas State line to Houston and Dallas, to set aside an order of the Interstate Commerce Commission, on the ground that it exceeded its authority. The order was made in a proceeding initiated by the Railroad Commission of Louisiana before the Commission. The complaint in that proceeding was that the carriers maintained unreasonable rates from Shreveport, Louisiana, to various points in Texas, and that the carriers, in the adjustment of their rates over their respective lines, discriminated in favor of traffic within the State of Texas and against similar traffic between Shreveport and Texas points; that Shreveport competed in business with Houston and Dallas, and that the rates from Dallas and Houston east to intermediate points in Texas were much less, according to distance, than from Shreveport westward to the same points, with conditions similar in all respects. The difference was substantial, and injuriously affected the commerce of Shreveport. The Commission found that interstate rates out of Shreveport to main Texas points were unreasonable, and it fixed maximum rates for that traffic. It also found that the rates from Houston and Dallas [431] eastward to Texas points were so low as to be a discrimination and an undue and unlawful preference against Shreveport and against its interstate commerce. Accordingly, the carriers were directed to desist from charging higher rates from Shreveport to Dallas and Houston, respectively, and intermediate points, than were contemporaneously charged for the same carriage from Dallas and Houston to Shreveport for equal distances. The Commerce Court sustained the order, and so did this Court, leaving it to the Railroad Company to bring about the equality required either by decreasing the rates from Shreveport to the Texas points between that city and Dallas and Houston, or by increasing the intrastate rates from Houston and Dallas eastward to the Texas points between those cities and Shreveport. This Western Classification, which the carrier applied in this case, was adopted by the railroads under the authority of the Interstate Commerce Commission thus sustained in the *Shreveport* case. That authority rested on the supremacy of federal authority in respect to interstate commerce. The intrastate rates fixed by the Texas State Railway Commission from Houston and Dallas eastward to Texas points were a discrimination against the interstate traffic between Shreveport and those same points; and,

therefore, it was held to be within the power of the Interstate Commerce Commission, in preventing such unlawful discrimination under the Interstate Commerce Act, to direct the railways to ignore the Texas Commission rates and to establish rates, not unduly discriminating against interstate commerce, in intrastate traffic. Such an order, of course, included classification as well as rates. The two are so bound together in the regulation of interstate commerce that the effect of both must be reasonable and without undue discrimination. The Interstate Commerce Commission, therefore, had full authority to issue this order for the adoption of the Western Classification [432] for intrastate points between Houston and Cisco, both in Texas. The conflict between the Revised Statutes of Texas and the order of the Interstate Commerce Commission can only be settled by recognition of the supremacy of the federal authority. It is plain from the agreed statements of facts that the only recovery which could be had under the Western Classification in this case was less than $60. The limitation of liability was in accordance with the second Cummins Amendment, was properly agreed to, and was binding upon the shipper as well as the carrier.

The judgment of the Court of Civil Appeals must be reversed and the cause remanded for further proceedings not inconsistent with this opinion.

Reversed.

Brooks v. United States

The Court's earlier decision in the child labor cases prompted a steady stream of challenges to other efforts by the federal government to exercise police powers via the Commerce Clause of Article I. Brooks was convicted of violating the National Motor Vehicle Theft Act of 1919 (the Dyer Act). Taft, for a unanimous Court, upheld the conviction and attempted to explain the differences between this and similar legislation, including the law struck down in *Hammer v. Dagenhart,* 247 U.S. 251 (1918).

Brooks v. United States

*Error to the District Court of the United States
for the District of South Dakota*

No. 286. Argued January 30, 1925—Decided March 9, 1925

267 U.S. 432 (1925)

[435]

MR. CHIEF JUSTICE TAFT delivered the opinion of the Court.

This is a writ of error to the District Court for the District of South Dakota brought by Rae Brooks to reverse a judgment against him of conviction under two indictments for violation of the Act of Congress, of October, 1919, known as the National Motor Vehicle Theft Act. . . .

* * * * *

[436] The objection to the Act can not be sustained. Congress can certainly regulate interstate commerce to the extent of forbidding and punishing the use of such commerce as an agency to promote immorality, dishonesty or the spread of any evil or harm to the people of other States from the State of origin. In doing this it is merely exercising the police power, for the benefit of the public, [437] within the field of interstate commerce. *Gloucester Ferry Co. v. Pennsylvania,* 114 U.S. 196, 215. In *Reid v. Colorado,* 187 U.S. 137, it was held that Congress could pass a law excluding diseased stock from interstate commerce in order to prevent its use in such a way as thereby to injure the stock of other States. In the *Lottery* case, 188 U.S. 321, it was held that Congress might pass a law punishing the transmission of lottery tickets from one State to another, in order to prevent the carriage of those tickets to be sold in other States and thus demoralize, through a spread of the gambling habit, individuals who were likely to purchase. In *Hipopolite Egg Co. v. United States,* 220 U.S. 45, it was held that it was within the regulatory power of Congress to punish the transportation in interstate commerce of adulterated articles which, if sold in other States than the one from which they were transported, would deceive or injure persons who purchased such articles. In *Hoke v. United States,* 227 U.S. 308, and *Caminetti v. United States,* 242 U.S. 470, the so-called White Slave Traffic Act, which was construed to punish any person engaged in enticing a woman from one State to another for immoral ends, whether for commercial purposes or otherwise, was valid because it was intended to prevent the use of interstate commerce to facilitate prostitution or concubinage, and other forms of immorality. In *Clark Distilling Co. v. Western Maryland Railway Co.,* 242 U.S. 311, it was held that Congress had power to forbid the introduction of intoxicating liquors into any State in which their use was prohibited, in order to prevent the use of interstate commerce to promote that which was illegal in the State. In *Weber v. Freed,* 239 U.S. 325, it was held that Congress had power to prohibit the

importation of pictorial representations of prize fights designed for public exhibition, because of the demoralizing effect of such exhibitions in the State of destination.

[438] In *Hammer v. Dagenhart,* 247 U.S. 251, it was held that a federal law forbidding the transportation of articles manufactured by child labor in one State to another was invalid, because it was really not a regulation of interstate commerce but a congressional attempt to regulate labor in the State of origin, by an embargo on its external trade. Articles made by child labor and transported into other States were harmless, and could be properly transported without injuring any person who either bought or used them. In referring to the cases already cited, upon which the argument for the validity of the Child Labor Act was based, this Court pointed out that, in each of them, the use of interstate commerce had contributed to the accomplishment of harmful results to people of other States, and that the congressional power over interstate transportation in such cases could only be effectively exercised by prohibiting it. The clear distinction between authorities first cited and the *Child Labor* case leaves no doubt where the right lies in this case. It is known of all men that the radical change in transportation of persons and goods effected by the introduction of the automobile, the speed with which it moves, and the ease with which evil-minded persons can avoid capture, have greatly encouraged and increased crimes. One of the crimes which have been encouraged is the theft of the automobiles themselves and their immediate transportation to places remote from homes of the owners. Elaborately organized conspiracies for the theft of automobiles and the spiriting them away into some other State, and their sale or other disposition far away from the owner and his neighborhood, have roused Congress to devise some method for defeating the success of these widely spread schemes of larceny. The quick passage of the machines into another State helps to conceal the trail of the thieves, gets the stolen property into another police jurisdiction [439] and facilitates the finding of a safer place in which to dispose of the booty at a good price. This is a gross misuse of interstate commerce. Congress may properly punish such interstate transportation by any one with knowledge of the theft, because of its harmful result and its defeat of the property rights of those whose machines against their will are taken into other jurisdictions.

* * * * *

[441] *Affirmed.*

Barclay & Co. v. Edwards

The adoption of the federal income tax prompted numerous suits. In this case, Chief Justice Taft expounded on the broad power to tax he viewed the federal government as possessing.

Barclay & Company, Incorporated, v. Edwards, Collector of Internal Revenue for the Second District of New York

Error to the District Court of the United States for the Southern District of New York

No. 547. Argued November 24, 1924—Decided December 15, 1924

267 U.S. 442 (1924)

[446]

MR. CHIEF JUSTICE TAFT delivered the opinion of the Court.

On December 15, 1924, Mr. Justice McKenna delivered the opinion of this Court in the case of the National Paper and Type Company against Frank K. Bowers, Collector, [266 U.S. 373] No. 320 of the present Term. That case was heard at the same time with this. They were suits to recover taxes which it was claimed had been illegally collected, for the reason that the statutes under which they had been exacted deprived the taxpayers of their property without due process of law. The statute attacked in No. 320 was the income tax of 1921, that in this case was the income tax of 1918.

The plaintiffs in the two cases were corporations of this country engaged in the business of the purchase and manufacture of personal property within the United States, and the sale thereof without the United [447] States. Their objection to the taxes, both of 1921 and of 1918, was that they were subjected to a tax on all of their net income, including profits made by them in the sale of their goods abroad, while foreign corporations, engaged in the same business of buying and manufacturing goods in this country and selling them abroad, were not taxed upon their whole net income but were exempted from a tax on all or a part of it.

Another objection to the tax was that the tax in both instances was a tax on exports. That was disposed of by this Court in opinion No. 320 by reference to the case of *Peck & Company v. Lowe*, 247 U.S. 165.

* * * * *

[450] The power of Congress in levying taxes is very wide, and where a classification is made of taxpayers that is reasonable, and not merely arbitrary and capricious, the Fifth Amendment can not apply. As this Court said, speaking of the taxing power of Congress, in *Evans v. Gore,* 253 U.S. 245, 256: "It may be applied to every object within its range 'in such measure as Congress may determine'; enables that body 'to select one calling and omit another, to tax one class of property and to forbear to tax another'; and may be applied in different ways to different objects so long as there is 'geographical uniformity' in the duties, imposts and excises imposed. *McCulloch v. Maryland,* 4 Wheat. 316, 431. . . .

[451] The power of Congress to make a difference between the tax on foreign corporations and that on domestic corporations is not measured by the same rule as that for determining whether taxes imposed by one State upon the profits of a manufacturing corporation are an imposition of tax upon a subject matter not within the jurisdiction of the taxing State. . . . Considerations of policy toward foreign countries may very well justify an exemption of the foreign corporations from taxes that might legitimately be imposed on them, but which Congress does not think it wise to exact. Such considerations justify a different classification of foreign corporations doing business in the United States, either of manufacture or of purchase, and making profit out of that business in other countries, from that which would apply to its own corporations. The injustice thought to be worked upon domestic corporations engaged in sales abroad, by a different classification, for purposes of taxation, of foreign corporations similarly engaged, is an argument, not for the constitutional invalidity of the law before a court, but for its repeal before Congress.

The opinion of Mr. Justice McKenna applying the same principles in this case to those applied in No. 320 was entirely justified, and the petition for rehearing is

Overruled.

Western & Atlantic Railroad v. Georgia Public Service Commission

Western & Atlantic Railroad sought to have a decision by the Georgia Public Service Commission overturned on the grounds that only the Interstate Commerce Commission could rule in the situation. Taft disagreed, finding that such an argument was contrary to the federal Transportation Act of 1920.

Western & Atlantic Railroad v. Georgia Public Service Commission et al.

Appeal from the District Court of the United States for the Northern District of Georgia

No. 209. Argued January 20, 1925—Decided April 13, 1925

267 U.S. 493 (1925)

[494]

MR. CHIEF JUSTICE TAFT delivered the opinion of the Court.

The Western & Atlantic Railroad Company, an interstate common carrier, filed this bill in the District Court of the United States for the Northern District of Georgia against the Georgia Public Service Commission and its members, to enjoin the enforcement of an order of the Commission requiring the railroad to furnish switching service on an industrial siding to the National Bonded Warehouse, Inc., of Atlanta, Georgia.

* * * * *

On August 2, 1923, the Railroad Company notified the Warehouse Company, that unless it signed a standard form of contract in respect to the sidetrack, its use and maintenance, which had been submitted to it, the service would be discontinued after August 15th. The Warehouse Company made complaint to the Public Service Commission. The Commission advised the Railroad Company that no application from the Company had been made to the Commission for such authority, which, under its Rule 14, was necessary before the service could be discontinued. However, on August 28th a full hearing was held by the Commission with the parties present, and as a result of such hearing it was ordered that effective [495] immediately on receipt of the order, the Railroad Company should restore the service. . . .

* * * * *

The bill further alleges that the side track is out of repair and that in order to put it in proper condition it will require an expenditure of $440, that the receipts from the switching are but a small part of the cost of it and that enforced compliance with the order will thus deprive the Company of its property without due process of law.

* * * * *

[496] It is said that the requirement of the continuance of the service deprived the Company of its property without due process of law, in viola-

tion of the Fourteenth Amendment, because the service rendered by the sidetrack was much greater in out-of-pocket cost than the compensation. This can not be sustained. The service has been rendered for years. It was a voluntary arrangement, and under its statutory powers (§ 2664, Georgia Code, 1910) was made irrevocable by the Public Service Commission under Rule 14, except by consent of the Commission. . . .

[497] It seems to be the contention of the Company that, since 85 per cent. of the business done on the side track is interstate commerce, the power to order its establishment or abandonment is vested in the Interstate Commerce Commission, and that the state commission is without authority in the premises. Such a claim is in the teeth of the Transportation Act of 1920, 41 Stat. 456, c. 91, § 402, par. 22, which provides that the authority of the commission conferred by § 402 over the extension or abandonment of interstate railway lines shall not extend to the construction of spur industrial or side tracks. See *Railroad Commission v. Southern Pacific Co.*, 264 U.S. 331, 345.

The question whether the continuance of the service on this industrial track violates the Interstate Commerce Act as unduly discriminatory, is one that involves issues not primarily for the courts, but is for the Interstate Commerce Commission. It requires a consideration by experts of the benefit of the use of such a siding as compared with that of other sidings, in connection with the rates in interstate commerce, to determine whether there is undue discrimination between shippers. The Railroad Company is therefore in no position to appeal to the courts on this ground until it has invoked the investigation and decision of the Interstate Commerce Commission upon the concrete facts in a proper manner. . . .

[498] *Affirmed.*

Steele v. United States No. 1

Steele arose from the enforcement by federal agents of the Volstead Act and called upon the Court to pass on the requirements for "probable cause," particularity, and reasonableness in conducting searches.

Steele v. United States No. 1

*Appeal from the District Court of the United States
for the Southern District of New York*

No. 235. Argued March 11, 1925—Decided April 13, 1925

267 U.S. 498 (1925)

[499]

MR. CHIEF JUSTICE TAFT delivered the opinion of the Court.

This is an appeal, under § 238 of the Judicial Code, direct from the District Court, being a case involving the application of the Federal Constitution. The judgment complained of denied a petition of Steele for an order vacating a search warrant, by authority of which Steele's premises were searched and a large amount of whiskey and other intoxicating liquor was found and seized. He contends that the search warrant violated the Fourth Amendment, because not issued upon probable cause, and not particularly describing the place to be searched or the property to be seized; and because the search conducted under the warrant was unreasonable. . . .

* * * * *

[502] The facts developed before the Commissioner on hearing this petition for return of the seized goods were these: Einstein and Moe Smith were prohibition agents. They saw a truck depositing cases in a garage on the opposite side of 46th Street from where they were. Einstein crossed the street and saw they were cases stenciled as whiskey. Einstein left his companion to remain in the neighborhood until he could get the warrant, and in somewhat more than an hour returned with it and made the seizure. The building searched was a four-story building in New York City on the south side of West 46th Street, with a sign on it: "Indian Head Auto Truck Service— Indian Head Storage Warehouse, No. 609 and 611." It was all under lease to Steele. It was entered by three entrances from the street, one on the 609 side, which is used, and which leads to a staircase running up to the four floors. On the 611 side there is another staircase of a similar character, which is closed, and in the middle of the building is an automobile entrance from the street into a garage, and opposite to the entrance on the south side is an elevator reaching to the four stories, of sufficient size to take up a Ford machine. There is no partition between 611 and 609 on the ground or garage floor, and there were only partial partitions above, and none which prevented access to the elevator on any floor from either the 609 or 611 side. The evidence left no doubt that, though the building had two numbers, the garage business covering the whole first floor and the storage business above were of such a character and so related to the elevator that there was no real [503] division in fact or in use of the building into separate halves. The places searched and in which the liquor was found were all rooms connected

with the garage by the elevator. One of them was a room on the second floor with a door open toward the elevator, in which, when Einstein made his search, three men were bottling and corking whiskey. There was a room on one of the floors, flimsily boarded off, in which an employee had a cot and a cook stove. The prohibition agents seized 150 cases of whiskey, 92 bags of whiskey, and one 5-gallon can of alcohol, on the third floor on the 609 side. On the second floor, 33 cases of gin were seized on the 609 side and six 5-gallon jugs of whiskey, 33 cases of gin, 102 quarts of whiskey, and two 50-gallon barrels of whiskey, and a corking machine, were taken on the 611 side of the building.

The description of the building as a garage and for business purposes at 611 W. 46th Street clearly indicated the whole building as the place intended to be searched. It is enough if the description is such that the officer with a search warrant can with reason able effort ascertain and identify the place intended. . . .

Nor did the search go too far. A warrant was applied for to search any building or rooms connected or used in connection with the garage, or the basement or subcellar beneath the same. It is quite evident that the elevator of the garage connected it with every floor and room in the building and was intended to be used with it.

The attempt to give the building the character of a dwelling house by reason of the fact that an employee slept and cooked in a room on one of the floors was of [504] course futile. Section 25 of the Prohibition Act forbids the search of any private dwelling unless it is used for the unlawful sale of intoxicating liquor, or unless it is in part used for some business purpose, such as a store, shop, saloon, restaurant, hotel or boarding house. It provides that "private dwelling" is to be construed to include the room or rooms used and occupied not transiently but solely as a residence in an apartment house, hotel or boarding house. Certainly the room occupied in this case was not a private dwelling within these descriptions, but more than this, it was not searched and no liquor was found in it. . . .

* * * * *

Finally it is said there was no probable cause for the warrant and the seizure. Einstein, a man of experience in such prosecutions and in such seizures, saw the name "whiskey" stenciled on cases and said they looked like whiskey cases. He ascertained by his own investigation of the official records that there was no permit for the legal storage of whiskey on these premises. In a recent case we have had occasion to lay down what is probable cause for a search. *Carroll v. United States*, 267 U.S. 132. "If the facts and circumstances before the officer are such as to warrant a man of prudence and caution in [505] believing that the offense has been committed, it is sufficient." What Einstein saw and ascertained was quite sufficient to warrant a man of prudence and caution and his experience in believing that the offense had been committed of possessing illegally whiskey and intoxicating liquor, and that it was in the building he described.

The search warrant fully complied with the statutory and constitutional requirements as set forth above, the liquor was lawfully seized and the District Court rightly held that it should not be returned.

The decree is affirmed.

Affirmed.

Steele v. United States No. 2

In addition to the Fourth Amendment issues raised in the previous case, *Steele No. 2* raised the issue of whether Prohibition agents were "civil officers" of the United States. The Court found that they were.

Steele v. United States No. 2

Error to the District Court of the United States for the Southern District of New York

No. 636. Argued March 11, 1925—Decided April 13, 1925

267 U.S. 505 (1925)

[506]

MR. CHIEF JUSTICE TAFT delivered the opinion of the Court.

. . . In addition to the grounds urged in the last case, the validity of seizure is attacked because the search warrant was issued to a general prohibition agent, when under § 6 of Title XI of the Espionage Act of June 15, 1917, (c. 30, 40 Stat. 217, 228), such a warrant must be issued "to a civil officer of the United States duly authorized to enforce or assist in enforcing any law thereof."

The argument is that the prohibition agent is appointed by the Commissioner of Internal Revenue, and therefore is only an employee and not a civil officer of the government in the constitutional sense, because such an officer under Article 2, Section 2 of the Constitution [507] can only be appointed either by the President and the Senate, the President alone, the courts of law or the heads of departments.

* * * * *

. . . We think that the expression "civil officer of the United States duly authorized to enforce, or assist in enforcing, any law thereof," as used in the Espionage Act, does not mean an officer in the constitutional sense; that Congress in incorporating the provision in § 25, Title II, of the National Prohibition Act, did not so construe it and had no intention thus to limit persons authorized to receive and serve search warrants. It is quite true that the words "officer of the United States," when employed in the statutes of the United States, is to be taken usually to have the limited constitutional meaning. *Burnap v. United States,* 252 U.S. 512; *United States v. Mouat,* 124 U.S. 303; *United States v. Smith,* 124 U.S. 525. But we find that this Court in consideration of the context has sometimes given it an enlarged meaning and has found it to include others than those appointed by the President, heads of departments, and courts. . . .

* * * * *

[510] The question whether a prohibition agent has the power and right to serve a search warrant as provided in the Espionage Act, and § 25 of Title II of the National Prohibition Act, has led to some difference of opinion among the judges of the Circuit Courts of Appeals and also of the District Courts, but the weight of authority as indicated by the decisions is strongly in favor of the broader construction which vests the power and duty to receive and serve a search warrant in prohibition agents appointed by the Commissioner of Internal Revenue.

* * * * *

[511] The judgment of the District Court is affirmed.

Affirmed.

Cooke v. United States

The power of judges to punish for contempt of court is seen as a necessary concomitant to judicial independence. According to Taft, however, this power is not without limits. In this particular case the grounds for contempt were found in a letter written by Cooke to a federal judge. Taft believed that the fact that the contempt was made in private and not in open court gave Cooke the right to present a "defense by witnesses and argument."

Cooke v. United States

Certiorari to the Circuit Court of Appeals for the Fifth Circuit

No. 311. Argued March 20, 1925—Decided April 13, 1925

267 U.S. 517 (1925)

[532]
MR. CHIEF JUSTICE TAFT, after stating the case as above, delivered the opinion of the Court.

The first objection to the sentence of the court, made on behalf of the petitioner, is that the letter written to the judge is not a contempt of the court. . . .

* * * * *

[533] It is said that all that the petitioner intended to do by this letter was to advise the court of the desire of his client to have another judge try the four cases yet to be heard, and of his own desire to avoid the necessity of filing an affidavit of bias under the above section in those cases by inducing the regular judge voluntarily to withdraw. Had the letter contained no more than this, we agree with the Circuit Court of Appeals that it would not have been improper.

But we also agree with that court that the letter as written did more than this. The letter was written the morning after the verdict in the heat of the petitioner's evident indignation at the judge's conduct of the case and the verdict. . . .

[534] . . . Though the writer addressed the judge throughout as "Your Honor," this did not conceal but emphasized the personal reflection intended. The expression of disappointed hope that the judge was big enough and broad enough to overcome his personal prejudice against petitioner's client and that the client would have the privilege of rebutting the whispered slanders to which the judge had lent his ear, and the declaration that his confidence in the judge had been rudely shattered, were personally condemnatory and were calculated to stir the judge's resentment and anger. Considering the circumstances and the fact that the case was still before the judge, but without intending to foreclose the right of the petitioner to be heard

with witnesses and argument on this issue when given an opportunity, we agree with the Circuit Court of Appeals that the letter was contemptuous.

But while we reach this conclusion, we are far from approving the course of the judge in the procedure, or absence of it, adopted by him in sentencing the petitioner. He treated the case as if the objectionable words had been uttered against him in open court.

To preserve order in the court room for the proper conduct of business, the court must act instantly to suppress disturbance or violence or physical obstruction or disrespect to the court when occurring in open court. There is no need of evidence or assistance of counsel before punishment, because the court has seen the offense. Such summary vindication of the court's dignity and authority is necessary. It has always been so in the courts of the common law and the punishment imposed is due process of law. Such a case had great consideration in the decision of this Court in *Ex parte Terry,* 128 U.S. 289. It was there held that a court of the United States upon the commission of a contempt in open court [535] might upon its own knowledge of the facts without further proof, without issue or trial, and without hearing an explanation of the motives of the offender, immediately proceed to determine whether the facts justified punishment and to inflict such punishment as was fitting under the law.

The important distinction between the *Terry* case and the one at bar is that this contempt was not in open court. . . .

* * * * *

[536] When the contempt is not in open court, however, there is no such right or reason in dispensing with the necessity of charges and the opportunity of the accused to present his defense by witnesses and argument. . . .

* * * * *

[537] Due process of law, therefore, in the prosecution of contempt, except of that committed in open court, that the accused should be advised of the charges and have a reasonable opportunity to meet them by way of defense or explanation. We think this includes the assistance of counsel, if requested, and the right to call witnesses to give testimony, relevant either to the issue of complete exculpation or in extenuation of the offense and in mitigation of the penalty to be imposed. See *Hollingsworth v. Duane,* 12 Fed. Cases 359, 360; *In re Stewart,* 118 La. 827; *Ex parte Clark,* 208 Mo. 121.

The proceeding in this case was not conducted in accordance with the foregoing principles. . . .

After the court elicited from the petitioner the admission that he had written the letter, the court refused him time to secure and consult counsel, prepare his defense and call witnesses, and this although the court itself [538] had taken time to call in counsel as a friend of the court. The presence of the United States District Attorney also was secured by the court on the ground that it was a criminal case.

The court proceeded on the theory that the admission that the petitioner had written the letter foreclosed evidence or argument. In cases like this, where the intention with which acts of contempt have been committed must necessarily and properly have an important bearing on the degree of guilt and the penalty which should be imposed, the court can not exclude evidence in mitigation. It is a proper part of the defense. There was a suggestion in one of the remarks of the petitioner to the court that, while he had dictated the letter he had not read it carefully, and that he had trusted to the advice of his partner in sending it; but he was not given a chance to call witnesses or to make a full statement on this point.

* * * * *

[540] Judgment of the Circuit Court of Appeals is reversed and the case is remanded to the District Court for further proceedings in conformity with this opinion.

Reversed.

Omitted Taft Opinions

Shewan & Sons v. United States, 267 U.S. 86 (1925)—admiralty case.

Nahmeh v. United States, 267 U.S. 122 (1925)—admiralty case.

Merchants Liability Co. v. Smart, 267 U.S. 126 (1925)—challenge to state insurance law.

Work v. Rives, 267 U.S. 175—writ of *mandamus* not applicable to discretionary act of secretary of the interior.

Work v. Chestatee Corp., 267 U.S. 185 (1925)—same as above.

Pennsylvania Brotherhood of Railway Clerks v. Pennsylvania Railroad, 267 U.S. 219—identical to 267 U.S. 203.

Wells v. Bodkin, 267 U.S. 474 (1925)—estate issue.

Bohler v. Callaway, 267 U.S. 479 (1925)—jurisdiction of federal court in state tax assessment issue.

Santa Fe Pacific Railroad Company v. Work, 267 U.S. 571 (1925)—land rights.

VOLUME 268

Coronado Coal Co. v. United Mine Workers

In the first *Coronado* case, 259 U.S. 344 (1922), the Court had ruled that trade unions could be sued under sections 7 and 8 of the Sherman Antitrust Act. Armed with this decision, the Coronado Coal Company pressed on with its case, introducing further evidence that the United Mine Workers had intended to impede the interstate shipment of coal. In reaching his decision, Taft had to grapple with whether the facts demonstrated that the union's actions posed a remote or indirect threat to interstate commerce, in which case there was no violation of federal law, or whether there was evidence that the destruction of property by the union was intended to impair interstate commerce. If it could be so shown, then he concluded that the union could be held to be in violation of the antitrust act.

Coronado Coal Company et al. v. United Mine Workers of America et al.

Error to the Circuit Court of Appeals for the Eighth Circuit

No. 671. Argued January 7, 1925—Decided May 25, 1925

268 U.S. 295 (1925)

[296]

MR. CHIEF JUSTICE TAFT delivered the opinion of the Court.

This is a suit for damages for the effect of an alleged conspiracy of the defendants unlawfully to restrain and prevent plaintiffs' interstate trade in coal in violation of the first and second sections of the Federal Anti-Trust Act. The charge is that the defendants, in 1914, for the purpose of consummating the conspiracy, destroyed valuable mining properties of the plaintiffs. Treble damages and an attorney's fee are asked under the seventh section of the Act. . . . The original [297] complaint was filed in September, 1914. It was demurred to, and the demurrer sustained. On error in the Court of Appeals the ruling was reversed. *Dowd v. United Mine Workers of America*, 235 Fed. 1. The case then came on for trial on the third amended complaint and the answers of the defendants. The trial resulted in a verdict of $200,000 for the plaintiffs, which was trebled by the court, and a counsel fee of $25,000 and interest to the date of the judgment were added. The Court of Appeals reversed the judgment as to interest, but in other respects affirmed it. 258 Fed. 829. On error from this Court under § 241 of the Judicial Code, the judgments of both courts were reversed, and the cause remanded to the District Court for further proceedings. The opinion is reported in 259th United States, 344. The new trial, in October, 1923, resulted in a directed verdict and judgment for the defendants, which was affirmed by the Circuit Court of Appeals. The case is here on error for a second time.

In our previous opinion we held that the International Union, known as the United Mine Workers of America, the union known as United Mine Workers, District No. 21, and the subordinate local unions which were made defendants, were, though unincorporated associations, subject to suit under the Anti-Trust Act, but that there was not sufficient evidence to go to the jury to show participation by the International Union in the conspiracy and the wrongs done. We found evidence tending to show that District No. 21 and other defendants were engaged in the conspiracy and the destruction of the property, but not enough to show an intentional restraint of interstate trade and a violation of the Anti-Trust Act. The plaintiffs contend that they have now supplied the links lacking at the first trial against each of the principal defendants.

[298] . . . District No. 21 was a regional organization of the United Mine Workers which included Arkansas, Texas and Oklahoma. Mr. Bache as manager of the plaintiffs' mines had been operating them for a number of years with union labor and under a District No. 21 contract and scale of wages, which did not expire until July 1, 1914. In March of that year he determined to run his mines thereafter on a non-union or open basis, and notified Pete Stewart, the president of the District No. 21, that he intended to do so. He shut down his mines and prepared to open them on an open shop basis on April 6th. He anticipated trouble. He employed three guards from the Burns Detective Agency and a number of others to aid him. He bought a number of Winchester rifles and ammunition, and surrounded his principal mining plant at Prairie Creek, No. 4, with cables strung on posts. . . .

The people in all that part of the country were urged by the members of the local unions to come to a meeting at the school house, a short distance from the Prairie Creek mine, for a public protest. The meeting appointed a committee to visit the superintendent and insist that the mine remain a union mine. The guards, directed not to use their guns save to defend their own lives, were at the mercy of the union miners, who assaulted them, took their guns away and injured a number of them. The employees deserted the mine, which filled with water upon the stopping of the pumps. One of the crowd went up to the top of the coal tipple and planted a flag on which was the legend, "This is a union man's country."

* * * * *

[299] First. Is there any evidence in the present record tending to show that the International Union of the United Mine Workers participated?

* * * * *

[300] It does not appear that the International Convention or Executive Board ever authorized this strike or took any part in the preparation for it or in its maintenance, or that they ratified it by paying any of the expenses. It came within the definition of a local strike in the constitutions of both the national and district organizations. . . .

There were introduced at both trials long accounts of speeches and votes at national conventions of the International Union and meetings between union operators and representatives of the International Union from 1898 to 1914, revealing a constant effort on the part of the [301] operators to force wages down to meet the competition of non-union mines, accompanied by assurances by the union representatives that they would do everything to unionize the competing non-union mines and enable the union mine operators to maintain the scale insisted on.

We thought at the first hearing and we think now that none of this evidence tends to establish the participation of the International in the Prairie Creek strike and disturbances.

The new evidence adduced for the purpose is chiefly the testimony of one James P. McNamara. He was the secretary of Local Union No. 1526 at Hartford. . . .

His testimony at the second trial was that in May, 1914, between the riot of April and the July battle, he went to Fort Smith to see Pete Stewart, the President of District No. 21, who was ill; that Stewart told him that he had been to Kansas City and had a talk with White, the International President, and that they had arranged a plan there to prevent Bache from producing coal.

* * * * *

[303] McNamara further testified that he saw between three and four hundred guns in boxes at Hartford and that part of them were distributed to the union miners and part returned to the secretary of District No. 21 at McAlester, Oklahoma.

* * * * *

[304] Giving the fullest credence to all that McNamara says, it is clear that White did not intend by what he did to make the Prairie Creek difficulty a national affair. The International Board had not approved as the constitution required that they should do in order to make it so. It is quite true that White himself personally can be held as a defendant, if McNamara's evidence is to be believed, for urging and abetting the destruction of the plaintiffs' property; but according to McNamara's testimony, repeated by him several times, White was particular to insist that he did not wish to be regarded as acting for the International in the matter or to involve it in the Prairie Creek difficulties. In our previous opinion we held that a trades-union, organized as effectively as this United Mine Workers' organization was, might be held liable, and all its funds raised for the purpose of strikes might be levied upon to pay damages suffered through illegal methods in carrying them on; but certainly it must be clearly shown in order to impose such a liability on an association of 450,000 men that what was done was done by their agents in accordance with their fundamental agreement of association.

* * * * *

[305] The action of the trial court in its direction of a verdict for the defendant, the International Union, must be affirmed.

Second. The tendency of the evidence to show that District No. 21 through its authorized leaders and agents and certain of its subordinate local unions organized and carried through the two attacks of April 6th and July 17th is so clear that it does not need further discussion. The only issue is whether the outrages, destruction and crimes committed were intentionally directed toward a restraint of interstate commerce. On the first trial we held that the evidence did not show this. . . .

The hostility of the head of District No. 21 and that of his men seemed sufficiently aroused by the coming of non-union men into that local community, by Mr. Bache's alleged breach of his contract with District No. 21 in employing non-union men three months before it expired, by his charged evasion of it through a manipulation of his numerous corporations, by his advertised anticipation of trespass and violence in his warning notices, in his enclosing his mining premises with a cable, and in stationing guards with guns to defend them. These preparations in the heart of a territory that had been completely unionized for years were likely to stir a bitterness of spirit in the neighborhood. Bache [306] had himself foreseen such a spirit when he took part in the formulation of a letter to his stockholders for his superintendent to sign, in which it was said: "To do this means a bitter fight, but in my opinion it can be accomplished by proper organization." He testified that he was entering into a matter he knew was perilous and dangerous to his companies. In view of these circumstances, we said in the previous opinion

"Nothing of this is recited to justify in the slightest the lawlessness and outrages committed, but only to point out that as it was a local strike within the meaning of the International and District constitutions, so it was in fact a local strike, local in its origin and motive, local in its waging, and local in its felonious and murderous ending."

Were we concerned only with the riot of April 6th, we should reach the same conclusion now; but at the second trial plaintiffs were able to present a large amount of new evidence as to the attitude and purpose of the leaders and members of District No. 21. . . .

Part of the new evidence was an extract from the convention proceedings of District No. 21 at Fort Smith, Arkansas, in February, 1914, in which the delegates discussed the difficulties presented in their maintenance of the union scale in Arkansas, Oklahoma and Texas because of the keen competition from the non-union fields of Southern Colorado and the non-union fields of the South in Alabama and Tennessee.

* * * * *

[308] In addition to this, the testimony of McNamara, already discussed, while ineffective to establish the complicity of the International Union with this conspiracy, contains much, if credited, from which the jury could reasonably infer that the purpose of the union miners in District No. 21 and the local unions engaged in the plan was to destroy the power of the owners and lessees of the Bache-Denman mines to send their output into interstate commerce to compete with that of union mines in Oklahoma, in Kansas, in Louisiana markets and elsewhere. It appeared that 80 per cent. of all the product of the mines in Sebastian County went into other States.

* * * * *

[310] The mere reduction in the supply of an article to be shipped in interstate commerce by the illegal or tortious prevention of its manufacture or production is ordinarily an indirect and remote obstruction to that commerce. But when the intent of those unlawfully preventing the manufacture or production is shown to be to restrain or control the supply entering and moving in interstate commerce, or the price of it in interstate markets, their action is a direct violation of the Anti-Trust Act. *United Mine Workers v. Coronado Co.,* 259 U.S. 344, 408, 409; *United Leather Workers v. Herkert,* 265 U.S. 457, 471; *Industrial Association v. United States, ante,* p. 64. We think there was substantial evidence at the second trial in this case tending to show

that the purpose of the destruction of the mines was to stop the production of non-union coal and prevent its shipment to markets of other States than Arkansas, where it would by competition tend to reduce the price of the commodity and affect injuriously the maintenance of wages for union labor in competing mines, and that the direction by the District Judge to return a verdict for the defendants other than the International Union was erroneous.

We affirm the judgment of the District Court and the Circuit Court of Appeals in favor of the International Union of United Mine Workers of America, and reverse that in favor of District No. 21 and the other local unions and the individual defendants and remand the cause as to them for a new trial.

Affirmed in part and reversed in part.

Selzman v. United States

The 1920s witnessed efforts by a thirsty public to explore the use of alcoholic beverages that had not been on the menu prior to Prohibition. Denatured alcohol was one such drink. Selzman argued that control of denatured alcohol was reserved to the states since it was not usable as a beverage. The federal authorities disagreed, and Chief Justice Taft concurred, giving a broad reading to the scope of federal legislation enacted under the terms of the Eighteenth Amendment.

Selzman v. United States

Error to the United States District Court for the Northern District of Ohio

No. 998. Submitted April 27, 1925—Decided June 1, 1925

268 U.S. 466 (1925)

[466]

MR. CHIEF JUSTICE TAFT delivered the opinion of the Court.

Meyer Selzman was tried and convicted on two indictments in the District Court. The first charged him, Martin Bracker, Harry Porter and others with a violation of § 37 of the Criminal Code in conspiring to violate [467] § 15, Title III, of the National Prohibition Act (enacted October 28, 1919, c. 85, 41 Stat. 305) and the regulations relating to the manufacture and distribution of industrial alcohol prescribed by the Commissioner of Internal Revenue, pursuant to the provisions of Title III of the Act. . . .

* * * * *

It is said that the Eighteenth Amendment prohibits the manufacture, sale and transportation of intoxicating liquor for beverage purposes only, and that, as denatured alcohol is not usable as a beverage, the amendment does not give to Congress authority to prevent or regulate its sale, and that such authority remains with the States and is within their police power exclusively.

* * * * *

[468] The argument is without force.

In order that the uses of alcohol might not be lost to the arts by reason of the then heavy internal revenue tax, Congress made provisions (Act of June 7, 1906, c. 3047, 34 Stat. 217, Act of March 2, 1907, c. 2571, 34 Stat. 1250, and Act of October 3, 1913, c. 16, § IV, N, subsect. 2, 38 Stat. 114, 199) by which alcohol was made tax free if denatured so that it could not be used for a beverage and evade the federal tax on the potable article. Any attempt to recover the alcohol thus denatured for beverage purposes was punished. The plaintiff in error's suggestion is that this was then within the power of Congress because necessary to protect its power of levying an excise tax on liquor under Section 8, Art. 1, of the Constitution; but that as there is now no tax upon alcohol to protect, denatured alcohol has passed out of the domain of Congressional action. But surely the denaturing of alcohol is now as necessary in maintaining its use in the arts and prohibiting its use as a beverage, as it was formerly needed to permit its use in the arts and to prevent its consumption as a beverage without paying the tax. The power of the Federal Government, granted by the Eighteenth Amendment, to enforce the prohibition of the manufacture, sale and transportation of intoxicating liquor carries with it power to enact any legislative [469] measures reasonably adapted to promote the purpose. The denaturing in order to render the making and sale of industrial alcohol compatible with the enforcement of prohibition of alcohol for beverage purposes is not always effective. The ignorance of some, the craving and the hardihood of others, and the fraud and cupidity of still others, often tend to defeat its object. It helps the main purpose of the Amendment, therefore, to hedge about the making and disposition of the denatured article every reasonable precaution and penalty to prevent the proper industrial use of it from being perverted to drinking it. The conclusion is fully supported by the decisions of this Court in *Jacob Ruppert v. Cafey,* 251 U.S. 264, 282, and *National Prohibition Cases,* 253 U.S. 350, Par. 11. See also *Huth v. United States,* 295 Fed. 35, 38.

Affirmed.

Maple Flooring Manufacturing Ass'n v. United States

Maple Flooring triggered one of the rare Taft dissents. The Maple Flooring Manufacturing Association had been charged with a violation of the Sherman Act. The majority, speaking though Associate Justice Harlan Fiske Stone, reversed the conviction. Taft, along with Justices Sanford and McReynolds, dissented. Stone's opinion represented a reversal of an earlier precedent from which Justices Holmes and Brandeis had dissented. It was Stone's first opinion since joining the Court and earned him praise from both of the earlier dissenters: "Holmes called it 'good sense and good law.'"[1]

Note

1. Mason, *Stone,* 219.

Maple Flooring Manufacturers Association et al. v. United States

Appeal from the District Court of the United States for the Western District of Michigan

No. 342. Argued December 1, 2, 1924; reargued March 3, 1925—Decided June 1, 1925

268 U.S. 563 (1925)

[565]

MR. JUSTICE STONE delivered the opinion of the Court.

By bill in equity filed March 5, 1923, the United States asked an injunction restraining the defendants, who are appellants here, from violating § 1 of the Act of Congress of July 2, 1890, entitled, "An Act to Protect Trade and Commerce Against Unlawful Restraints and Monopolies" (c. 647, 26 Stat. 209), commonly known as the Sherman Act.

The defendants are the Maple Flooring Manufacturers Association, an unincorporated "trade association"; twenty-two corporate defendants, members of the Association, engaged in the business of selling and shipping maple, beech and birch flooring in interstate commerce. . . .

* * * * *

[586] We decide only that trade associations or combinations of persons or corporations which openly and fairly gather and disseminate information

as to the cost of their product, the volume of production, the actual price which the product has brought in past transactions, stocks of merchandise on hand, approximate cost of transportation from the principal point of shipment to the points of consumption, as did these defendants, and who, as they did, meet and discuss such information and statistics without however reaching or attempting to reach any agreement or any concerted action with respect to prices or production or restraining competition, do not thereby engage in unlawful restraint of commerce.

The decree of the District Court is reversed.

MR. CHIEF JUSTICE TAFT and MR. JUSTICE SANFORD dissent from the opinions of the majority of the Court in these two cases on the ground that in their judgment the evidence in each case brings it substantially within the rules stated in the *American Column Co.* and *American Linseed Oil Co.* cases, the authority of which, as they understand, is not questioned in the opinions of the majority of the Court.

[587] The separate opinion of MR. JUSTICE MCREYNOLDS.

These causes disclose carefully developed plans to cut down normal competition in interstate trade and commerce. Long impelled by this purpose, appellants have adopted various expedients through which they evidently hoped to defeat the policy of the law without subjecting themselves to punishment.

They are parties to definite and unusual combinations and agreements, whereby each is obligated to reveal to confederates the intimate details of his business and is restricted in his freedom of action. It seems to me that ordinary knowledge of human nature and of the impelling force of greed ought to permit no serious doubt concerning the ultimate outcome of the arrangements. We may confidently expect the destruction of that kind of competition long relied upon by the public for establishment of fair prices, and to preserve which the Anti-trust Act was passed.

United States v. American Linseed Oil Co., 262 U.S. 371, states the doctrine which I think should be rigorously applied. Pious protestations and smug preambles but intensify distrust when men are found busy with schemes to enrich themselves through circumventions. And the Government ought not to be required supinely to await the final destruction of competitive conditions before demanding relief through the courts. The statute supplies means for prevention. Artful gestures should not hinder their application.

I think the courts below reached right conclusions and their decrees should be affirmed.

Omitted Taft Opinions

North Carolina Railroad v. Story, 268 U.S. 288 (1925)—injuries suffered on railroad.
United States v. Fish, 268 U.S. 607 (1925)—tariff issue.
United States v. Noce, 268 U.S. 613 (1925)—army salary dispute.

October Term, 1925

William Howard Taft, Chief Justice
Oliver Wendell Holmes
Willis Van Devanter
James Clark McReynolds
Louis D. Brandeis
George Sutherland
Pierce Butler
Edward T. Sanford
Harlan Fiske Stone

VOLUME 269

Donegan v. Dyson

Congress in 1913 abolished the Commerce Court, but provided that its judges would remain as judges. Donegan, who had been convicted of a banking offense, claimed that his rights were violated for having been tried before one of the judges of the former Commerce Court. The issue in *Donegan* thus was the power of the chief justice to assign such judges to other duties. Taft ruled in favor of such a power.

Donegan v. Dyson, U.S. Marshal

*Appeal from the District Court of the United States
for the Southern District of Florida*

No. 185. Motion submitted October 5, 1925—Decided November 16, 1925

269 U.S. 49 (1925)

[50]

MR. CHIEF JUSTICE TAFT delivered the opinion of the Court.

This is an appeal from a judgment in a *habeas corpus* case remanding the petitioner. It is brought under § 238 of the Judicial Code, on the ground that it involves the construction or application of the Constitution of the United States.

March 5, 1919, Donegan was indicted in the United States District Court for the Southern District of Florida, in the Tampa Division, charged with the offense of misapplication and abstraction of funds of a National Bank in violation of the banking laws of the United States. At a subsequent term he was tried, convicted and sentenced to a term of three years' imprisonment in the Atlanta Penitentiary. On a writ of error his conviction was affirmed by the Circuit Court of Appeals for the Fifth Circuit. He applied for a writ of certiorari in this Court, which was denied. 265 U.S. 585. While in the custody [51] of the United States marshal, after the coming down of the mandate of the Circuit Court of Appeals, he filed this petition for the writ of *habeas corpus.* The ground for the petition is that United States Circuit Judge Julian W. Mack, who presided in the cause in which the petitioner was convicted, had no power or jurisdiction to act as judge in the District Court for the Southern District of Florida. Judge Mack, as the petition avers, was one of the five additional United States circuit judges appointed at the time of the creation of the Court of Commerce, by virtue of the Act of June 18, 1910. . . .

* * * * *

[52] The original Act creating the Commerce Court had this provision (36 Stat. 541, c. 309):

"If, at any time, the business of the commerce court does not require the services of all the judges, the Chief Justice of the United States may, by writing, signed by him and filed in the Department of Justice, terminate the assignment of any of the judges or temporarily assign him for service in any circuit court or circuit court of appeals."

When, by the Judicial Code, the circuit courts were abolished (36 St. 1087), and in Chapter 13 the powers of the circuit courts were conferred upon the district courts. . . .

* * * * *

In addition to these provisions, § 201 of the Judicial Code provided expressly as follows (36 Stat. 1087,1147):

"Sec. 201. The five additional circuit judges authorized by the Act to create a Commerce Court, and for other purposes, approved June eighteenth, nineteen hundred and ten, shall hold office during good behavior, and from [53] time to time shall be designated and assigned by the Chief Justice of the United States for service in the district court of any district, or the circuit court of appeals for any circuit, or in the Commerce Court, *and when so designated and assigned for service in a district court or circuit court of appeals shall have the powers and jurisdiction in this Act conferred upon a circuit judge in his circuit.*"

The Commerce Court was abolished by the Act of October 22, 1913, c. 32, 38 Stat. 208, 219. While the court was abolished, no attempt was made to abolish the offices of the judges. More than that, there was this special saving clause in the Act abolishing the Commerce Court, 38 Stat. 219:

"Nothing herein contained shall be deemed to affect the tenure of any of the judges now acting as circuit judges by appointment under the terms of said Act, but such judges shall continue to act under assignment, as in the said Act provided, as judges of the district courts and circuit courts of appeals."

* * * * *

It is . . . submitted that . . . the circuit judge surviving the Court of Commerce is a judge without a circuit and that, when assigned to the Fifth Circuit or any other circuit, he goes to the circuit as *pro tempore* a judge of that circuit, and has only the powers and jurisdiction of such circuit judge provided in § 201, which are the powers and jurisdiction conferred in the Judicial Code "upon a circuit judge in his circuit." Now it is said that a regularly appointed circuit judge in a circuit can exercise power and jurisdiction in a district [54] court of his circuit only after designation and assignment by the circuit justice of his judicial circuit, or by the senior circuit judge thereof. . . .

* * * * *

. . . It is urged, therefore, that, after the Chief Justice had under § 201 assigned this former commerce court circuit judge to the 5th circuit, it was, in addition, necessary that the circuit justice of the 5th circuit, or the senior circuit judge of that circuit, should then assign him as a *pro tempore* circuit judge of the 5th circuit to the particular district court of that circuit in which he was to exercise the duties of a district judge. We think such reasoning is making complex a very simple statute and going out of the way to create confusion. . . .

* * * * *

[55] The action of the District Court in dismissing the petition and remanding the prisoner is

Affirmed.

Central Union Telephone Co. v. City of Edwardsville

An Illinois statute provided that if a party elected to take a particular avenue of appeal, by doing so it waived its right subsequently to raise either state or federal constitutional issues. The Supreme Court of the United States, *per* Taft, found no constitutional defect in the statute.

Central Union Telephone Co. v. City of Edwardsville

Error to the Supreme Court of the State of Illinois

No. 37. Argued October 13, 1925—Decided November 23, 1925

269 U.S. 190 (1925)

[192]

MR. CHIEF JUSTICE TAFT delivered the opinion of the Court.

The City of Edwardsville, in July 1882, by ordinance granted to the Central Union Telephone Company a right in its streets to erect and maintain the necessary poles and wires for the operation of a telephone system. The Central Telephone Company transferred its rights to the Central Union Telephone Company. Later the city council adopted a resolution requesting the Central Union Telephone Company to furnish to the city, free of charge, one telephone and such additional telephones as the city council might call for at a reduction of 25 per cent. from the regular rates, and the right to attach, without charge, fire and police alarm wires to the top cross-arm of each pole. The company filed its acceptance of this resolution as provided in the resolution. It maintains 1000 poles in the City of Edwardsville. The city in 1914 passed an ordinance which in effect imposes a tax of 50 cents a pole upon every person, firm or corporation owning, controlling or occupying any such poles in the streets of Edwardsville. The city brought [193] suit for the amount due under the tax law at 50 cents a pole. A jury was waived, and after a hearing the court entered judgment for $3,000 against the company. The Circuit Court held that neither the ordinance by which the Central Telephone Company was permitted to occupy the streets, nor the subsequent resolution accepted by the Central Union Telephone Company, constituted a contract, and that the tax law was not therefore a violation of the Constitution of the United States in impairing a contract, or in depriving the company of property without due process of law. Upon this record an appeal was taken to the Appellate Court of the State for the Fourth Circuit. That court transferred the case to the Supreme Court of Illinois, on the ground that the Appellate Court had no jurisdiction of it. *City of Edwardsville v. Central Union Telephone Co.,* 302 Ill. 362. The Supreme Court held that as the appeal had been taken to the Appellate Court and errors assigned which that court had jurisdiction to hear, the case was improperly transferred to the Supreme Court, and remanded it to the Appellate Court, which gave judgment affirming the Circuit Court. The plaintiff . . . obtained a certiorari from the Supreme Court to review the decision of the Appellate Court, and in that hearing the Supreme Court declined to hear the constitutional questions on the ground that they had been waived by the failure to carry the case from the Circuit Court directly to the Supreme Court to review those questions.

* * * * *

[195] The construction of this statute has been uniformly held to be, that where a question involves the Constitution, it must be taken on error or appeal to the Supreme Court, and that if it be taken to the Appellate Court on other grounds, the party taking the appeal or suing out the writ of error shall be held to have waived the constitutional questions. . . .

* * * * *

It is objected on behalf of the plaintiff in error that the words "validity of a statute or construction of the Constitution" refer to the constitution of Illinois and not to the Federal Constitution. The Supreme Court of Illinois has held otherwise in this case. 309 Ill. 482, 483, 484.

But counsel for plaintiff in error insist that it is for this Court to determine finally whether a litigant in a state court has waived his federal right. . . .

* * * * *

It seems to us that the practice under the statute of Illinois above quoted is entirely fair. If the litigant has a constitutional question, federal or state, he may take the case directly to the Supreme Court and have that question decided, together with all the other questions in the case, and then, if the federal constitutional question is decided against him, he may bring it here by writ of error or application for certiorari. If he elects to take his case to the Appellate Court, he may have the non-constitutional questions considered and decided, but he gives up the right to raise constitutional objections in any court. . . .

[196] *The motion to dismiss the writ of error is granted.*

Omitted Taft Opinions

Buckeye Co. v. Hocking Valley Co., 269 U.S. 42 (1925)—jurisdiction of federal courts in anti-trust cases.
Southern Electric Co. v. Stoddard, 269 U.S. 186 (1925)—bankruptcy.
Matthews v. Huwe, 269 U.S. 262 (1925)—nature of a writ of error.
Henderson Water Co. v. Corporation Commission, 269 U.S. 278 (1925)—exhaustion of remedies.
Independent Wireless Telegraph Co. v. RCA, 269 U.S. 459 (1926)—patent case.

VOLUME 270

Maryland v. Soper No. 1

Four federal Prohibition agents and their driver were charged by Maryland authorities with murder. The agents, in their defense, claimed they were performing their official duties. The state of Maryland applied to the Supreme Court to issue a writ of *mandamus* requiring that United States District Court Judge Morris Soper turn over the agents to state authorities. After reviewing the facts, Taft granted the writ.

Maryland v. Soper, Judge, No. 1

Petition for a Writ of Mandamus

No. 23, Original. Argued December 7, 1925—Decided February 1, 1926

270 U.S. 9 (1926)

[20]

MR. CHIEF JUSTICE TAFT delivered the opinion of the Court.

This is a petition by the State of Maryland for a writ of mandamus against Morris A. Soper, the United States District Judge for Maryland, directing him to remand an indictment for murder, found in the Circuit Court for [21] Harford County, Maryland, against four prohibition agents and their chauffeur, which was removed to the United States District Court. . . .

The indictment, found February 10, 1925, charged as follows:

"The jurors of the State of Maryland, for the body of Harford County, do on their oath present that Wilton L. Stevens, John M. Barton, Robert D. Ford, E. Franklin Ely, and William Trabing, late of Harford County aforesaid, on the nineteenth day of November, in the year of our Lord nineteen hundred and twenty-four, at the County aforesaid, feloniously, wilfully, and of their deliberately premeditated malice aforethought did kill and murder Lawrence Wenger; contrary to the form of the Act of Assembly in such case made and provided; and against the peace, government, and dignity of the State."

[22] The defendants were arrested, and on February 11, 1925, filed a petition in the United States District Court for the District of Maryland, in which they averred that they were Federal prohibition agents, except Trabing, who was their chauffeur, and was assisting them and was acting under the authority of the Prohibition Director, and that the act or acts done by Trabing, as chauffeur and helper, as well as by the other defendants, at the time when they were alleged to have been guilty of the murder of Lawrence Wenger, which charge they all denied, were done in the discharge of their official duties as prohibition agents, and as officers of the internal revenue in

the discharge of their duty. Thereupon an order of removal, together with a writ of certiorari, and *habeas corpus cum causa,* pursuant to § 33, was made by Judge Soper of the District Court. On March 12th, the State of Maryland, by its Attorney General and the State's Attorney for Harford County, appeared specially and made a motion to quash the writ and rescind the order. . . .

* * * * *

[26] A motion to quash the amended petition, April 11, 1925, was based on the ground, among others, that the allegations of the amended petition did not disclose a state of facts entitling the defendants to have the writ issue, or to have the charge against them removed. On May 5, 1925, Judge Soper denied the motion to quash, and directed that the order of court removing the indictment be ratified and confirmed. On the same day, the following stipulation was entered into by the parties:

> "It is stipulated by and between the parties hereto that Robert D. Ford, John M. Barton, Wilton L. Stevens and E. Franklin Ely, during the month of November, in the year 1924, and prior to said time, and at the time of the matters and facts charged in the indictment in the [27] Circuit Court for Harford County, were Federal Prohibition Officers, holding a commission under the Commissioner of Internal Revenue, and countersigned by the Federal Prohibition Commissioner, in the form following, that is to say:
>
> 'This certifies that ———— is hereby, employed as a Federal Prohibition Officer to act under the authority of and to enforce the National Prohibition Act and Acts supplemental thereto and all Internal Revenue Laws, relating to the manufacture, sale, transportation, control, and taxation of intoxicating liquors, and he is hereby authorized to execute and perform all the duties delegated to such officers by law.'
>
> "And that William Trabing was, at the time of the acts alleged in the indictment in the Circuit Court for Harford County, a chauffeur of the Reliable Transfer Company, engaged and employed by Edmund Budnitz, Federal Prohibition Director of the State of Maryland, in the capacity of chauffeur for the Prohibition Agents above named."

* * * * *

[34] In invoking the protection of a trial of a state offense in a federal court under § 33, a federal officer abandons his right to refuse to testify because accused of crime, at least to the extent of disclosing in his application

for removal all the circumstances known to him out of which the prosecution arose. The defense he is to make is that of his immunity from punishment by the State, because what he did was justified by his duty under the federal law, and because he did nothing else on which the prosecution could be based. He must establish fully and fairly this defense by the allegations of his petition for removal before the federal court can properly grant it. . . .

We think that the averments of the amended petition in this case are not sufficiently informing and specific to make a case for removal under § 33. We have set forth the account the defendants gave in their amended petition of what they saw and did, but the only averments important in directly connecting the prosecution with their act are at the opening and close of their petition. They refer to the death of Wenger only by incorporating the indictment in the petition, and then say that "the acts [i. e. the killing of Wenger] alleged to have been done by petitioners Robert D. Ford, John M. Barton, Wilton L. Steven and E. Franklin Ely, are alleged to have been at a time when they were engaged in the discharge of their official duties as Federal Prohibition Officers, and in making and attempting to make an investigation concerning a violation of the National Prohibition Act and other Internal [35] Revenue Laws and in reporting the results of said investigation, and in protecting themselves in the discharge of their duty." . . .

These averments amount to hardly more than to say that the homicide on account of which they are charged with murder was at a time when they were engaged in performing their official duties. They do not negative the possibility that they were doing other acts than official acts at the time and on this occasion, or make it clear and specific that whatever was done by them leading to the prosecution was done under color of their federal official duty. They do not allege what was the nature of Wenger's fatal wound, whether gunshot or otherwise, whether they had seen him among those who brought the still and fled, or whether they heard, or took part in any shooting. They do not say what they did, if anything, in pursuit of the fugitives. It is true that, in their narration of the facts, their nearness to the place of Wenger's killing and their effort to arrest the persons about to engage in alleged distilling are circumstances possibly suggesting the reason and occasion for the criminal charge and the prosecution against them. But they should do more than this in order to satisfy the statute. In order to justify so exceptional a procedure, the person seeking the benefit of it should be candid, specific and positive in explaining his relation to the transaction growing out of which he has been indicted, and in showing that his relation to it was confined to his acts as an officer. As the defendants in their statement have not clearly fulfilled this requirement, we must grant the writ of mandamus.

Oregon-Washington Railroad & Navigation Company v. Washington

The state of Washington had established a quarantine to protect its agricultural industry. Chief Justice Taft struck the state order down as interfering with federal legislation on agricultural quarantines. To do this, Taft relied on the famous Marshall opinion in the case of *Gibbons v. Ogden,* 9 Wheat. (22 U.S.) 1 (1824). Since the federal government had authorized the United States Department of Agriculture to order quarantines, any similar regulations by the states must give way to federal authority. The federal government having occupied the field, there was no room for state enforcement.

Oregon-Washington Railroad & Navigation Company v. State of Washington

Error to the Supreme Court of the State of Washington

No. 187. Argued January 28, 1926—Decided March 1, 1926

270 U.S. 87 (1926)

[90] MR. CHIEF JUSTICE TAFT delivered the opinion of the Court.

* * * * *

[93] In the absence of any action taken by Congress on the subject matter, it is well settled that a State in the exercise of its police power may establish quarantines against human beings or animals or plants, the coming in of which may expose the inhabitants or the stock or the trees, plants or growing crops to disease, injury or destruction thereby, and this in spite of the fact that such quarantines necessarily affect interstate commerce.

Chief Justice Marshall, in *Gibbons v. Ogden,* 9 Wheat. 1, speaking of inspection laws, says at p. 203:

"They form a portion of that immense mass of legislation, which embraces everything within the territory of a state, not surrendered to the general government: all which can be most advantageously exercised by the states themselves. Inspection laws, quarantine laws, health laws of every description, as well as laws for regulating the [94] internal commerce of a state, and those which respect turnpike roads, ferries, etc., are component parts of this mass."

Again, he says at p. 205:

"The acts of congress, passed in 1796 and 1799 (1 Stat. 474, 619), empowering and directing the officers of the general government to conform to, and assist in the execution of the quarantine and health laws of a state, proceed, it is said, upon the idea that these laws are constitutional. It is undoubtedly true, that they do proceed upon that idea; and the constitutionality of such laws has never, so far as we are informed, been denied. But they do not imply an acknowledgment that a state may rightfully regulate commerce with foreign nations, or among the states; for they do not imply that such laws are an exercise of that power, or enacted with a view to it. On the contrary, they are treated as quarantine and health laws, are so denominated in the acts of congress, and are considered as flowing from the acknowledged power of a state, to provide for the health of its citizens. But, as it was apparent that some of the provisions made for this purpose, and in virtue of this power, might interfere with, and be affected by the laws of the United States, made for the regulation of commerce, congress, in that spirit of harmony and conciliation, which ought always to characterize the conduct of governments standing in the relation which that of the Union and those of the states bear to each other, has directed its officers to aid in the execution of these laws; and has, in some measure, adapted its own legislation to this object, by making provisions in aid of those of the states. But, in making these provisions, the opinion is unequivocally manifested, that Congress may control the state laws, so far as it may be necessary to control them, for the regulation of commerce."

* * * * *

[96] The second objection to the validity of this Washington law and the action of the State officers, however, is more formidable. Under the language used in *Gibbons v. Ogden, supra,* and the *Minnesota Rate Cases, supra,* the exercise of the police power of quarantine, in spite of its interfering with interstate commerce, is permissible under the Interstate Commerce clause of the Federal Constitution "subject to the paramount authority of Congress if it decides to assume control."

By the Act of Congress of August 20, 1912, 37 Stat. 315, c. 308, as amended by the Act of March 4, 1917, 39 Stat. 1165, c. 179, it is made unlawful to import or offer for entry into the United States, any nursery stock unless permit had been issued by the Secretary of Agriculture under regulations prescribed by him.

* * * * *

[97] Section 8 of the Act was amended by the Agricultural Appropriation Act of March 4, 1917, and reads as follows:

"Sec. 8. That the Secretary of Agriculture is authorized and directed to quarantine any State, Territory, or District of the United States, or any portion thereof, when he shall determine that such quarantine is necessary to prevent the spread of a dangerous plant disease or insect infestation. . . .

* * * * *

[98] It is impossible to read this statute and consider its scope without attributing to Congress the intention to take over to the Agricultural Department of the Federal Government the care of the horticulture and agriculture of the States, so far as these may be affected injuriously by the transportation in foreign and interstate commerce of anything which by reason of its character can convey disease to and injure trees, plants or crops. All the sections look to a complete provision for quarantine against importation into the country and quarantine as between the States under the direction and supervision of the Secretary of Agriculture.

* * * * *

[102] It follows that, pending the existing legislation of Congress as to quarantine of diseased trees and plants in interstate commerce, the statute of Washington on the subject can not be given application. It is suggested that the States may act in the absence of any action by the Secretary of Agriculture; that it is left to him to allow the States to quarantine, and that if he does not act there is no invalidity in the state action. Such construction as that can not be given to the federal statute. The obligation to act without respect to the States is put directly upon the Secretary of Agriculture whenever quarantine, in his judgment, is necessary. When he does not [103] act, it must be presumed that it is not necessary. With the federal law in force, state action is illegal and unwarranted.

The decree of the Supreme Court of Washington is

Reversed.

MR. JUSTICE MCREYNOLDS and MR. JUSTICE SUTHERLAND, dissenting.

We cannot think Congress intended that the Act of March 4, 1917, without more should deprive the States of power to protect themselves against threatened disaster like the one disclosed by this record.

If the Secretary of Agriculture had taken some affirmative action the problem would be a very different one. Congress could have exerted all the power which this statute delegated to him by positive and direct enactment. If it had said nothing whatever, certainly the State could have resorted to the quarantine; and this same right, we think, should be recognized when its agent has done nothing.

It is a serious thing to paralyze the efforts of a State to protect her people against impending calamity and leave them to the slow charity of a far-off and perhaps supine federal bureau. No such purpose should be attributed to Congress unless indicated beyond reasonable doubt.

Omitted Taft Opinions

Maryland v. Soper (No. 2), 270 U.S. 36 (1926)—same as 270 U.S. 9 (1926).

Maryland v. Soper (No. 3), 270 U.S. 44 (1926)—same as 270 U.S. 9 (1926).

Interocean Oil Co. v. United States, 270 U.S. 65 (1926)—contract dispute over war work.

Independent Wireless Co. v. Radio Corp., 270 U.S. 84 (1926)—patent case.

Southern Pacific Company v. United States, 270 U.S. 103 (1926)—Supreme Court jurisdiction over contract case from Court of Claims.

Cincinnati, Indianapolis & Western Railroad Company v. Indianapolis Union Railway Company, 270 U.S. 107 (1926)—bankruptcy.

Goldsmith v. United States Board of Tax Appeals, 270 U.S. 117 (1926)—notice required by Board to individuals deemed not qualified to practice before Board.

United States v. Swift & Company, 270 U.S. 124 (1926)—contract dispute.

Morse v. United States, 270 U.S. 151 (1926)—procedures for Court of Claims.

Rogers v. United States, 270 U.S. 154 (1926)—procedures for military court of inquiry.

Girard Trust Company v. United States, 270 U.S. 163 (1926)—interest on tax refunds.

Cherokee Nation v. United States, 270 U.S. 476 (1926)—determination of interest owed Cherokee nation.

Luckett v. Delpark, 270 U.S. 496 (1926)—patent case.

United States v. Koenig Coal Co., 270 U.S. 512 (1926)—definition of guilt under Elkins Act.

United States v. Michigan Portland Cement Company, 270 U.S. 521 (1926)—definition of guilt under Elkins Act.

VOLUME 271

Booth Fisheries Co. v. Industrial Commission of Wisconsin

Booth Fisheries challenged the Workmen's Compensation Act of Wisconsin, arguing that it violated the Fourteenth Amendment by limiting judicial review of decisions of the industrial commission. Taft, for a unanimous Court, found no constitutional problem, since the company had voluntarily accepted the jurisdiction of the commission.

Booth Fisheries Company et al. v. Industrial Commission of Wisconsin et al.

Error to the Supreme Court of the State of Wisconsin

No. 313. Argued May 5, 1926—Decided May 24, 1926

271 U.S. 208 (1926)

[209]

MR. CHIEF JUSTICE TAFT delivered the opinion of the Court.

This was a suit begun in the Circuit Court of Dane County, Wisconsin, to review and set aside the findings and award under the Wisconsin Workman's Compensation Act of a death benefit in favor of Mary McLaughlin as widow of William McLaughlin, against his employer, the Booth Fisheries Company. . . .

The only question raised on the appeal to the Supreme Court of Wisconsin was the constitutionality under the Fourteenth Amendment of the Workman's Compensation Act of Wisconsin in its limitation of the judicial review of the findings of fact of the Industrial Commission to cases in which "the findings of fact by the Commission do not support the order or award" (Wisconsin Statutes, 1921, §§ 2394–19). This limitation has been held by the state Supreme Court to mean that the findings of fact [210] made by the Industrial Commission are conclusive, if there is any evidence to support them. . . .

It is argued that the employer in a suit for compensation under the Act is entitled under the Fourteenth Amendment to his day in court, and that he does not secure it unless he may submit to a court the question of the preponderance of the evidence on the issues raised.

A complete answer to this claim is found in the elective or voluntary character of the Wisconsin Compensation Act. That Act provides that every employer who has elected to do so shall become subject to the Act, that such election shall be made by filing a written statement with the Commission, which shall subject him to the terms of the law for a year and until July 1st following, and to successive terms of one year unless he withdraws. Wisconsin Stat. § 2394—3, 4, 5. It is conceded by the counsel for the plaintiffs in error that the Act is elective, and that it is so is shown by the decisions of the Wisconsin court in *Borgnis v. Falk Company,* 147 Wis. 327, 350, and in the present case. 185 Wis. 127. If the employer elects not to accept the provisions of the compensation Act, he is not bound to respond in a proceeding before the Industrial Commission under the Act, but may await a suit for damages for injuries or wrongful death by the person claiming recovery therefor, and make his defense at law before a court in which the issues of fact and law are to be tried by jury. In view of such an [211] opportunity for choice, the employer who elects to accept the law may not complain that, in the plan for assessing the employer's compensation for injury sustained, there is no particular form of judicial review. . . .

* * * * *

The judgment of the Supreme Court of Wisconsin is

Affirmed.

Appleby v. City of New York

Article I, Section 10, Clause 1 of the Constitution states that "no State shall . . . pass any Law impairing the Obligation of Contracts." Several major decisions of the Marshall Court turned on this provision, including *Fletcher v. Peck,* 6 Cranch (10 U.S.) 87 (1810) and *Dartmouth College v. Woodward,* 4 Wheat. (17 U.S.) 518 (1819). In *Appleby v. City of New York* Taft found that, as interpreted by the New York courts, certain state laws ran afoul of the Constitution's limitation on a state's power to impair contracts.

Appleby et al. v. City of New York et al.

Error to the Supreme Court of the State of New York

No. 15. Argued October 7, 1925;
reargued March 1, 2, 1926—Decided June 1, 1926

271 U.S. 364 (1926)

[389]

MR. CHIEF JUSTICE TAFT . . . delivered the opinion of the Court.

The plaintiffs in their writ of error charge that the judgment of the Supreme Court of New York, as affirmed by the Court of Appeals, has interpreted and enforced the Acts of 1857 and 1871 in such a way as to impair the obligation of the contract in their deeds.

* * * * *

[391] If we are right in our conclusion as to the effect of these deeds under the law of New York at the time of their execution, then there can be no doubt that the laws of 1857 and 1871 as enforced in this case impair the contract made by the city with the grantees of these deeds.

* * * * *

[399] Our conclusions are that Appleby and Latou were vested with the fee simple title in the lots conveyed, and with a grant of the wharfage at the ends of the lots on the river; that with respect to the water over those lots and the wharfage, the State and the city had parted with the *jus publicum* and the *jus privatum;* and that the city can only be revested with them by a condemnation of the rights granted.

What, then, is the effect upon the rights of the parties of the fact that the grantees only filled the part of lots [400] conveyed east of 12th Avenue? The plaintiffs are not in default in this, because there was no covenant on their part to fill. . . .

The rights of the plaintiff with reference to the use of the water over their lots lying between the bulkhead line and 12th Avenue are not affected by the order of the Secretary of War. The evidence shows that for 100 feet or more inside the line the water over these lots is made part of the slip and city mooring place for the city's pier; that in order to adapt it to such a purpose the soil in the lots is being constantly dredged, the dredging having increased the depth of the water from three feet to sixteen and twenty feet.

This has been done by the city on the assumption that, because it is water connected with the river, the city may improve its navigation. As the city has parted with the *jus publicum* in respect of these lots, it may not exercise this power, and must be content with sailing over it with boats as it finds it. The dredging of the mud to a depth of fifteen feet in their lots is a trespass upon the plaintiffs' rights. They have a right, at [401] their convenience, to fill both lots from the bulkhead line easterly to 12th Avenue and beyond. And we know from a record in a related case, argued with this and to be decided this day, that they have applied for permission to fill the lots and are pressing their right to do so. So, too, the use of the water over these lots inside the bulkhead line, for mooring places, berths or slips, by the city and its tenants, as we have shown, violates the rights of the plaintiffs. They are entitled to an injunction against both.

The order of the Secretary of War, of 1890, fixing the bulkhead line 150 feet west of 12th Avenue, and allowing pier extensions far beyond 13th Avenue, to 700 feet from the bulkhead line, does not take away the right of the plaintiffs to object to the city's dredging their lots or to its using the water over their lots for what is in effect an exclusive slip and mooring place. The order did not restore to the city the power, as against these plaintiffs, to regulate navigation over their lots, and so did not make the Act of 1857 and the Act of 1871 with respect to the spacing of 100 feet between piers and for mooring places adjoining the piers effective to defeat those deeds. The action of the city in making these deeds and covenants was of course subject to the dominant right of the Government of the United States to control navigation, but the exercise of that dominant right did not revest in the city a control and proprietary right which it had parted with by solemn deed and covenant to these plaintiffs.

* * * * *

[402] The lots have been bought and paid for subject only to control by the General Government in the interest of navigation. The General Government, through its agent, says it does not require open water for navigation, but is sufficiently satisfied by piers on piles extending over the water. The city has by deed granted to the Applebys the wharfage and cranage rights upon these lots. What is there to prevent the Applebys, by the construction of piers on piles over their lots, in conformity to the Secretary of War's order, from enjoying the profit from that wharfage?

* * * * *

[403] The application of the Acts of 1857 and 1871 by the courts of New York would reduce the rights which were intended to be conveyed in these deeds to practically nothing, and would leave the grantees only the privilege of paying taxes for something quite unsubstantial. The qualification of those rights by the order of the Secretary of War still leaves value in the deeds, if the Acts of 1857 and 1871 are invalid, as we hold them to be when applied as they have been in this case.

The judgment of the Supreme Court of New York is reversed for further proceedings not inconsistent with this opinion.

Reversed.

Appleby v. Delaney

This case arises from the same circumstances as the case immediately preceding it.

Appleby et al. v. Delaney, Commissioner

Error to the Supreme Court of the State of New York

No. 16. Argued October 7, 1925;
reargued March 1, 2, 1926—Decided June 1, 1926

271 U.S. 403 (1926)

[409]

Mr. Chief Justice Taft . . . delivered the opinion of the Court.

The relators base their writ upon the alleged impairment of their contract rights contained in the grant and covenants of their deeds by the plan, adopted in 1916, under the Act of 1871, by the Dock Department, and approved by the Sinking Fund trustees, the execution of which the Dock Commissioner is enforcing by a formal refusal to grant permission, as requested by the relators, to fill up their lots. The authority of the Dock Commissioner and the Sinking Fund trustees, under the Act of 1871, is such as to make the plan and the refusal equivalent to a statute of the State, and, assuming that it is in conflict with the grant and covenants of relators' deeds, it is a law of the State impairing a contract obligation under § 10, Article I, of the Federal Constitution. . . .

* * * * *

[413] It is not reasonable to suppose that the grantees would pay $12,000, in 1852 and 1853 and leave to the city authorities the absolute right completely to nullify the chief consideration for seeking this property in making dry land, or that the parties then took that view of the transaction. In addition to the down payment, the grantees or their successors have paid the taxes assessed by the city for seventy-five years, which have evidently amounted to much more than $70,000. It does not seem fair to us, after these taxes have been paid for sixty years, in the confidence, justified by the decision of the highest state court, that there was the full right to fill in at the pleasure of the grantees and without the consent of the city, now to hold that all this expenditure may go for naught at the pleasure of the city.

If the Sinking Fund ordinance is to be applied at all to the filling in of the land in the limits within the deeds, it should in our judgment be regarded as a mere police [414] requirement of a permit incident to the filling and to supervising its execution by regulation as to time and method, so that it should not disturb the public order. . . .

The judgment of the Supreme Court is reversed and the case remanded for further proceedings not inconsistent with this opinion.

Reversed.

Thornton v. United States

Thornton and his associates were charged with murdering an employee of the federal Bureau of Animal Industry, wounding and assaulting other employees, and dynamiting a federal facility. Their defense was that the law under which the employees of the bureau were acting was unconstitutional since it affected activities reserved to the states under the Tenth Amendment, and that therefore their crimes could be punished only by a state. Taft rejected this argument, holding that it was necessary for interstate commerce for the federal government to take measures to suppress ticks in cattle and that it was a federal crime to interfere with them in pursuit of this function.

Thornton et al. v. United States

Certiorari to the Circuit Court of Appeals for the Fifth Circuit

No. 255. Argued April 20, 1926—Decided June 1, 1926

271 U.S. 414 (1926)

[417]

MR. CHIEF JUSTICE TAFT delivered the opinion of the Court.

This case comes here by certiorari from the Circuit Court of Appeals of the Fifth Circuit. 267 U.S. 589. The judgment is one of conviction of the petitioners under an indictment found in the District Court for the Southern District of Georgia, charging the petitioners and sixteen others with the crime of conspiracy under § 37 of the Criminal Code to commit the offense against the United States denounced in § 62 of the same Code. Section 62 punishes anyone who shall assault or interfere with an employee of the Bureau of Animal Industry of the Agricultural Department in the execution of his duties. . . .

* * * * *

[421] The evidence for the Government at the trial showed that Echols County, where this conspiracy was formed and the overt acts took place, was on the line between Georgia and Florida; that cattle ranged between one state and the other in that region; that the Department of Agriculture had quarantined in interstate transportation the cattle coming from Echols County because of the presence of the cattle tick among them; that under the Act an agreement had been made between the Secretary of Agriculture and the Georgia authorities acting under a Georgia statute, by which the regulations of the Secretary had been accepted as guidance for the state employees engaged in attempting to suppress the disease by requiring tick infested cattle to be dipped; that spray pens and dipping vats had been erected in Echols County at the expense of the United States, to carry out the duties of the Bureau of Animal Industry; that the state law authorized and directed the county and state officers to enforce the dipping of cattle in the counties which were tick infested, by process served in the name of the State, and that the state officers served such processes upon cattle-owners in the county; that the cattle which were [422] thoroughly dipped were marked with indelible paint; that United States inspectors were not always present at the dipping, but usually supervised what was done to gain a knowledge of what the state officers were doing in enforcing the state law, so that if successful the quarantine against cattle for shipment

out of Georgia against Echols County could be discontinued; that this was only one instance of the investigations required under the Act of 1884 by the Bureau of Animal Industry employees to help cattle movements from the southern States to the north in promotion of interstate commerce; that it was while these activities of the employees of the Federal Bureau were progressing that the defendants and others, residents of Echols County, owners of cattle and neighbors, resenting the necessity for dipping, dynamited the spray pens and the dipping vats and assaulted the United States employees of the Bureau, wounded several and killed one by gun shot.

* * * * *

[423] It is . . . objected that there were no allegations in the indictment that the cattle being dipped were the subject matter of interstate commerce or had in any way under the law become subject to the supervision or control of the Secretary of Agriculture, or that what the employees were doing was to prevent the spread of communicable disease among the cattle from one state to another. . . .

The assaults upon the employees of the Bureau of Animal Industry and the interference with their duties were described in the indictment as having to do with the inspection of suspected cattle and the supervision of their dipping. As their duties in connection with suspected and diseased cattle were described in the statute as imposed for the purpose of preventing the spread of [424] contagious cattle disease from one state to another, it is sufficient certainty to a common intent to describe generally that they were performing their duties under the statute in the supervision and dipping of cattle, without further definition.

It is finally urged against this conviction that the statute of 1884 *supra* is unconstitutional in that Congress had no power to make it a duty of a federal employee to dip cattle and suppress disease among cattle within a State; that such power is vested in the Legislature of the State under the reservations of the Tenth Amendment to the Federal Constitution; and that such legislation by Congress can not be sustained as a regulation of interstate commerce, because it is not confined to interstate commerce and the cattle treated were not in interstate commerce.

It is very evident from the Act of 1884 and the subsequent legislation and the regulations issued under them that everything authorized to be done was expressly intended to prevent the spread of disease from one State to another by contagion, which of course means by the passage of diseased cattle from one state to another. This is interstate commerce.

* * * * *

[425] More than this, it is established by *United States v. Ferger,* 250 U.S. 199, that the authority of Congress over interstate commerce extends to dealing with and preventing burdens to that commerce and the spread of disease from one state to another by such cattle ranging would clearly be such a burden, if it were not to be regarded as commerce itself, and is therefore properly within the congressional inhibition. *Stafford v. Wallace,* 258 U.S. 495.

Judgment affirmed.

Yu Cong Eng v. Trinidad

The Philippine legislature had adopted a measure, supposedly to fight fraud, entitled the Chinese Bookkeeping Act. The law was challenged as being in violation of the guarantees of both equal protection and due process of law. In an opinion that seems to speak to the contemporary controversy of English-only laws, Taft found the statute unconstitutional.

Yu Cong Eng et al. v. Trinidad, Collector, et al.

Certiorari to the Supreme Court of the Philippine Islands

No. 623. Argued April 12, 13, 1926—Decided June 7, 1926

271 U.S. 500 (1926)

[506]

MR. CHIEF JUSTICE TAFT prepared the opinion of the Court.[1]

This case comes here on a writ of certiorari to review a decision of the Supreme Court of the Philippine Islands denying an original petition for prohibition against the enforcement by criminal prosecution of Act No. 2972 of the Philippine Legislature, known as the Chinese Bookkeeping Act, on the ground of its invalidity. . . .

* * * * *

[508] "Section 1. It shall be unlawful for any person, company, partnership or corporation engaged in commerce, industry or any other activity for the purpose of profit in the Philippine Islands, in according with existing

law, to keep its account books in any language other than English, Spanish, or any local dialect.

"Section 2. Any person violating the provisions of this Act shall, upon conviction, be punished by a fine of not more than ten thousand pesos, or by imprisonment for not more than two years, or both.

* * * * *

[510] The petitioners aver that the Act, if enforced, will deprive the petitioners, and the twelve thousand Chinese merchants whom they represent, of their liberty and property without due process of law, and deny them the equal protection of the laws, in violation of the Philippine Autonomy Act of Congress of August 29, 1916, c. 416, sec. 3, 39 Stat. 546.

An amendment to the petition set up the rights of the petitioners under the treaty now in force between the United States and China, alleging that under it the petitioners are entitled to the same rights, privileges and immunities as the citizens and subjects of Great Britain and Spain, and that the treaty has the force and effect of a law of Congress, which this law violates.

* * * * *

[512] There are 85,000 merchants in the Philippines to whom the bookkeeping law applies. Of these, 71,000 are Filipinos who may use their own dialects; 1,500 are Americans, or British or Spanish subjects; 500 are of other foreign nationalities most of whom know the Spanish or English language. The remainder, some 12,000 in number, are Chinese. The aggregate commercial business transacted by these is about 60 per cent. of the total business done by all the merchants in the Islands. . . .

In 1913, certain revenue statistics were reported by the then collector of internal revenue to the Court of First Instance in the case of *Young v. Raferty,* 33 Philippine Reports, 556, in which the validity of an order by the collector requiring the keeping of certain books by tax payers in Spanish and English was at issue. The figures given above are based on this report. The report showed that Chinese merchants paid about 60 per cent. of the taxes; but this is [513] now in dispute and evidence was introduced by the present collector to show that the proportion of taxes paid by them in 1918 and 1922 was much less, and that examination of the books of four hundred Chinese tax payers showed a very considerable loss probably due to evasion and fraud.

* * * * *

[517] The court in effect concludes that what the Legislature meant to do was to require the keeping of such account books in English, Spanish or

the Filipino dialects as would be reasonably adapted to the needs of the taxing officers in preventing and detecting evasion of taxes, and that this might be determined from the statutes and regulations then in force. What the court really does is to change the law from one which, by its plain terms, forbids the Chinese merchants to keep their account books in any language except English, Spanish or the Filipino dialects, and thus forbids them to keep account books in the Chinese, into a law requiring them to keep certain undefined books in the permitted languages. This is to change a penal prohibitive law to a mandatory law of great indefiniteness, to conform to what the Court assumes was, or ought to have been, the purpose of the Legislature, and which in the change would avoid a conflict with constitutional restriction.

It would seem to us, from the history of the legislation and the efforts for its repeal or amendment, that the Philippine Legislature knew the meaning of the words it used, and intended that the Act as passed should be prohibitory and should forbid the Chinese merchants from keeping the account books of their business in Chinese.

* * * * *

[518] We fully concede that it is the duty of a court in considering the validity of an act to give it such reasonable construction as can be reached to bring it within the fundamental law. But it is very clear that amendment may not be substituted for construction, and that a court may not exercise legislative functions to save the law from conflict with constitutional limitation.

One of the strongest reasons for not making this law a nose of wax to be changed from that which the plain language imports, is the fact that it is a highly penal statute authorizing sentence of one convicted under it to a fine of not more than 10,000 pesos, or by imprisonment for not more than two years, or both. If we change it to meet the needs suggested by other laws and fiscal regulations and by the supposed general purpose of the legislation, we are creating by construction a vague requirement, and one objectionable in a criminal statute. We are likely thus to trespass on the provision of the Bill of Rights that the accused is entitled to demand the nature and cause of the accusation against him; and to violate the principle that a statute which requires the doing of an act so indefinitely described that men must guess at its meaning, violates due process of law. . . .

* * * * *

[522] The suggestion has been made in argument that we should accept the construction put upon a statute of the Philippine Islands by their Supreme Court, as we would the construction of a state court in passing upon the federal constitutionality of a state statute. . . .

[523] It is very true that, with respect to questions turning on questions of local law, or those properly affected by custom inherited from the centuries of Spanish control, we defer much to the judgment of the Philippine or Porto Rican courts. . . .

* * * * *

The question of applying American constitutional limitations to a Philippine or Porto Rican statute dealing with the rights of persons living under the government established by the United States, is not a local one, especially when the persons affected are subjects of another sovereignty with which the United States has made a treaty promising to make every effort to protect their rights. The fundamental law we administer in the Philippine bill of rights was a marked change from that which prevailed in the Islands before we took them over, and is to be enforced in the light of the construction by this Court of such limitations as it has recognized them since the foundation of our own government. In its application here, we must determine for ourselves the necessary meaning of a statute officially enacted in English, and its conformity with fundamental limitations.

* * * * *

[524] We can not give any other meaning to the Bookkeeping Act than that which its plain language imports, making it a crime for anyone in the Philippine Islands engaged in business to keep his account books in Chinese. This brings us to the question whether the law thus construed to mean what it says is invalid.

The Philippine Bill of Rights, already referred to, provides that:

"No law shall be enacted in said islands which shall deprive any person of life, liberty, or property without due process of law, or deny to any person therein the equal protection of the laws."

In *Serra v. Mortiga,* 204 U.S. 470, at 474, this Court said:

"It is settled that by virtue of the bill of rights enacted by Congress for the Philippine Islands, 32 Stat. 691, 692, that guarantees equivalent to the due process and equal protection of the law clause of the Fourteenth Amendment, the twice in jeopardy clause of the Fifth Amendment, and the substantial guarantees of the Sixth Amendment, exclusive of the right to trial by jury, were extended to the Philippine Islands. It is further settled that the guarantees which Congress has extended to the Philippine Islands are to be interpreted as meaning what the like provisions meant at the time when Congress made them applicable, to the Philippine Islands. *Kepner v. United States,* 195 U.S. 100.

"For the purpose, therefore, of passing on the errors assigned we must test the correctness of the action of the court below by substantially the same criteria which we would apply to a case arising in the United States and controlled by the bill of rights expressed in the amendments to the Constitution of the United States."

In view of the history of the Islands and of the conditions there prevailing, we think the law to be invalid, because it deprives Chinese persons—situated as they are, [525] with their extensive and important business long established—of their liberty and property without due process of law, and denies them the equal protection of the laws.

* * * * *

[526] In the case of *Meyer v. Nebraska,* 262 U.S. 390, this Court considered the validity of state legislation making it unlawful to teach a foreign language to children, adopted on the theory that the State had the right to protect children likely to became citizens from study of a particular language, in which they might read and learn doctrine inimical to the Constitution of the United States and to the Nation, and forbidding the teachers of the language from pursuing their occupation on this account, and held it invalid. The Court said:

"While this Court has not attempted to define with exactness the liberty thus guaranteed, the term has received much consideration and some of the included things have been definitely stated. Without doubt it denotes not merely freedom from bodily restraint but also the right of the individual to contract, to engage in any of the common occupations of life, to acquire useful knowledge, to marry, establish a home and bring up children, to worship God according to the dictates of his own conscience, and generally to enjoy those privileges long recognized at common law as essential to the orderly pursuit of happiness by free men. . . . The established doctrine is that this liberty may not be interfered with under the guise of [527] protecting the public interest, by legislative action which is arbitrary or without reasonable relation to some purpose within the competency of the State to effect. Determination by the legislature of what constitutes proper exercise of police power is not final or conclusive but is subject to supervision by the courts."

The same principle is laid down in *Pierce v. Society of Sisters,* 268 U.S. 510, in *Truax v. Raich,* 239 U.S. 33, and in *Adams v. Tanner,* 244 U.S. 590, in which this Court has held legislative attempts arbitrarily and oppressively to interfere with the liberty of the individual in the pursuit of lawful occupations to involve a lack of due process.

* * * * *

[528] We hold the law in question to be invalid.

Judgment reversed.

Note

1. The opinion was announced by Mr. Justice Holmes, the Chief Justice being absent.

Goltra v. Weeks

Goltra **presented the Court with an incident in which military officials clearly acted in a highly arbitrary fashion. At the same time, the facts also established that the military ultimately had a right to the ships in question. Taft ruled for the military. Justice McReynolds dissented.**

Goltra v. Weeks, Secretary of War, et al.

Certiorari to the Circuit Court of Appeals for the Eighth Circuit

No. 718. Argued April 27, 28, 1926—Decided June 7, 1926

271 U.S. 536 (1926)

[538]

MR. CHIEF JUSTICE TAFT prepared the opinion of the Court.[1]

This was a suit in equity brought in the United States District Court for the Eastern District of Missouri, and reaches here from the Circuit Court of Appeals for the [539] Eighth Circuit by certiorari. The general purpose of the bill filed by Edward F. Goltra, petitioner here, was to enjoin the seizure of a fleet of towboats and barges on the Mississippi River which had been held by him as lessee. It charged that the Secretary of War, the Chief of Engineers, and Colonel T. Q. Ashburn, Chief, Inland and Coastwise Waterways Service, were engaged in a conspiracy unlawfully to deprive him of the boats. He sought to enjoin the threatened seizure of them and to have those of them which had already been taken restored to his possession.

* * * * *

[541] . . . [T]he whole fleet had been taken over by Colonel Ashburn under an order of the Secretary of War. The taking over was on Sunday, and

there was a purpose on the part of Colonel Ashburn, anticipating an [542] injunction, to remove such of the fleet as were in St. Louis, across the river, to be out of the jurisdiction of the Missouri District Court. All of the defendants filed returns to the rule setting out defenses. A hearing was had on the motion for a temporary injunction, evidence was taken, and the District Court found that the fleet had been improperly seized and should be restored to the plaintiffs, and the defendants be enjoined from any attempt to resume possession until a final hearing of the case.

* * * * *

[543] The Circuit Court of Appeals reversed the action of the District Court in restoring the fleet to Goltra and enjoining the defendants, and held that the motion to dismiss and to quash the temporary restraining order should have been granted, on the ground that the United States was a necessary party and could not be sued in such an action.

[544] We can not agree with the Circuit Court of Appeals that the United States was a necessary party to the bill. The bill was suitably framed to secure the relief from an alleged conspiracy of the defendants without lawful right to take away from the plaintiff the boats of which by lease or charter he alleged that he had acquired the lawful possession and enjoyment for a term of five years. He was seeking equitable aid to avoid a threatened trespass upon that property by persons who were government officers. If it was a trespass, then the officers of the Government should be restrained whether they professed to be acting for the Government or not. Neither they nor the Government which they represent could trespass upon the property of another, and it is well settled that they may be stayed in their unlawful proceeding by a court of competent jurisdiction, even though the United States for whom they may profess to act is not a party and can not be made one. By reason of their illegality, their acts or threatened acts are personal and derive no official justification from their doing them in asserted agency for the Government. . . .

* * * * *

[546] Much has been said on behalf of the Government with reference to the special power of a government officer to act in such a case, and without judicial assistance forcibly to repossess himself of government property, which we might find it difficult to agree with but which it is unnecessary for us to consider. Our conclusion is based on the law as it is administered between private persons. Colonel Ashburn took possession without notification to Goltra other than that which had been communicated to him by the Secretary of War terminating the contract, and it is clear from the evidence that Colonel Ashburn was anxious to take possession of the property before a writ

of injunction could be sued out by Goltra, and that he sought to take the fleet out of the jurisdiction of the court where he feared the injunction. He was not directed to make the seizure by the Secretary of War against the opposition of Goltra, but in such case he was directed to resort to legal proceedings. He stands upon the statement that he took possession without violence and therefore was rightly in possession when the order of the court was served. He took possession, whether he took it violently or not. Concede that he did it with a show of force which was coercive. Concede that it was a seizure without process, and wrong. But even so, an injunction looks only to the future. At the hearing it was made plain that Goltra was not entitled to the possession, and the court—one of equity—would not go through the idle form of restoring the property to Goltra by way of correcting the Colonel's wrong, and then requiring a redelivery to the lessor.

* * * * *

[550] If Colonel Ashburn committed a breach of the peace or illegally injured any person in his taking possession, he is responsible to proper authority and to the person injured; but that does not affect the rights of the lessor under this lease or the vindication of them in this review.

The reversal of the injunction of the District Court by the Circuit Court of Appeals is affirmed, and the cause is remanded to the District Court for further proceedings in conformity with this opinion.

Affirmed.

The separate opinion of MR. JUSTICE McREYNOLDS.

Theoretically, everybody in this land is subject to the law. But of what value is the theory if performances like those revealed by this record go unrebuked?

[551] An army officer, having inflated himself into judge and executioner, decided that a fleet of towboats and barges lying in the Mississippi River at St. Louis ought no longer to remain in the custody of a private citizen who held possession of them under a solemn lease and contract of sale from the United States and who, in order to make them operative, had expended upon them forty thousand dollars of his own money. Then, waiting until a Sunday arrived, he proceeded to grab the vessels by force and endeavored to run them beyond the jurisdiction of the court.

Action like that is familiar under autocracies, but the prevalent idea has been that we live under a better system.

The trial court, after taking an ample indemnifying bond, issued a temporary injunction requiring that possession of the vessels be restored and remain as before the seizure until the rights of all parties could be properly considered and determined. The Circuit Court of Appeals reversed this interlocutory order, and from its decree the cause came here by certiorari.

As a fitting climax to the high-handed measures pursued by the officer, special counsel for the United States appeared at our bar and gravely announced—"Where the executive power has pronounced its finding or judgment within its proper sphere of action, a judicial judgment is not necessary to the enforcement of the executive one, for the reason that all the compulsive power of the government is in the executive department and may be exercised by it in execution of its own processes and judgment, just as it is exercised by it in the execution of judicial process and judgment."

It is easy enough for us to smile at such stuff, but, unfortunately, the evil effects are not dissipated by gentle gestures. There should be condemnation forceful enough to prevent repetition so long as men have eyes to read.

[552] In the Circuit Court of Appeals Judge Sanborn presented a well-considered dissenting opinion and pointed out that the only judicable question before that court was whether or not the order for the injunction and the record disclosed an unlawful, improvident or abusive use of the sound discretion which the trial judge was required to exercise. 7 Fed. (2d) 838; 851; and see *Ex parte United States,* 263 U. S 389. He could find no such abuse, and neither can I. The trial court did no more than the circumstances permitted. We should approve its action with commendation of the impelling courage and good sense.

Note

1. Mr. Justice Holmes announced the opinion, the Chief Justice being absent.

Omitted Taft Opinions

Sun Ship Co. v. United States, 271 U.S. 96 (1926)—contract dispute.
Union Insulating Co. v. United States, 271 U.S. 121 (1926)—contract dispute.
Iselin v. United States, 271 U.S. 136 (1926)—contract dispute.
Early v. Daniel Company, 271 U.S. 140 (1926)—contract dispute.
United States v. Minnesota Investment Co., 271 U.S. 212 (1926)—contract dispute.
Alejandrino v. Quezon, 271 U.S. 528 (1926)—issue of suspension of a member of Philippine Senate held to be moot since suspension was ended.

October Term, 1926

William Howard Taft, Chief Justice
Oliver Wendell Holmes
Willis Van Devanter
James Clark McReynolds
Louis D. Brandeis
George Sutherland
Pierce Butler
Edward T. Sanford
Harlan Fiske Stone

VOLUME 272

Myers v. United States

Professor William Howard Taft, in his lectures at Yale Law School, given during the period between his unhappy tenure as president and his happy assumption of the long-hoped-for post of chief justice, took a generally narrow view of the powers of the president, one usually cited as representing the constitutional theory of presidential power. "There is no residuum of power upon which the President can draw."[1] For Taft, thus, executive powers were limited to those that could be fairly traced to the words of the Constitution or to statutes passed by Congress. Louis Brownlow has speculated that the narrow view of presidential powers expressed by Taft in the Yale lectures "may have been tinged by a sense of personal frustration" and dissatisfaction with the first four years of the administration of President Woodrow Wilson.[2] Whatever the reason or reasons may have been, as chief justice Taft's opinions on executive power tended strongly to favor the president. Chief Justice Taft was the mirror image of Professor Taft!

In 1926 Chief Justice Taft had his most important opportunity to speak to the nature of presidential power. At issue was the presidential power to remove executive officers. Taft's opinion in *Myers* seemed totally to contradict the views he earlier expressed in *Our Chief Executive and His Powers.*

The lengthy opinion (seventy-one pages in *The United States Reports*) found both historical and constitutional bases for striking down an 1876 law that restricted the president's power to remove postmasters without senatorial consent. Not content with simply striking this law down, Taft proceeded to offer the opinion that the Tenure of Office Act passed by the Radical Republicans to limit President Andrew Johnson was also unconstitutional.

More than possibly any of Taft's other opinions, *Myers* was a labor of love, and those who dared to disagree with it drew from the Chief more than the usual scorn he visited upon those who dissented. In a letter to his brother, Taft castigated Justices Brandeis and McReynolds, both of whom had written lengthy dissents from the Taft opinion, as "belong[ing] to a class of people who have no loyalty to the court and sacrifice almost everything to the gratification of their own publicity."[3] Surprisingly, Holmes appears to have escaped Taft's written volley of criticism, though in an opinion of three paragraphs that was dwarfed by the opinions of Taft, Brandeis, and McReynolds, Holmes cut to the heart of the matter for many who read his opinion, pointing out that concerning "an office that owes its existence to Congress and that Congress may abolish tomorrow," Congress may quite appropriately set the terms for the removal of the person who holds the office.

A unanimous Court significantly cut back on much of the breadth of Taft's holding in the subsequent case of *Humphrey's Executor v. United States,* 295 U.S. 602 (1935), by limiting the removal power to persons performing solely executive functions and ruling that officials performing quasi-legislative or quasi-judicial duties could not be removed arbitrarily by a president.

Notes

1. William Howard Taft, *Our Chief Magistrate and His Powers* (New York: Columbia University Press, 1916); reprinted in The President and His Powers *and* The United States and Peace, ed. W. Carey McWilliams and Frank X. Gerrity, vol. 6 of *The Collected Works of William Howard Taft* (Athens: Ohio University Press, 2003), 104.

2. Louis Brownlow, *The President and the Presidency* (Chicago: Public Administration Service, 1949), as cited in Rocco Tresolini, *American Constitutional Law* (New York: The MacMillan Company, 1959), 247–48.

3. Pringle, *Life and Times,* 2:1025.

Myers, Administratrix, v. United States

Appeal from the Court of Claims

No. 2. Argued December 5, 1923; reargued April 13, 14, 1925—
Decided October 25, 1926

272 U.S. 52 (1926)

[106]

MR. CHIEF JUSTICE TAFT delivered the opinion of the Court.

This case presents the question whether under the Constitution the President has the exclusive power of removing executive officers of the United States whom he has appointed by and with the advice and consent of the Senate.

Myers, appellant's intestate, was on July 21, 1917, appointed by the President, by and with the advice and consent of the Senate, to be a postmaster of the first class at Portland, Oregon, for a term of four years. On January 20, 1920, Myers' resignation was demanded. He refused the demand. On February 2, 1920, he was removed from office by order of the Postmaster General, acting by direction of the President. . . . In August, 1920, the President made a recess appointment of one Jones, who took office September 19, 1920.

[107] The Court of Claims gave judgment against Myers, and this is an appeal from that judgment. . . .

By the 6th section of the Act of Congress of July 12, 1876, 19 Stat. 80, 81, c. 179, under which Myers was appointed with the advice and consent of the Senate as a first-class postmaster, it is provided that

"Postmasters of the first, second and third classes shall be appointed and may be removed by the President by and with the advice and consent of the Senate and shall hold their offices for four years unless sooner removed or suspended according to law."

The Senate did not consent to the President's removal of Myers during his term. If this statute, in its requirement that his term should be four years unless sooner removed by the President by and with the consent of the [108] Senate, is valid, the appellant, Myers' administratrix, is entitled to recover his unpaid salary for his full term, and the judgment of the Court of Claims must be reversed. The Government maintains that the requirement is invalid, for the reason that under Article II of the Constitution the President's power of removal of executive officers appointed by him with the advice and consent of the Senate is full and complete without consent of the Senate. If this view is sound, the removal of Myers by the President without the Senate's consent was legal and the judgment of the Court of Claims against the appellant was correct and must be affirmed, though for a different reason from that given by that court. We are therefore confronted by the constitutional question and can not avoid it.

The relevant parts of Article II of the Constitution are as follows:

"Section 1. The executive Power shall be vested in a President of the United States of America. . . .

"Section 2. The President shall be Commander in Chief of the Army and Navy of the United States, and of the Militia of the several States, when called into the actual Service of the United States; he may require the Opinion, in writing, of the principal Officer in each of the executive Departments, upon any subject relating to the duties of their respective Offices, and he shall have Power to grant Reprieves and Pardons for Offences against the United States, except in Cases of Impeachment.

"He shall have Power, by and with the Advice and Consent of the Senate, to make Treaties, provided two thirds of the Senators present concur; and he shall nominate, and by and with the Advice and Consent of the Senate, shall appoint Ambassadors, other public Ministers and Consuls, Judges of the Supreme Court, and all other Officers of the United States whose Appointments are not herein otherwise provided for, and which shall be [109] established by Law: but the Congress may by Law vest the Appointment of such inferior Officers, as they think proper, in the President alone, in the Courts of Law, or in the Heads of Departments.

"The President shall have Power to fill up all Vacancies that may happen during the Recess of the Senate, by granting Commissions which shall expire at the End of their next Session.

"Section 3. He shall from time to time give to the Congress information of the State of the Union and recommend to their consideration such measures as he shall judge necessary and expedient; he may, on extraordinary occasions, convene both Houses or either of them, and in case of disagreement between them with respect to the time of adjournment, he may adjourn them to such time as he shall think proper; he shall receive Ambassadors and other public Ministers; he shall take Care that the Laws be faithfully executed, and shall Commission all the Officers of the United States.

"Section 4. The President, Vice President and all civil Officers of the United States, shall be removed from Office on Impeachment for, and

Conviction of, Treason, Bribery, or other High Crimes and Misdemeanors."

Section 1 of Article III, provides:

"The judicial power of the United States shall be vested in one Supreme Court and in such inferior courts as the Congress may from time to time ordain and establish. The judges, both of the Supreme and inferior Courts, shall hold their offices during good behavior. . . ."

[110] The question where the power of removal of executive officers appointed by the President and by and with the advice and consent of the Senate was vested, was presented early in the first session of the First Congress. There is no express provision respecting removals in the Constitution, except as Section 4 of Article II, above quoted, provides for the removal from office by impeachment. The subject was not discussed in the Constitutional Convention.

* * * * *

[111] In the House of Representatives of the First Congress, on Tuesday, May 18, 1789, Mr. Madison moved in the Committee of the Whole that there should be established three executive departments—one of Foreign Affairs, another of the Treasury, and a third of War—at the head of each of which there should be a Secretary, to be appointed by the President by and with the advice and consent of the Senate, and to be removable by the President. The committee agreed to the establishment of a Department of Foreign Affairs, but a discussion ensued as to making the Secretary removable by the President. 1 Annals of Congress, 370, 371. "The question was now taken and carried, by a considerable majority, in favor [112] of declaring the power of removal to be in the President." 1 Annals of Congress, 383.

* * * * *

[114] It is very clear from this history that the exact question which the House voted upon was whether it should recognize and declare the power of the President under the Constitution to remove the Secretary of Foreign Affairs without the advice and consent of the Senate. That was what the vote was taken for. Some effort has been made to question whether the decision carries the result claimed for it, but there is not the slightest doubt, after an examination of the record, that the vote was, and was intended to be, a legislative declaration that the power to remove officers appointed by the President and the Senate vested in the President alone, and until the

Johnson Impeachment trial in 1868, its meaning was not doubted even by those who questioned its soundness.

* * * * *

[118] It is quite true that, in state and colonial governments at the time of the Constitutional Convention, power to make appointments and removals had sometimes been lodged in the legislatures or in the courts, but such a disposition of it was really vesting part of the executive power in another branch of the Government. In the British system, the Crown, which was the executive, had the power of appointment and removal of executive officers, and it was natural therefore, for those who framed our Constitution to regard the words "executive power" as including both. *Ex Parte Grossman,* 267 U.S. 87, 110. Unlike the power of conquest of the British Crown, considered and rejected as a precedent for us in *Fleming v. Page,* 9 How. 603, 618, the association of removal with appointment of executive officers is not incompatible with our republican form of Government.

* * * * *

[119] Under Section 2 of Article II, however, the power of appointment by the Executive is restricted in its exercise by the provision that the Senate, a part of the legislative branch of the Government, may check the action of the Executive by rejecting the officers he selects. Does this make the Senate part of the removing power? And this, after the whole discussion in the House is read attentively, is the real point which was considered and decided in the negative by the vote already given.

The history of the clause by which the Senate was given a check upon the President's power of appointment makes it clear that it was not prompted by any desire to limit removals. As already pointed out, the important purpose of those who brought about the restriction was to lodge in the Senate, where the small States had equal [120] representation with the larger States, power to prevent the President from making too many appointments from the larger States. Roger Sherman and Oliver Ellsworth, delegates from Connecticut, reported to its Governor: "The equal representation of the States in the Senate and the voice of that branch in the appointment to offices will secure the rights of the lesser as well as of the greater States." 8 Farrand, 99. The formidable opposition to the Senate's veto on the President's power of appointment indicated that, in construing its effect, it should not be extended beyond its express application to the matter of appointments.

* * * * *

[131] As Mr. Madison said in the debate in the First Congress:

"Vest this power in the Senate jointly with the President, and you abolish at once that great principle of unity and responsibility in the Executive department, which was intended for the security of liberty and the public good. If the President should possess alone the power of removal from office, those who are employed in the execution of the law will be in their proper situation, and the chain of dependence be preserved; the lowest officers, the middle grade, and the highest, will depend, as they ought, on the President, and the President on the community." 1 Annals of Congress, 499.

* * * * *

[132] Made responsible under the Constitution for the effective enforcement of the law, the President needs as an indispensable aid to meet it the disciplinary influence upon those who act under him of a reserve power of removal. . . .

[133] The extent of the political responsibility thrust upon the President is brought out by Mr. Justice Miller, speaking for the Court in *Cunningham v. Neagle*, 135 U.S. 1 at p. 63:

"The Constitution, section 3, Article 2, declares that the President 'shall take care that the laws be faithfully executed,' and he is provided with the means of fulfilling this obligation by his authority to commission all the officers of the United States, and by and with the advice and consent of the Senate to appoint the most important of them and to fill vacancies. He is declared to be commander-in-chief of the army and navy of the United States. The duties which are thus imposed upon him he is further enabled to perform by the recognition in the Constitution, and the creation by Acts of Congress, of executive departments, which have varied in number from four or five to seven or eight, the heads of which are familiarly called cabinet ministers. These aid him in the performance of the great duties of his office and represent him in a thousand acts to which it can hardly be supposed his personal attention is called, and thus he is enabled to fulfill the duty of his great department, expressed in the phrase that 'he shall take care that the laws be faithfully executed.'"

* * * * *

[134] In all such cases, the discretion to be exercised is that of the President in determining the national public interest and in directing the action to be taken by his executive subordinates to protect it. In this field his cabinet

officers must do his will. He must place in each member of his official family, and his chief executive subordinates, implicit faith. The moment that he loses confidence in the intelligence, ability, judgment or loyalty of any one of them, he must have the power to remove him without delay. To require him to file charges and submit them to the consideration of the Senate might make impossible that unity and coordination in executive administration essential to effective action.

The duties of the heads of departments and bureaus in which the discretion of the President is exercised and which we have described, are the most important in the whole field of executive action of the Government. There is nothing in the Constitution which permits a distinction between the removal of the head of a department or a bureau, when he discharges a political duty of the President or exercises his discretion, and the removal of executive officers engaged in the discharge of their other normal duties. The imperative reasons requiring an unrestricted power to remove the most important of his subordinates in their most important duties must, therefore, control the interpretation of the Constitution as to all appointed by him.

* * * * *

[159] It is further pressed on us that, even though the legislative decision of 1789 included inferior officers, yet under the legislative power given Congress with respect to such officers, it might directly legislate as to the method of their removal without changing their method of appointment by the President with the consent of the Senate. We do not think the language of the Constitution justifies such a contention.

Section 2 of Article II, after providing that the President shall nominate and with the consent of the Senate [160] appoint ambassadors, other public ministers, consuls, judges of the Supreme Court and all other officers of the United States whose appointments are not herein otherwise provided for, and which shall be established by law, contains the proviso "but the Congress may by law vest the appointment of such inferior officers as they think proper in the President alone, in the courts of law or in the heads of departments." In *United States v. Perkins,* 116 U.S. 483, a cadet engineer, a graduate of the Naval Academy, brought suit to recover his salary for the period after his removal by the Secretary of the Navy. It was decided that his right was established by Revised Statutes 1229, providing that no officer in the military or naval service should in time of peace be dismissed from service, except in pursuance of a sentence of court-martial. The section was claimed to be an infringement upon the constitutional prerogative of the Executive. The Court of Claims refused to yield to this argument. . . .

* * * * *

[163] Summing up, then, the facts as to acquiescence by all branches of the Government in the legislative decision of 1789, as to executive officers, whether superior or inferior, we find that from 1789 until 1863, a period of 74 years, there was no act of Congress, no executive act, and no decision of this Court at variance with the declaration of the First Congress, but there was, as we have seen, clear, affirmative recognition of it by each branch of the Government.

Our conclusion on the merits, sustained by the arguments before stated, is that Article II grants to the [164] President the executive power of the Government, i.e., the general administrative control of those executing the laws, including the power of appointment and removal of executive officers—a conclusion confirmed by his obligation to take care that the laws be faithfully executed; that Article II excludes the exercise of legislative power by Congress to provide for appointments and removals, except only as granted therein to Congress in the matter of inferior offices; that Congress is only given power to provide for appointments and removals of inferior officers after it has vested, and on condition that it does vest, their appointment in other authority than the President with the Senate's consent; that the provisions of the second section of Article II, which blend action by the legislative branch, or by part of it, in the work of the executive, are limitations to be strictly construed and not to be extended by implication; that the President's power of removal is further established as an incident to his specifically enumerated function of appointment by and with the advice of the Senate, but that such incident does not by implication extend to removals the Senate's power of checking appointments; and finally that to hold otherwise would make it impossible for the President, in case of political or other differences with the Senate or Congress, to take care that the laws be faithfully executed.

We come now to a period in the history of the Government when both Houses of Congress attempted to reverse this constitutional construction and to subject the power of removing executive officers appointed by the President and confirmed by the Senate to the control of the Senate—indeed, finally, to the assumed power in Congress to place the removal of such officers anywhere in the Government.

This reversal grew out of the serious political difference between the two Houses of Congress and President Johnson. [165] There was a two-thirds majority of the Republican party in control of each House of Congress, which resented what it feared would be Mr. Johnson's obstructive course in the enforcement of the reconstruction measures, in respect of the States whose people had lately been at war against the National Government. This led the two Houses to enact legislation to curtail the then acknowledged powers of the President. . . .

* * * * *

[166] But the chief legislation in support of the reconstruction policy of Congress was the Tenure of Office Act, of March 2, 1867, 14 Stat 430, c. 154, providing that all officers appointed by and with the consent of the Senate should hold their offices until their successors should have in like manner been appointed and qualified, and that certain heads of departments, including the Secretary of War, should hold their offices during the term of the President by whom appointed and one month thereafter subject to removal by consent of the Senate. The Tenure of Office Act was vetoed, but it was passed over the veto. The House of Representatives preferred articles of impeachment against President Johnson for refusal to comply with, and for conspiracy to defeat, the legislation above referred to, but he was acquitted for lack of a two-thirds vote for conviction in the Senate. . . .

* * * * *

[167] After President Johnson's term ended, the injury and invalidity of the Tenure of Office Act in its radical innovation were immediately recognized by the Executive and objected to. General Grant, succeeding Mr. Johnson [168] in the Presidency, earnestly recommended in his first message the total repeal of the act. . . .

* * * * *

While, in response to this, a bill for repeal of that act passed the House, it failed in the Senate, and, though the law was changed, it still limited the Presidential power of removal. The feeling growing out of the controversy with President Johnson retained the act on the statute book until 1887, when it was repealed. . . .

* * * * *

[169] The attitude of the Presidents on this subject has been unchanged and uniform to the present day whenever an issue has clearly been raised.

* * * * *

[172] The fact seems to be that all departments of the Government have constantly had in mind, since the passage of the Tenure of Office Act, that

the question of power of removal by the President of officers appointed by him [173] with the Senate's consent, has not been settled adversely to the legislative action of 1789 but, in spite of Congressional action, has remained open until the conflict should be subjected to judicial investigation and decision.

* * * * *

[174] What, then, are the elements that enter into our decision of this case? We have first a construction of the Constitution made by a Congress which was to provide by legislation for the organization of the Government in accord with the Constitution which had just then been adopted, and in which there were, as representatives and senators, a considerable number of those who had been members of the Convention that framed the Constitution and presented it for ratification. It was the Congress that launched the Government. It was the Congress that rounded out the Constitution itself by the proposing of the first ten amendments which had in effect been promised to the people as a consideration for the ratification. It was the Congress in which Mr. Madison, one of the first in the framing of the Constitution, led also in the organization of the Government under it. It was a Congress whose constitutional decisions have always been regarded, as they should be regarded, as of the greatest [175] weight in the interpretation of that fundamental instrument. This construction was followed by the legislative department and the executive department continuously for seventy-three years, and this although the matter, in the heat of political differences between the Executive and the Senate in President Jackson's time, was the subject of bitter controversy, as we have seen. This Court has repeatedly laid down the principle that a contemporaneous legislative exposition of the Constitution when the founders of our Government and framers of our Constitution were actively participating in public affairs, acquiesced in for a long term of years, fixes the construction to be given its provisions. . . .

We are now asked to set aside this construction, thus buttressed, and adopt an adverse view, because the Congress of the United States did so during a heated political difference of opinion between the then President and the majority leaders of Congress over the reconstruction measures adopted as a means of restoring to their proper status the States which attempted to withdraw from the Union at the time of the Civil War. The extremes to which the majority in both Houses carried legislative measures in that matter are now recognized by all who calmly review the history of that episode in our Government, leading to articles of impeachment against President Johnson, and his acquittal. Without [176] animadverting on the character of the measures taken, we are certainly justified in saying that they should not be given the weight affecting proper constitutional construction to be accorded to that reached by the First Congress of the United States during a political calm and acquiesced in by the whole Government for three-quarters of a century, especially when the new construction contended for has never been acquiesced in by either the executive or the judicial departments. While this Court has studiously avoided deciding the issue until it was presented in such a way that it could not be avoided, in the references it has made to the history of the question, and in the presumptions it has indulged in favor of a statutory construction not inconsistent with the legislative decision of 1789, it has indicated a trend of view that we should not and can not ignore. When, on the merits, we find our conclusion strongly favoring the view which prevailed in the First Congress, we have no hesitation in holding that conclusion to be correct; and it therefore follows that the Tenure of Office Act of 1867, in so far as it attempted to prevent the President from removing executive officers who had been appointed by him by and with the advice and consent of the Senate, was invalid, and that subsequent legislation of the same effect was equally so.

For the reasons given, we must therefore hold that the provision of the law of 1876, by which the unrestricted power of removal of first class postmasters is denied to the President, is in violation of the Constitution, and invalid. This leads to an affirmance of the judgment of the Court of Claims.

Before closing this opinion, we wish to express the obligation of the Court to Mr. Pepper for his able brief and argument as a friend of the Court. Undertaken at our request, our obligation is none the less if we find ourselves obliged to take a view adverse to his. The strong presentation of arguments against the conclusion of the Court [177] is of the utmost value in enabling the Court to satisfy itself that it has fully considered all that can be said.

Judgment affirmed.

Hughes Bros. Timber Co. v. Minnesota

Hughes Brothers again required the Court to defend interstate commerce from efforts by states to tax it. As he had done earlier in *Champlain Realty Company v. Town of Brattleboro*, 260 U.S. 366 (1922), Taft found the tax to be unconstitutional as applied.

Hughes Brothers Timber Company v. Minnesota

Certiorari to the Supreme Court of Minnesota

No. 170. Argued October 6, 7, 1926—Decided November 23, 1926

272 U.S. 469 (1926)

[471]

MR. CHIEF JUSTICE TAFT delivered the opinion of the Court.

This was a special proceeding in the District Court of Cook County, Minnesota, by the State, through the county treasurer, to collect taxes on personal property owned by the Hughes Bros. Timber Company. With the penalty and fees and costs, the amount sued for was $2,919.50. The amount claimed by items appeared in a delinquent list furnished by the treasurer to the sheriff of the county for collection for the year 1922. It included a tax upon 10,000 cords of pulp wood of the assessed value of $21,233. In its answer as amended, the Timber Company pleaded that the pulp wood was not subject to taxation in the State of Minnesota at the time it was assessed, May 1, 1922, but was at that time in actual transit in interstate commerce by continuous route from the State of Minnesota to the State of Michigan. . . .

* * * * *

[472] The Timber Company was a partnership, having its office headquarters at Hovland, Cook County, Minnesota. The Swamp River flows through the county and empties into the Pigeon River. The latter forms the boundary between Cook County, Minnesota, and the Province of Ontario, Canada, and empties into Lake Superior. The Timber Company's pulp wood was cut and gathered at various places in the county, but was hauled to the Swamp River and piled up on the ice and on its banks at a point about two miles and a half above its discharge into the Pigeon River. In October, 1921, the Timber Company had made a contract with the Central Paper Company of Muskegon, Michigan. By that contract the Timber Company agreed to deliver to the Paper Company, over the rail of the Paper Company's vessels at the mouth of the Pigeon River, approximately 10,000 cords of spruce pulp wood. The Timber Company agreed to load the wood into them as promptly as possible after its arrival. . . .

* * * * *

[473] The Timber Company was under contract to float the timber down from the place of piling on the Swamp River and deliver it as promptly as possible. The Paper Company by payment of $3.00 a ton had acquired a

qualified ownership in the timber even before it was segregated and put to float. Had the Timber Company or some one claiming under it attempted to stop the drive after it had begun, and interfered with the passage of the timber [474] down the Swamp or Pigeon River, it would have been a breach of the contract of sale. All this characterizes what was being done in the drive between the Swamp River entrepot and the mouth of the Pigeon River. That was the beginning or first leg of the interstate journey. The obligations of both parties accorded with that view. The change in the method of transportation by floating to carriage on a vessel did not affect the continuity of the interstate passage. . . .

The case seems to us to come within the ruling of this Court in the case of *Champlain Company v. The Town of Brattleboro*, 260 U.S. 366. That was a tax case like this. There the owner had cut pulpwood in several towns in Vermont. The wood was placed upon the banks of the West River and its tributaries, to be floated down into the Connecticut River and thence to its destination at the mill of the owner in Hinsdale on the New Hampshire side of the river. Four thousand of the cords had been floated down the West River on the high water and reached a boom at the mouth of the West River, but it was thought not safe, in view of the high water, then to let the wood into the Connecticut. It was contended that the logs which were held in the boom at the mouth of the West River were taxable there. We held otherwise; that the interstate journey of the logs had already begun when [475] the boom was reached, that the boom was not a depot for the gathering of logs preparatory for the final journey, that it was a safety appliance in the course of the final journey, a harbor of refuge from danger to a shipment on its way; that it was not used by the owner for any beneficial purpose of his own except to facilitate the safe delivery of the wood in New Hampshire on the other side of the Connecticut River.

* * * * *

[476] The judgment of the Supreme Court of Minnesota is reversed and remanded for further proceedings not inconsistent with this opinion.

Reversed.

Hanover Fire Insurance Co. v. Harding

The power to tax is a power possessed by both the federal government and the governments of the states. The state power to tax, however, may not be employed in a manner designed to discriminate in favor of domestic corporations as against out-of-state or foreign corporations. Ensuring that out-of-state and foreign firms pay their fair share for doing business in a state while also ensuring that they are not taxed unfairly is a burden the Supreme Court has wrestled with and continues to wrestle with. Taft found the particular tax imposed by Illinois to discriminate unconstitutionally against out-of-state insurance firms.

Hanover Fire Insurance Company
v. Harding, County Treasurer

Error to the Supreme Court of the State of Illinois

No. 179. Argued October 18, 1926—Decided November 23, 1926

272 U.S. 494 (1926)

[501]

MR. CHIEF JUSTICE TAFT delivered the opinion of the Court.

* * * * *

[510] In subjecting a law of the State which imposes a charge upon foreign corporations to the test whether such a charge violates the equal protection clause of the Fourteenth Amendment, a line has to be drawn between the burden imposed by the State for the license or privilege to do business in the State, and the tax burden which, having secured the right to do business, the foreign corporation must share with all the corporations and other taxpayers of the State. With respect to the admission fee, so to speak, which the foreign corporation must pay, to become a quasi citizen of the State and entitled to [511] equal privileges with citizens of the State, the measure of the burden is in the discretion of the State, and any inequality as between the foreign corporation and the domestic corporation in that regard does not come within the inhibition of the Fourteenth Amendment; but, after its admission, the foreign corporation stands equal, and is to be classified with domestic corporations of the same kind.

In this class of cases, therefore, the question of the application of the equal protection clause turns on the stage at which the foreign corporation is put on a level with domestic corporations, in engaging in business within the State. To leave the determination of such a question finally to a state court would be to deprive this Court of its independent judgment in determining whether a federal constitutional limitation has been infringed. While we may not question the meaning of the tax law, as interpreted by the state court, in the manner and effect in which it is to be enforced, we must re-examine the question passed upon by the state court, as to whether the law complained of is a part of the condition upon which admission to do business of the State is permitted and is merely a regulating license by the State to protect the State and its citizens in dealing with such corporation, or whether it is a tax law for the purpose of securing contributions to the revenue of the State as they are made by other taxpayers of the State. . . .

* * * * *

[516] We thus reach the question whether a tax imposed upon foreign fire, marine and inland navigation insurance companies on the net receipts of all their business, whether fire, marine, inland navigation or other risks, is a denial of the equal protection of the laws, when domestic insurance companies pay no taxes on such net receipts. Under the previous decisions of the Supreme Court of Illinois, when the net receipts were treated as personal property and the assessment thereon as a personal property tax subjected to the same reductions for equalization and debasement, it might well have been said that there was no substantial inequality as between domestic corporations and foreign corporations, in that the net receipts were personal property acquired during the year and removed by foreign companies out of the State, and could be required justly to yield a tax fairly equivalent to that which the domestic companies would have to pay on all their personal property, including their net receipts or what they were invested in. It was this view, doubtless, which led to the acquiescence by the state authorities and the foreign insurance companies in such a construction of § 30, and in the practice under it. But an occupation tax imposed upon 100 per cent. of the net receipts of foreign insurance companies admitted to do business in Illinois, is a heavy discrimination in favor of domestic insurance companies of the same class and in the same business, which pay only a tax on the assessment of personal property at a valuation reduced to one-half of 60 per cent. of the full value of that property. . . .

[517] One argument urged against our conclusion is that the relation of a foreign insurance company to the State which permits it to do business within its limits, is contractual, and that, by coming into the State and engaging in business on the conditions imposed, it waives all constitutional restrictions, and can not object to a condition or law regulating its obligations, even though, as a statute operating *in invitum,* it may be in conflict with constitutional limitations. This argument can not prevail in view of the decisions of this Court . . .

The judgment of the Supreme Court of Illinois must be reversed and the case remanded for further proceedings not inconsistent with this opinion.

Reversed.

Federal Trade Commission v. Western Meat Co

These cases involved questions about the power of the Federal Trade Commission to take action under the Clayton Act. The Court divided five to four, with Justice Brandeis writing a dissenting opinion upholding the powers of the FTC to act in which Chief Justice Taft joined.

Federal Trade Commission v. Western Meat Company

Certiorari to the Circuit Court of Appeals for the Ninth Circuit

Thatcher Manufacturing Company
v. Federal Trade Commission

Certiorari to the Circuit Court of Appeals for the Third Circuit

Swift & Company v. Federal Trade Commission

Certiorari to the Circuit Court of Appeals for the Seventh Circuit

Nos. 96, 213, 231. Argued October 25, 26, 1926—
Decided November 23, 1926

272 U.S. 554 (1926)

[556]

MR. JUSTICE MCREYNOLDS delivered the opinion of the Court.

I

These causes necessitate consideration of the power of the Federal Trade Commission where it finds that one corporation has acquired shares of a competitor contrary to the inhibition of the Clayton Act. . . .

* * * * *

[563] . . . As all property and business of the two competing companies were acquired by the petitioner prior to the filing of the complaint, it is evident that no practical relief could be obtained through an order merely directing petitioner to divest itself of valueless stock. As stated in number 213, we are of opinion that under §§ 7 and 11 of the Clayton Act the Commission is without authority to require one who has secured actual title and possession of physical property before proceedings were begun against it to dispose of the same, although secured through an unlawful purchase of stock. The courts must administer whatever remedy there may be in such situation. The order of the Commission should have been reviewed and set aside; and judgment to that effect will be entered here.

Reversed.

MR. JUSTICE BRANDEIS, dissenting in part.

In my opinion, the purpose of § 7 of the Clayton Act was not, as stated by the Court, merely "to prevent continued holding of the stock and the peculiar evils incident thereto." It was also to prevent the peculiar evils resulting therefrom. The institution of a proceeding before the Commission under § 7 does not operate, like an injunction, to restrain a company from acquiring the assets of the controlled corporation by means of the stock held in violation of that section. If, in spite of the commencement of such a proceeding, the company took a transfer of the assets, the Commission could, I assume, require a retransfer of the assets, so as to render effective the order of divestiture of the stock. I see no reason why it should not, likewise, do this although the company succeeded in securing the assets of the controlled corporation before [564] the Commission instituted a proceeding. Support for this conclusion may be found in § 11, which provides for action by the Commission whenever it "shall have reason to believe that any person is violating *or has violated* any of the provisions" of the earlier sections. (Italics ours.)

I think that the decrees in Nos. 213 and 231 should be affirmed.

THE CHIEF JUSTICE, MR. JUSTICE HOLMES and MR. JUSTICE STONE join in this dissent.

Omitted Taft Opinions

United States v. General Electric Co., 272 U.S. 476 (1926)—patent case.
Wright v. Ynchausti & Co., 272 U.S. 640 (1926)—dispute from the Philippines over money collected improperly for imports.

Eastern Transportation Company v. United States, 272 U.S. 675 (1927)—admiralty.
Postum Cereal Co. v. California Fig Nut Co., 272 U.S. 693 (1927)—trademark.
Los Angeles Brush Manufacturing Corporation v. James, District Judge, 272 U.S. 693 (1927)—
power of Supreme Court to mandamus district court.

VOLUME 273

Tumey v. Ohio

Tumey was convicted of violating Ohio's Prohibition act. He was tried before the mayor of the village of North College Hill. Ohio law provided that half of the fine assessed would be retained by the village and that the mayor would be compensated for his costs in hearing the case. Tumey claimed that this arrangement violated his right to due process as guaranteed by the Fourteenth Amendment. Taft and the Court agreed and unanimously reversed the conviction.

Tumey v. Ohio

Error to the Supreme Court of Ohio

No. 527. Argued November 29, 30, 1926—Decided March 7, 1927

273 U.S. 510 (1927)

[514]

MR. CHIEF JUSTICE TAFT delivered the opinion of the Court.

The question in this case is whether certain statutes of Ohio, in providing for the trial by the mayor of a village of one accused of violating the Prohibition Act of the State, deprive the accused of due process of law and violate the Fourteenth Amendment to the Federal [515] Constitution, because of the pecuniary and other interest which those statutes give the mayor in the result of the trial.

Tumey, the plaintiff in error, hereafter to be called the defendant, was arrested and brought before Mayor Pugh, of the Village of North College

Hill, charged with unlawfully possessing intoxicating liquor. He moved for his dismissal because of the disqualification of the Mayor to try him, under the Fourteenth Amendment. The Mayor denied the motion, proceeded to the trial, convicted the defendant of unlawfully possessing intoxicating liquor within Hamilton County, as charged, fined him $100, and ordered that he be imprisoned until the fine and costs were paid. . . .

* * * * *

[517] . . . [T]he Village Council of North College Hill passed Ordinance No. 125, as follows:

* * * * *

[518] "Section I. That fifty per cent of all moneys hereafter paid into the treasury of said village of North College Hill, Ohio, that is one-half of the share of all fines collected and paid into and belonging to said village of North College Hill, Ohio, received from fines collected under any law of the state of Ohio, prohibiting the liquor traffic, shall constitute a separate fund to be called the Secret Service Fund to be used for the purpose of securing the enforcement of any prohibition law.

* * * * *

[519] "Section V. That the mayor of the village of North College Hill, Ohio, shall receive or retain the amount of his costs in each case, in addition to his regular salary, as compensation for hearing such cases.

* * * * *

The duties of the Mayor of a village in Ohio are primarily executive. . . .

* * * * *

[520] The fees which the Mayor and Marshal received in this case came to them by virtue of the general statutes of the state applying to all state cases, liquor and otherwise. The Mayor was entitled to hold the legal fees taxed in his favor. Ohio General Code, § 4270; *State v. Nolte*, 111 o. S. 486. Moreover, the North College Hill village council sought to remove all doubt on this point by providing (§ 5, Ord. 125, *supra*), that he should receive or retain the amount of his costs in each case, in addition to his regular salary, as compensation for hearing such cases. But no fees or costs in such cases are paid him except by the defendant if convicted. . . .

* * * * *

[523] The Mayor of the Village of North College Hill, Ohio, had a direct, personal, pecuniary interest in convicting the defendant who came before him for trial, in the twelve dollars of costs imposed in his behalf, which he would not have received if the defendant had been acquitted. This was not exceptional, but was the result of the normal operation of the law and the ordinance.

* * * * *

[532] But the pecuniary interest of the Mayor in the result of his judgment is not the only reason for holding that due process of law is denied to the defendant here. The statutes were drawn to stimulate small municipalities in the country part of counties in which there are large cities, to organize and maintain courts to try persons accused of violations of the Prohibition Act everywhere in the county. The inducement is offered of dividing between [533] the State and the village the large fines provided by the law for its violations. The trial is to be had before a mayor without a jury, without opportunity for retrial and with a review confined to questions of law presented by a bill of exceptions, with no opportunity by the reviewing court to set aside the judgment on the weighing of evidence, unless it should appear to be so manifestly against the evidence as to indicate mistake, bias or willful disregard of duty by the trial court. . . .

* * * * *

[535] It is finally argued that the evidence shows clearly that the defendant was guilty and that he was only fined $100, which was the minimum amount, and therefore that he can not complain of a lack of due process, either in his conviction or in the amount of the judgment. The plea was not guilty and he was convicted. No matter what the evidence was against him, he had the right to have an impartial judge. He seasonably raised the objection and was entitled to halt the trial because of the disqualification of the judge, which existed both because of his direct pecuniary interest in the outcome, and because of his official motive to convict and to graduate the fine to help the financial needs of the village. There were thus presented at the outset both features of the disqualification.

The judgment of the Supreme Court of Ohio must be reversed and the cause remanded for further proceedings not inconsistent with this opinion.

Judgment reversed.

Shields v. United States

Shields was convicted for violation of the Volstead Act. At his trial in United States District Court, the jury returned to the courtroom to ask for additional instructions on the issue of entrapment. Neither Shields nor his attorney were present when the judge gave the jury additional instructions. Taft found this to constitute reversible error.

Shields v. United States

On Petition for a Writ of Certiorari to the Circuit Court of Appeals for the Third Circuit

No. 944. Petition submitted March 21, 1927—Decided April 11, 1927

273 U.S. 583 (1927)

[583]

MR. CHIEF JUSTICE TAFT delivered the opinion of the Court.

* * * * *

[584] Shields, the petitioner, was indicted and tried with eight or nine others for conspiracy to violate the Prohibition Act. . . . Shortly after the opening of the court, the jury returned for additional instructions on the subject of entrapment, and having received the same, retired for further deliberation. At 2.30 o'clock that afternoon, the jury again returned to court, in the absence of petitioner and his counsel, and reported that they could not agree. What instructions, if any, were then given the jury the record does not disclose. It appears that the jury again retired to deliberate, and between 4.30 and 5.00 o'clock in the afternoon sent from their jury room to the judge in chambers the following written communication:

"We, the jury, find the defendants John G. Emmerling, Charles Lynch not guilty on all counts, E. W. Hardison, J. E. Hunter and J. L. Simler guilty on all counts. Daniel J. Shields, Harry Widman, J. M. Gastman unable to agree.

Signed, E. B. MILLIGAN,
Foreman."

The judge from his chambers sent back the following written reply:

"The jury will have to find also whether Shields, Widman and Gastman are guilty or not guilty.

F. P. SCHOONMAKER,
Judge."

[585] These communications were not made in open court, and neither the petitioner Shields nor his counsel was present, nor were they advised of them. Shortly after, the jury returned in court and announced the following verdict:

"We, the jury, find that the defendants John G. Emmerling, Charles Lynch, not guilty on all counts. E. W. Hardison, J. L. Simler, J. E. Hunter guilty on all four counts. Daniel J. Shields, Harry Widman, J. M. Gastman guilty on first count and recommended to mercy of court. Not guilty on 2nd, 3rd and 4th counts, this 13th day of February, 1926.

E. B. MILLIGAN,
Foreman."

* * * * *

[588] In the case of *Fillippon v. Albion Vein Slate Co.,* 250 U.S. 76, which was a suit for damages for personal injuries, it appeared that, after the trial judge had completed his instructions and the jury had retired for deliberation, and while they were deliberating, they sent to the judge a written inquiry on the question of contributory negligence, to which the trial judge replied by sending a written instruction to the jury room, in the absence of the parties and their counsel and without their consent, and without calling the jury into open court. A new trial was ordered on this account. The Court said:

"Where a jury has retired to consider of its verdict, and supplementary instructions are required, either because asked for by the jury or for other reasons, they ought to be given either in the presence of counsel or after notice and an opportunity to be present; and written instructions ought not to be sent to the jury without notice to counsel and an opportunity to object."

If this be true in a civil case, *a fortiori* is it true in a criminal case. The request made to the court jointly by the counsel for the defendant and for the Government did not justify exception to the rule of orderly conduct [589] of jury trial entitling the defendant, especially in a criminal case, to be present from the time the jury is impaneled until its discharge after rendering the verdict. We reverse the judgment without reference to the other causes of error assigned.

Reversed.

Kelley v. Oregon

Kelley was convicted of killing a guard during a prison escape and sentenced to death. He appealed, claiming a violation of the Fourteenth Amendment. He claimed that by executing him the state would prevent him from serving out the term to which he had previously been sentenced. The Court disagreed.

Kelley v. Oregon

Error to the Supreme Court of the State of Oregon

No. 827. Argued March 9, 1927—Decided April 11, 1927

273 U.S. 589 (1927)

[589]

MR. CHIEF JUSTICE TAFT delivered the opinion of the Court.

* * * * *

[590] At the time of the commission of the crime set forth in the indictment, Kelley and the two others accused with him were prisoners in the Oregon State Penitentiary at Salem, Oregon, and the crime was committed by them in their escape from that institution. John Sweeney, named in the indictment, was a guard at the institution and was slain in his attempt to prevent the escape.

* * * * *

[592] It is contended that this construction of the statute, in permitting one who has committed a murder while a convict in the penitentiary to be

executed before his term has expired, deprives him of a right secured by the Fourteenth Amendment, in that due process of law secures to him as a privilege the serving out of his sentence before he shall be executed. It is doubtful whether this exception and assignment can be said to be directed to a ruling of the Supreme Court of Oregon such as to draw in question the validity of a statute of Oregon on the ground of its repugnancy to the Constitution, treaties or laws of the [593] United States and sustain it, as required in § 237a of the Judicial Code, as amended, c. 229, 43 Stat. 936, 937, permitting a writ of error. But assuming that it does, or, if not, treating the writ of error as an application for certiorari, there is not the slightest ground for sustaining the assignment.

A prisoner may certainly be tried, convicted and sentenced for another crime committed either prior to or during his imprisonment, and may suffer capital punishment and be executed during the term. The penitentiary is no sanctuary, and life in it does not confer immunity from capital punishment provided by law. He has no vested constitutional right to serve out his unexpired sentence. . . .

The writ of error is dismissed and the certiorari is denied.

Ford v. United States

The *Ford* case is yet another example of how the issue of Prohibition helped fill the Court's docket in the 1920s. The defendants sought to exclude the evidence against them by contending that the seizure was illegal because it occurred outside U.S. territorial waters as prescribed by a treaty with the United Kingdom. Taft carefully examined the treaty and concluded that there was no evidence that the United Kingdom meant that the treaty should operate in a way that would interfere with the ability of the United States to enforce its laws against the importation of liquor.

Ford et al. v. United States

Certiorari to the Circuit Court of Appeals for the Ninth Circuit

No. 312. Argued October 26, 27, 1926—Decided April 11, 1927

273 U.S. 593 (1927)

[600]

MR. CHIEF JUSTICE TAFT delivered the opinion of the Court.

This is a review by certiorari of the conviction of George Ford, George Harris, J. Evelyn, Charles H. Belanger and Vincent Quartararo, of a conspiracy, contrary to § 37 of the Criminal Code, to violate the National Prohibition Act. . . . The trial and conviction resulted largely from the seizure of the British vessel Quadra, hovering in the high seas off the Farallon Islands, territory of the United States, twenty-five miles west from San Francisco. The ship, her officers, her crew and cargo of liquor were towed into the port of San Francisco. The seizure was made under the authority of the treaty between Great Britain and the United States, proclaimed by the President May 22, 1924, 43 Stat. 1761, as a convention to aid in the prevention of the smuggling of intoxicating liquors into the United States.

The main questions presented are, first, whether the seizure of the vessel was in accordance with the treaty; second, whether the treaty prohibits prosecution of the persons, subjects of Great Britain, on board the seized vessel brought within the jurisdiction of the United States upon the landing of such vessel, for illegal importation of liquor; third, whether the treaty authorizes prosecution of such persons, not only for the substantive offense of illegal importation or attempt to import, but also for conspiracy to effect it; and, fourth, whether such persons, [601] without the United States, conspiring and cooperating to violate its laws with other persons who are within the United States and to commit overt acts therein, can be prosecuted therefor when thereafter found in the United States.

* * * * *

[604] There was a preliminary motion to exclude and suppress the evidence of the ship and cargo. It was contended that the seizure was unlawful because not within the zone of the high seas prescribed by the treaty; and that the officers of the Quadra being prosecuted were protected [605] against its use as evidence against them under the Fourth and Fifth Amendments to the Federal Constitution. The motion was heard by the District Court without a jury and was denied in an opinion reported in 3 Fed. (2d) 643. The evidence of the Government showed that the Quadra was seized at a distance from the Farallon Islands of 5.7 miles, and a test made later of the speed of the motor boat C-55, caught carrying liquor from her, showed that it could traverse 6.6 miles in an hour. There was a conflict as to the exact position of the Quadra at the time of the seizure. It was further objected that

the speed of the motor boat was not made under the same conditions as those which existed at the time of the seizure.

The question of the evidential weight of the test as well as of all the circumstances was for the judgment of the trial court. As it has been affirmed by the Circuit Court of Appeals, we see no reason to reverse it.

* * * * *

[607] The defendants contend that on the face of the indictment and the treaty they are made immune from trial. This requires an examination and construction of the treaty.

The preamble of the treaty recites that the two nations, being desirous of avoiding any difficulties which might arise between them in connection with the laws in force in the United States on the subject of alcoholic beverages, have decided to conclude a convention for the purpose.

* * * * *

"ARTICLE II.

"(1) His Britannic Majesty agrees that he will raise no objection to the boarding of private vessels under the British flag outside the limits of territorial waters by the authorities of the United States, its territories or possessions in order that enquiries may be addressed to those on board and an examination be made of the ship's papers for the purpose of ascertaining whether the vessel or those on board are endeavoring to import or have imported alcoholic beverages into the United States, its territories or possessions in violation of the laws there in force. [608] When such enquiries and examination show a reasonable ground for suspicion, a search of the vessel may be instituted.

"(2) If there is reasonable cause for belief that the vessel has committed or is committing or attempting to commit an offense against the laws of the United States, its territories or possessions prohibiting the importation of alcoholic beverages, the vessel may be seized and taken into a port of the United States, its territories or possessions for adjudication in accordance with such laws."

* * * * *

[610] . . . The treaty provides for the disposition of the vessel after seizure. It has to be taken into port for adjudication. What is to be adjudicated? The vessel. What does that include? The inference that both ship and those on

board are to be subjected to prosecution on incriminating evidence is fully justified by paragraph 1 of Article II, in specifically permitting examination of the ship papers and inquiries to those on board to ascertain whether, not only the ship, but also those on board, are endeavoring to import, or have imported, liquor into the United States. If those on board are to be excluded, then by the same narrow construction the cargo of liquor is to escape adjudication, though it is subject to search as the persons on board are to inquiry into their guilt. It is no straining of the language of the article therefore to interpret the phrase "the vessel may be seized and taken into a port of the United States . . . for adjudication in accordance with such laws," as intending that not only the vessel but that all and everything on board are to be adjudicated. The seizure and the taking into port necessarily include the cargo and persons on board. They can not be set adrift or thrown overboard. They must go with the ship—they are identified with it. Their immunity on the high seas from seizure or being taken into port came from the immunity of the vessel by reason of her British nationality. When the vessel lost this immunity, they lost it too, and when they were brought into a port of the United States and into the jurisdiction of its District Court, they were just as much subject to its [611] adjudication as the ship. If they committed an offense against the United States and its liquor importation laws, they can not escape conviction, unless the treaty affirmatively confers on them immunity from prosecution. There certainly are no express words granting such immunity. Why should it be implied? If it was intended by the parties why should it not have been expressed?

* * * * *

[612] What reason could Great Britain have for a stipulation clothing with immunity either contraband liquor which should be condemned or the guilty persons aboard, when the very object of the treaty was to help the United States in its effort to protect itself against such liquor and such persons, from invasion by the sea? To give immunity to the cargo and the guilty persons on board would be to clear those whose guilt should condemn the vessel and to restore to them the liquor, and thus release both for another opportunity to flout the laws of a friendly government which it was the purpose of the [613] treaty to discourage. The owner of the vessel would thus alone be subjected to penalty, and he would suffer for the primary guilt of the immunized owner of the liquor. . . .

Nor have we been advised that Great Britain has ever suggested that under this treaty a crew of a vessel lawfully seized could not be brought into port or tried according to our laws. Diligent as the representatives of that nation have always been in guarding the rights of their people, such a construction of the treaty has not been advanced. It is said by the Solicitor General without contradiction that, following a number of seizures of British ships on our coasts under the treaty, those on board have been indicted and tried for offenses against the laws relating to intoxicating beverages, and that the State Department records show no objection of immunity therefrom to have been claimed for them by the British Government. . . .

* * * * *

[625] The judgment of conviction of the Court of Appeals is

Affirmed.

Omitted Taft Opinions

Hartford Accident Co. v. Southern Pacific Co., 273 U.S. 207 (1927)—admiralty case.
Charleston Mining Co. v. United States, 273 U.S. 220 (1927)—rule for reviewing finding of fraud by lower federal courts.
Barrett Co. v. United States, 273 U.S. 227 (1927)—contract dispute.
DeForest Co. v. United States, 273 U.S. 236 (1927)—patent case.
Hellmich v. Missouri Pacific, 273 U.S. 242 (1927)—tax on telegraph service.
Oklahoma Natural Gas Co. v. Oklahoma, 273 U.S. 257 (1927)—effect of dissolution of company on litigation.
United States v. Shelby Iron Co., 273 U.S. 571 (1927)—contract dispute.

VOLUME 274

Morris v. Duby

Ordinarily, Chief Justice William Howard Taft could be depended upon in conflicts between the power of the federal government and that of a state to rule in favor of the federal government. This case was a notable exception. The Oregon Highway Commission, after hearings, had lowered the maximum load on trucks using a postal road that went to the state of Washington. A trucking company challenged the new restriction, arguing that it was both unreasonable and an invasion of the federal government's power under I-8–3 (the Commerce Clause). Taft found for the state, holding that the decision was a reasonable exercise of the state's legitimate police powers.

Morris et al. v. Duby et al., Commissioners

Appeal from the District Court of the United States for the District of Oregon

No. 372. Argued October 29, 1926—Decided April 18, 1927

274 U.S. 135 (1927)

[139]

MR. CHIEF JUSTICE TAFT delivered the opinion of the Court.

The plaintiffs below, the appellants here, owned and operated for hire, under proper license, motor trucks on the Columbia River Highway in Oregon, from the east boundary of Multnomah County to the west limits of the city of Hood River, a distance of 22.11 miles. This Highway extends from Portland to The Dalles, Oregon, and is a rural post road. The plaintiffs have complied with all the state rules and regulations respecting the operation of motor trucks upon the Highway, and under previous regulations carried a combined maximum load of not exceeding 22,000 pounds. The Highway Commission, under a law of Oregon, has reduced the maximum to 16,500 pounds, by an order in which the Commission recites that the road is being damaged by heavier loads. The plaintiffs filed this bill to enjoin the enforcement of the order, on the ground that it invades their federal constitutional rights.

The case was heard under § 266 of the Judicial Code, as amended by the Act of February 13, 1925, c. 229, 43 Stat. 926, before a court of three judges, on an order to show cause why a preliminary injunction should not issue restraining the Commission from enforcing the order. . . .

[140] The Secretary of Agriculture, by virtue of three Acts of Congress, one of July 11, 1916, c. 241, 39 Stat. 355, an amendment thereto of February 28, 1919, c. 69, 40 Stat. 1189, 1200, and the Federal Highway Act of November 9, 1921, c. 119, 42 Stat. 212, is authorized to cooperate with the States, through their respective highway departments, in the construction of rural post roads. These require that no money appropriated under their provisions shall be expended in any State until it shall by its legislature have assented to

the provisions of the Acts. They provide that the Secretary of Agriculture and the state highway department of each State shall agree upon the roads to be constructed therein and the character and method of their construction. The construction work in each State is to be done in accordance with its laws, and under the supervision of the state highway department, subject to the inspection and approval of the Secretary and in accord with his rules and regulations made pursuant to the federal acts. The States are required to maintain the roads so constructed according to their laws.

* * * * *

[142] The order complained of, set forth as an exhibit to the amended bill of complaint, recites that the Commission, as a result of due investigation, finds that the road is being damaged and injured on account of the kind and character of traffic now being hauled over it, and that the loads of maximum weight moved at the maximum speed are breaking up, damaging and deteriorating the road, and that it will therefore be for the best interests of the state highway that the maximum weight be reduced from 20,000 to 16,500, and that changes be made with respect to tires and their width.

The amended bill gives a history of the highway and its continued use for a weight of 22,000 pounds for four years, which has been availed of by the appellants as common carriers and as members of an Auto Freight Transportation Association of Oregon and Washington with costly terminals in Portland established by requirement of that city; it alleges that the twenty-two miles [143] of the Columbia River Highway here involved is a part of the interstate highway from Astoria, Oregon, into the State of Washington, and all subject to the Federal Highway Acts, and that this order will interfere with interstate commerce thereon. The amended bill denies the damage to the road as found by the Highway Commission, and says that the reduction of the limit will be unreasonable, arbitrary and discriminatory. It avers that the plaintiffs have been engaged in active competition with steam railroads paralleling the Columbia River Highway and charging rates of traffic which, unless the appellants can use trucks combined with loads of 22,000 pounds, will prevent their doing business except at a loss. . . .

An examination of the acts of Congress discloses no provision, express or implied, by which there is withheld from the State its ordinary police power to conserve the highways in the interest of the public and to prescribe such reasonable regulations for their use as may be wise to prevent injury and damage to them. In the absence of national legislation especially covering the subject of interstate commerce, the State may rightly prescribe uniform regulations adapted to promote safety upon its highways and the conservation of their use, applicable alike to vehicles moving in interstate commerce and those of its own citizens.

* * * * *

[144] The mere fact that a truck company may not make a profit unless it can use a truck with load weighing 22,000 or more pounds does not show that a regulation forbidding it is either discriminatory or unreasonable. That it prevents competition with freight traffic on parallel steam railroads may possibly be a circumstance to be considered in determining the reasonableness of such a limitation, though that is doubtful, but it is necessarily outweighed when it appears by decision of competent authority that such weight is injurious to the highway for the use of the general public and unduly increases the cost of maintenance and repair. In the absence of any averments of specific facts to show fraud or abuse of discretion, we must accept the judgment of the Highway Commission upon this question, which is committed to their decision, as against merely general averments denying their official finding.

* * * * *

[145] . . . Regulation as to the method of use, therefore, necessarily remains with the State and can not be interfered with unless the regulation is so arbitrary and unreasonable as to defeat the useful purposes for which Congress has made its large contribution to bettering the highway systems of the Union and to facilitating the carrying of the mails over them. There is no averment of the bill or any showing by affidavit making out such a case.

The temporary injunction was rightly refused and the motion to dismiss the bill was properly granted.

Affirmed.

Federal Trade Commission v. Claire Furnace Co.

Twenty-two companies sought to enjoin the Federal Trade Commission from enforcing orders against them, claiming that the activities involved did not involve interstate commerce and as a result were beyond the scope of FTC power. Speaking for the Court, Taft concluded that this particular issue should be passed on by the attorney general before a court ruled on it. McReynolds wrote a separate opinion urging the Court to have done with the issue immediately, since clearly the evidence showed that the firms' activities were not within the ambit of interstate commerce.

Federal Trade Commission et al.
v. Claire Furnace Company et al.

Appeal from the Court of Appeals of the District of Columbia

No. 1. Argued December 6, 1923; reargued November 24, 1925—Decided April 18, 1927

274 U.S. 160 (1927)

[165]

MR. CHIEF JUSTICE TAFT delivered the opinion of the Court.

This was a bill in equity brought in the Supreme Court of the District of Columbia on behalf of twenty-two companies of Ohio, Pennsylvania, West Virginia, New York, Delaware, New Jersey and Maryland, in the coal, steel and related industries, to enjoin the Federal Trade Commission from enforcing or attempting to enforce orders issued by that Commission against the complainant [166] companies, requiring them to furnish monthly reports of the cost of production, balance sheets, and other voluminous information in detail, upon a large variety of subjects relating to the business in which complainant corporations are engaged. . . .

* * * * *

[167] Purporting to proceed under this resolution, the Commission served separate notices upon the twenty-two appellees and many other corporations, engaged in mining, manufacturing, buying and selling coal, coke, ore, iron and steel products, etc., which directed them to furnish monthly reports in the form prescribed showing output of every kind, itemized cost of production, sale prices, contract prices, capacity, buying orders, depreciation, general administration and selling expenses, income, general balance sheet, etc., etc. Elaborate questionnaires, accompanying these orders, asked for answers revealing the intimate details of every department of the business, both intrastate and interstate. A summary of these, printed in the margin, sufficiently indicates their contents. The concluding paragraph of the notice [168] declared—"The purpose of this report is to compile in combined or consolidated form the data received from individual companies and to issue currently in such form accurate and comprehensive information regarding

changes in the conditions of the industry both for the benefit of the industry and of the public."

Appellees did not comply with the inquiries in the notices but filed in the Supreme Court, District of Columbia, their joint bill against the Commission and its members, wherein they set out its action, alleged that it had exceeded its powers, and asked that all defendants be restrained "from the enforcement of said orders, and from requiring answers to said questionnaires, and from taking any proceedings whatever with reference to the enforcement of compliance with said orders and answers to said questionnaires." . . .

* * * * *

[170] . . . The trial court concluded that, as the propounded questions were not limited to interstate commerce, but asked also for detailed information concerning mining, manufacture and intrastate commerce, they were beyond the Commission's authority. "The power claimed by the Commission is vast and unprecedented. The mere fact that a corporation engaged in mining ships a portion of its product to other States does not subject its business of production or its intrastate commerce to the powers of Congress." It accordingly held the answer insufficient and, as defendants declined to amend, granted the injunction as prayed. The Court of Appeals affirmed this action. . . .

* * * * *

The action of the commission here challenged must be justified, if at all, under the paragraphs of §§ 6 and 9, Act of September 26, 1914, copied below, and the only [171] methods prescribed for enforcing orders permitted by any of these paragraphs are specified in §§ 9 and 10. They are applications to the Attorney General to institute an action for mandamus, and proceedings by him to recover the prescribed penalties.

* * * * *

[174] . . . It was intended by Congress in providing this method of enforcing the orders of the Trade Commission to impose upon the Attorney General the duty of examining the scope and propriety of the orders, and of sifting out of the mass of inquiries issued what in his judgment was pertinent and lawful before asking the Court to adjudge forfeitures for failure to give the great amount of information required or to issue a mandamus against those whom the orders affected and who refused to comply. The wide scope and variety of the questions, answers to which are asked in these orders, show the wisdom of requiring the chief law officer of the Govern-

ment to exercise a sound discretion in designating the inquiries to enforce which he shall feel justified in invoking the action of the court. In a case like this, the exercise of this discretion will greatly relieve the court and may save it much unnecessary labor and discussion. The purpose of Congress in this requirement is plain, and we do not think that the court below should have dispensed with such assistance. Until the Attorney General acts, the defendants can not suffer, and when he does act, they can promptly answer and have full opportunity to contest the legality of any prejudicial proceeding against them. That right being adequate, they were not in a position to ask relief by injunction. The bill should have been dismissed for want of equity.

[175] This conclusion leads to a reversal of the decree of the District Court of Appeals and a remanding of the case to the Supreme Court of the District with direction to dismiss the bill.

Reversed.

MR. JUSTICE SUTHERLAND and MR. JUSTICE BUTLER took no part in the consideration or decision of this case.

The separate opinion of MR. JUSTICE MCREYNOLDS. [(Omitted.)]

Cline v. Frank Dairy Co.

Fourteenth Amendment challenges to state regulation of property during the era of the "Old Court," the pre-"switch-in-time-that-saved-nine" Court, regularly revolved around the issue of substantive due process. This doctrine was developed by the Court in the late 1800s and was used by the Court to void state legislation on the basis not of procedural defects, but because the substance of the law was seen as depriving persons of property.

This particular Colorado case involved a challenge to that state's antitrust legislation. Taft found it defective, but his reasoning was very much along the lines of procedural due process: the terms of the law were not clear, and their vagueness constituted procedural unfairness.

Cline, District Attorney, v. Frank Dairy Company et al.

Appeal from the United States District Court for the District of Colorado

No. 304. Argued April 29, 1927—Decided May 31, 1927

274 U.S. 445 (1927)

[449]

MR. CHIEF JUSTICE TAFT delivered the opinion of the Court.

This is a direct appeal under § 238 of the Judicial Code, as amended by the Act of February 13, 1925, c. 229, 43 Stat. 936, from a final decree of the United States District Court of Colorado, three Judges sitting, granting a permanent injunction against the enforcement by a state officer of a state law, on the ground of its unconstitutionality. . . .

The bill alleges that the suit involves for decision the question of the validity under the Constitution of the United States of what is known as the Colorado Anti-Trust Act. . . .

* * * * *

[451] The first question is whether the practice and precedents in equity justified the granting of relief by injunction, where one criminal prosecution had been begun and where many others, together with suits for forfeiture of corporate franchises, were threatened. The general rule is that a court of equity is without jurisdiction to restrain criminal proceedings to try the same right that is in issue [452] before it; but an exception to this rule exists when the prevention of such prosecutions under alleged unconstitutional enactments is essential to the safeguarding of rights of property, and when the circumstances are exceptional and the danger of irreparable loss is both great and immediate. . . .

* * * * *

[453] We agree with the view of the dissenting Judge that the injunction is too broad, in so far as it restrains proceedings actually pending, and that it must be accordingly modified.

This brings us to the consideration of the constitutionality of the Anti-Trust Act. We think that the act is so vague and uncertain in its description of what shall constitute its criminal violations that it is invalid under the Fourteenth Amendment. It in this respect violates due process and can not be distinguished from the case [454] of *United States v. Cohen Grocery Company,* 255 U.S. 81. The law there under consideration was the fourth section of the Lever Act, re-enacted in 1919. . . .

* * * * *

[455] The Colorado Anti-Trust law denounces conspiracies and combinations of persons and corporations, 1st, to create and carry out restrictions in trade or commerce preventing the full and free pursuit of any lawful business in the State; 2d, to increase or reduce the price of merchandise, products or commodities; 3rd, to prevent competition in the making, transportation,

sale or purchase of commodities or merchandise; 4th, to fix any standard of figures whereby the price shall be controlled or established; 5th, to make or execute any contract or agreement to bind the participants not to sell below a common standard, or to keep the price of the article at a fixed or graded figure, or establish or settle the price between themselves so as to preclude a free and unrestricted competition among themselves, or to pool, combine or unite any interest they may have in such business of making, selling or transporting that the price of the article may be affected. The foregoing language sufficiently describes [456] for purposes of a criminal statute the acts which it intends to punish; but the Colorado law does not stop with that: it is accompanied by two provisos which materially affect its purport and effect. They are as follows:

> "And all such combinations are hereby declared to be against public policy, unlawful and void; provided that no agreement or association shall be deemed to be unlawful or within the provisions of this act, the object and purposes of which are to conduct operations at a reasonable profit or to market at a reasonable profit those products which can not otherwise be so marketed; provided further that it shall not be deemed to be unlawful, or within the provisions of this act, for persons, firms, or corporations engaged in the business of selling or manufacturing commodities of a similar or like character to employ, form, organize or own any interest in any association, firm, or corporation having as its object or purpose the transportation, marketing or delivering of such commodities; . . ."

The effect of the first proviso is that combinations, with the purposes defined in the 1st, 2nd, 3rd, 4th and 5th paragraphs of § 1, and declared thereby to be unlawful and void, are not to be regarded as unlawful if their purpose shall be to obtain only a reasonable profit in such products or merchandise as can not yield a reasonable profit except by marketing them under the combinations previously condemned. The second is like the first in declaring that it shall not be unlawful or within the condemnatory provisions of the Act for persons engaged in the business of selling or manufacturing commodities of a class that can only be dealt with at a reasonable profit by such previously condemned trust methods, to employ or own interests in an association having as its object the transportation, marketing or delivering of such commodities at a reasonable profit. These provisos make the line [457] between lawfulness and criminality to depend upon, first what commodities need to be handled according to the trust methods condemned in the first part of the Act to enable those engaged in dealing in them to secure a reasonable profit therefrom; second, to determine what generally would be a reasonable profit for such a business; and third, what would be a reasonable profit for the defendant under the circumstances of his particular business. It would, therefore, be a complete defense for the defendant to prove in this case that it is impossible to sell milk or milk products, except by trust methods and make a reasonable profit, if he also showed that by such methods he had in fact only made a reasonable profit.

We have examined the opinions of the Supreme Court of Colorado in reference to the construction and operation of these provisos in the Colorado Anti-Trust law. *Campbell v. The People,* 72 Colo., 213; *Johnson v. The People, Id.,* 218; *People v. Apostolos,* 73 Colo., 71; and we find nothing there which is in conflict with our construction of them. Such an exception in the statute leaves the whole statute without a fixed standard of guilt in an adjudication affecting the liberty of the one accused. An attempt to enforce the section will be to penalize and punish all combinations in restraint of trade in a commodity when in the judgment of the court and jury they are not necessary to enable those engaged in it to make it reasonably profitable, but not otherwise. Such a basis for judgment of a crime would be more impracticable and complicated than the much simpler question in the *Cohen Grocery* case, whether a price charged was unreasonable or excessive. The real issue which the proviso would submit to the jury would be legislative, not judicial. To compel defendants to guess on the peril of an indictment, whether one or more of the restrictions of the statute will destroy all profit or [458] reduce it below what would be reasonable, would tax the human ingenuity in much the same way as that which this Court refused to allow as a proper standard of criminality. . . .

* * * * *

[463] The principle of due process of law requiring reasonable certainty of description in fixing a standard for exacting obedience from a person in advance has application as well in civil as in criminal legislation, *Small Company v. American Sugar Refining Company,* 267 U.S. 233, 238, et seq.; but the fact that it is often necessary to [464] investigate and decide certain questions in civil cases is not controlling or persuasive as to whether persons may be held to civil or criminal liability for not deciding them rightly in advance. On questions of confiscatory rates for public utilities, for instance, courts must examine in great detail the circumstances and reach a conclusion as to a reasonable profit. But this does not justify in such a case holding the average member of society in advance to a rule of conduct measured by his judgment and action in respect to what is a reasonable price or a reasonable profit. . . .

* * * * *

[465] But it will not do to hold an average man to the peril of an indictment for the unwise exercise of his economic or business knowledge involving so many factors of varying effect that neither the person to decide in advance nor the jury to try him after the fact can safely and certainly judge the result. When to a decision whether a certain amount of profit in a complicated business is reasonable is added that of determining whether detailed restriction of particular antitrust legislation will prevent a reasonable profit in the case of a given commodity, we have an utterly impracticable standard for a jury's decision. A legislature must fix the standard more simply and more definitely before a person must conform or a jury can act.

We conclude that the Anti-Trust statute of Colorado is void in that those who are prosecuted and convicted under it will be denied due process of law.

[466] The decree of the District Court to enjoin proceedings which the defendant threatens to bring under the Act against the plaintiffs should be affirmed, but the decree below is modified and reversed so far as it purports to enjoin the defendant from proceeding further in prosecuting the information under that Act against the plaintiffs now pending in the state criminal court.

The decree is in part reversed and in part affirmed.

Weedin v. Chin Bow

Among the prominent attorneys who regularly appeared before the Taft Court in the 1920s, few were more distinguished than former associate justice Charles Evans Hughes. Hughes had resigned from the Court in 1916 to accept the Republican nomination for president. He later would serve as secretary of state and, in 1930, would be named to succeed Taft as chief justice. Hughes appeared as counsel for Chin Bow.

Bow had arrived in Seattle from China and claimed to be a United States citizen on the basis of his father's being a United States citizen. The government rejected this claim, but its decision was, in turn, rejected by the United States District Court, and this latter decision was sustained by the Court of Appeals for the Ninth Circuit. Taft reversed and found for the government, arguing that the broad interpretation the lower courts had given to the relevant congressional legislation was unwarranted.

Weedin, Commissioner of Immigration, v. Chin Bow

Certiorari to the Circuit Court of Appeals for the Ninth Circuit

No. 237. Argued March 16, 1927—Decided June 6, 1927

274 U.S. 657 (1927)

[658]

MR. CHIEF JUSTICE TAFT delivered the opinion of the Court.

* * * * *

Chin Bow applied for admission to the United States at Seattle. The board of special inquiry of the Immigration Bureau at that place denied him admission on the ground that, though his father is a citizen, he is not a citizen, because at the time of his birth in China his father had never resided in the United States. Chin Bow was born March 29, 1914, in China. His father, Chin Dun, [659] was also born in China, on March 8, 1894, and had never been in this country until July 18, 1922. Chin Dun was the son of Chin Tong, the respondent's grandfather. Chin Tong is forty-nine years old and was born in the United States.

* * * * *

"All children heretofore born or hereafter born out of the limits and jurisdiction of the United States, whose fathers were or may be at the time of their birth citizens thereof, are declared to be citizens of the United States; but the rights of citizenship shall not descend to children whose fathers never resided in the United States."

The rights of Chin Bow are determined by the construction of this section.

* * * * *

[660] The United States contends that the proviso of § 1993 "but the rights of citizenship shall not descend to children whose fathers never resided in the United States" must be construed to mean that only the children whose fathers have resided in the United States before their birth become citizens under the section. It is claimed for the respondent that the residence of the father in the United States at any time before his death entitles his son, whenever born, to citizenship. These conflicting claims make the issue to be decided.

* * * * *

[666] Only two constructions seem to us possible, and we must adopt one or the other. The one is that the descent of citizenship shall be regarded as taking place at the birth of the person to whom it is to be transmitted, and that the words "have never been resident in the United States" refer in point of time to the birth of the person to whom the citizenship is to descend. This is the adoption of the rule of *jus sanguinis* in respect of citizenship, and that emphasizes the fact and time of birth as the basis of it. We think the words "the right of citizenship shall not descend to persons whose fathers have never been resident in the United States" are equivalent to saying that fathers may not have the power of transmitting by descent the right of citizenship until they shall become residents in the United States. The other view is that the words "have never been resident in the United States" have reference to the whole life of the father until his death, and therefore that grandchildren of native-born citizens, even after they, having been born abroad, have lived abroad to middle age and without residing at all in the United States, will become citizens, if their fathers, born abroad and living until old age abroad, shall adopt a residence in the United States just before death. We are thus to have two generations of citizens who have been born abroad, lived abroad, the first coming to old age and the second to maturity and bringing up of a family, without any relation to the United States at all until the father shall, in his last days, adopt a new residence. We do not think that such a construction accords with the probable attitude of Congress at the time of the adoption of this proviso into the statute. Its [667] construction extends citizenship to a generation whose birth, minority and majority, whose education, and whose family life, have all been out of the United States and naturally within the civilization and environment of an alien country. The beneficiaries would have evaded the duties and responsibilities of American citizenship. They might be persons likely to become public charges or afflicted with disease, yet they would be entitled to enter as citizens of the United States. Van Dyne, Citizenship of the United States, p. 34.

As between the two interpretations, we feel confident that the first one is more in accord with the views of the First Congress. . . .

* * * * *

Now, if this Congress had construed § 1993 to permit the residence prescribed to occur after the birth of such children, we think that it would have employed appropriate words to express such meaning, as for example "All children born who are or may become citizens." The present tense is used, however, indicating that citizenship is determined at the time of birth. Moreover, such foreign-born citizens are required, upon reaching the age of eighteen years, to record their intention to become residents and remain citizens of the United States, and take [668] the oath of allegiance to the United States upon attaining their majority. If the residence prescribed for the parent may occur after the birth of the children, the father may remain abroad and not reside in the United States until long after such children attain their majority. Thus they could not register or take the oath of allegiance, because the rights of citizenship could not descend to them until their fathers had resided in the United States. This class of foreign-born children of American citizens could not, then, possibly comply with the provisions of the Act of 1907. Nor could such children "remain citizens," since they are expressly denied the rights of citizenship. We may treat the Act of 1907 as being *in pari materia* with the original act, and as a legislative declaration of what Congress in 1907 thought was its meaning in 1790. . . .

* * * * *

[675] This leads to a reversal of the judgment of the Circuit Court of Appeals and a remanding of the respondent.

Reversed.

Omitted Taft Opinions

Federal Trade Commission v. Klesner, 274 U.S. 148 (1927)—jurisdiction of U.S. Court of Appeals for the District of Columbia over the FTC.

Kadow v. Paul, 274 U.S. 175 (1927)—property assessment.

Timken Roller Bearing Co. v. Pennsylvania Railroad Co., 274 U.S. 181 (1927)—jurisdiction of District Court over contract dispute with railroad.

United States v. Stone & Downer Co., 274 U.S. 225 (1927)—judgments of Court of Customs Appeals not *res judicata.*

Posados v. Manila, 274 U.S. 410 (1927)—right to secure a writ of *mandamus* to compel Philippine Collector of Internal Revenue to countersign tax receipts.

Overland Motor Company v. Packard Motor Company et al., 474 U.S. 417 (1927)—patent case.

Messel v. Foundation Co., 274 U.S. 427 (1927)—injury subject to state and not federal law.

Rhea v. Smith, 274 U.S. 434 (1927)—real estate lien.

October Term, 1927

William Howard Taft, Chief Justice
Oliver Wendell Holmes
Willis Van Devanter
James Clark McReynolds
Louis D. Brandeis
George Sutherland
Pierce Butler
Edward T. Sanford
Harlan Fiske Stone

VOLUME 275

Gong Lum v. Rice

Race, "an American dilemma" according to Swedish sociologist Gunnar Myrdal, did not pass the Taft Court by. As is typical of his decisions, Chief Justice Taft devoted much of this one to a careful reliance on precedent and copious quotations from previous justices. In upholding the decision of the Supreme Court of Mississippi requiring a Chinese student to attend the school reserved for the "colored race," Taft quoted approvingly a decision by Justice John Marshall Harlan that allowed a state to maintain schools only for whites.

Gong Lum et al. v. Rice et al.

Error to the Supreme Court of the State of Mississippi

No. 29. Submitted October 12, 1927—Decided November 21, 1927

275 U.S. 78 (1927)

[79]

MR. CHIEF JUSTICE TAFT delivered the opinion of the Court.

* * * * *

Gong Lum is a resident of Mississippi, resides in the Rosedale Consolidated High School District, and is the father of Martha Lum. He is engaged in the mercantile business. Neither he nor she was connected with the consular service or any other service of the government of China, or any other government, at the time of her birth. [80] She was nine years old when the petition was filed, having been born January 21, 1915, and she sued by her next friend, Chew How, who is a native born citizen of the United States and the State of Mississippi. The petition alleged that she was of good moral character and between the ages of five and twenty-one years, and that, as she was such a citizen and an educable child, it became her father's duty under the law to send her to school; that she desired to attend the Rosedale Consolidated High School; that at the opening of the school she appeared as a pupil, but at the noon recess she was notified by the superintendent that she would not be allowed to return to the school; that an order had been issued by the Board of Trustees, who are made defendants, excluding her from attending the school solely on the ground that she was of Chinese descent and not a member of the white or Caucasian race, and that their order had been made in pursuance to instructions from the State Superintendent of Education of Mississippi, who is also made a defendant.

The petitioners further show that there is no school maintained in the District for the education of children of Chinese descent, and none established in Bolivar County where she could attend.

The Constitution of Mississippi requires that there shall be a county common school fund, made up of poll taxes from the various counties, to be retained in the counties where the same is collected, and a state common school fund to be taken from the general fund in the state treasury, which together shall be sufficient to maintain a common school for a term of four months in each scholastic year, but that any county or separate school district may levy an additional tax to maintain schools for a longer time than a term of four months. . . .

[81] The petition alleged that, in obedience to this mandate of the Constitution, the legislature has provided for the establishment and for the pay-

ment of the expenses of the Rosedale Consolidated High School, and that the plaintiff, Gong Lum, the petitioner's father, is a taxpayer and helps to support and maintain the school; that Martha Lum is an educable child, is entitled to attend the school as a pupil, and that this is the only school conducted in the District available for her as a pupil; that the right to attend it is a valuable right; that she is not a member of the colored race nor is she of mixed blood, but that she is pure Chinese; that she is by the action of the Board of Trustees and the State Superintendent discriminated against directly and denied her right to be a member of the Rosedale School; that the school authorities have no discretion under the law as to her admission as a pupil in the school, but that they continue without authority of law to deny her the right to attend it as a pupil. For these reasons the writ of mandamus is prayed for against the defendants commanding them and each of them to desist from discriminating against her on account of her race or ancestry and to give her the same rights and privileges that other educable children between the ages of five and twenty-one are granted in the Rosedale Consolidated High School.

The petition was demurred to by the defendants on the ground, among others, that the bill showed on its face that plaintiff is a member of the Mongolian or yellow race, and [82] therefore not entitled to attend the schools provided by law in the State of Mississippi for children of the white or Caucasian race.

The trial court overruled the demurrer and ordered that a writ of mandamus issue to the defendants as prayed in the petition.

The defendants then appealed to the Supreme Court of Mississippi, which heard the case. *Rice v. Gong Lum,* 139 Miss. 760. In its opinion, it directed its attention to the proper construction of § 207 of the State Constitution of 1890, which provides:

"Separate schools shall be maintained for children of the white and colored races."

The Court held that this provision of the Constitution divided the educable children into those of the pure white or Caucasian race, on the one hand, and the brown, yellow and black races, on the other, and therefore that Martha Lum of the Mongolian or yellow race could not insist on being classed with the whites under this constitutional division. The Court said:

"The legislature is not compelled to provide separate schools for each of the colored races, and, unless and until it does provide such schools and provide for segregation of the other races, such races are entitled to have the benefit of the colored public schools. . . ."

* * * * *

[84] We must assume then that there are school districts for colored children in Bolivar County, but that no colored school is within the limits of the Rosedale Consolidated High School District. This is not inconsistent with there being, at a place outside of that district and in a different district, a colored school which the plaintiff Martha Lum, may conveniently attend. If so, she is not denied, under the existing school system, the right to attend and enjoy the privileges of a common school education in a colored school. If it were otherwise, the petition should have contained an allegation showing it. Had the petition alleged specifically that there was no colored school in Martha Lum's neighborhood to which she could conveniently go, a different question would have been presented, and this, without regard to the State Supreme Court's construction of the State Constitution as limiting the white schools provided for the education of children of the white or Caucasian race. But we do not find the petition to present such a situation.

[85] The case then reduces itself to the question whether a state can be said to afford to a child of Chinese ancestry born in this country, and a citizen of the United States, equal protection of the laws by giving her the opportunity for a common school education in a school which receives only colored children of the brown, yellow or black races.

The right and power of the state to regulate the method of providing for the education of its youth at public expense is clear. In *Cumming v. Richmond County Board of Education,* 175 U.S. 528, 545, persons of color sued the Board of Education to enjoin it from maintaining a high school for white children without providing a similar school for colored children. which had existed and had been discontinued. Mr. Justice Harlan, in delivering the opinion of the Court, said:

"Under the circumstances disclosed, we cannot say that this action of the state court was, within the meaning of the Fourteenth Amendment, a denial by the State to the plaintiffs and to those associated with them of the equal protection of the laws, or of any privileges belonging to them as citizens of the United States. We may add that while all admit that the benefits and burdens of public taxation must be shared by citizens without discrimination against any class on account of their race, the education of the people in schools maintained by state taxation is a matter belonging to the respective States, and any interference on the part of Federal authority with the management of such schools can not be justified except in the case of a clear and unmistakable disregard of rights secured by the supreme law of the land."

* * * * *

[86] In *Plessy v. Ferguson,* 163 U.S. 537, 544, 545, in upholding the validity under the Fourteenth Amendment of a statute of Louisiana requiring the separation of the white and colored races in railway coaches, a more difficult question than this, this Court, speaking of permitted race separation, said:

"The most common instance of this is connected with the establishment of separate schools for white and colored children, which has been held to be a valid exercise of the legislative power even by courts of States where the political rights of the colored race have been longest and most earnestly enforced."

The case of *Roberts v. City of Boston, supra,* in which Chief Justice Shaw of the Supreme Judicial Court of Massachusetts, announced the opinion of that court upholding the separation of colored and white schools under [87] a state constitutional injunction of equal protection, the same as the Fourteenth Amendment, was then referred to, and this Court continued:

"Similar laws have been enacted by Congress under its general power of legislation over the District of Columbia, Rev. Stat. D. C. §§ 281, 282, 283, 310, 319, as well as by the legislatures of many of the States, and have been generally, if not uniformly, sustained by the Courts," citing many of the cases above named.

Most of the cases cited arose, it is true, over the establishment of separate schools as between white pupils and black pupils, but we can not think that the question is any different or that any different result can be reached, assuming the cases above cited to be rightly decided, where the issue is as between white pupils and the pupils of the yellow races. The decision is within the discretion of the state in regulating its public schools and does not conflict with the Fourteenth Amendment. The judgment of the Supreme Court of Mississippi is

Affirmed.

Segurola v. United States

This involved a criminal appeal from Puerto Rico. Taft's experience in the Philippines may explain his concern that the defendants be provided with a copy of the information filed. He, however, did not find this error to require a new trial and moved swiftly through the defendants' other claims of constitutional violations, the right to confront their accusers, and the issue of probable cause in the search of their auto's trunk.

Segurola et al. v. United States

Certiorari to the Circuit Court of Appeals for the First Circuit

No. 195. Argued October 12, 1927—Decided November 21, 1927

275 U.S. 106 (1927)

[107]

MR. CHIEF JUSTICE TAFT delivered the opinion of the Court.

* * * * *

[109] The case was carried upon writ of error to the Circuit Court of Appeals for the First Circuit. 16 Fed. (2d) 563. That Court affirmed the judgment, holding that the refusal to furnish a copy of the information without payment of a fee to the clerk was right and, even if erroneous, was, under the circumstances, a harmless error; that the refusal to permit cross-examination of the officer as to his informant in respect to the coming of Segurola and the contents of his car was in accord with approved public policy and that the circumstances constituted probable cause for a legal seizure.

The error assigned to the failure to direct the delivery of a copy of the information rests on the second section of the Organic Act of Porto Rico— Act of March 2, 1917, c. 145, 39 Stat. 951, U.S. C., Title 48, § 737, in which it is provided that "in all criminal prosecutions the accused shall enjoy the right to have the assistance of counsel for his defense, to be informed of the nature and cause of the accusation, to have a copy thereof, to have a speedy and public trial, to be confronted with the witnesses against him, and to have compulsory process for obtaining witnesses in his favor." The district judge held that this did not mean that the defendant was to have a copy of the information without paying the regular copying fees to the clerk. We think this was an erroneous construction of the statute. It was enacted by Congress to apply in a country where there were two languages, and in which a [110] criminal procedure, new in some of its aspects, was to be put into effect. It was not strange, therefore, that it was thought necessary *ex industria* to emphasize the means by which the accused could be advised of the charge made against him. . . . We think, therefore, that the court was wrong in not directing that a copy be furnished to each defendant. But that is very different from saying that because of the failure of the court to issue this order, the trial which ensued should be held for naught and a new trial had. . . .

* * * * *

[111] As there was no evidence introduced by the defendants to refute or deny the testimony unobjected to, which clearly showed the illegal transportation of the liquor and sustained the verdict, the admission in evidence of the liquor and the refusal to permit cross-examination of Ceballos worked no prejudice for which a reversal can be granted. Moreover, the principle laid down by this Court in *Adams v. New York,* 192 U.S. 585, and recognized as proper in *Weeks v. United States,* 232 U.S. 383, 395, and in *Marron v. United States, post,* p. 192, applies to render unavailing, under the circumstances of this case, the objection to the use of the liquor as evidence based on the Fourth Amendment. This principle is that, except where there has been no opportunity to present the matter in advance of trial, *Gouled v. United States,* 255 U.S. 298, 305; *Amos v. United States,* 255 U.S. 313, 316; *Agnello v. United States,* 269 U.S. 20, 34, a court, when engaged in trying a criminal case, will not take notice of [112] the manner in which witnesses have possessed themselves of papers or other articles of personal property, which are material and properly offered in evidence, because the court will not in trying a criminal cause permit a collateral issue to be raised as to the source of competent evidence. To pursue it would be to halt in the orderly progress of a cause and consider incidentally a question which has happened to cross the path of such litigation and which is wholly independent of it. In other words, in order to raise the question of illegal seizure, and an absence of probable cause in that seizure, the defendants should have moved to have the whiskey and other liquor returned to them as their property and as not subject to seizure or use as evidence. To preserve their rights under the Fourth Amendment, they must at least have seasonably objected to the production of the liquor in court. This they did not do, but waited until the liquor had been offered and admitted and then for the first time raised the question of legality of seizure and probable cause as a ground for withdrawing the liquor from consideration of the jury. This was too late.

* * * * *

[113] The judgment is

Affirmed.

Atlantic Coast Line Railroad Co. v. Standard Oil

The question posed by this case was whether shipments of oil by Standard Oil Company from Florida ports to destinations within Florida should be classified as intrastate commerce and charged at lower rates or whether the railroad was justified in charging the higher interstate rates. The Court found, based on the facts, that the intrastate rates were appropriate and ruled for the Standard Oil Company.

Atlantic Coast Line Railroad Company v. Standard Oil Company of Kentucky

Standard Oil Company, Incorporated in Kentucky, v. Atlantic Coast Line Railroad Company

Certiorari to the Circuit Court of Appeals for the Sixth Circuit

Nos. 176 and 177. Argued October 4, 1927—Decided November 28, 1927

275 U.S. 257 (1927)

[261]

MR. CHIEF JUSTICE TAFT delivered the opinion of the Court.

* * * * *

[262] The bill avers that since June 15, 1923, the defendant railroad company has refused to accept shipments of the complainant from Port Tampa, Tampa and Jacksonville, Florida, to other points within the state at intrastate rates, and has compelled the complainant to pay thereon higher interstate rates, which it has done under protest; that according to the records of the complainant it has already overpaid to the defendant, between June 15, 1923, and April 17, 1925, the sum of $63,000.

* * * * *

[266] The District Court held that all the transportation of oil by the defendant for the plaintiff, after the oil reaches the storage tanks or tank cars, in Tampa, Port Tampa or Jacksonville, is intrastate commerce, and that the plaintiff is entitled to secure the transportation necessary in that commerce at intrastate rates. 13 F. (2d) 633. The Circuit Court of Appeals modified the order of the District Court, 16 F. (2d) 441, and held that the fuel oil landed at Port Tampa is a continuous foreign and interstate shipment from Tampico to its ultimate destination in Florida where it is used; that the gasoline and kerosene shipments through to Port Tampa must also be classified as interstate shipments from Baton Rouge to the bulk stations where they

are distributed; that the lubricating oils [267] received at Port Tampa must be treated as distributed from the Tampa and Jacksonville storage tanks, and that from those places its transportation is to be regarded as intrastate; that as to gasoline and kerosene in Jacksonville, as 13 per cent. of it received into the tanks is used locally at Jacksonville, it must all be regarded as intrastate; that as to Jacksonville fuel oil the record is obscure and the case must be sent back to the trial court for further evidence.

* * * * *

It seems very clear to us on a broad view of the facts that the interstate or foreign commerce in all this oil ends upon its delivery to the plaintiff into the storage tanks or the storage tank cars at the seaboard, and that from there its distribution to storage tanks, tank cars, bulk stations and drive-in stations, or directly by tank wagons to customers, is all intrastate commerce. This distribution is the whole business of the plaintiff in Florida. There is no destination intended and arranged for with the ship carriers in Florida at any point beyond the deliveries from the vessels to the storage tanks or tank cars of the plaintiff. There is no designation of any particular oil for any particular place within Florida beyond the storage receptacles or storage tank cars into which the oil is first delivered by the ships. The title to the oil in bulk passes to the plaintiff as it is thus delivered. When the oil reaches these storage places along the Florida seaboard, it is within the control and ownership of the plaintiff for use for its particular purposes in Florida. . . .

[268] The question whether commerce is interstate or intrastate must be determined by the essential character of the commerce, and not by mere billing or forms of contract, although that may be one of a group of circumstances tending to show such character. The reshipment of an interstate or foreign shipment does not necessarily establish a continuity of movement or prevent the shipment to a point within the same state from having an independent or intrastate character, even though it be in the same cars. . . .

* * * * *

[272] Reliance is put on *Stafford v. Wallace*, 258 U.S. 495, to sustain the claim that this transportation of plaintiff's oil in Florida is interstate commerce. In that case the question under consideration was the validity of the Packers and Stockyards Act of Congress of 1921, c. 64, 42 Stat. 159, providing for the supervision by Federal authority of the business of the commission men and of the live stock dealers in the great stock yards of the country, and it was held that for the purpose of protecting interstate commerce from the power of the packers to fix arbitrary prices for live stock and meat through their monopoly of its purchase, preparation in meat, and sales, Congress had

power to regulate the business done in the stockyards, although there was a good deal of it which was, strictly speaking, only intrastate commerce. It was held that a reasonable fear upon the part of Congress, that acts usually affecting only intrastate commerce when occurring alone, would probably and more or less constantly be performed in aid of conspiracies against interstate commerce, or constitute a direct and undue obstruction and restraint of it, would serve to bring such acts within lawful Federal statutory restraint.

The Court relied much on the case of *United States v. Ferger,* 250 U.S. 199, where the validity of an act of Congress, punishing forgery and utterance of bills of lading for fictitious shipments in interstate commerce, was in question. It was there contended that there was and could be no commerce on a fraudulent and fictitious bill of lading, and therefore that the power of Congress could not embrace such pretended bill. In upholding the act, this Court, speaking through Chief Justice White, answered the objection by saying:

"But this mistakenly assumes that the power of Congress is to be necessarily tested by the intrinsic existence of commerce in the particular subject dealt with, instead of by the relation of that subject to commerce and its [273] effect upon it. We say mistakenly assumes, because we think it clear that if the proposition were sustained it would destroy the power of Congress to regulate, as obviously that power, if it is to exist, must include the authority to deal with obstructions to interstate commerce (*In re Debs,* 158 U.S. 564) and with a host of other acts which, because of their relation to and influence upon interstate commerce, come within the power of Congress to regulate, although they are not interstate commerce in and of themselves."

The use of this authority as a basis for the conclusion in *Stafford v. Wallace* clearly shows that the case can not be cited to show what is interstate and what is intrastate commerce in a controversy over rates to determine whether they come normally within the regulation of Federal or State authority.

Our conclusion is that, in all the cases presented by the plaintiff in its bill, intrastate rates should have been applied and should be applied in the future, so long as the facts remain as they are now. This leads to a reversal of the decision of the Sixth Circuit Court of Appeals as to fuel oil from Port Tampa, as to gasoline and kerosene from Tampa, and an affirmation of its decision as to lubricating oil through Port Tampa; an affirmation of its decision as to gasoline from Jacksonville, as to kerosene from Jacksonville, and as to lubricating oil from Jacksonville. As to fuel oil from Jacksonville, the Circuit Court of Appeals left the matter undetermined. We think that fuel oil also from Jacksonville should be treated as subject to intrastate rates. The result is that the decision of the Circuit Court of Appeals is partly affirmed and partly reversed, that of the District Court is wholly affirmed, and the case is remanded to the District Court for further proceedings.

Affirmed in part; reversed in part.

United States v. Murray

Cook and Murray were both convicted for violating the Volstead Act and sentenced to prison. They were subsequently put on probation. The question presented by the cases was whether the probation act gave federal judges the power to put a person on probation after the individual had begun serving a sentence. Taft ruled that judges did not have such a power.

United States v. Murray

Certificate from the Circuit Court of Appeals for the Eighth Circuit

Cook v. United States

Certiorari to the Circuit Court of Appeals for the Fifth Circuit

Nos. 394, 539. Argued November 22, 23, 1927—Decided January 3, 1928

275 U.S. 347 (1928)

[350]

MR. CHIEF JUSTICE TAFT delivered the opinion of the Court.

These cases involve the construction of the Act of March 4, 1925, c. 521, 43 Stat. 1259, which provides a probation system for United States Courts.

* * * * *

On October 22, 1926, in the District Court of the United States for the District of Nebraska, the defendant, Glen Murray, pleaded guilty to certain violations of the National Prohibition Act. On October 25, 1926, he was sentenced to three months' imprisonment at the Douglas [351] County jail, at Omaha. On the same day he was delivered by the United States Marshal, in pursuance of the sentence, to the jail keeper, and commenced serving it. On October 26th, the next day, and during the same term of court, the district court entered an order placing him on probation. [Cook was convicted of fraud and also given probation after he had begun serving his sentence.] . . .

* * * * *

[352] The first question which we must consider, and which if we decide in favor of the Government controls both cases and disposes of them, is whether there is any power in the federal courts of first instance to grant probation under the Probation Act, after the defendant has served any part of his sentence. . . .

* * * * *

[356] The Probation Act gives power to grant probation to a convict after his conviction or after a plea of guilty, by suspending the imposition or suspending execution of the sentence. This probation is to be after conviction or plea of guilty. The question is—Before what time must it be granted? Two answers to this latter question are possible. It must either be grantable at any time during his whole sentence or be limited to a time before execution of the sentence begins. If the first answer is adopted, it would confer very comprehensive power on the district judges in the exercise of what is very like that of executive clemency in all cases of crime or misdemeanor. It would cover in most cases the period between the imposition of the sentence and the full execution of it. It would cover a period in which not only clemency by the President under the Constitution might be exercised but also the power of parole by a Board of Parole abating judicial punishment to the extent of two-thirds of it as to all crimes punishable by imprisonment for more than one year. It seems quite unlikely that Congress would have deemed it wise or necessary thus to make applicable to the same crimes at the same time three different methods of mitigation.

Nor can we suppose that Congress would wish to grant such extended power in all but life and capital cases to the district judges and thus subject each to the applications of convicts during the entire time until the full ending of the sentences. This would seem unnecessary for [357] the hard worked district judges with their crowded dockets. A more reasonable construction is to reconcile the provisions for probation, parole and executive clemency, making them as little of a repetition as we can.

* * * * *

[358] This Act has been before courts of first instance and circuit courts of appeals a number of times, but we have found only one reported case, in addition to the decisions by the district courts in the instant cases, in which it has been held that probation may be granted after the service of the sentence has

begun. That case is *United States v. Chafina,* 14 Fed. (2d) 622, a district court case. The other cases brought to our attention are not inconsistent with our ruling. . . .

[359] With this interpretation of the statute it must be decided that the district court neither in the *Glen Murray* case nor in the *Cook* case had power to grant probation. It is true that there was but one day of execution of the sentence in the *Murray* case, but the power passed immediately after imprisonment began and there had been one day of it served. The cause is remanded to the district court with instructions to reverse the order placing Murray upon probation and for further proceedings. In the Cook case the action of the Circuit Court of Appeals reversing the order of the district court of the United States for the Northern District of Texas granting to Cook probation is affirmed.

No. 394, reversed,

No. 539, affirmed.

Omitted Taft Opinions

Fairmont Creamery Co. v. Minnesota, 275 U.S. 70 (1927)—power of Supreme Court to impose costs against a state.

Compañia General de Tabacos v. Collector of Internal Revenue, 275 U.S. 87 (1927)—power of the government of the Philippines to tax.

Wickshire v. Reinecke, 275 U.S. 101 (1927)—inheritance issue.

Temco Electric Motor Co. v. Apco Manufacturing Co., 275 U.S. 319 (1928)—patent issue.

Richmond Co. v. United States, 275 U.S. 331 (1928)—patent case.

VOLUME 276

Wuchter v. Pizzutti

Throughout his tenure, Chief Justice Taft showed a special concern for protecting the rights of property. Although such an attitude sounds old-fashioned today, clearly the framers of the Constitution were aware that one of the reasons ancient democracies failed was the tendency of democratic majorities to use their powers to attack the rights of the propertied. Although property rights are, at bottom, the issue in this case, the more immediate concern for the Court was whether the challenged New Jersey statute provided adequate procedural due process to out-of-state drivers involved in accidents in New Jersey. The dissents of Justices Stone and Brandeis (with whom Holmes concurred) urged self-restraint upon the Court, arguing that from the facts it was not at all clear that the statute actually denied out-of-state drivers due process. For Taft, however, the procedural flaw was quite clear.

Wuchter v. Pizzutti

Error to the Court of Errors and Appeals of New Jersey

No. 142. Argued January 5, 1928—Decided February 20, 1928

276 U.S. 13 (1928)

[15]

MR. CHIEF JUSTICE TAFT delivered the opinion of the Court.

This case involves the validity, under the Fourteenth Amendment, of a statute of New Jersey providing for service of process on non-residents of the State in suits for injury by the negligent operation of automobiles on its highways.

Pizzutti was driving a team of horses attached to a wagon on a public highway in New Jersey. Wuchter was a resident of Pennsylvania who was following the wagon with his automobile. Wuchter drove his car so as to crash into the rear of the wagon, damaging it, and injuring Pizzutti and his horses. Pizzutti instituted a suit against Wuchter in the Supreme Court of New Jersey. Wuchter was served with process under the provisions of the Act known as Chapter 232 of the Laws of 1924, (P. L. 1924, p. 517) by leaving process with the Secretary of State. Wuchter interposed no defense. A judgment interlocutory was taken against him and a writ of inquiry of damages was issued. Although the statute did not [16] require it, notice of its proposed execution was actually served personally on Wuchter in Pennsylvania. Wuchter did not appear. A final judgment was entered. Wuchter then appealed to the court below, contending that the Act under which the process was served upon him was unconstitutional, because it deprived him of his property without due process of law, in contravention of section 1 of the Fourteenth Amendment to the Federal Constitution.

* * * * *

[18] It is settled by our decisions that a state's power to regulate the use of its highways extends to their use by non-residents as well as by residents. *Hendrick v. Maryland,* 235 U.S. 610, 622. We have further held that, in advance of the operation of a motor vehicle on its highways by a non-resident, a state may require him to take out a license and to appoint one of its officials as his agent, on whom process may be served in suits growing out of accidents in such operation. This was under the license act of New Jersey, last above referred to, and not No. 232. *Kane v. New Jersey,* 242 U.S. 160, 167. We have also recognized it to be a valid exercise of power by a state, because of its right to regulate the use of its highways by non-residents, to declare, without exacting a license, that the use of the highway by the non-resident may by statute be treated as the equivalent of the appointment by him of a state official as agent on whom process in such a case may be served. *Hess v. Pawloski,* 274 U.S. 352.

The question made in the present case is whether a statute, making the Secretary of State the person to receive the process, must, in order to be valid, contain a provision making it reasonably probable that notice of the service on the Secretary will be communicated to the non-resident defendant who is sued. Section 232 of the Laws of 1924 makes no such requirement. . . .

[19] A provision of law for service that leaves open such a clear opportunity for the commission of fraud (*Heinemann v. Pier,* 110 Wis. 185) or injustice is not a reasonable provision, and in the case supposed would certainly be depriving a defendant of his property without due process of law. . . .

* * * * *

Judgment reversed.

[25] MR. JUSTICE BRANDEIS (with whom MR. JUSTICE HOLMES concurs), dissenting.

The rule of general law stated by the Court seems to me sound. But I think the judgment should be affirmed. The objection sustained by the Court—that the statute is void because it fails to provide that the Secretary of State shall notify the non-resident defendant—is an objection taken for the first time in this Court. It was not made or considered below; and it is not to be found in the assignments of error filed in this Court. . . .

* * * * *

[26] For aught that appears, it may have been the uniform practice of the Secretary to give notice whenever the address of the defendant was ascertainable. Such an administrative construction would carry great weight

with the courts of New Jersey, *State v. Kelsey,* 44 N. J. L. 1; *Stephens v. Civil Service Commission,* 101 N. J. L. 192, 194, as it would with this Court. *United States v. Cerecedo Hermanos y Compania,* 209 U.S. 337. Moreover, the rule that a construction which raises a serious doubt as to the constitutionality of a statute will not be adopted if some other construction is open, is a rule commonly acted upon by the courts of New Jersey.

* * * * *

[28] MR. JUSTICE STONE, dissenting.

I agree that the judgment should be reversed and the cause remanded, but with leave to the state court to determine whether the notice given to the plaintiff in error by the Secretary of State was required by the statute.

Nigro v. United States

The decision in *Bailey v. Drexel Furniture Company,* 259 U.S. 20 (1922), continued to be invoked by those who sought to rein in what they saw to be the unconstitutional development of a federal police power bottomed on the federal government's power "to lay and collect taxes." The Harrison Anti-Narcotic Act of 1914 was the basis upon which Nigro was convicted. Nigro claimed that the law was not a taxing measure, but rather was designed to give to the federal government a power that could be rightfully exercised only by states.

Taft's efforts to draw a distinction between this tax and the tax on child labor held unconstitutional in *Bailey* failed to persuade the three dissenters, Justices Butler, McReynolds, and Sutherland.

Nigro v. United States

Certificate from the Circuit Court of Appeals for the Eighth Circuit

No. 600. Argued January 11, 12, 1928—Decided April 9, 1928

276 U.S. 332 (1928)

[337]

MR. CHIEF JUSTICE TAFT delivered the opinion of the Court.

This case comes here by certificate of the Circuit Court of Appeals of the Eighth Circuit, and is intended to submit to us, for answer, certain questions concerning the validity and proper construction of the Anti-Narcotic

Act of December 17, 1914, c. 1, 38 Stat. 785, as amended in the Revenue Act
of 1918, February 24, 1919, § 1006, 18, 40 Stat. 1057, 1130.

* * * * *

[341] In interpreting the Act, we must assume that it is a taxing measure, for otherwise it would be no law at all. If it is a mere act for the purpose of regulating and restraining the purchase of the opiate and other
drugs, it is beyond the power of Congress and must be regarded as invalid,
just as the Child Labor Act of Congress was held to be, in *Bailey, Collector,
v. Drexel Furniture Company,* 259 U.S. 20. Everything in the construction of
§ 2 must [342] be regarded as directed toward the collection of the taxes imposed in § 1 and the prevention of evasion by persons subject to the tax. If
the words can not be read as reasonably serving such a purpose, § 2 can not
be supported.

[343] The importation, preparation and sale of the opiate, or other like
drugs, and their transportation and concealment in small packages, are ex-
ceedingly easy and make the levy and collection of a tax thereon correspond-
ingly [344] difficult. More than this, use of the drug for other than medicinal
purposes leads to addiction and causes the addicts to resort to so much cunning, deceit and concealment in the procurement and custody of the drug,
and to be willing to pay such high prices for it that, to be efficient, a law for
taxing it needs to make thorough provision for preventing and discovering
evasion of the tax—as by requiring that sales, purchases and other transactions in the drug be so conducted and evidenced that any dealing in it where
the tax has not been paid, may be detected and punished and that opportunity for successful evasion may be lessened as far as may be possible.

* * * * *

[350] Section 2 of the Anti-Narcotic Act introduces into the Act the feature of the required and stamped order form to accompany each sale. It is to
bear the name of the purchaser, and is addressed to the seller, with other data.
Recorded as the law requires it to be, it constitutes a registry of purchasers as
distinguished from that of sellers. Congress intended not only to punish sales
without registration under the first section, but also to punish them without
order forms from the purchaser to the seller, as a means of making it difficult
for the unregistered seller to carry through his unlawful sales to those who
could not get order forms. Thus an illegal unregistered seller might wish to
clothe his actual unregistered sales with order forms that would give the
transaction a specious appearance of legality. To punish him for this misuse

of an order form is not to punish him for not [351] recording his own crime. It is to punish him for an added crime—that of deceiving others into the belief that the sale is a lawful sale. There is no incongruity in increasing the criminal liability of the non-registered seller who fails to use an order form in his sales, or who misuses it. Both the registered and the non-registered seller are, under our construction of the section, punished for not using the order forms as the statute requires, or for misusing them. The order form is not a mere record of a past transaction—it is a certificate of legality of the transaction being carried on, or else it is a means of discovering the illegality and is useful for the latter purpose. We think the resemblance of the Katz case and this case is superficial and that they are distinguishable.

We are of opinion, therefore, that the provision which is contained in the first sentence of § 2 of the Act is not limited in its application to those persons who by § 1 are required to register and pay the tax. We answer the first question in the negative.

This brings us to the second question, which is " . . . is the provision as so construed, constitutional?" It was held to be constitutional in *United States v. Doremus,* 249 U.S. 86, 94. In that case the validity of the Anti-Narcotic Drug Act, as it was enacted, December 17, 1914, 38 Stat. 785, was under examination by this Court. The inquiry was whether § 2, in making sales of the drugs unlawful except to persons giving orders on forms issued by the Commissioner of Internal Revenue, to be preserved for official inspection, and forbidding any person to obtain the drugs by means of such order forms for any other purpose than use, sale or distribution in the conduct of a lawful business, or in the legitimate practice of his profession, bore a reasonable relation to the enforcement of the tax provided by § 1 and did not exceed the power of Congress. It was held that § 2 aimed to confine sales to [352] registered dealers, and to those dispensing the drugs as physicians, and to those who come to dealers with legitimate prescriptions of physicians; that Congress, with full power over the subject, inserted these provisions in an Act specifically providing for the raising of revenue. Considered of themselves, the Court thought that they tended to keep the traffic aboveboard and subject to inspection by those authorized to collect the revenue; that they tended to diminish the opportunity of unauthorized persons to obtain the drugs and sell them clandestinely without paying the tax imposed by the federal law. This Court said in the *Doremus* case:

"This case well illustrates the possibility which may have induced Congress to insert the provisions limiting sales to registered dealers and requiring patients to obtain these drugs as a medicine from physicians or upon regular prescriptions. Ameris, being as the indictment charges an addict, may not have used this great number of doses for himself. He might sell some to others without paying the tax, at least Congress may have deemed it wise to prevent such possible dealings because of their effect upon the collection of the revenue."

* * * * *

[353] Four members of the Court dissented in the *Doremus* case, because of opinion that the court below had correctly held the Act of Congress, in so far as it embraced the matters complained of, to be beyond its constitutional power, and that the statute, in § 2, was a mere pretext as a tax measure and was in fact an attempt by Congress to exercise the police power reserved to the States and to regulate and restrict the sale and distribution of dangerous and noxious narcotic drugs. Since that time, this Court has held that Congress by merely calling an Act a taxing act can not make it a legitimate exercise of taxing power under § 8 of Article I of the Federal Constitution, if in fact the words of the act show clearly its real purpose is otherwise. *Child Labor Tax Case,* 259 U.S. 20, 38. By the Revenue Act of 1918, the Anti-Narcotic Act was amended so as to increase the taxes under § 1, making an occupation tax for a producer of narcotic drugs of $24 a year, for a wholesale dealer, $12, for a retail dealer, $6.00, and for a physician administering the narcotic, $3.00. The amendment also imposes an excise tax of one cent an ounce on the sale of the drug. Thus the income from the tax for the Government becomes substantial. Under the Narcotic Act, as now amended, the tax amounts to about one million dollars a year, and since the amendment in 1919 it has benefited the Treasury to the extent of nearly nine million dollars. If there was doubt as to the character of this Act—that it is not, as alleged, a subterfuge—it has been removed by the change whereby what was a nominal tax before was made a substantial one. It is certainly a taxing act now as we held in the *Alston* case. [354] It may be true that the provisions of the Act forbidding all but registered dealers to obtain the order forms has the incidental effect of making it more difficult for the drug to reach those who have a normal and legitimate use for it. . . . But, this effect . . . should not render the order form provisions void as an infringement on state police power where these provisions are genuinely calculated to sustain the revenue features. Section 2 was once sustained by this Court some nine years ago, with more formidable reason against it than now exists under the amended statute. Its provisions have been enforced for those years. Whatever doubts may have existed respecting the Act have been removed by the amendment made in 1919.

We said in the *Child Labor Tax Case,* 259 U.S. 20, 38:

"Taxes are occasionally imposed in the discretion of the legislature on proper subjects with the primary motive of obtaining revenue from them and with the incidental motive of discouraging them by making their continuance onerous. They do not lose their character as taxes because of the incidental motive."

In this case, the qualification of the right of a resident of State to buy and consume opium or other narcotic without restraint by the Federal Government, is subject to the power of Congress to lay a tax by way of excise on its sale. Congress does not exceed its power if the object is laying a tax and the interference with lawful purchasers and users of the drug is reasonably adapted to securing the payment of the tax. Nor does it render such qualification or interference with the original state right an invasion of it because it may incidentally discourage some in the harmful use of the thing taxed. *License Tax* cases, 5 Wall. 462; *Nicol v. Ames,* 173 U.S. 509, 524; *Knowlton v. Moore,* 178 U.S. 41, 60, 61; *In re Kollock,* 165 U.S. 526, 536.

* * * * *

The separate opinion of MR. JUSTICE MCREYNOLDS.

[355] Nigro, not alleged to be registered as a dealer, was charged with violating § 2 of the Harrison Anti-Narcotic Act by selling opium (whether in or from an original stamped package does not appear) to Raithel, not a dealer, without an order upon a form issued by the Commissioner of Internal Revenue.

* * * * *

[357] The habit of smoking tobacco is often deleterious. Many think it ought to be suppressed. The craving for diamonds leads to extravagance and frequently to crime. Silks are luxuries and their use abridges the demand for cotton and wool. Those who sell tobacco, or diamonds, or silks may be taxed by the United States. But, surely, a provision in an act laying such a tax which limited sales of cigars, cigarettes, jewels, or silks to some small class alone authorized to secure official blanks would not be proper or necessary in order to enforce collection. The acceptance of such a doctrine would bring many purely local matters within the potential control of the Federal Government. The admitted evils incident to the use of opium cannot justify disregard of the powers "reserved to the States respectively, or to the people."

MR. JUSTICE SUTHERLAND concurs in these views.

MR. JUSTICE BUTLER, dissenting. [Omitted.]

Hampton & Co. v. United States

Hampton involved the constitutionality of Title III, section 315 (a) of the Tariff Act of 1922, which gave to the president the power to adjust tariffs either up or down, based on findings of what was needed to protect American manufacturers. The provision was attacked as an unconstitutional delegation of legislative power to the executive. This allegation was to prove a highly effective weapon to opponents of early New Deal legislation. It did not work, however, in the *Hampton* case. Taft ruled in favor of executive power.

J. W. Hampton, Jr., & Company v. United States

Certiorari to the United States Court of Customs Appeals

No 242. Argued March 1, 1928—Decided April 9, 1928

276 U.S. 394 (1928)

[400]

MR. CHIEF JUSTICE TAFT delivered the opinion of the Court.

J. W. Hampton, Jr., & Company made an importation into New York of barium dioxide, which the collector of customs assessed at the dutiable rate of six cents per pound. This was two cents per pound more than that fixed by statute, par. 12 ch. 356, 42 Stat. 858, 860. The rate was raised by the collector by virtue of the proclamation of the President, 45 Treas. Dec. 669, T. D. 40216, issued under, and by authority of, § 315 of Title III of the Tariff Act of September 21, 1922, ch. 356, 42 Stat. 858, 941, which is the so-called flexible tariff provision.

* * * * *

[404] The issue here is as to the constitutionality of § 315, upon which depends the authority for the proclamation of the President and for two of the six cents per pound duty collected from the petitioner The contention of the taxpayers is two-fold—first, they argue that the section is invalid in that it is a delegation to the President of the legislative power, which by Article I, § 1 of the Constitution, is vested in Congress, the power being that declared in § 8 of Article I, that the Congress shall have power to lay and collect taxes, duties, imposts and excises. The second objection is that, as § 315 was enacted with the avowed intent and for the purpose of protecting the industries of the United States, it is invalid because the Constitution gives power to lay such taxes only for revenue.

First. It seems clear what Congress intended by § 315. Its plan was to secure by law the imposition of customs duties on articles of imported merchandise which should equal the difference between the cost of producing in a foreign country the articles in question and laying them down for sale in the United States, and the cost of producing and selling like or similar articles in the United States, so that the duties not only secure revenue but at the same time enable domestic producers to compete on terms of equality with foreign producers in the markets of the United States. It may be that it is difficult to fix with exactness this difference, but the difference which is sought in the statute is perfectly clear and perfectly intelligible. Because of the difficulty in practically determining what that difference is, Congress seems to have [405] doubted that the information in its possession was such as to enable it to make the adjustment accurately, and also to have apprehended that with changing conditions the difference might vary in such a way that some readjustments would be necessary to give effect to the principle on which the statute proceeds. To avoid such difficulties, Congress adopted in § 315 the method of describing with clearness what its policy and plan was and then authorizing a member of the executive branch to carry out this policy and plan, and to find the changing difference from time to time, and to make the adjustments necessary to conform the duties to the standard underlying that policy and plan. As it was a matter of great importance, it concluded to give by statute to the President, the chief of the executive branch, the function of determining the difference as it might vary. . . .

The Tariff Commission does not itself fix duties, but before the President reaches a conclusion on the subject of investigation, the Tariff Commission must make an investigation and in doing so must give notice to all parties interested and an opportunity to adduce evidence and to be heard.

The well-known maxim *"Delegata potestas non potest delegari,"* applicable to the law of agency in the general and common law, is well understood and has had wider [406] application in the construction of our Federal and State Constitutions than it has in private law. The Federal Constitution and State Constitutions of this country divide the governmental power into three branches. The first is the legislative, the second is the executive, and the third is the judicial, and the rule is that in the actual administration of the government Congress or the Legislature should exercise the legislative power, the President or the State executive, the Governor, the executive power, and the Courts or the Judiciary the judicial power, and in carrying out that constitutional division into three branches it is a breach of the National fundamental law if Congress gives up its legislative power and transfers it to the President, or to the Judicial branch, or if by law it attempts to invest itself or its members with either executive power or judicial power. This is not to say that the three branches are not co-ordinate parts of one government and that each in the field of its duties may not invoke the action of the two other branches in so far as the action invoked shall not be an assumption of the constitutional field of action of another branch. In determining what it may do in seeking assistance from another branch, the extent and character of that assistance must be fixed according to common sense and the inherent necessities of the governmental co-ordination.

The field of Congress involves all and many varieties of legislative action, and Congress has found it frequently necessary to use officers of the Executive Branch, within defined limits, to secure the exact effect intended by its acts of legislation, by vesting discretion in such officers to make public regulations interpreting a statute and directing the details of its execution, even to the extent of providing for penalizing a breach of such regulations. . . .

[407] Congress may feel itself unable conveniently to determine exactly when its exercise of the legislative power should become effective, because dependent on future conditions, and it may leave the determination of such time to the decision of an Executive, or, as often happens in matters of state legislation, it may be left to a popular vote of the residents of a district to be effected by the legislation. While in a sense one may say that such residents are exercising legislative power, it is not an exact statement, because the power has already been exercised legislatively by the body vested with that power under the Constitution, the condition of its legislation going into effect being made dependent by the legislature on the expression of the voters of a certain district. . . .

* * * * *

[409] . . . If Congress shall lay down by legislative act an intelligible principle to which the person or body authorized to fix such rates is directed to conform, such legislative action is not a forbidden delegation of legislative power. If it is thought wise to vary the customs duties according to changing conditions of production at home and abroad, it may authorize the Chief Executive to carry out this purpose, with the advisory assistance of a Tariff Commission appointed under Congressional authority. . . .

* * * * *

[411] Second. The second objection to § 315 is that the declared plan of Congress, either expressly or by clear implication, formulates its rule to guide the President and his advisory Tariff Commission as one directed to a tariff system of protection that will avoid damaging competition to the

country's industries by the importation of goods from other countries at too low a rate to equalize foreign and domestic competition in the markets of the United States. It is contended that the only power of Congress in the levying of customs duties is to create revenue, and that it is unconstitutional to frame the customs duties with any other view than that of revenue raising. It undoubtedly is true that during the political life of this country there has been much discussion between parties as to the wisdom of the policy of protection, and we may go further and say as to its constitutionality, but no historian, whatever his view of the wisdom of the policy of protection, would contend that Congress, since the first revenue Act, in 1789, has not assumed that it was within its power in making provision for the collection of revenue, to put taxes upon importations and to vary the subjects of such taxes or rates in an effort to encourage the growth of the industries of the Nation by protecting home production against foreign competition. It is enough to point out that the second act adopted by the Congress of the United States, July 4, 1789, ch. 2, 1 Stat. 24, contained the following recital.

"SEC. 1. Whereas it is necessary for the support of government, for the discharge of the debts of the United States, and the encouragement and protection of [412] manufactures, that duties be laid on goods, wares and merchandises imported: Be it enacted, etc."

In this first Congress sat many members of the Constitutional Convention of 1787. . . .

* * * * *

So long as the motive of Congress and the effect of its legislative action are to secure revenue for the benefit of the general government, the existence of other motives in the selection of the subjects of taxes can not invalidate Congressional action. As we said in the *Child Labor Tax Case,* 259 U.S. 20, 38: "Taxes are occasionally imposed in the discretion of the legislature on proper subjects with the primary motive of obtaining revenue from them, and with the incidental motive of discouraging them by making their continuance onerous. They do not lose their character as taxes because of the incidental motive." [413] And so here, the fact that Congress declares that one of its motives in fixing the rates of duty is so to fix them that they shall encourage the industries of this country in the competition with producers in other countries in the sale of goods in this country, can not invalidate a revenue act so framed. Section 315 and its provisions are within the power of Congress. The judgment of the Court of Customs Appeals is affirmed.

Affirmed.

Omitted Taft Opinions

In re Gilbert, 276 U.S. 6 (1928)—role of special master and fees paid to him.

Linstead v. Chesapeake & Ohio Railway, 276 U.S. 28 (1928)—interpretation of the Employers' Liability Act.

Harkin v. Brundage, 276 U.S. 36 (1928)—concurrent jurisdiction of federal and state courts.

In re Gilbert, 276 U.S. 294 (1928)—disbarment of attorney.

Corona Co. v. Dovan Corp., 276 U.S. 358 (1928)—patent case.

Krauss Brothers v. Mellon, 276 U.S. 386 (1928)—procedural issue.

VOLUME 277

Blodgett v. Silberman

This case involved the power of the state of Connecticut to levy transfer taxes on the property of a decedent, which property was no longer located in the state. The Connecticut Supreme Court of Errors had held that both the decedent's interest in a New York partnership and United States government bonds situated in New York were immune from the tax. Taft upheld the former ruling, but found that the bonds were subject to the Connecticut tax.

Blodgett v. Silberman et al.
Silberman et al. v. Blodgett

Certiorari and Error to the Superior Court of Fairfield County, Connecticut

Nos. 190 and 191. Argued March 12, 13, 1928—Decided April 16, 1928

277 U.S. 1 (1928)

[3]

MR. CHIEF JUSTICE TAFT delivered the opinion of the Court.

These two cases, which are really one, grow out of the operation of a transfer tax by the State of Connecticut. They are brought to this Court, one by certiorari, and one by writ of error. The questions presented are whether the tax on the transfer of certain parts of the large estate of Robert B. Hirsch was in violation of the due process clause of the Fourteenth Amendment to the Federal Constitution in that they were tangible property in New York and not in Connecticut. . . .

* * * * *

[6] The Supreme Court of Errors held, first, that the interest of the decedent in the partnership was a chose in action and intangible and the transfer thereof was subject to the tax imposed by the law of the decedent's domicile; second, that the bonds and certificates of the United States were tangible property having a *situs* in New York and were not within the taxable jurisdiction of Connecticut, but were to be regarded as in the same class of tangibles as the paintings, works of art and furniture considered in the case of *Frick v. Pennsylvania,* 268 U.S. 473. In that case, Pennsylvania, the State of Mr. Frick's domicil, sought to impose a transfer or succession tax on the paintings and other tangible personalty, which had always been in New York City, and it was held that they had an actual *situs* in New York and that, under the Fourteenth Amendment, Pennsylvania could impose no transfer or succession tax in respect of them. Applying what it conceived to be the principle of that case to the bonds of the United States and certificates of its indebtedness in this, the Supreme Court of Errors held that their transfer could not be taxed in Connecticut.

The Superior Court, following the advice of the Supreme Court of Errors, entered a judgment giving full effect to it. That is the final judgment in the case and it is the judgment now to be reviewed.

* * * * *

[7] Had the Supreme Court of Errors put its ruling against the validity of part of the tax on the construction of the State Constitution or statute, we could not review that ruling, because it would have involved only a question of state law, but so far as the ruling was put on the ground that the State could not impose the tax consistently with the due process of law clause of the Fourteenth Amendment, a federal question is presented which we may consider, and when we have determined the federal questions, the cause will go back to the state court for further proceedings not inconsistent with our views on such federal questions.

* * * * *

[12] It thus clearly appears that both under the partnership agreement and under the laws of the State of New York the interest of the partner was the right to receive a sum of money equal to his share of the net value of the partnership after a settlement, and this right to his share is a debt owing to him, a chose in action, and an intangible. We concur with the Supreme Court of Errors that as such it was subject to the transfer tax of Connecticut.

We come then to the second question, whether bonds of the United States and certificates of indebtedness of the United States deposited in a safe deposit box in New York City, and never removed from there, owned by the [13] decedent at the time of his death, were intangibles which come within the rule already stated.

* * * * *

[17] The discussion . . . shows what this Court meant in the *Frick* case in holding that personal property in the form of paintings and furniture having an actual *situs* in one State could not be subjected to a transfer tax in another State, and emphasizes the inference that it did not apply to anything having as its essence an indebtedness or a chose in action and could not apply to property in the form of specialties or bonds or other written evidences of indebtedness whether governmental or otherwise, even though they passed from hand to hand. The analogy between furniture and bonds cannot be complete because bonds are representative only and are not the thing represented. They are at most choses in action and intangibles.

We think therefore that the Supreme Court of Errors in extending the rule of the *Frick* case from tangible personal property, like paintings, furniture or cattle, to bonds, is not warranted, and to that extent we must reverse its conclusion in denying to Connecticut the right to tax the transfer of the bonds and Treasury certificates.

[18] Of course this reasoning necessarily sustains the different view of that court that the transfer of certificates of stock in corporations of other States than Connecticut was taxable in the latter as the transfer of choses in action.

* * * * *

The results thus stated lead to our reversing the judgment of the Superior Court of Connecticut, in respect to the tax on the transfer of the bonds and certificates of indebtedness of the United States, and to our affirming the judgment in other respects.

* * * * *

Dugan v. Ohio

Dugan was convicted in a mayor's court of a liquor violation. He challenged the role of the mayor as being in violation of the Fourteenth Amendment's guarantee to due process, contending that the mayor had an interest in the fines that were assessed as a result of his conviction. Taft upheld the conviction, distinguishing this situation from that of *Tumey v. Ohio,* 273 U.S. 510 (1927), in which the Court had found a mayor's role to be a violation of due process because he stood to gain financially from the conviction. Since there was no direct financial gain for the mayor like in this case, Taft found no violation of due process.

Dugan v. Ohio

Error to the Supreme Court of Ohio

No. 766. Argued April 10, 1928—Decided May 14, 1928

277 U.S. 61 (1928)

[62]

MR. CHIEF JUSTICE TAFT delivered the opinion of the Court.

M. J. Dugan was convicted before the Mayor's Court of the city of Xenia, Greene County, Ohio, for the unlawful possession of intoxicating liquor under Section 6212–15 of the General Code of Ohio. The conviction was sustained by the Common Pleas Court of Greene County, Ohio, by the Court of Appeals of the same county, and by the Supreme Court of the State. The defendant has duly raised the question of the constitutional impartiality of the mayor to try the case. This is the only issue for our consideration. The objection is based on the ground that for the mayor to act in this case was a violation of the Fourteenth Amendment to the Federal Constitution, in that the mayor occupied in the city government two practically and seriously inconsistent positions, one partisan and the other judicial; that as such mayor he had power under the law to convict persons without a jury of the offense of the possession of intoxicating liquor and punish them by substantial fines, half of which were paid into the city treasury, and as a member of the city commission he had a right to vote on the appropriation and the spending of city funds; and further that while he received only a fixed salary and did not receive any fees, yet all the fees taxed and collected under his convictions were paid into the city treasury [63] and were contributions to a general fund out of which his salary as mayor was payable.

The defendant, in February, 1924, pleaded guilty and was fined $400 for possessing intoxicating liquor, and thereafter was convicted and fined $1,000 for a subsequent similar offense. This is a review of the second conviction.

The city of Xenia is a charter city, and has a commission form of government, with five commissioners. The charter provides that a member of the city commission shall also be mayor. The mayor has no executive, and exercises only judicial, functions. The commission exercises all the legislative power of the city, and together with the manager exercises all its executive powers. The manager is the active executive. The mayor's salary is fixed by the votes of the members of the commission other than the mayor, he having no vote therein. He receives no fees. . . .

* * * * *

[64] As the plaintiff in error contends, however, the mayor's individual pecuniary interest in his conviction of defendants was not the only reason in the *Tumey* case for [65] holding the Fourteenth Amendment to be violated. Another was that a defendant brought into court might with reason complain that he was not likely to get a fair trial or a fair sentence from a judge who as chief executive was responsible for the financial condition of the village, who could and did largely control the policy of setting up a liquor court in the village with attorneys, marshals and detectives under his supervision, and who by his interest as mayor might be tempted to accumulate from heavy fines a large fund by which the running expenses of a small village could be paid, improvements might be made and taxes reduced. This was thought not to be giving the defendant the benefit of due process of law.

No such case is presented at the bar. The mayor of Xenia receives a salary which is not dependent on whether he convicts in any case or not. While it is true that his salary is paid out of a fund to which fines accumulated from his court under all laws contribute, it is a general fund, and he receives a salary in any event, whether he convicts or acquits. There is no reason to infer on any showing that failure to convict in any case or cases would deprive him of or affect his fixed compensation. The mayor has himself as such no executive but only judicial duties. His relation under the Xenia charter, as one of five members of the city commission, to the fund contributed to by his fines as judge, or to the executive or financial policy of the city, is remote. We agree with the Supreme Court of Ohio in its view that the principles announced in the *Tumey* case do not cover this.

Judgment affirmed.

Compañia de Navegacion v. Fireman's Fund Insurance Co.

A tugboat that had been built for inland waterway work took a contract to sail on open water. It had procured insurance policies to protect it against "perils of the sea." The insurance companies had charged premiums for the policies and had had the tug carefully inspected for "seaworthiness." Despite the precautions, the tug sunk and the insurance companies refused to pay. Taft, in reversing the lower court decision, found that the terms "seaworthiness" and "perils of the sea" were relative terms and that the higher premiums required attested to this fact.

Compañia de Navegacion, Interior, S. A., v. Fireman's Fund Insurance Company

Certiorari to the Circuit Court of Appeals for the Fifth Circuit

Nos. 510 to 520, inclusive. Argued April 19, 1928—Decided May 14, 1928

277 U.S. 66 (1928)

[70]

MR. CHIEF JUSTICE TAFT delivered the opinion of the Court.

These are eleven libels filed in the District Court of the United States for the Eastern District of Louisiana by a Mexican corporation known as the Compañia de Navegacion, against as many different insurance companies, English and American, on eleven separate policies, insuring the tug "Wash Gray" in favor of the libelant as owner in different sums aggregating $85,000, and covering a voyage of the tug while in tow from Tampico, Mexico, to Galveston, Texas.

The tug was designed for inland waters. She was 87 1/2 feet long, with 19 feet beam, 9 feet depth of hold, and was of 105 tons. She was insured specially for this sea voyage, to be towed as agreed with the Insuring Companies by the "Freeport Sulphur No. 1," a vessel engaged in regular trade on the Gulf of Mexico, and measuring 309 feet in length, 45 feet beam, with 22 1/2 feet depth, and of approximately 3,000 tons displacement.

[71] When application was made for insurance, the underwriters required an inspection for seaworthiness, general fitness and towing arrangements for that voyage. For that purpose two well known marine surveyors, representing the various underwriters, made a thorough, critical inspection, followed by recommendations for preparations for the voyage, including

certain overhauling, particularly of her towing bitts and decking, and for the planking up of doors, ports, and other openings. They reported in writing to the underwriters that the requirements had been complied with, and certified her seaworthiness, and her fitness for the particular voyage. Because of the extra hazardous risk involved in the transit of this small inland vessel in tow at sea, the premiums were much increased by the underwriters. . . .

* * * * *

[78] The fourth objection claimed by the respondents is that no recovery could be had because the loss of the "Wash Gray" was not caused by any peril insured against. These policies all contained a clause like the following:

"It is the intent of this insurance company by this policy to fully indemnify the insured against the adventures and perils of the harbors, bays, sounds, seas, rivers and other waters above named."

It is urged by the Insurance Companies that weather when the wind did not exceed a velocity of twenty-five miles, though with squalls, and with a cross current and swell producing a choppy sea with waves five feet high and breaking over the head of the vessel, did not constitute a peril of the sea.

* * * * *

[79] . . . [I]t is contended on behalf of the insurance companies that the phrase "perils of the sea" has not a varying but an absolute meaning, and they rely on the language of Mr. Justice Story in the *Reeside,* 20 Federal Cases, No. 11,657, p. 458 (2 Sumn. 567).

[80] . . . A contract of maritime insurance is usually not different from any other contract except that the words and phrases used may have a technical nautical meaning to be understood by the parties and enforced accordingly. We have seen however from the cases that the term "seaworthiness" varies with the circumstances and the exceptional features of the risk known to both parties. The view of the Circuit Court of Appeals that "perils of the sea" has an absolute meaning and may not be varied by the knowledge of the parties as to the circumstances and must be maintained stiffly in favor of the insurance companies and against the insured, is not necessary or reasonable. The variation in the significance of "seaworthy," as shown by the above authorities, when caused by exceptional circumstances known to both parties, applies as well to the meaning of perils of the sea as to that of seaworthiness. . . .

* * * * *

[81] We find ourselves unable to follow this distinction. In all these cases the recovery was on the contract, and the question was of the construction

of the contract. Its construction was affected necessarily by the special circumstances surrounding the contract known to both parties and acted on by them in charging and paying an increased compensation for the risk run. The circumstances in this case are very like those shown in the cases cited. They certainly justify the conclusion to which we have come.

The judgment of the Circuit Court of Appeals is reversed.

Gaines v. Washington

In the case of *Gitlow v. New York,* 268 U.S. 652 (1925), the Supreme Court held that the First Amendment's guarantee of freedom of speech was carried over onto the states by the due process clause of the Fourteenth Amendment. Gaines was convicted of murder in a Washington state court. Among the issues he raised on appeal was whether his conviction was invalid because he had been denied the right to a public trial (Sixth Amendment) and had been proceeded against by means of an information and not an indictment (Fifth Amendment). Taft, for a unanimous Court, rejected both claims.

In doing so Taft did explore whether the Fourteenth Amendment's guarantee of due process made the Sixth Amendment's right to a public trial applicable to the states. Interestingly, Taft did not explicitly deny that it did. Rather, he found that the facts on the record of the case did not show that Gaines had been denied a public trial. As for the use of an information rather than an indictment, this, for Taft, was settled by the Court's prior ruling in *Hurtado v. California,* 110 U.S. 516 (1884).

Gaines v. Washington

Error to the Supreme Court of Washington

No. 841. Submitted April 23, 1928—Decided May 14, 1928

277 U.S. 81 (1928)

[82]

MR. CHIEF JUSTICE TAFT delivered the opinion of the Court.

The defendant was charged by information with the crime of murder in the first degree in the Superior Court of King County in the State of Washington. The trial resulted in a verdict of guilty as charged and a finding by the jury that the death penalty should be inflicted. Motions for a new trial and in arrest of judgment were made and overruled, and the judgment was entered upon the verdict.

* * * * *

[84] In obedience to the rule, the petitioner, Wallace C. Gaines, has filed a return in which he avers that the first federal question upon which he asks a writ of certiorari arises because of the action of the trial judge, as shown by the record as follows:

"At the close of the afternoon session on the ninth day of the trial, to wit, August 11th, Judge Jones, the trial judge, said:

"Before adjourning, I will state that the atmosphere is pretty unbearable. I know the jury must also feel it. I assume there is a certain part of the members of the Bar who from the standpoint of students desire to hear the testimony, but with those exceptions, court officers and members of the Bar, the general public will be excluded beginning tomorrow."

This action, the return alleges, was a violation of the Sixth Amendment to the Constitution of the United States, and of the due process clause of the Fourteenth Amendment to the same Constitution, and that this error [85] was duly urged in the trial court and the State Supreme Court, on both grounds.

The Sixth Amendment to the Constitution provides in part that "In all criminal prosecutions the accused shall enjoy the right to a speedy and public trial by an impartial jury of the state and district wherein the crime shall have been committed." Many state constitutions contain a substantially similar guaranty and restriction. . . .

But we are relieved from considering or reconciling the different views taken in these cases by the fact that the Sixth Amendment to the Federal Constitution does not apply to the trial of criminal prosecutions by a State. It has been well settled for years that the first ten Amendments apply only to the procedure and trial of causes in the federal courts and are not limitations upon those in state courts. *Spies v. Illinois,* 123 U.S. 131, 166, and cases cited.

It is contended, however, that due process of law exacted in the Fourteenth Amendment in causes tried in state courts must be construed as equivalent to the Sixth Amendment in federal trials. The question has not arisen in any case cited to us. It would involve a consideration of whether due process requires more than a trial that is not private or secret, or whether due process would not be satisfied except by such a restriction upon the discretion of the court in regulating attendance as the [86] defendant here insists upon and as is held in some of the authorities cited above in enforcing the Sixth Amendment and similar constitutional provisions of an affirmative character. But we need not pass on that question now.

For even if the due process clause requires the same kind of public trial as that contended for by the petitioner, the record does not disclose facts which would justify us in bringing the case before us for our review. The order of the court complained of was oral only. No formal order was entered, neither was there a minute entry nor a specific mention to any particular officer to see that it was executed so far as the record discloses. The State before the Supreme Court contended that the order to exclude the general public was never executed. This was an issue of fact before both Washington courts. After the fullest examination of affidavits filed by both sides upon the motion for a new trial the State Supreme Court's conclusion was as follows:

"Believing that the statement of the Court was not carried out but that the general public were admitted to the courtroom to the extent of its seating capacity during the trial, the rights of the appellant as guaranteed by the constitution of this state and by the Fourteenth Amendment to the Constitution of the United States were not invaded."

From an examination of the record, we find no reason for rejecting this conclusion of fact reached by the unanimous judgment of that court.

Another question raised on behalf of the defendant concerns the filing of the information for murder by the prosecuting attorney. Prosecution by information instead of by indictment is provided for by the laws of Washington. This is not a violation of the Federal Constitution. *Hurtado v. California,* 110 U.S. 516.

* * * * *

The order will be entered dismissing the writ of error and denying the application for a certiorari.

Writ of error dismissed. Certiorari denied.

Olmstead v. United States

Olmstead was handed down by the Court at a time when Taft's ability to "mass the Court" is generally thought to have been in decline. As Taft had feared he would, Justice Stone now regularly voted with Holmes and Brandeis. In *Olmstead* they were joined by Pierce Butler, whose general antipathy toward government often made him a defender of the rights of the accused. But with his health failing, the now seventy-year-old Taft should perhaps be given credit for keeping Justices Sutherland and McReynolds on board.

Despite the narrowness of the majority he put together (5–4), Taft's opinion would survive almost to the end of the Warren Court (1953–69). It was finally explicitly overturned only in *Katz v. United States,* 389 U.S. 347 (1967).

Like the *Carroll* case, *Olmstead* was the product of the enforcement of Prohibition. Federal authorities had placed a tap on the phone lines going into Olmstead's dwelling. In contrast to the famous Brandeis dissent—which in many ways anticipated the *Katz* opinion by stressing the importance of the concept of privacy in understanding the Fourth Amendment's guarantees—Taft's opinion emphasized the fact that there had been no physical trespass by government agents. Furthermore, Taft allowed that if Congress wanted to give special protection to telephone communications and restrict or limit wiretapping, that was a decision for Congress and not the Court to make. In 1934, with Prohibition over, Congress finally accepted Taft's suggestion when it adopted the Federal Communications Act.

Olmstead et al. v. United States
Green et al. v. Same
McInnis v. Same

Certiorari to the Circuit Court of Appeals for the Ninth Circuit

Nos. 493, 532 and 533. Argued February 20, 21, 1928—Decided June 4, 1928

277 U.S. 438 (1928)

[455]

MR. CHIEF JUSTICE TAFT delivered the opinion of the Court.

* * * * *

[456] Olmstead was the leading conspirator and the general manager of the business. He made a contribution of $10,000 to the capital; eleven others contributed $1,000 each. The profits were divided one-half to Olmstead and the remainder to the other eleven. . . .

The information which led to the discovery of the conspiracy and its nature and extent was largely obtained by intercepting messages on the telephones of the conspirators by four federal prohibition officers. Small [457] wires were inserted along the ordinary telephone wires from the residences of four of the petitioners and those leading from the chief office. The insertions were made without trespass upon any property of the defendants. They were made in the basement of the large office building. The taps from house lines were made in the streets near the houses.

The gathering of evidence continued for many months. Conversations of the conspirators of which refreshing stenographic notes were currently made, were testified to by the government witnesses. . . .

The Fourth Amendment provides—"The right of the people to be secure in their persons, houses, papers, and effects against unreasonable searches and seizures shall not be violated; and no warrants shall issue but upon probable cause, supported by oath or affirmation and particularly describing the place to be searched and the persons or *things* to be seized." . . .

[458] It will be helpful to consider the chief cases in this Court which bear upon the construction of these Amendments.

* * * * *

[Having reviewed the major cases, Taft concluded]

The well known historical purpose of the Fourth Amendment, directed against general warrants and writs of assistance, was to prevent the use of governmental force to search a man's house, his person, his papers and his effects; and to prevent their seizure against his will. This phase of the misuse of governmental power of compulsion is the emphasis of the opinion of the Court in the *Boyd* case. This appears too in the *Weeks* case, in the *Silverthorne* case and in the *Amos* case.

* * * * *

[464] The Amendment itself shows that the search is to be of material things—the person, the house, his papers or his effects. The description of the warrant necessary to make the proceeding lawful, is that it must specify the place to be searched and the person or things to be seized.

It is urged that the language of Mr. Justice Field in *Ex parte Jackson,* already quoted, offers an analogy to the interpretation of the Fourth Amendment in respect of wire tapping. But the analogy fails. The Fourth Amendment may have proper application to a sealed letter in the mail because of the constitutional provision for the Postoffice Department and the relations between the Government and those who pay to secure protection of their sealed letters. See Revised Statutes, §§ 3978 to 3988, whereby Congress monopolizes the carriage of letters and excludes from that business everyone else, and § 3929 which forbids any postmaster or other person to open any letter not addressed to himself. It is plainly within the words of the Amendment to say that the unlawful rifling by a government agent of a sealed letter is a search and seizure of the sender's papers or effects. The letter is a paper, an effect, and in the custody of a Government that forbids carriage except under its protection.

The United States takes no such care of telegraph or telephone messages as of mailed sealed letters. The Amendment does not forbid what was done here. There was no searching. There was no seizure. The evidence was secured by the use of the sense of hearing and that only. There was no entry of the houses or offices of the defendants.

[465] By the invention of the telephone, fifty years ago, and its application for the purpose of extending communications, one can talk with another at a far distant place. The language of the Amendment can not be extended and expanded to include telephone wires reaching to the whole world from the defendant's house or office. The intervening wires are not part of his house or office any more than are the highways along which they are stretched.

This Court in *Carroll v. United States,* 267 U.S. 132, 149, declared:

"The Fourth Amendment is to be construed in the light of what was deemed an unreasonable search and seizure when it was adopted and in a manner which will conserve public interests as well as the interests and rights of individual citizens."

Justice Bradley in the *Boyd* case, and Justice Clark in the *Gouled* case, said that the Fifth Amendment and the Fourth Amendment were to be liberally construed to effect the purpose of the framers of the Constitution in the interest of liberty. But that can not justify enlargement of the language employed beyond the possible practical meaning of houses, persons, papers, and effects, or so to apply the words search and seizure as to forbid hearing or sight.

* * * * *

Congress may of course protect the secrecy of telephone messages by making them, when intercepted, inadmissible in evidence in federal criminal trials, by direct legislation, [466] and thus depart from the common law of evidence. But the courts may not adopt such a policy by attributing an enlarged and unusual meaning to the Fourth Amendment. The reasonable view is that one who installs in his house a telephone instrument with connecting wires intends to project his voice to those quite outside, and that the wires beyond his house and messages while passing over them are not within the protection of the Fourth Amendment. Here those who intercepted the projected voices were not in the house of either party to the conversation.

Neither the cases we have cited nor any of the many federal decisions brought to our attention hold the Fourth Amendment to have been violated as against a defendant unless there has been an official search and seizure of his person, or such a seizure of his papers or his tangible material effects, or an actual physical invasion of his house "or curtilage" for the purpose of making a seizure.

We think, therefore, that the wire tapping here disclosed did not amount to a search or seizure within the meaning of the Fourth Amendment.

What has been said disposes of the only question that comes within the terms of our order granting certiorari in these cases. But some of our number, departing from that order, have concluded that there is merit in the two-fold objection overruled in both courts below that evidence obtained through intercepting of telephone messages by government agents was inadmissible because the mode of obtaining it was unethical and a misdemeanor under the law of Washington. To avoid any misapprehension of our views of that objection we shall deal with it in both of its phases.

* * * * *

[468] A standard which would forbid the reception of evidence if obtained by other than nice ethical conduct by government officials would make society suffer and give criminals greater immunity than has been known heretofore. In the absence of controlling legislation by Congress, those who realize the difficulties in bringing offenders to justice may well deem it wise that the exclusion of evidence should be confined to cases where rights under the Constitution would be violated by admitting it.

* * * * *

[469] The judgments of the Circuit Court of Appeals are affirmed. The mandates will go down forthwith under Rule 31.

Affirmed.

Omitted Taft Opinion

Gaineville v. Brown-Crummer Co., 277 U.S. 54 (1928)—diversity of citizenship cases in federal courts.

October Term, 1928

William Howard Taft, Chief Justice
Oliver Wendell Holmes
Willis Van Devanter
James Clark McReynolds
Louis D. Brandeis
George Sutherland
Pierce Butler
Edward T. Sanford
Harlan Fiske Stone

VOLUME 278

Lehigh Valley Railroad Co.
v. Board of Public Utility Commissioners

The New Jersey Public Utility Commission ordered the Lehigh Valley Railroad Company to make improvements to two grade crossings within the state. The railroad refused. It argued that the action of the commission invaded the powers of Congress under the Interstate Commerce Act, violated the due process and equal protection guarantees of the Fourteenth Amendment by requiring an unreasonable expenditure of money, impaired the obligation of contract, and failed to allow an independent review of the commission's findings by a court. Writing the opinion of the Court, Taft rallied all but the cantankerous Justice James McReynolds in upholding the order of the New Jersey Public Utility Commission, finding there was the possibility for judicial review and that the order was not unreasonable given the state's valid interest in exercising its police powers to improve the safety of its citizens.

Lehigh Valley Railroad Company v. Board of Public Utility Commissioners et al.

Appeals from the District Court of the United States for the District of New Jersey

Nos. 24 and 54. Argued October 10, 11, 1928—Decided November 19, 1928

278 U.S. 24 (1928)

[28]

MR. CHIEF JUSTICE TAFT delivered the opinion of the Court.

These are two appeals from orders of a circuit judge and two district judges of the United States sitting in the District Court of New Jersey, denying to the Lehigh Valley Railroad Company injunctions sought by it in that court under § 380, United States Code, Title 28; § 266 of the Judicial Code. The defendants were the Board of Public Utility Commissioners, the Attorney General, and Francis L. Bergen, Prosecutor of the Pleas of Somerset County, all of New Jersey. The order sought to be enjoined was one made by the Board of Public Utility [29] Commissioners requiring the Railroad Company to eliminate two railroad grade crossings in Hillsborough Township, Somerset County, New Jersey, and to substitute for both of them one overhead crossing, to cost the railroad company $324,000. It was alleged that the change would involve unreasonable expenditure and thereby violate Par. 2, § 15, of the Act of Congress to Regulate Commerce, as amended by the Transportation Act of 1920, by interposing a direct interference with interstate commerce and imposing a direct burden thereon; that it would confiscate the property of the railroad company, deny it the equal protection of the laws and impair the obligation of a contract between the company and the State Highway Commission. The three federal judges heard the application for a temporary injunction and denied it, and on final hearing entered a decree dismissing the bill.

* * * * *

In December, 1922, negotiations were opened between the Railroad Company and the State Highway Commission for the purpose of considering a plan for these eliminations. The negotiations continued until March 11, [30] 1924, when the State Highway Commission adopted a resolution approving a plan of their engineer. There was public objection to it, and the negotiations continued, until finally the engineering staff of both the Company and the Highway Commission agreed on Plan C, to cost $109,000. The Railroad Company expended some $5,000 in preliminary preparation for its execution.

No contract was ever signed, either by the Railroad or the Commission. The Highway Commission had statutory power to make such a contract, but none was made other than the informal agreement between the engineering staffs.

The matter was then taken up in 1926 by the Board of Public Utility Commissioners, which was vested with authority to order railroad companies to eliminate grade crossings and to direct how they should be constructed. On November 24, the Board of Public Utilities issued an order to the Railroad Company providing for a different plan from that considered by the Highway Commission, to cost $324,000.

* * * * *

[31] It is objected by the Railroad Company that the expense of the crossing of $324,000 is unreasonable, when it might have been constructed by an expenditure of at least $100,000 less.

The State of New Jersey, lying between New York and Philadelphia and the West, has always been a thoroughfare for intrastate and interstate commerce. The State has issued bonds to the extent of $70,000,000 for the improvements of its roads, and they now aggregate 1,500 miles in length. The highway with which we are concerned is known as Route 16, and is one of the chief arteries of travel between central New Jersey and the lake and mountain regions of the northern part of the State, northeastern Pennsylvania and the lower counties of New York. In connection with two other highway routes, it has become one of the principal roads between New York and Philadelphia. . . .

Two plans for elimination of the two crossings were finally presented, one by the chief engineer of the Board of Public Utility Commissioners, and one, called Plan C by the Railroad Company. The plan of the Board provided for keeping the highway straight, carrying it under a bridge of the railroad tracks with a width of 66 feet, elevating the tracks for clearance, and dividing the [32] highway by a central pier of 5 feet, two roadways of 20 feet each, and two sidewalks of 10 feet 6 inches each.

Plan C provided for the vacation and abandonment of the highway where it crosses the railroad right of way, so that Route 16 would come to a dead end both north and south of the railroad. It provides further for the laying out and establishing of a new stretch of highway which would cross the railroad about 400 feet east of the present crossing. It would first have a 6 degree curve to the east. It would then have a straight course of about 250 feet to the entrance of the tunnel under the railroad tracks. A short distance beyond the tunnel a second 6 degree curve to the west would begin, and then a third 6 degree curve to the east and the roadway would join Route 16 at a point about 1,000 feet south of the intersection of the route with the center line of the railroad. It would thus have three 6 degree curves in it in about half a mile, with cuts, which at stations 100 feet apart would have 7 feet of depth at one, 10 feet of depth at another, 7 1/2 feet of depth at a third, and 5 feet at a fourth.

* * * * *

[33] The witnesses for the Railroad testify that 6 degree curves are not dangerous, and that the additional cost of $100,000 for preserving the straight road is not within the limit of reasonableness. The advantage of straightness in such a road through a tunnel is clear. The curves in the cuts of from 5 to 10 feet in the railroad plan would tend to increase the embarrassment of driving and to obscure the clearness with which the drivers could see those ahead in and through the tunnel and the curves. This highway is not infrequently crowded with vehicles. When Route No. 29 is completed, it will certainly be more crowded. The immediate prospect of using new Route 29 makes greater room in the roadways most desirable. The large expenditure to secure such advantages does not seem to be arbitrary or wasteful when made for two busy highways instead of one.

It is not for the Court to cut down such expenditures merely because more economical ways suggest themselves. The Board has the discretion to fix the cost. The function of the Court is to determine whether the outlay involved in the order of the Board is extravagant in the light of all the circumstances, in view of the importance of the crossing, of the danger to be avoided, of the probable permanence of the improvement and of the prospect of enlarged capacity to be required in the near future, and other considerations similarly relevant.

An increase from $200,000 to $300,000 for a railroad crossing might well, under different circumstances from [34] those here, be regarded as so unreasonable as to make the order a violation of the company's constitutional rights and to be in the nature of confiscation. The protection of the

Fourteenth Amendment in such cases is real and is not to be lightly regarded. A railroad company, in maintaining a path of travel and transportation across a State, with frequent trains of rapidity and great momentum, must resort to reasonable precaution to avoid danger to the public. This Court has said that where railroad companies occupy lands in the State for use in commerce, the State has a constitutional right to insist that a highway crossing shall not be dangerous to the public, and that where reasonable safety of the public requires abolition of grade crossings, the railroad can not prevent the exercise of the police power to this end by the excuse that such change would interfere with interstate commerce or lead to the bankruptcy of the railroad. *Erie R. R. v. Board,* 254 U.S. 394. This is not to be construed as meaning that danger to the public will justify great expenditures unreasonably burdening the railroad, when less expenditure can reasonably accomplish the object of the improvements and avoid the danger. If the danger is clear, reasonable care must be taken to eliminate it and the police power may be exerted to that end. But it becomes the duty of the Court, where the cost is questioned, to determine whether it is within reasonable limits.

* * * * *

[36] The final objection to the order is that the statute providing for the elimination of grade crossings by the Board of Public Utilities impinges on the constitutional rights of the Company, because it makes no provision for appeal from the decision of the Board of Public Utilities to a court with jurisdiction judicially to determine independently, on the law and facts, whether the property of the Company is being confiscated, in violation of the Fourteenth Amendment to the Federal Constitution. *Ohio Valley Water Co. v. Ben Avon Borough,* 253 U.S. 287.

* * * * *

[37] We do not think the *Ben Avon* case applies here. In this case Chapter 195 of the Laws of 1911 of New Jersey created a Board of Public Utility Commissioners and prescribed its duties and powers. By §§ 21 and 22 of that Act, the Board is vested with authority to protect the traveling public at grade crossings by directing the Railroad Company to install such protective device or devices, and adopt such other reasonable provision for the protection of the traveling public at such crossing, as in the discretion of the Board shall be necessary.

Section 38 of this Act, as amended by Chapter 130 of the Laws of 1918, provides that any order made by the Board may be reviewed upon certiorari after notice, and the Supreme Court is given jurisdiction to review the order, and to set it aside when it clearly appears that there was no evidence before the Board reasonably to support the same, or that the same was without the jurisdiction of the Board. . . .

* * * * *

[41] We are of opinion that the infirmity in the Pennsylvania statute which was pointed out in *Ohio Valley Co. v. Ben-Avon Borough* is not present in the New Jersey statutes.

Affirmed.

MR. JUSTICE MCREYNOLDS is of opinion that the action of the Board of Public Utility Commissioners was unreasonable and arbitrary and should be set aside. To permit the Commissioners to impose a charge of $100,000 upon the Railroad under the pretense of objection to a six per cent. curve in a country road is to uphold what he regards as plain abuse of power.

Oriel v. Russell

The Court in these cases addressed the amount of evidence necessary for issuing a turnover order and for a finding of contempt.

Oriel et al. v. Russell, Trustee
Prela v. Hubshman, Trustee

Certiorari to the Circuit Court of Appeals for the Second Circuit

Nos. 92 and 91. Argued November 20, 21, 1928—Decided January 14, 1929

278 U.S. 358 (1929)

[360]

MR. CHIEF JUSTICE TAFT delivered the opinion of the Court.

* * * * *

[362] The cases are brought here on the ground of error in the District Court in holding that the turnover order could not be collaterally attacked and that the only evidence which was relevant on the motion to commit for contempt was evidence tending to show that since the turnover order, circumstances had happened disclosing the inability of the bankrupts to com-

ply with the order. It was urged that a finding of contempt required a greater weight of evidence than a turnover order, and hence that the former could not be predicated upon the latter without a reëxamination of all the evidence. These rulings present the question before us.

We think a proceeding for a turnover order in bankruptcy is one the right to which should be supported by clear and convincing evidence. The charge upon which the order is asked is that the bankrupt, having possession of property which be knows should have been delivered by him to the trustees, refuses to comply with his obligation in this regard. It is a charge equivalent to one of fraud, and must be established by the same kind of evidence required in a case of fraud in a court of equity. A mere preponderance of evidence in such a case is not enough.

* * * * *

[365] A number of cases can be found in the decisions of the Circuit Courts of Appeal and the District Courts indicating a hesitation and great reluctance to issue orders of commitment where there is any reasonable doubt of the ability of the bankrupt to comply with the turnover order. *Kirsner v. Taliaferro,* 202 Fed. 51; *Stuart v. Reynolds,* 204 Fed. 709; *In re Haring,* 193 Fed. 168. We think it would be going too far to adopt the severer rule of criminal cases and would render the bankruptcy system less effective. We find ourselves in general accord on this subject with the remarks of the late Circuit Judge McPherson, of the Third Circuit, who used the following language in the case of *Epstein v. Steinfeld,* 206 Fed. 568 [p. 569]:

"In the case in hand, the consequence is that, as the order to pay or deliver stands without sufficient reply, it [366] remains what it has been from the first—an order presumed to be right, and therefore an order that ought to be enforced. In the pending case, or in any other, the court may believe the bankrupt's assertion that he is not now in possession or control of the money or the goods, and in that event the civil inquiry is at an end; but it is also true that the assertion may not be believed, and the bankrupt may therefore be subjected to the usual pressure that follows willful disobedience of a lawful command, namely, the inconvenience of being restrained of his liberty. No doubt this may be unpleasant; it is intended to be unpleasant, but I see no reason why the proceeding should be condemned, as if it interfered with the liberty of the citizen without sufficient reason or excuse. I have known a brief confinement to produce the money promptly, thus justifying the court's incredulity, and I have also known it to fail. Where it has failed, and where a reasonable interval of time has supplied the previous defect in the evidence, and has made sufficiently certain what was doubtful before, namely, the bankrupt's inability to obey the order, he has always been released, and I need hardly say that he would always have the right to be released, as soon as the fact becomes clear that he can not obey. Actual or virtual imprisonment for debt has ceased, but imprisonment to compel obedience to a lawful judicial order (if it appear that obedience is being willfully refused) has not yet ceased and ought not to cease, unless it should be thought expedient to destroy all respect for the courts by stripping them of power to enforce their lawful decrees."

In the two cases before us, the contemnors had ample opportunity in the original hearing to be heard as to the fact of concealment, and in the motion for the contempt to show their inability to comply with the turnover order. They did not succeed in meeting the burden which was necessarily theirs in each case, and we think, [367] therefore, that the orders of the Circuit Court of Appeals in affirming the judgments of the District Court were the proper ones.

The judgments are affirmed.

Wisconsin v. Illinois

Article III of the Constitution gives the Supreme Court both appellate and original jurisdiction. The latter is defined to include "all Cases affecting Ambassadors, other public Ministers and Consuls, and those in which a State shall be a Party." Generally in such cases the Court appoints a special master with the responsibility of hearing the facts and making a report based on these facts as to what the law requires.

The dispute in this case arose from the action of the Sanitary District of Chicago in diverting water from Lake Michigan in order to dispose of Chicago sewage. The result was to lower the water level of all but one of the Great Lakes. The affected states sued to stop the diversion. States along the Mississippi intervened to support the action of the sanitary district, since the diverted water flowed into the Mississippi, improving the navigability of the river. The Court appointed former associate justice Charles Evans Hughes as special master. Hughes ruled against the sanitary district and Chief Justice Taft's opinion hewed closely to Hughes's report.

State of Wisconsin et al. v. State of Illinois and Sanitary District of Chicago et al.
State of Michigan v. Same
State of New York v. Same

Nos. 7, 11, and 12 Original. Argued April 23, 24, 1928— Decided January 14, 1929

278 U.S. 367 (1929)

[399]

Mr. Chief Justice Taft delivered the opinion of the Court.

These are amended bills by the States of Wisconsin, Minnesota, Michigan, Ohio, Pennsylvania and New York, praying for an injunction against the State of Illinois and the Sanitary District of Chicago from continuing to withdraw 8,500 cubic feet of water a second from Lake Michigan at Chicago.

The Court referred the cause to Charles Evans Hughes as a Special Master, with authority to take the evidence, and to report the same to the Court with his findings of fact, conclusions of law and recommendations for a decree, all to be subject to approval or other disposal by the Court. The Master gave full hearings and filed and submitted his report November 23, 1927, to which the complainants duly lodged exceptions, which have been elaborately argued.

* * * * *

[400] The amended bills herein averred that the Chicago diversion had lowered the levels of Lakes Michigan, Huron, Erie and Ontario, their connecting waterways, and of the St. Lawrence River above tidewater, not less than six inches, to the serious injury of the complainant States, their citizens and property owners; that the acts of the defendants had never been authorized by Congress but were violations of the rights of the complainant States and their people; that the withdrawals of the water from Lake Michigan were for the purpose of taking care of the sewage of Chicago and were not justified by any control Congress had attempted to exercise or could exercise in interstate commerce over the waters of Lake Michigan; and that the withdrawals were in palpable violation of the Act of Congress of March 3, 1899. The bills prayed that the defendants be enjoined from permanently diverting water

from Lake Michigan or from dumping or draining sewage into its waterways which would render them unsanitary or obstruct the people of the complainant States in navigating them.

The State of Illinois filed a demurrer to the bills and the Sanitary District of Chicago an answer, which included a motion to dismiss. The States of Missouri, Kentucky, Tennessee and Louisiana, by leave of Court, became intervening co-defendants, on the same side as Illinois, and moved to dismiss the bills. The demurrer of Illinois was overruled and the motions to dismiss were denied, without prejudice. Thereupon the intervening defendants and the defendants, the Sanitary District and the State of Illinois, filed their respective answers. The States of [401] Mississippi and Arkansas were also permitted to intervene as defendants, and adopted the answers of the other interveners. The answers of the defendants denied the injuries alleged, and averred that authority was given for the diversion under the acts of the Legislature of Illinois and under acts of Congress and permits of the Secretary of War authorized by Congress in the regulation of interstate commerce. All the answers stressed the point that the diversion of water from Lake Michigan improved the navigation of the Mississippi River and was an aid to the commerce of the Mississippi Valley and sought the preservation of this aid. They also set up the defense of laches, acquiescence and estoppel, on the ground that the purposes of the canal and the diversion were known to the people and the officials of the complainant States, and that no protest or complaint had been made in their behalf prior to the filing of the original bills herein.

The Master has made a comprehensive review of the evidence before him in regard to the history of the canal, the extent and effect of the diversion, the action of the State and Federal Governments, the plans for the disposal of the sewage and waste of Chicago and the other territory within the Sanitary District, as well as the character and feasibility of works proposed as a means of compensating for the lowering of lake levels. From this review we shall take what will assist us in the consideration of the issues deemed necessary to be considered on the exceptions to the report.

* * * * *

[408] The Master finds that the damage due to the diversion at Chicago relates to navigation and commercial interests, to structures, to the convenience of summer resorts, to fishing and hunting grounds, to public parks and other enterprises, and to riparian property generally, but does not report that injury to agriculture is established. . . .

* * * * *

[409] The controversies have taken a very wide range. The exact issue is whether the State of Illinois and the Sanitary District of Chicago by diverting 8,500 cubic feet from the waters of Lake Michigan have so injured the riparian and other rights of the complainant States bordering the Great Lakes and connecting streams by lowering their levels as [410] to justify an injunction to stop this diversion and thus restore the normal levels. Defendants assert that such a diversion is the result of Congressional action in the regulation of interstate commerce; that the injury, if any, resulting is *damnum absque injuria* to the complaining States. Those States reply that the regulation of interstate commerce under the Constitution does not authorize the transfer by Congress of any of the navigable capacity of the Great Lake System of Waters to the Mississippi basin, that is from one great watershed to another; second, that the transfer is contrary to the provision of the Constitution forbidding the preference of the ports of one State over those of another; and, third, that the injuries to the complainant States deprive them and their citizens and property owners of property without due process of law and of the natural advantages of their position, contrary to their sovereign rights as members of the Union. If one of these issues is decided in favor of the complaining States, it ends the case in their favor and the diversion must be enjoined. But in the view which we take respecting what actually has been done by Congress some of these objections need not be considered or passed upon.

The complainants, even apart from their constitutional objections, contend that Congress has not by statute or otherwise authorized the Lake Michigan diversion, that it is therefore illegal and that injuries by it to the complainant States and their people should be forbidden by decree of this Court. The diversion of 8,500 cubic feet a second is now maintained under a permit of the Secretary of War of March 3, 1925, acting under Section 10 of the Act of 1899, which it is contended by the complainants vests no such authority in him. They claim that the diversion is based on a purpose not to regulate navigation of the Lake, but merely to get rid of the sewage of Chicago, that this is a State purpose, not a Federal function, and should be enjoined to save the rights of complainants.

* * * * *

[420] The intervening States on the same side with Illinois, in seeking a recognition of asserted rights in the navigation of the Mississippi, have answered denying the rights of the complainants to an injunction. They really seek affirmatively to preserve the diversion from Lake Michigan in the interest of such navigation and interstate commerce though they have made

no express prayer therefor. In our view of the permit of March 3, 1925, and in the absence of direct authority from Congress for a waterway from Lake Michigan to the Mississippi, they show no rightful interest in the maintenance of the diversion. Their motions to dismiss the bills are overruled and so far as their answer may suggest affirmative relief, it is denied.

In increasing the diversion from 4,167 cubic feet a second to 8,500, the Sanitary District defied the authority of the National Government resting in the Secretary of War. And in so far as the prior diversion was not for the purposes of maintaining navigation in the Chicago River it was without any legal basis, because made for an inadmissible purpose. It therefore is the duty of this Court by an appropriate decree to compel the reduction of the diversion to a point where it rests on a legal basis and thus to restore the navigable capacity of Lake Michigan to its proper level. The Sanitary District authorities, relying on the argument with reference to the health of its people, have much too long delayed the needed substitution of suitable sewage plants as a means of avoiding the diversion in the future. Therefore they can not now complain if an immediately heavy burden is placed upon the District because of their attitude and course. The situation requires the District to devise proper methods for providing sufficient money and to construct and put in operation with all reasonable expedition adequate plants for the [421] disposition of the sewage through other means than the Lake diversion.

Though the restoration of just rights to the complainants will be gradual instead of immediate it must be continuous and as speedy as practicable, and must include everything that is essential to an effective project.

The Court expresses its obligation to the Master for his useful, fair, and comprehensive report.

To determine the practical measures needed to effect the object just stated and the period required for their completion there will be need for the examination of experts; and the appropriate provisions of the necessary decree will require careful consideration. For this reason, the case will be again referred to the Master for a further examination into the questions indicated. He will be authorized and directed to hear witnesses presented by each of the parties, and to call witnesses of his own selection, should he deem it necessary to do so, and then with all convenient speed to make report of his conclusions and of a form of decree.

It is so ordered.

Larson v. South Dakota

South Dakota had granted Larson an exclusive lease to operate a ferry. Subsequently, the state built a bridge that offered an alternative means of crossing the river. Larson sued, claiming that by allowing the construction of a railroad bridge the state had violated Article I's contract clause guarantee. The case caused Taft to discuss the case of *Charles River Bridge v. Warren Bridge*, 11 Pet. (36 U.S.) 420 (1837), and Chief Justice Roger Taney's opinion upholding the power of the state to grant a second company the power to build a bridge across the Charles River. Taft held for the state.

Larson v. South Dakota

Appeal from the Supreme Court of South Dakota

No. 102. Argued January 8, 1929—Decided February 18, 1929

278 U.S. 429 (1929)

[432]

The petitioner contended in the state court, and contends here, that the acts of the state Legislature, under which the bridge was constructed, impaired the obligation of the contract embodied in his ferry leases or franchises and therefore were void as being in conflict with the contract clause of the Constitution of the United States.

* * * * *

MR. CHIEF JUSTICE TAFT, after stating the case, delivered the opinion of the Court.

The exclusive ferry leases were contracts between the State and the petitioner. *The Binghamton Bridge,* 3 Wall. 51. Was the building of the bridge a breach of them?

The Supreme Court of the State has had the meaning of "exclusive ferry franchise" before it twice before this case, in *Nixon v. Reid,* 8 S. D. 507, and in *Chamberlain Ferry & Cable Bridge v. King,* 41 S. D. 246; but these cases did not require consideration of the effect of the term as applied to anything but ferries.

* * * * *

[433] The petitioner relies on the contract clause of the Federal Constitution, and is not prevented from invoking from this Court an independent

consideration of what the contract means, and whether by a proper construction, the building of a bridge impairs its obligation.

* * * * *

[435] . . . The leading case on the subject in Federal jurisprudence is that of *Charles River Bridge v. Warren Bridge,* 11 Pet. 420, 547. In that case the Legislature of Massachusetts incorporated a company to build a bridge over the Charles River where a ferry stood, granting it tolls. Years after, the Legislature incorporated another company for the erection of another bridge within 800 feet of the original one. The new bridge was to become free after a few years, and at the time of the litigation it had become actually free. The Charles River Bridge was deprived of the tolls and its value was destroyed. Its proprietors filed a bill against the proprietors of the Warren Bridge, for an injunction against the use of the bridge as an act impairing the obligations of a contract and repugnant to the Constitution of the United States. The Supreme Court of Massachusetts dismissed the bill and the case was brought by error to this Court, which affirmed the judgment of the Massachusetts court. The principle of the case is that public grants are to be strictly construed, that nothing passes to the grantee by implication.

* * * * *

[436] Chief Justice Taney, delivering the opinion in the *Charles River Bridge* case, said [p. 547]:

"But the object and end of all government is to promote the happiness and prosperity of the community by which it is established; and it can never be assumed that the government intended to diminish its power of accomplishing the end for which it was created. And in a country like ours, free, active, and enterprising, continually advancing in numbers and wealth, new channels of communication are daily found necessary, both for travel and trade, and are essential to the comfort, convenience and prosperity of the people. A state ought never to be presumed to surrender this power, because, like the taxing power, the whole community have an interest in preserving it undiminished. And when a corporation alleges that a state has surrendered for seventy years its power of improvement and public accommodation, in a great and important line of travel, along which a vast number of its citizens must daily pass, the community have a right to insist, in the language of this Court above quoted, 'that its abandonment ought not to be presumed in a case in which the deliberate purpose of the state to abandon does not appear.'"

* * * * *

[438] The great weight of authority holds that a contractual term forbidding a ferry or a toll bridge does not exclude a railroad bridge. . . .

* * * * *

The strongest case for the appellant is *Mason v. Harper's Ferry Bridge Co.,* 17 W. Va. 396 (1880), where a statute forbidding other ferries was held to give an exclusive right to transportation over the river and hence to prohibit rival bridges as well, but the court said that the Legislature could take away at any time all the exclusive privileges of the proprietors theretofore existing.

* * * * *

[439] We can hardly say, therefore, from the weight of authority, that an exclusive grant of a ferry franchise, without more, would prevent a legislature from granting the right to build a bridge near the ferry. Following the cases in this Court in its limited and careful construction of public grants, it is manifest that we must reach in this case the same conclusion.

The judgment of the Supreme Court of South Dakota is

Affirmed.

Arlington Hotel Co. v. Fant

The Arlington Hotel Company leased land from the federal government in Hot Springs, Arkansas. A fire at the hotel caused Fant and other plaintiffs to lose their property. The hotel company claimed that under Arkansas law they were not liable for the losses unless it could be shown that the fire was caused by their negligence. Taft found against the hotel company, ruling that Hot Springs Park, where the hotel was located, was under the exclusive jurisdiction of the United States and that under federal law the company was liable for the damages suffered by Fant.

Arlington Hotel Company v. Fant et al.

Error to the Supreme Court of Arkansas

No. 157. Argued January 17, 1929—Decided February 18, 1929

278 U.S. 439 (1929)

[445]
MR. CHIEF JUSTICE TAFT delivered the opinion of the Court.

These are three suits brought in the Circuit Court of Garland County, Arkansas, against the Arlington Hotel Company, a corporation of Arkansas, in which the plaintiffs seek to recover for the losses they sustained, when guests of the hotel, in the destruction by fire of their personal property. The hotel was in Hot Springs National Park.

The complaints averred that the United States in 1904 acquired from Arkansas exclusive jurisdiction over Hot Springs Park and that under the common law, which was there in force (*Pettit v. Thomas,* 103 Ark. 593), an innkeeper was an insurer of his guests' personal property against fire. In 1913, the Arkansas Legislature enacted a law relieving innkeepers from liability to their guests [446] for loss by fire, unless it was due to negligence. The complainants contended that this act had no force in Hot Springs Park as it was within the exclusive jurisdiction of the United States.

* * * * *

[453] Counsel for the plaintiffs in the present case insist that the United States has the constitutional authority to maintain exclusive jurisdiction over the tract here in [454] question as a national park, and that as the Government undoubtedly may use its control over all land within its exclusive jurisdiction to provide national parks, it may, where land is ceded by a State to the exclusive jurisdiction of the National Government, treat land thus ceded by the State for such a purpose as it would treat national public land which had never come within the jurisdiction of the State; that as by virtue of Article 4 of the Constitution, Section 3, Congress has power to dispose of and make all needful rules and regulations respecting the territory or other property belonging to the United States, it may treat land ceded to it by a State for the purposes of making a national park exactly as it would treat land which had always been within its exclusive jurisdiction and subject to its disposition for park purposes. This issue may in the future become a subject of constitutional controversy, because some twenty or more parks have been created by Congress, in a number of which exclusive jurisdiction over the land has been conferred by act of cession of the State.

We do not find it necessary, however, now to examine this question. We think that the history of this Hot Springs National Park, as shown by the legislation leading to its establishment and circumstances which the Court may judicially notice, is such that the small tract whose jurisdiction is here in question may be brought within the principle of the *Lowe* case and other cases already cited.

The Hot Springs are mentioned as remarkable by Thomas Jefferson in a message to Congress on February 19, 1806, in which he transmitted a report containing a description of them. Messages, Reports, etc., 1st Sess. 9th Cong., 1806, pp. 202, 344. Their known value for remedial purposes and the appreciation of that value by Congress were shown in the Act of 1832, already cited, by which the land surrounding them was reserved for the future disposal of the United States. The purpose was evidently to make use of them for national public needs.

The analysis of the forty-four springs indicated that [455] these waters were of a special excellence with respect to diseases likely to be treated in a military hospital. Therefore it was that in 1882 an appropriation of $100,000 was made for the construction of an adequate hospital under the War Department. That hospital has been enlarged by appropriations from time to time since its original establishment. It was certainly a wise prevision which with the consent of the State brought within exclusive national jurisdiction the hospital buildings and accessories and all the forty-four springs from which the healing waters came in order to secure to the Government their complete police protection, preservation and control. This justified acquisition of the springs and hospital for the exclusive jurisdiction of the United States under clause 17, Section 8, Article I of the Constitution. Nor is the constitutional basis for acquisition any less effective because the springs thus kept safely available for the Federal purpose do in the abundance of their flow also supply water sufficient to furnish aid to the indigent and to those of the public of the United States who are able to pay for hotel accommodation on the little park surrounding the hospital and the springs. *Benson v. United States, supra,* and *Williams v. Arlington Hotel Co.,* 22 F. (2d) 669.

The cases relied on by the defendant are clearly distinguishable. *Williams v. Arlington Hotel Co.,* 15 F. (2d) 412, was overruled by the Circuit Court of Appeals, as above. In *Crook, Horner & Co. v. Old Point Comfort Hotel Co.,* 54 Fed. 604, there was an express reverter clause in the act of cession, which limited the use of the land to defensive purposes. *Renner v. Bennett,* 21 Ohio St. 431, and *State v. Board of Commissioners,* 153 Ind. 302, were cases where Congress had receded jurisdiction to the State. In *La Duke v. Melin,* 45 N. D. 349, there had been complete abandonment of a military reservation, which by Act of Congress had been opened to homesteaders.

Affirmed.

Omitted Taft Opinions

Weil v. Neary, 278 U.S. 160 (1929)—bankruptcy case.
Exchange Trust Co. v. Drainage District, 278 U.S. 421 (1929)—state annexation of land.

VOLUME 279

County of Spokane v. United States

Taft's opinion in this case revisited disputes over taxing powers that dated back to the era of Chief Justice John Marshall. The taxing power is a concurrent power— a power that can be exercised by both the federal and state governments. A Washington state trial court had interpreted a federal statute as giving priority to a county's lien against an estate over the claims of the federal government. Writing for a unanimous Court, Taft made quick work of this claim, upholding the decision of the Supreme Court of Washington, which had also ruled in favor of the federal government.

County of Spokane, Washington, et al. v. United States

Certiorari to the Supreme Court of Washington

No. 164. Argued February 20, 21, 1929—Decided April 8, 1929

279 U.S. 80 (1929)

[85]

MR. CHIEF JUSTICE TAFT delivered the opinion of the Court.

This case presents the question of the priority of payment of debts due to the United States, over those due to a State or its agencies against the same fund for state taxes, under § 3466 of the Revised Statutes of the United States.

* * * * *

[86] The funds in the hands of the receiver are insufficient to pay in full the claims of the United States, and Spokane and Whitman counties. By proper pleadings, issues were made, presenting the question of the comparative priorities in distribution of the fund in his hands. The Superior Court held that the two counties were entitled to priority, not only as to the county taxes levied against the corporation, but for the county taxes for 1923–26 assessed on the money in the receiver's hands. On an appeal to the Supreme Court of Washington, the judgment was reversed and priority awarded to the United States. 147 Wash. 176.

Section 3466 of the Revised Statutes provides in part that "whenever any person indebted to the United States is insolvent, or whenever the estate of any deceased debtor in the hands of the executors or administrators, is insufficient to pay all the debts due from the deceased, the debts due to the United States shall be first satisfied."

The Constitution, Article 1, Section 8, provides that Congress shall have power to lay and collect taxes and to make all laws which shall be necessary and proper to carry this and its other powers into execution. Article IV of [87] the Constitution declares that the Constitution and the laws made in pursuance thereof shall be the supreme law of the land.

The constitutional validity of the priority of claims of the United States against insolvent debtors, declared in § 3466, was established by this Court very early in the history of the Government. *United States v. Fisher*, 2 Cranch 358. But it was not established as between debts owing to the States and debts owing to the United States until after a critical controversy between those who looked to the maintenance of the supremacy of the national government and those who were anxious to sustain undiminished the power of the States.

Section 3466 R. S. was § 5 of an Act entitled "An Act to provide more effectually for the settlement of accounts between the United States and receivers of public money," enacted in 1797, c. 20; 1 Stat. 515. It was amended by an Act of 1799, § 65, c. 22; 1 Stat. 676.

The language has been varied very little since these original enactments. The whole Act of 1797 came up for consideration in *United States v. Fisher.* There seems to have been a division among the Judges. Chief Justice Marshall delivered the opinion of the Court, which upheld the priority of the United States as against the claims of the States, and held that the Act extended not only to revenue officers and persons, accountable for public money, but to debtors generally. The Chief Justice said (p. 396):

"If the act has attempted to give the United States a preference in the case before the court, it remains to inquire whether the constitution obstructs its operation. . . .

"The government is to pay the debt of the Union, and must be authorized to use the means which appear to itself most eligible to effect that object. It has, consequently, a right to make remittances by bills or otherwise [88] and to take those precautions which will render the transaction safe.

"This claim of priority on the part of the United States will, it has been said, interfere with the right of the state sovereignties respecting the dignity of debts, and will defeat the measures they have a right to adopt to secure themselves against delinquencies on the part of their own revenue officers. But this is an objection to the constitution itself. The mischief suggested, so far as it can really happen, is the necessary consequence of the supremacy of the laws of the United States on all subjects to which the legislative power of congress extends."

This case was decided in 1805. Later that year the question arose in a Pennsylvania state court. *United States v. Nicholls,* 4 Yeates 251. Nicholls was indebted to the United States, and on June 9, 1798, executed a mortgage to the United States supervisor of the revenue for the use of the United States. There was a levy upon the lands of Nicholls and they were sold for $14,530. The money was deposited in the hands of the prothonotary of the court, subject to the court's order. Nicholls made an assignment for the benefit of his creditors and a commission of bankruptcy issued against him. The Attorney General relied on this same 5th section of the Act of 1797, and the issue arose whether in the distribution of that fund the laws of Pennsylvania, giving a preference to that State in the payment, should prevail over the federal act of 1797. Mr. Justice Yeates, speaking for the Court, said, p. 259:

"Congress have the concurrent right of passing laws to protect the interest of the union, as to debts due to the government of the United States arising from the public revenue; but in so doing, they can not detract from the uncontrollable power of individual states to raise their own revenue, nor infringe on, or derogate from the sovereignty of any independent state. . . . The rights of [89] the general government to priority of payment, and the rights of individual states, are contemplated as subsisting at the same time, and as perfectly compatible with each other. This can only be effected by giving preference to each existing lien, according to its due priority in point of time. I know of no other mode whereby the several conflicting claims can with justice be protected and secured."

The colleagues of Judge Yeates concurred with him, but one of them expressed regret that the opinion in the *Fisher* case, *supra,* delivered previously, had not been furnished for comparison. The decisions in the *Fisher* and the *Nicholls* cases created much popular excitement, and, united with other issues of a similar character as between the supporters of the federal government and the state governments, led to much concern over the open defiance of the decisions of this Court, until the issues were disposed of in the case of *United States v. Judge Peters;* 5 Cranch 115. See the account of the litigation in Charles Warren's Supreme Court in United States History, vol. 1, pp. 372, 538 *et seq.* Four years after the decision in the *Nicholls* case, a review of that case was sought in this Court on a writ of error. When it came to be heard, after nine years more of inaction, it was dismissed for lack of jurisdiction, on the ground that the record did not disclose the insolvency of the debtor so as to make § 3466 applicable; and thus was eliminated the federal question. 4 Wheat. 311.

No question of the construction of § 3466 seems to have come before this Court again until, in *Field v. United States,* 9 Pet. 182, it was sought to make certain trustees liable from their own funds, because they had made disbursements out of a bankrupt's estate, as to which the United States was entitled to priority. It was objected that the distribution had been made under order of the parish court in an action in which the United States was [90] not a party. This Court held that the United States was not bound to become a party, and said, p. 201:

"The local laws of the state could not, and did not, bind them [the United States] in their rights. They could not create a priority in favor of other creditors, in cases of insolvency, which should supersede that of the United States."

The power of the Congress of the United States, in giving preference to the debts of the Government of the United States over those of the separate States, is very clearly brought out in *Lane County v. Oregon,* 7 Wall. 71, which may well be referred to here, because there are some expressions in that opinion which, taken away from their context, have been used to give an erroneous view.

After discussing the taxing powers of the national and state governments, the Court, speaking by Chief Justice Chase, said of the state power of taxation, p. 77:

"It is indeed a concurrent power, and in the case of a tax on the same subject by both governments, the claim of the United States, as the supreme authority, must be preferred; but with this qualification it is absolute. The extent to which it shall be exercised, the subjects upon which it shall be exercised, and the mode in which it shall be exercised, are all equally within the discretion of the legislatures to which the States commit the exercise of the power. That discretion is restrained only by the will of the people expressed in the State constitutions or through elections, and by the condition that it must not be so used as to burden or embarrass the operations of the national government."

* * * * *

[93] The foregoing citations certainly make it clear that the United States has power, in order to collect its taxes and its revenues and debts due it, to confer priority for them over those of the States.

There remains only to determine what priority it has conferred. It may withhold it or vary it, and it has sometimes done so. When, in this case, did the priority attach and apply? It was said in *United States v. Oklahoma*, 261 U.S. 253, 260, that in a case like this it applied when the receiver was appointed. The appointment was on August 28, 1922. The taxes and penalties due the United States, amounting to $70,268.58, were assessed on February 28, 1923, and May 2, 1923, and therefore the priority of the United States attached on or before those dates. No assessment by the counties upon specific property in the hands of the receiver was made until September 23, 1924. The claim of the United States, therefore, had priority over such claims.

* * * * *

[94] . . . I think a critical reading of the revenue legislation of the respective sovereignties, the United States and the state, and the record in this case showing the manner of levying in these respective taxes, will render this plain. The revenue legislation of each has prescribed procedure by which its personam tax debts may be made specific liens upon property of one personally owing such tax debt. This record, I think, warrants the conclusion that neither the United States, the state of Washington nor Spokane County for the state of Washington has ever, by the prescribed statutory procedure, perfected its inchoate tax lien right against any of the property of which the funds here in question are the proceeds. I therefore view these respective tax debts wholly apart from any supporting lien right. Thus I think the question of which shall be first satisfied out of these funds is determinable by the language of § 3466, [95] quoted in the majority opinion, and hence must be determinable in favor of the United States.

Whatever might have been the effect of more completed procedure in the perfecting of the liens under the law of the State, upon the priority of the

United States herein, the attitude of the state court relieves us of consideration of it.

Judgment affirmed.

Carson Petroleum Co. v. Vial

Another issue that surfaced during the Marshall Court involved the power of states to tax goods intended for shipment to another state or to a foreign country. This raised questions not simply of the taxing powers of the two levels of government but also of the power of the federal government over interstate commerce. The matter continues to vex the Court even in our time, with more recent decisions expanding the powers of state government to levy taxes. In *Carson,* Taft ruled in favor of the petroleum company's not having to pay the Louisiana tax. For a seven to two Court, Taft found the Louisiana tax to be an infringement on interstate commerce and therefore unconstitutional.

Carson Petroleum Company v. Vial, Sheriff and Tax Collector, et al.

Certiorari to the Supreme Court of Louisiana

No. 306. Argued February 28, 1929—Decided April 8, 1929

279 U.S. 95 (1929)

[98]

MR. CHIEF JUSTICE TAFT delivered the opinion of the Court.

This was a petition by the Carson Petroleum Company, a corporation of Delaware, to enjoin Leon C. Vial, sheriff and tax collector of the Parish of St. Charles, Louisiana, R. A. De Broca, assessor for the Parish, and the Louisiana Tax Commission, from laying and levying against it an alleged illegal assessment of duties on a quantity of oil in storage tanks at St. Rose in the Parish. They were ad valorem duties levied on all the property of the petitioner subject to taxation. The taxation was objected to because it was deemed an interference with interstate and foreign commerce.

The District Court granted the injunction on the ground that the oil was in transit from another State to a foreign country, and was halted only temporarily at St. Rose, and had no situs in the Parish or State. The Supreme Court of Louisiana reversed the decree and ordered that the tax be collected, with the penalties imposed by law. [99] 166 La. 398. There is no dispute about the facts. We avail ourselves of the statement made by the Chief Justice of the Supreme Court of Louisiana, which is a clear and fair representation of the case:

"The Petroleum Import & Export Corporation is a subsidiary of the Carson Petroleum Company, and owns and operates the system of tanks and pumping equipment for receiving the contents of the railroad tank cars of oil into the tanks owned by the Petroleum Import & Export Corporation and afterwards loading it into ships for export. The Port of New Orleans has no facility or equipment for assembling or receiving from railroad tank cars cargoes of oil and loading it aboard ships for export. The tanks and equipment at St. Rose, a few miles above New Orleans, were constructed for that purpose. No oil is sold at St. Rose except what is exported. The only business conducted there is the unloading of oil from railroad tank cars into the storage tanks and the loading of the oil from the storage tanks aboard the tankers for shipment to England, France, and other foreign ports. The oil is bought by the Carson Petroleum Company from the refiners in the Mid-Continent Field, comprising Kansas, Oklahoma and Texas, and is shipped to St. Rose, Louisiana, in railroad tank cars consigned to the Carson Petroleum Company. The shipments are not on through bills of lading, but on an export rate, which is lower than the domestic rate. The oil is a higher grade of gasoline than is used in this country generally, and is made especially for export, because the automobiles in England, France and other foreign countries require a higher grade of gasoline than that which is used in this country. The Carson Petroleum Company takes orders for cargoes of oil from the foreign buyers, who charter the vessels to transport the oil from St. Rose to the foreign ports. The company always has orders on hand in excess of the quantity of oil at St. Rose, and buys the oil in the Mid-Continent Field for the [100] purpose of filling orders already received from the foreign buyers. . . .

* * * * *

[101] The crucial question to be settled in determining whether personal property or merchandise moving in interstate commerce is subject to local taxation is that of its continuity of transit. The leading case is that of *Coe v. Errol,* 116 U.S. 517, in which Mr. Justice Bradley for this Court laid down the principles that should be applied. It was a case of floating logs. There were two lots, one where the logs were cut in Maine, and were floated down the Androscoggin on their way to Lewiston, Maine, but after starting on the trip were detained for a season in New Hampshire by low water. It was held that

they were free from local taxation in New Hampshire because they had begun the interstate trip and the cause of detention was to be found in the necessities of the passage and trip back to Maine, which was held to be continuous. [102] This ruling, which was by the state court of New Hampshire, was approved by this Court. But, in respect to the other lot, this Court found that the logs were gathered in New Hampshire in what the Court termed an "entrepôt," looking to ultimate transportation to another State, but that when taxed they had not started on their final and continuous journey, and hence were not in interstate commerce, and were taxable.

* * * * *

[104] Another case is that of *General Oil Co. v. Crain,* 209 U.S. 211. The company conducted a large oil business in Memphis, where it gathered from the North much oil and maintained an establishment for its distribution. It had tanks of various sizes from which the oil was put in barrels or other small vessels to be sold locally or in other States, or to fill orders already received from customers in Arkansas, Louisiana and Mississippi. For years the company had unloaded its oil from its tank cars on arrival into large stationary tanks indiscriminately, and had sold and distributed it as required in its business. After a time, in order to escape the local inspection tax, part of the oil was deposited in a stationary tank No. 1 [105] marked "Oil already sold in Arkansas, Louisiana and Mississippi," while the local oil and that yet to be sold was kept in other tanks. The oil in No. 1 was divided, according to the orders already received, into barrels and larger containers, to be forwarded by rail to customers in the three States named, It was contended that oil of tank No. 1 was on a continuous trip through Memphis from sources in the North to the ascertained customers in Arkansas, Louisiana and Mississippi, and was not taxable at Memphis. It was held that the doings of the company, in thus separating the oil after it reached Memphis into various amounts in different containers, was itself a local business in Memphis, and that the delivery into Memphis of the oil, and its subsequent shipment made two separate interstate shipments and permitted local taxation on the oil while it awaited the second shipment. The Court seemed to regard the redistribution of the oil at Memphis as a rest interrupting the journey, and the Memphis yard for the tanks as an assembling entrepôt like that described by Mr. Justice Bradley in *Coe v. Errol.*

The Court was divided and there was very vigorous dissent. The case has caused discussion, and it must be admitted that it is a close one and might easily have been decided the other way. The result was probably affected by the impression created by the original situation and the somewhat artificial rearrangement of tanks in a large entrepôt for redistribution of oil to avoid previous taxability.

We do not think, in deciding the case at bar, that we should give the *Crain* case the force claimed for it by the court below and by counsel for the State. Since its decision this Court has had to consider several cases where there was transshipment of the commodity from local carriage in a State to a ship at an export port and conveyance thence to a foreign destination. There has been a liberal [106] construction of what is continuity of the journey, in cases where the Court finds from the circumstances that export trade has been actually intended and carried through.

* * * * *

[107] In *Texas & New Orleans R. R. v. Sabine Tram Co.*, 227 U.S. 111, the question was whether the rates charged on shipments of lumber on local bills of lading from one point in Texas to another, but destined for export, were intrastate or foreign commerce. The exporter purchased the lumber from other mills in Texas with which to supply its sales in part. It did not know, when any particular car of lumber left the starting point, into which ship or to what particular destination the contents of the car would ultimately go, or on which sale it would be applied; this not being found out until its agents inspected the invoice mailed to and received by him after shipment. The lumber remained after arrival at the shipping port, in the slips or on the dock, until a ship chartered by the exporter arrived, when the exporter selected the lumber suited for that cargo and shipped it to its destination. There was no local market for lumber at the port of shipment, the population of which did not exceed fifty, and the exporter had never done any local business at that point. This Court held that the shipments to the point of shipment from other points of Texas were in interstate and foreign commerce and should pay rates accordingly. . . .

* * * * *

[108] We do not think the *Sabine Tram* case can be distinguished from the one before us. It has been suggested that, in the present case, there was a failure to fix the exact point of destination abroad before shipment, and that this prevents the continuity required in a continuous exportation. But there was the same indefiniteness on this point in the *Sabine Tram* case. Then, it is said, there was no separation of the various shipments of oil from the interior points to the tanks and thence to ships at the port of shipment. But in the *Sabine Tram* case cars of lumber were sent to the transshipment point

without regard to the filling of one order or another. In both cases the delay in transshipment was due to nothing but the failure of the arrival of the subject to be shipped at the same [109] time as the arrival of the ships at the port of transshipment. The use of the tanks at the point of transshipment can not be distinguished from the storing of the lumber on the docks, or in the slips between them, till the vessel to carry it should be ready. The quickness of transshipment in both cases was the chief object each exporter plainly sought. In both cases the selection of the point of shipment and the equipment at that point were solely for the speedy and continuous export of the product abroad, and for no other purpose. No lumber or oil was sold there but that to be exported. There was no possibility of any other business there. Whatever hesitation might be prompted in deciding this case, if the *Crain* case stood alone, the effect of the decisions of this Court since is such as to make it inapplicable to the case before us.

The judgment is reversed.

MR. JUSTICE MCREYNOLDS and MR. JUSTICE SANFORD are in favor of affirming the judgment on the authority of *General Oil Co. v. Crain,* 209 U.S. 211.

Sutter Butte Canal Co. v. Railroad Commission

The division of powers that characterizes the government of the United States reserves to the states the so-called police powers—the power to enact legislation designed to advance the health, welfare, and safety of their citizens. Until the adoption of the Fourteenth Amendment in 1868, there were only two constitutional bases for limiting state police powers. The first comes out of Section 10 of Article I and specifically prohibits the states from engaging in certain activities. The second is the supremacy clause of Article VI. This provides that when the federal government is exercising its powers, any conflict between such actions and state legislation results in the state legislation being struck down.

The Fourteenth Amendment's guarantee that "no . . . State [shall] deprive any person of life, liberty, or property, without due process of law" was to alter significantly the power of the federal judiciary over state legislation. Not only was the Court now able to overturn arbitrary or irrational acts of states as being in violation of due process, but by the end of the nineteenth century it had developed the doctrine commonly known as "substantive due process," under which it could void state legislation that it found to invade the rights of property, no matter how unarbitrary and rational the legislation might in fact be. In the instant case, the Sutter Butte Canal Company claimed that the result of the California Railroad Commission's ruling was "confiscatory" in that its effect was to produce "a net return of less than 5 1/2%" (from the statement of facts). Taft found for the power of the California Railroad Commission and rejected the opportunity to second guess the state body.

Sutter Butte Canal Company
v. Railroad Commission of California

Error to the Supreme Court of California

No. 403. Argued March 6, 7, 1929—Decided April 8, 1929

279 U.S. 125 (1929)

[131]

MR. CHIEF JUSTICE TAFT delivered the opinion of the Court.

This is a writ of error to an order of the Supreme Court of California reviewing on certiorari an order of the Railroad Commission of the State fixing water rates and contracts. 202 Cal. 179. The Sutter Butte Canal Company, a corporation of the State, petitioned for a review and the annulment of an order of the Railroad Commission designated as decision No. 16289, made on March 20, 1926, relating to water rates, the valuation of its property for rate-fixing purposes, the rate of return thereon and the modification and practical abrogation of certain continuous contracts for the furnishing of water held by it with a certain class of consumers.

* * * * *

[132] The Canal Company is a public utility subjected by law to the power and direction of the State Railroad Commission and is in possession of a water right dedicated to the public use. Its consumers are divided into two classes—contract consumers and non-contract consumers. The water was originally furnished to the contract consumers under water right contracts which were continuous supply contracts, whereby the consumer paid an initial amount, which varied somewhat, and agreed to pay a stipulated rate for irrigation water service each year thereafter upon the total acreage covered by the contract, and the Company on its part agreed to furnish water as required for all of the acres covered thereby. Non-contract consumers, or applicants, pursuant to the order of the Commission made in

March, 1918, were served upon the basis only of applications for water made from year to year.

In December, 1924, a decision, numbered 14422, on application by the Company, further increased the water rates over those allowed under a decision of 1922, and abolished the differential in rates which had theretofore existed between contract and non-contract consumers. . . .

[133] This, however, was not a satisfactory adjustment, as the Commission ultimately determined, and in 1925 there was a completely new investigation by the Commission of the rates, charges, classifications, contracts, rules, regulations and service of the Canal Company, in view of existing protests and dissatisfaction. . . .

The proceedings resulting in decision No. 16289, modified the previous rules so as to give each continuous contract holder the right, at his option, either (1) to obtain water under applications for so much of his land as he desired to irrigate, similarly with applicants generally who were not holders of continuous contracts, or (2) to obtain water under his continuous contract. . . .

* * * * *

[134] The substance of this was to release all contract consumers. The contracts might be retained at the election of the consumer, but the whole plan was really to get rid of the troublesome dual situation and to abolish all distinction between the two classes of consumers and put them on a parity, in order that there might be removed from controversy this source of friction and trouble. . . .

In view of the finding of the Supreme Court that the record does not disclose any substantial evidence which would impeach the findings of the Railroad Commission upon the subject of a fair rate-base and a proper return to the Company, with which we agree, our decision will be limited to a consideration of the charge that the decision here under review is a violation of the Fourteenth Amendment by taking away from the Company its contract rights and depriving it of payment to it for water service for all the lands which under the original contract the land owners were to pay for, whether the water was used or not.

The case made on behalf of the Commission and its decision is that there has been delegated by the State to the Commission the regulation for the public benefit of the [135] rates and revenue to be received by the public utility for the service it renders to the public; that included in such power of regulation is the modification and qualification of the original contracts held by the public utility corporation in this public service; that in being a public utility under the California Constitution it necessarily submits itself to the police power of the State for the benefit of the public; that the ordinary rules that apply to the protection of contracts as between private persons under the Constitution of the United States or to the maintenance of due process of law under the Fourteenth Amendment and the rights of property as between individuals, do not apply, but that, by the acquisition of such contracts and property, knowing that the police power controls in their regulation, the owner holds them without the usual sanctions of the Fourteenth Amendment of the Federal Constitution between individuals. This power is said to operate upon property and property rights, including contracts, to the extent necessary for the protection of the public health, safety, morals and welfare, and its exercise has been committed to the Railroad Commission in regulating the public utilities in California.

* * * * *

[137] The power to increase charges for service had been twice exercised by the Railroad Commission at the behest of the Canal Company, and the times and terms of payment under the contracts had been changed by the same power, and so far as the petitioner was concerned, its privileges and emoluments under the contract had been greatly increased. So far as the consumer was concerned, the contract has slight, if any, benefit to him left in it. The consumer of water who came in last, and who had no contract, was really served with water upon less onerous terms than the contract consumer, and he might satisfy all demands made against him in three years, if not sooner, and be completely released. This the Supreme Court held was a discrimination. It decided that it was within the power of the Commission to remove it. The only provision of the contract which had not been theretofore modified by the Commission or the Court was the one with respect to the duration of the contract. As the contract was necessarily made in view of the power of the Commission to change its terms, to avoid discrimination in dealing with the consumers of water of a public utility, it is very difficult to see why the situation may not be reduced to a uniform one under the power of the Commission, if that body deems it equitable and fair to do so in the interest of the public. The record shows with much clearness the complicated situation that must continue unless the duration of the obligations of the so-called contract and non-contract consumers be made the same. This change would seem to be well within the police power, subject to which these con-

tracts were made, and there is no such difference between the fixing of rates [138] and the modification of the duration of a contract as would prevent the application of the police power to the one and not to the other.

* * * * *

[139] The judgment of the Supreme Court of California is

Affirmed.

Alberto v. Nicolas

Taft's assignment of *Alberto v. Nicolas* to himself was no surprise given its nature. The case came from the Philippines, where Taft had served as governor-general from 1901 to 1904 and involved both the question of judicial independence, a matter close to Taft's heart and one of the issues that had ruptured his friendship with Theodore Roosevelt, as well as questions dealing with executive power. The Supreme Court of the Philippine Islands had reversed the action of the governor-general in reassigning a justice of the peace, a power given to the governor-general by the Philippine legislature. Taft reversed the Philippine supreme court, distinguishing justices of the peace from other higher members of the judiciary. Justices of the peace were subject to the executive power of the governor.

Alberto v. Nicolas

Certiorari to the Supreme Court of the Philippine Islands

No. 364. Argued March 6, 1929—Decided April 8, 1929

279 U.S. 139 (1929)

[140]

MR. CHIEF JUSTICE TAFT delivered the opinion of the Court.

This is a certiorari to the Supreme Court of the Philippine Islands, to bring here for review an order of ouster in *quo warranto* brought by Bonifacio Nicolas against Severino Alberto to test the right of Alberto to hold the office of justice of the peace of the town of Angat, province of Bulacan, in those Islands. The issue is the legal right [141] of the Governor-General to transfer a justice of the peace from one municipality to another without the consent of the Philippine Senate.

After issue made, the parties, through their counsel, signed a stipulation of facts, from which it appears that on February 9, 1920, the plaintiff was appointed a justice of the peace of Angat, Bulacan, by the Governor-General with the advice and consent of the Philippine Senate; that he qualified, took possession, and exercised the office on and since February 14, 1920, up to August 19, 1927, when he was forced to surrender its possession to the defendant. On February 28, 1918, the defendant was appointed justice of the peace of San José del Monte, Bulacan, by the Governor-General, with the advice and consent of the Senate; he qualified for and exercised the office since then up to August 19, 1927, when, pursuant to an order transferring him to the office of justice of the peace of Angat, Bulacan, he exercised, and has since exercised, the latter office. There was a proceeding by the municipal president of Angat against the plaintiff, which was investigated by the Judge of First Instance of Bulacan, resulting in a report which disclosed unsatisfactory conditions and political partisanship, but with which the president of Angat was not content because the plaintiff was not removed. The matter was appealed to the Secretary of Justice. Thereafter, on July 2, 1927, the Governor-General transferred the plaintiff from Angat to San José del Monte, and also transferred the defendant to the municipality of Angat. There were protests by plaintiff against the transfer, and applications by him for reconsideration; and, finally, through proceedings before the Court of First Instance of Bulacan, the plaintiff yielded up his office under protest, on August 19, 1927, and since that time the defendant has exercised the office of justice of the peace of Angat, excluding the plaintiff therefrom.

[142] The Supreme Court, after the hearing, rendered an opinion by a vote of six judges to three, granting against Alberto a judgment of ouster, to which an application for certiorari to this Court has been duly made and granted. 278 U.S. 593.

Our jurisdiction in this case is questioned. The Act of February, 13, 1925, § 7, c. 229, 43 Stat. 940, provides that a certiorari may be issued by this Court to the Supreme Court of the Philippine Islands in any case "wherein the Constitution or any statute or treaty of the United States is involved." The effect of the Philippine Organic Act of Congress, approved August 29, 1916, by § 21, c. 416, 39 Stat. 545, 552, is that an appointment of a justice of the peace by the Governor-General must be consented to by the Senate of the Islands. Section 206 of the Philippine Administrative Code of 1917, as amended by Act 2768, approved March 5, 1918, enacts a proviso that "in case the public interest requires it, a justice of the peace of one municipality may be transferred to another." The point in question is whether that proviso is to be construed as impliedly requiring the consent of the Philippine Senate to the transfer, or whether it was intended to avoid that necessity.

In reaching the conclusion that the proviso of § 206, as properly construed, required the consent of the Senate, the Supreme Court used these words:

"The body of the section sanctions the holding of office by justices of the peace during good behavior. The proviso qualifies this by providing 'That in case the public interest requires it, a justice of the peace of one municipality may be transferred to another.' At once it is noted that the law is silent as to the office or entity which may make the transfer. The law does not say may be transferred 'by the Governor-General.' The insertion of the words 'by the Philippine Senate' would be as justifiable. [143] The more reasonable inference, indeed the only possible legal inference permissible without violating the constitution, is that the justice of the peace may be transferred by the exercise of the appointing power, and the appointing power consists of the Governor-General acting in conjunction with the Philippine Senate."

In other words, the interpretation that the court gives to the amended law, with the proviso, depends clearly on what the court calls the Constitution, that is, on the Organic Act, and therefore, even if its construction of the proviso of § 206 could be sustained, it still involved the Organic Act. We have jurisdiction.

In order to understand the scope of this case, we should point out that the Organic Act provided, by §§ 6, 7, 8 and 12, that the laws then in force in the Philippines were to remain in effect, except as altered by the Act itself, until altered, amended or repealed by the legislative authority provided in the Act, or by an Act of Congress; that the legislative authority therein provided had power, when not inconsistent with the Act, to amend, alter, modify or repeal any law, civil or criminal, continued in force by the Act as it might see fit; and that the general legislative powers in the Philippines, except as otherwise provided in the Act, were vested in the Philippine Legislature, consisting of an Assembly and a Senate.

Section 21 provided that the Governor-General of the Philippines should be the supreme executive power in the Philippines, and that he should, unless otherwise provided in the Act, appoint, by and with the consent of the Senate, such officers as might then be appointed by the Governor-General, or such as he was authorized by that Act to appoint, or whom he might thereafter be authorized by law to appoint; that he should have general supervision and control of all the departments and bureaus of the government in the Philippine Islands as far as [144] not inconsistent with the provisions of the Act, and that he should be responsible for the faithful execution of the laws of the Philippine Islands and of the United States operative within those Islands; that all executive functions of the government must be directly under the Governor-General, or within one of the executive departments under the supervision and control of the Governor-General. *Springer v. Philippine Islands,* 277 U.S. 189.

* * * * *

[146] It is to be observed that the Legislature of the Philippines made legislative provision for as close observation of the conduct of justices of the peace as is practicable. They are not like justices of the peace in this country, generally elected by the people. They are selected by the Governor-General and occupy positions of considerable power in these local communities, and exercise a control in the remote districts that makes it of the highest importance that they should be closely under the discipline of the chief executive. They are judicial officers, it is true, but these [147] provisions indicate how marked a difference there is and must be between the justices of the peace under our system and that of the Philippines. With respect to this matter we may take judicial notice that while the justices of the peace are to be treated as an important force for the preservation of local order and the administration of police court justice, they are subject to restraint by the Governor-General to prevent the abuses of their offices by the ease with which such local official authority lends itself in the Islands to the creation of caciques or local bosses exercising oppressive control over ignorant neighborhoods. This is the reason why their conduct is not only to be closely inquired into by the courts of first instance, but also why the Governor-General is given absolute power of removal or suspension, and the enlargement or restriction of their districts by merging them, and now in this last amendment, by rearranging their jurisdictions by transfer in the public interest.

The objection now is made that while, through the Governor-General, the districts under existing justices of the peace may be merged, combined, increased or decreased, an existing justice of the peace may not be transferred from one district to another, unless there is a new appointment of a justice with a new consent by the Senate.

This brings us to a consideration of the proper construction of the proviso of § 206 here in question. This proviso was the result of an amendment by § 1 of Act No. 2768 in February, 1918. The original bill was Senate Bill No. 163, providing that § 206 of the Administrative Code lie amended by adding the proviso, "that a justice of the peace of one municipality may be transferred to another when the government deems it wise." An amendment was offered in the Philippine Senate adding thereto the words, "provided further that his appointment by virtue of the transfer be confirmed by the Senate." With this [148] amendment the bill passed the Senate. When the bill came to the House, the House Committee recommended that the amendment made in the Senate be dropped. It so passed the House, and was then, on February 8, 1918, submitted to the Senate, and the amendment of the House was accepted. A purpose on the part of the Legislature to eliminate from such a transfer the consent of the Senate could hardly be more clearly established.

The majority of the Supreme Court seems to think otherwise. It is sufficient to say that its suggested implication that the consent of the Senate was to be retained, although express provision for it was expressly stricken out, is not convincing. Nor is the significance attached by the majority of the Supreme Court to the silence of the proviso as to the person intended to make the transfer at all impressive. Nor will the suggestion that the Philippine Senate alone might be intended to make the transfer suffice. The history of the legislation as well as the general trend of it with reference to the powers of the Governor-General in the discipline of justices of the peace, their suspension, their removal, the current extension of their jurisdiction by him pending their incumbency, all are convincing that, however invalid the exclusion of the Senate from the consent to the transfer, the purpose of the Legislature was certainly intended to effect that very result.

This brings us therefore to the final issue—whether the consent was necessary to the transfer, even though the Senate and the House, acting together as the Legislature, eliminated it by the proviso. It is to be borne in mind that we are dealing with the Philippine Legislature, which has full power to make legislative provision for the appointment of justices of the peace, to provide for their duties, for the payment of their salaries, for their removal, their suspension, their jurisdiction, and the changes in their jurisdiction, and to vest in the Governor-General, [149] as the executive, the exercise of the powers it thus creates, or indeed to abolish justices of the peace and substitute some other system. To take a possible example. Suppose that the Philippine Legislature had created the office of justice of the peace, had provided that the Governor-General should appoint forty justices of the peace for certain described districts in the Philippines, and had directed that the Governor-General should designate for them their districts, but that he might change the designation originally fixed by him for their distribution as the public benefit required. It seems to us clear that this would be quite within the power of the Legislature and that the Senate, by consenting to the appointment of each appointee, would be held legally to have confirmed his appointment, not only to act as justice of the peace under his first designation, but would have given him the right to continue to exercise his powers conferred by law in any other district to which he might be transferred, because the Senate would have had full notice as to the powers which he could enjoy and must be held to have consented to his exercise of those broader powers without further consideration and revision. This is the same case. When the Senate confirmed Severino Alberto to be a justice of the peace for San José del Monte, § 206, with the proviso, was in force; and when the Senate confirmed him it confirmed him with the knowledge of the possibility declared in the law that his powers and his functions as a justice of the peace, upon designation of the Governor-General, might be performed and exercised in another jurisdiction if the Governor-General should think it wise in the public interest in his regulation of the conduct of justices of the peace. There is no such necessary difference between the duties of a justice of the peace in one part of the Islands and those to be performed in another part as to make such enlargement or change of his jurisdiction, already provided for in existing law, unreasonably beyond the scope [150] of the consent to the original appointment. . . .

It is constantly to be borne in mind that this whole subject matter, in respect to the institution of justices of the peace as part of the government structure in the Philippines, is wholly within the control of the Legislature. If what they provide results in greater control by the Governor-General than is wise, the Legislature may repeal the provisions tomorrow and substitute some other limitations.

Some general observations were made by the Supreme Court with reference to the necessity of maintaining the independence of the judiciary, and expressions of opinion that this independence should be preserved strictly as it should be with respect to judges of superior court jurisdiction. It has always been recognized that justices of the peace, even in our system, are of less importance in the judiciary, and must be made to conform to greater regulation, than the judges of higher courts. *Capital Traction Co. v. Hof,* 174 U.S. 1, 17, 38. Justices of the peace are judicial officers, it is true, but they are much to be differentiated from judges of the courts of record. We do not think, therefore, that the case of *Borromeo v. Mariano,* 41 Phil. 322, with reference to the transfer and removal of a judge of the court of first instance, has application here.

The judgment is reversed.

Ex parte Worcester County National Bank

The highest court of Massachusetts, the Supreme Judicial Court, had ruled that as a result of a bank consolidation resulting from a federal act of February 25, 1927, the successor bank must reapply to the appropriate state probate court in order to continue to administer an estate. The Supreme Judicial Court also interpreted the language of section 3 of the federal act as violating both the Massachusetts and United States Constitutions. Taft upheld the decision of the state court on the first issue, but found that the Supreme Judicial Court's interpretation of section 3 was not required by the wording of the act and reversed the state court on this point.

Ex Parte Worcester County National Bank of Worcester

Appeal from the Probate Court for Worcester County, State of Massachusetts

No. 469. Argued April 11, 1929—Decided May 13, 1929

279 U.S. 347 (1929)

[353]

MR. CHIEF JUSTICE TAFT delivered the opinion of the Court.

The Worcester County National Bank is a consolidated banking corporation formed by uniting, on June 27, 1927, the Fitchburg Bank & Trust Company, a state institution of Massachusetts, and the Merchants National Bank of Worcester, a national bank of Worcester County, Massachusetts, under the Act of Congress of February 25, 1927, c. 191, 44 Stat. 1224, amending the Act of November 7, 1918, c. 209, 40 Stat. 1044. The amendment added a new section, 3, and this case turns chiefly on the construction, effect and validity of that new section.

The consolidated bank filed in the Probate Court of Worcester County a first and final account of the [354] Fitchburg Bank & Trust Company, executor of the last will and testament of Julia A. Legnard, late of Fitchburg in the county of Worcester. The account was for the period beginning April 21,1926, and ending February 9, 1928. The account was rendered by the Worcester County National Bank for the Fitchburg Bank & Trust Company to June 27, 1927, and thereafter as its own account.

The Fitchburg Bank & Trust Company had been appointed by the Probate Court executor of the will of Julia A. Legnard on April 21, 1926, and qualified by giving bond approved on that day.

The consolidated bank claimed that, in view of the proceedings, its right and duty was to render the account presented for allowance; and as all the parties interested had assented to it that it should be allowed by the court.

The Probate Court found that the account was in proper form for allowance and should be allowed as rendered, if the said Worcester County National Bank, as successor or otherwise, was executor of said will or had the right to render the account.

* * * * *

[355] The Probate Judge concluded the report as follows:

"Without action upon said account, I report the above facts and the question of law involved, for the consideration and determination of the Full Court, as to whether the petitioner is entitled to render said account."

"Fredk. H. Chamberlain,
Judge of Probate Court."

After a hearing on the report, a rescript of the Supreme Judicial Court was as follows:

"Ordered that the register of probate and insolvency in said county make the following entry under said case in the docket of said court, viz: The question reported, namely, 'Whether the petitioner is entitled to render said account,' is answered in the negative. Probate Court instructed accordingly."

* * * * *

[357] [The Supreme Judicial Court of Massachusetts] . . . considered what was the legal effect of the consolidation of the trust company and the national bank, and emphasized the explicit provision of § 3 that the consolidation was to be under the charter of the national bank. It referred again to the provision of the state law that upon the consolidation, the charter of the trust company should be "void except for the purpose of discharging existing obligations and liabilities." It held that the word "franchises" directed to be transferred to the national bank by virtue of § 3 did not mean its charter

or its right to be a corporation, for that would be in contravention of the law of the Commonwealth; that it was only the national bank that retained its corporate identity; that the certificate of the Comptroller did not constitute a charter, but only his approval of the consolidation; that the trust company had gone out of existence and all its property had become the property of the consolidated bank; and that the latter was not a newly-created organization, but an enlargement of the continuously existing national bank. Thus the court found that the [358] identity of the trust company had not been continued in a national bank, but had been extinguished. The court distinguished this case from cases of union where contract obligations had been held to pass from one of the uniting corporations to the other. Such cases were held not to be applicable to sustain the view that positions of trust like executor, administrator and other fiduciaries could be transferred to the national bank by the mere consolidation under Massachusetts law.

The court then set out at some length the reasons why under the Constitution and practice of Massachusetts the appointment of an executor was a judicial act, and that in the case before the court no one could succeed to the void and defunct State Trust Company as executor except by appointment by the Probate Court. The trust involved was highly personal. . . .

The third question the court discussed and decided was the validity and binding effect on courts of Massachusetts of the declaration in § 3 of the Act of Congress that the right of succession as trustee, executor or in any other fiduciary capacity would follow to the same extent as it was held and enjoyed by such state bank. It first inquired what was its meaning, and held that it meant that the original appointment of the state bank was to continue wholly unaffected by the fact that the state bank had ceased to be, and that another and different corporation, whose credit, standing and competency had never been the subject of judicial inquiry for this purpose must be substituted by virtue of § 3. The court found that [359] this result was in contravention of the law of the Commonwealth and contrary to the state and federal Constitutions.

The court found, however, that this provision was not the dominant part of § 3, that the clause was separable and distinct, that the rest of the section could stand independently and that there was no such connection between the two as to indicate that Congress would not have enacted the valid part without the other.

The court, therefore, held that the Worcester County National Bank of Worcester, the accountant and petitioner in the case at bar, had not succeeded the Fitchburg Bank & Trust Company as executor of the will of the testatrix and was not entitled to render an account as such executor; that it could only account as executor *de son tort,* and that the question of the Probate Court must be answered in the negative.

In passing on this appeal, we must observe that, in determining the policy of a State from its statutes and their construction, we of course follow the opinion of the state court except as it may be affected by the federal constitution. When, therefore, the state court holds that an executor, to act as such in the State, must be appointed by the Probate Court, this Court must respect that conclusion and act accordingly. But when the question arises as to what is the proper interpretation and construction of federal legislation, this Court adopts its own view.

It is very clear to us that Congress in the enactment of § 3 in the Act of February 25, 1927, was anxious even to the point of repetition to show that it wished to avoid any provision in contravention of the law of the State in which the state trust company and the national bank to be consolidated were located. So strongly manifest is this purpose that we do not hesitate to construe the effect of § 3 in Massachusetts to be only to transfer the property [360] and estate from the trust company to the national bank, to be managed and preserved as the state law provides, for administration of estates, and not to transfer the office of executor from the state trust company to the succeeding national bank. As this requires another judicial appointment by a probate court, it would become the duty of a consolidated national bank, after the union, immediately to apply for the appointment of itself as administrator, subject to the examination and approval of the proper probate court. . . .

These views lead us to agree with the conclusions of the Supreme Judicial Court in respect to the legality of the consolidation of the trust company and the national bank and only to differ from it in its construction of § 3, by which it would hold that section unconstitutional under the Constitution of Massachusetts, and so under the Constitution of the United States.

We think § 3 enjoins upon the national bank complete conformity with the Massachusetts law in its conduct of estates of deceased persons when acting as trustee or administrator thereof.

* * * * *

[362] Under the Massachusetts authorities, as already cited, the bank in attempting in this case to act as executor has become an executor *de son tort,* and that situation must be disposed of in accordance with the laws applicable in Massachusetts to such a situation. *Clabborn v. Phillips,* 245 Mass. 47. When the executor *de son tort* has been released, it would seem that applica-

tion might be made to the Probate Court for appointment of the national bank as administrator to close the estate. It seems to us that our construction of the Act of 1927, in differing from that of the Supreme Judicial Court of Massachusetts, makes it possible by the appointment of the Probate Judge if he approves, to enforce the requirements which the laws of that State impose in the execution of such trusts and still preserve the constitutional effectiveness of § 3.

This result requires us to affirm the dismissal of the petition of the Worcester County National Bank in seeking to render the first and final account of the Fitchburg Bank & Trust Company as executor of the last will and [363] testament of Julia A. Legnard, deceased, and its own account as executor of her will; but to remand the cause to the Probate Court for a proceeding by the petitioner as executor *de son tort,* and for such further proceedings as it may be advised and as are permissible by the laws of Massachusetts and the statutes of the United States, not inconsistent with this opinion.

And it is so ordered.

United States v. Fruit Growers Express Co.

The Interstate Commerce Act made it criminal for "any common carrier willfully [to] make any false entry in the accounts of any book of accounts or in any record or, memoranda kept by a carrier." The Fruit Growers Express Company was indicted under the act, charged with falsifying its records concerning icing of freight. A judge of the United States District Court for the Western District of Pennsylvania quashed the indictment. The federal government appealed this decision to the Supreme Court. Chief Justice Taft upheld the decision of the federal court judge, arguing that criminal statutes must be interpreted narrowly.

United States v. The Fruit Growers Express Company

*Appeal from the District Court of the United States
for the Western District of Pennsylvania*

No. 305. Argued December 3, 1928—Decided May 13, 1929

279 U.S. 363 (1929)

[365]

MR. CHIEF JUSTICE TAFT delivered the opinion of the Court.

* * * * *

This review is of an indictment of 75 counts against the Fruit Growers Express Company, a corporation of Delaware, engaged in icing and re-icing refrigerator cars containing shipments of perishable commodities transported to Pittsburgh by the Pennsylvania Railroad, for misreporting ice furnished and falsifying the official records of the Railroad Company showing expenditures made in those shipments. . . .

The Express Company, as provided in the contract, made and furnished written reports [366] of the quantity of ice placed by it in the bunkers of the cars for the Railroad Company at Pittsburgh. These reports were received and kept by the Railroad Company, and from them the Railroad Company prepared its reports of ice delivered, and rendered bills to the consignees of the shipments at Pittsburgh in accordance with its tariffs and schedules. . . .

[367] On behalf of the defendant, a motion was made and granted by the District Court, to quash the indictment in all its counts, on the ground, first, that the quoted §§ 10 and 20 relied on to support the indictment are really intended only to apply to common carriers, their directors, officers, agents and employees, or others acting for and in the interest of carriers or in collusion with them, and not to persons whose only relation to a carrier is that of an independent contractor acting adversely to the carrier's interest, in fraud of it and without its knowledge or acquiescence; and second, that the counts of the indictment only denounce the keeping of false or inaccurate official "records kept by the carrier" and do not include records not kept by the carrier, like bills, memoranda, and other data furnished by an independent contractor, intentionally misleading the carrier or its agents in keeping its official records.

* * * * *

[368] . . . [If] [369] the common carrier were privy to the furnishing of short ice, or to the making of false preliminary data by the independent contractor, both the carrier and the independent contractor would become criminally responsible for the shortage and for the misrepresentation of the official record. But that is not the case we have here. The Railroad Company having certain duties to perform in respect of the shipments, attempts to perform them by contract with an outside person not an agent of the carrier, and is itself deceived and defrauded by the contractor and outsider in his failure to perform his contract, so that by the falsification the carrier is led

into the making of the erroneous report. In such circumstances, is the outsider to be held guilty of criminality under the above statutory provisions? Congress of course could render these false statements by the defendant a crime; but has it done so in the absence of any collusion by the Railroad Company? It is a nice question, but the statute is a criminal one, and may lead to heavy penalties. A defendant under such circumstances is entitled to a reasonably strict construction of the language used to effect the particular purpose that Congress has in mind. We do not think that Congress was looking to protect an independent contractor against his servants or a common carrier against its independent contractor. . . .

If the independent contractor colludes with the common carrier by the false data it furnishes, and the common carrier knowingly uses them, of course the contractor is nothing but an aider and abettor, and so a principal, in the keeping of the false official records; but otherwise not.

The result is, therefore, that while the independent contractor might well be penalized by a different statute for [370] the fraud he has committed on the common carrier, we do not think that the present statutes bring them within the scope of the crime denounced, when the common carrier and its servants are innocent of offense.

It is clear to us that the words "record or memoranda kept by a carrier" contained in § 20 mean the official record kept by the carrier and do not refer to bills or memoranda kept by the contractor as a basis on which the carrier keeps its records. The defendant's bills or memoranda are not in that sense a record at all under § 20. They are not subject to the supervision of the Interstate Commerce Commission and it would seem that if the data proved to be dishonest and incorrect, the punishment for that, unless with the complicity of the common carrier, must be found elsewhere than in the provisions of the present Interstate Commerce Act.

This leads us necessarily to affirm the ruling of the District Court.

Affirmed.

United States v. John Barth Co.

The John Barth Company had contested a decision by the Internal Revenue Service as to its tax liability. As provided by statute, the company put up a bond in 1919 equal to twice the amount of taxes in dispute. The IRS commissioner made a decision in 1926 allowing some of the claims by the Barth Company, but rejecting most of its claims for tax abatement. The Barth Company refused to forfeit the bond posted, arguing that the five-year statute of limitations had passed. Both the district court and the Court of Appeals for the Seventh Circuit dismissed the IRS complaint against the Barth Company. Taft reversed, finding that the "plain language" of Congress required the complaint to stand.

United States v. The John Barth Company et al.

Certiorari to the Circuit Court of Appeals for the Seventh Circuit

No. 526. Argued April 18, 1929—Decided May 13, 1929

279 U.S. 370 (1929)

[371]
MR. CHIEF JUSTICE TAFT delivered the opinion of the Court.

* * * * *

[375] The plain purpose of par. 14 (a) was to effect a substitution for the obligation arising under the return and assessment to pay the tax, of the contract entered into in the bond to pay any part of the tax found to be due upon the subsequent determination of the Commissioner, and this with interest at the rate of 1 per cent. per month from the time the tax would have been due, had no such claim been filed. Of course, it is not difficult in the somewhat complicated provisions to suggest, as on behalf of respondent it has been suggested, that some other than the ordinary inference to be given to this set of facts should be drawn; but the common sense view of the return and the delay in the payment due after the claim of abatement and the giving of the bond, is as already stated. The making of the bond gives the United States a cause of action separate and distinct from an action to collect taxes which it already had. The statutes now pleaded to bar the suit can not be extended by implication to a suit upon a subsequent and substituted contract. The postponement of the collection of the taxes returned was a waiver of the statutory limitation of five years that would have applied had the voluntary return of the taxpayer stood and no bond been given. If there is any limitation applicable to a suit on the bond, it is conceded that it has not yet become effective.

Section 250 (d) of the Revenue Act of 1921, c. 136, 42 Stat. 227, 265, repeats the limitation of 1918, adding thereto "unless both the Commissioner and the taxpayer consent in writing to a later determination, assessment, and collection of the tax," and like § 250 (d) of the Act of 1918 has no relevancy or effect here. The Revenue Act of 1924, § 277 (a) (2), c. 234, 43 Stat. 253, repeats a similar limitation of five years. Section 1106 (a) of the [376] Revenue Act of 1926, c. 27, 44 Stat. 9, 113, provides that the bar of the statute of limitations against the United States in respect of any internal revenue tax shall not only operate to bar the remedy but shall extinguish the liability. This last Act was repealed as of the date of its enactment. See § 612, c. 852, 45 Stat. 791, 875.

The Government contends that this restores and gives life to the tax retroactively. It is not necessary for us to examine this claim, for the reason that the Act of 1926 does not affect, and was not intended to affect, the obligation arising out of the bond. Such bonds are not referred to in the amendments of 1921 or 1924 or 1926, nor in any way is the taxpayer expressly or impliedly relieved from such contracts. To avoid the result usually ensuing from the return which he himself made, the taxpayer was permitted by a bond temporarily to postpone the collection and to substitute for his tax liability his contract under the bond. The object of the bond was not only to prevent the immediate collection of the tax but also to prevent the running of time against the Government. The taxpayer has obtained his object by the use of the bond, and he should not object to making good the contract by which he obtained the delay he sought.

* * * * *

The judgment of the Circuit Court of Appeals should be reversed and the cause remanded for further proceedings.

Reversed.

Chesapeake & Ohio Railway Co. v. Stapleton

The Kentucky Court of Appeals had upheld a decision arising under the federal Employers' Liability Act of 1908, which broadly defined negligence on the part of an employer. Kentucky law prohibited employment of persons under sixteen years of age in certain occupations. Stapleton was employed in such a job and was severely injured while performing his duties. The state judge's charge to the jury was to the effect that if they found he was under sixteen when employed, then the railroad was negligent under federal statute. Chief Justice Taft, for a unanimous Court, reversed, holding that the definition of negligence under the act was for the federal courts to determine and that state precedents argued for a finding that the railroad was not negligent.

Chesapeake & Ohio Railway Company v. Stapleton

Certiorari to the Court of Appeals of Kentucky

No. 133. Submitted January 2, 1929. Restored to docket and argued April 9, 1929—Decided May 27, 1929

279 U.S. 587 (1929)

[588]

MR. CHIEF JUSTICE TAFT delivered the opinion of the Court.

Plaintiff is a citizen of Kentucky, and at the time of the suit was between 15 and 16 years of age. Marion Stapleton was his father and guardian. The Chesapeake and Ohio Railway Company is a railway corporation of Virginia, doing an interstate commerce business in Kentucky. The plaintiff and his father were employed by the defendant as section hands and were engaged in maintaining the railroad and the roadbed for interstate commerce. The plaintiff was directed by his father, who was his foreman, to get water for his companions. In returning with the water he passed between or under the cars of a train standing on a switch track. The train moved unexpectedly while he was under the cars, he was run over and sustained permanent injury. The evidence showed that the boy was large and well developed and had been working as a section hand and water carrier for nine months previously.

The law of Kentucky in force at the time of the accident was § 331a-9 Carroll's Kentucky Statutes, 1922, as follows:

"Children under sixteen; where not to work.

"No child under the age of sixteen years shall be employed, permitted or, suffered (1) to sew or assist in sewing belts in any capacity whatever; (2) nor to adjust any belt to machinery; . . . (6) nor to work upon any railroad whether steam, electric or hydraulic; (7) nor to operate or to assist in operating any passenger or freight elevator. . . ."

Section 331a-16 of the same statute provided:

"Whoever employs or suffers or permits a child under sixteen years of age to work, and any parent, guardian or any adult person under whose care or control a child under such age is, who suffers or permits such child to work, in violation of any of the provisions of this act, shall be [589] punished for the first offense by a fine of not less than fifteen dollars nor more than fifty dollars; for second offense by a fine of not less than fifteen dollars and nor [not] more than one hundred dollars, or by imprisonment for not more than thirty days, or by both such fine and imprisonment; for a third or any subsequent offense by a fine of not less than two hundred dollars, or by imprisonment for not less than thirty days, or by both such fine and imprisonment. . . ."

Suit was brought under the Federal Employers' Liability Act of April 22, 1908, c. 149, 35 Stat. 65. The case was tried to a jury and resulted in a verdict of $17,500. The Kentucky Court of Appeals affirmed the judgment. 233 Ky. 154. The case comes here on certiorari, and the error chiefly pressed is the giving of charge No. 3, as follows:

"The court instructs the jury that if they believe and find from the evidence that the defendant Chesapeake and Ohio Railway Company employed the plaintiff to work for it as a section hand at a time when he was under sixteen years of age, and if they further believe and find from the evidence that the plaintiff while working for it as a section hand in the course of said employment, was injured at a time when he was under the age of sixteen years, then the law is for the plaintiff, and the jury will so find. Unless they so believe they will find for the defendant."

The language of the Federal Employers' Liability Act shows unmistakably that the basis of recovery is negligence and that without such negligence no right of action is given under this Act. *New York Central R. R. v. Winfield,* 244 U.S. 147, 150; *Erie R. R. v. Winfield,* 244 U.S. 170, 172. The question squarely presented here is whether the employment by an interstate carrier in Kentucky in the business of interstate commerce of a worker under the age of sixteen years is by reason of the state statute [590] negligence justifying a recovery under the federal Act for injuries received during such employment. . . .

* * * * *

[592] The exclusive operation of the Federal Employers' Liability Act within the field of rights and duties as between an interstate commerce common carrier and its employees has been illustrated in opinions of this Court applying that Act by quotation of the words of Mr. Justice Story in *Prigg v. Pennsylvania,* 16 Pet. 539, 617, used in another association:

"If this be so, then it would seem, upon just principles of construction, that the legislation of Congress, if constitutional, must supersede all state legislation upon the same subject; and by necessary implication prohibit it. For, if Congress have a constitutional power to regulate a particular subject, and they do actually regulate it in a given manner, and in a certain form, it can not be that the state legislatures have a right to interfere, and, as it were, by way of complement to the legislation of Congress, to prescribe additional regulations, and what they may deem auxiliary provisions for the same purpose. In such a case, the legislation of Congress, in what it does prescribe, manifestly indicates, that it does not intend that there shall be any further legislation to act upon the subject-matter. Its silence as to what it does not do is as expressive of what its intention is as the direct provisions made by it. This doctrine was fully recognized by this Court, in the case of *Houston v. Moore,* 5 Wheat. 1, 21, 22, where it was expressly held that where Congress have exercised a power over a particular subject given them by the Constitution, it is not competent for state legislation to add to the provisions of Congress upon that subject; for that the will of Congress upon the whole subject is as clearly established by what it has not declared, as by what it has expressed."

[593] We come then to the specific question whether the violation of a statute of a State prohibiting the employment of workmen under a certain age and providing for punishment of such employment should be held to be negligence in a suit brought under the Federal Employers' Liability Act. That the State has power to forbid such employment and to punish the forbidden employment when occurring in intrastate commerce, and also has like power in respect of interstate commerce so long as Congress does not legislate on the subject, goes without saying. But it is a different question whether such a state Act can be made to bear the construction that a violation of it constitutes negligence *per se* or negligence at all under the Federal Employers' Liability Act. The Kentucky Act, as we have set it out above, is a criminal act and imposes a graduated system of penalties. There is nothing to indicate that it was intended to apply to the subject of negligence as between common carriers and their employees. It is true that in Kentucky and in a number of other States it is held that a violation of this or a similar state act is negligence *per se,* and such a construction of the Act by a state court is binding and is to be respected in every case in which the state law is to be enforced. *Louisville H. & St. L. Ry. v. Lyons,* 155 Ky. 396; *Terry Dairy Co. v. Nalley,* 146 Ark. 448; *Grand Rapids Trust Co. v. Petersen Beverage Co.,* 219 Mich. 208; *Elk Cotton Mills v. Grant,* 140 Ga. 727. But when the field of the relations between an interstate carrier and its interstate employees is the subject of consideration, it becomes a federal question and is to be decided exclusively as such.

We have not found any case in which this question has been presented to the federal courts, but there are three or four well-reasoned cases in state courts, wherein this exact point is considered and decided.

* * * * *

[595] The citations from these state cases, four of them, seem to show that their effect is confined to the government of the relation between the

employer and the employee, between the common carrier and the interstate commerce agent. A different rule might well apply where the issue and the litigation is with reference to the duties of the common carrier in dealing with the public, with passengers or with strangers. The cases cited were decided only after a full examination of the cases on the subject of the Federal Employers' Liability Act in this Court.

* * * * *

[597] We think that the statute of Kentucky limiting the age of employees and punishing its violation has no bearing on the civil liability of a railway to its employees injured in interstate commerce and that application of it in this case was error.

Reversed.

Old Colony Trust Co.
v. Commissioner of Internal Revenue

In 1924, Congress had set up the Board of Tax Appeals. In this and the following case, *United States v. Boston & Maine Railroad,* 279 U.S. 732 (1929), the board ruled that an employer's payment of taxes constituted income to an employee on which further taxes were due from the employee. The Court concurred in this finding. It also determined that appeals from the Board of Tax Appeals constituted "cases or controversies" under Article III and could, accordingly, be heard by federal courts.

Old Colony Trust Company et al.
v. Commissioner of Internal Revenue

Certificate from the Circuit Court of Appeals for the First Circuit

No. 130. Argued January 10, 11, 1929. Reargued April 15, 1929—Decided June 3, 1929

279 U.S. 716 (1929)

[718]

MR. CHIEF JUSTICE TAFT delivered the opinion of the Court.

* * * * *

[720] The question certified by the Circuit Court of Appeals for answer by this Court is:

"Did the payment by the employer of the income taxes assessable against the employee constitute additional taxable income to such employee?"

The first point presented to us is that of the jurisdiction of this Court to answer the question of law certified. It [721] requires us to examine the original statute providing for the Board of Tax Appeals under the Revenue Act of 1924, and the amending Act of 1926.

The Board of Tax Appeals, established by § 900 of the Revenue Act of 1924, Tit. IX, c. 234, 43 Stat. 253, 336, was created by Congress to provide taxpayers an opportunity to secure an independent review of the Commissioner of Internal Revenue's determination of additional income and estate taxes by the Board in advance of their paying the tax found by the Commissioner to be due. Before the Act of 1924 the taxpayer could only contest the Commissioner's determination of the amount of the tax after its payment. The Board's duty under the Act of 1924 was to hear, consider and decide whether deficiencies reported by the Commissioner were right.

* * * * *

[722] It is suggested that the proceedings before the Circuit Courts of Appeals or the District Court of Appeals on a petition to review are not and can not be judicial, for they involve "no case or controversy," and without this a Circuit Court of Appeals, which is a constitutional court (*Ex parte Bakelite Corporation, ante,* p. 438) is incapable of exercising its judicial function. This view of the nature of the proceedings we can not sustain. [723] The jurisdiction in this cause is quite like that of Circuit Courts of Appeals in review of orders of the Federal Trade Commission. . . .

It is not necessary that the proceeding to be judicial should be one entirely *de novo;* it is enough that, before the judgment which must be final has been invoked as an exercise of judicial power, it shall have certain necessary features. What these are has been often declared by this Court. Perhaps the most comprehensive definitions of them are set forth in *Muskrat v. United States,* 219 U.S. 346, 356, where this Court entered into the inquiry what was the exercise of judicial power as conferred by the Constitution. There was cited there a definition by Mr. Justice Field, in *Re Pacific Railway Commission,* 32 Fed. 241, 255, which has been generally accepted as accurate. He said:

"The judicial article of the Constitution mentions cases and controversies. The term 'controversies,' if distinguishable at all from 'cases,' is so in that it is less comprehensive than the latter; and includes only suits of a civil nature. *Chisholm v. Georgia,* 2 Dall. 431, 432; 1 Tuch. Bl. Comm. App. 420, 421. By cases and controversies are intended the claims of litigants brought before the courts for determination by such regular proceedings as are established by law or custom for the protection or enforcement of rights, or the prevention, redress, or punishment of wrongs. Whenever the claim of a party under the Constitution, laws or treaties of the United [724] States takes such a form that the judicial power is capable of acting upon it, then it has become a case. The term implies the existence of present or possible adverse parties whose contentions are submitted to the court for adjudication."

In *Osborn v. United States Bank,* 9 Wheat. 738, Chief Justice Marshall construed Article III of the Constitution as follows (p. 819):

"This clause enables the judicial department to receive jurisdiction to the full extent of the constitution, laws and treaties of the United States, when any question respecting them shall assume such a form that the judicial power is capable of acting on it. That power is capable of acting only when the subject is submitted to it, by a party who asserts his rights in the form prescribed by law. It then becomes a case, and the constitution declares, that the judicial power shall extend to all cases arising under the constitution, laws and treaties of the United States."

The Circuit Court of Appeals is a constitutional court under the definition of such courts as given in the *Bakelite* case, *supra,* and a case or controversy may come before it, provided it involves neither advisory nor executive action by it.

In the case we have here, there are adverse parties. The United States or its authorized official asserts its right to the payment by a taxpayer of a tax due from him to the Government, and the taxpayer is resisting that payment or is seeking to recover what he has already paid as taxes when by law they were not properly due. That makes a case or controversy, and the proper disposition of it is the exercise of judicial power. The courts are either the Circuit Court of Appeals or the District of Columbia Court of Appeals. The subject matter of the controversy is the amount of the tax claimed to be due or [725] refundable and its validity, and the judgment to be rendered is a judicial judgment.

The Board of Tax Appeals is not a court. It is an executive or administrative board, upon the decision of which the parties are given an opportunity to base a petition for review to the courts after the administrative inquiry of the Board has been had and decided.

* * * * *

[729] . . . Coming now to the merits of this case, we think the question presented is whether a taxpayer, having induced a third person to pay his income tax or having acquiesced in such payment as made in discharge of an obligation to him, may avoid the making of a return thereof and the payment of a corresponding tax. We think he may not do so. The payment of the tax by the employers was in consideration of the services rendered by the employee and was a gain derived by the employee from his labor. The form of the payment is expressly declared to make no difference. . . .

The taxes were paid upon a valuable consideration, namely, the services rendered by the employee and as part of the compensation therefor. We think therefore that the payment constituted income to the employee.

* * * * *

[731] Separate opinion of MR. JUSTICE McREYNOLDS.

The Board of Tax Appeals belongs to the executive department of the Government and performs administrative functions—the assessment of taxes. The statute attempts to grant a broad appeal to the courts and directs them to reconsider the Board's action—to do or to say what it should have done. This enjoins the use of executive power, not judicial. The duty thus imposed upon the courts is wholly different from that which arises upon the filing of a petition to annul or enforce the action of the Interstate Commerce Commission or the Federal Trade Commission.

I think the Circuit Court of Appeals was without jurisdiction.

United States v. Boston & Maine Railroad

The Court, following the *Old Colony* precedent, 279 U.S. 716 (1929), held that an employer's payment of taxes constituted taxable compensation to an employee. Taft wrote the opinion in both cases.

United States v. Boston & Maine Railroad

Certificate from the Circuit Court of Appeals for the First Circuit

No. 129. Argued January 10, 11, 1929; reargued April 15, 1929—
Decided June 3, 1929

279 U.S. 732 (1929)

[732]

MR. CHIEF JUSTICE TAFT delivered the opinion of the Court.

As indicated in *Old Colony Trust Co. v. Commissioner of Internal Revenue,* just decided, *ante,* p. 716, this case [733] comes here by certificate from the Circuit Court of Appeals for the First Circuit. . . .

* * * * *

[734] "Did the payment by the lessee of the net income taxes assessable against the lessor constitute additional taxable income to such lessor?"

The merits of this case must be disposed of in accord with the rule already laid down in the *Old Colony* case, just decided, *ante,* p. 716. Like that, it is one in which the lessee has paid to the Government the taxes due under the law from the lessor. The payment is made in accord with the contract of lease, and is merely a short cut whereby that which the lessee specifically agreed to pay as part of the rental effects that payment by discharging the obligation of the lessor to pay the tax to the Government.

* * * * *

Omitted Taft Opinion

London Co. v. Industrial Commission, 279 U.S. 109 (1929)—federal power over accidents at sea.

October Term, 1929

William Howard Taft, Chief Justice (resigned February 3, 1930)
Charles Evans Hughes, Chief Justice (joined the Court February 24, 1930)
Oliver Wendell Holmes
Willis Van Devanter
James Clark McReynolds
Louis D. Brandeis
George Sutherland
Pierce Butler
Edward T. Sanford
Harlan Fiske Stone

VOLUME 280

Colgate v. United States

Appropriately, one of Taft's last opinions was a decision that allowed him to incorporate a discussion of the Judges' Act of 1925, one of Taft's major accomplishments as chief. The facts of the case involved a suit by the estate of a dissatisfied patent holder suing the federal government for patent infringement. Congress had provided by a subsequent act that decisions of the United States Court of Claims could be appealed to the Supreme Court. The legal question that Taft addressed was whether this latter action by Congress expanded the types of appeals that the Court must hear or whether the only allowable appeal in this situation was to file a writ of *certiorari* (a discretionary writ), in which case the Court could refuse to hear the case unless it involved "a substantial federal question."

Colgate, Administrator, v. United States

Appeal from the Court of Claims

No. 74. Jurisdictional Statement Submitted October 14, 1929—
Decided November 4, 1929

280 U.S. 43 (1929)

[44]

MR. CHIEF JUSTICE TAFT delivered the opinion of the Court.

* * * * *

[45] We think the proper construction to be put upon this Special Act [of 1927] is that the review provided for was a petition for certiorari. One of the chief purposes of the General Act of February 13, 1925 . . . was to abolish appeals from the Court of Appeals to this Court and substitute therefore applications for writs of certiorari. . . . [46] It was intended by the Act of 1925 to give this Court an opportunity to determine in advance whether the case was one worthy of review here. To hold that the case may come here only by certiorari is to make it conform to the general purpose of the Act of February 13, 1925, in enlarging the use of certiorari as a method of review in this Court. . . .

* * * * *

[49] Unless a special reason in the Act [of 1927] providing foe appellate review indicates that the review is to be by technical appeal rather than by the ordinary method of certiorari, the latter method is the right one. This must lead to the dismissal of the present appeal.

Appeal dismissed.

Interstate Commerce Commission
v. United States ex rel. Los Angeles

Officials of the City of Los Angeles sought to have a court order the Interstate Commerce Commission to hear evidence on the wisdom of building a "union" station in Los Angeles that would serve both the Southern Pacific Company, the Atchison, Topeka & Santa Fe Railway Company, and the Los Angeles & Salt Lake Railroad

Company. The ICC claimed that they did not have such authority and prevailed in the trial court. The latter's decision was reversed by the United States Court of Appeals.

Interstate Commerce Commission v. United States ex rel. Los Angeles

Certiorari to the Court of Appeals for the District of Columbia

No. 54 Argued October 28, 29, 1929—Decided November 25, 1929

280 U.S. 52 (1929)

[60]

MR. CHIEF JUSTICE TAFT delivered the opinion of the Court.

* * * * *

[68] Without more specific and express legislative direction than is found in the [ICC] Act, we can not reasonably ascribe to Congress a purpose to compel the interstate carriers here to build a union passenger station. . . . If it was to be clothed with the power to require railroads to abandon their existing stations and terminal tracks . . . , that power we should expect to find in congressional legislation. . . .

* * * * *

[69] We can not agree with the Court of Appeals . . . [that vests] the Interstate Commerce Commission "with almost unlimited power in the matter of establishing terminals. . . ." The words "reasonable, proper and equal facilities" are of course comprehensive enough to included not only trackage but terminal facilities . . . , but hardly to give the Commission "unlimited power" in the building of union stations.

* * * * *

[71] The judgment of the Court of the District of Columbia is

Reversed.

United States v. Jackson

This was Chief Justice Taft's last opinion. Along with the *Luckenbach Steamship Company* case it was announced by Associate Justice Willis Van Devanter, a close Taft ally and a person Taft had nominated to the Court in 1911.

Jack Williams, an Indian, had acquired property under the Homestead Law. He died and his wife, also an Indian, inherited the land. She subsequently sold it to Jack Jackson, also an Indian. The latter transaction was never approved by the secretary of the interior. The secretary, however, had approved a will of the widow that left the land to another Indian, Bob Roberts. The United States government sued to establish Roberts's claim to the land under the terms of the approved will. The question was whether the status of Indians as wards of the federal government meant that even though this land had been acquired by Williams under the Homestead Act and not as an allotment given to Indians, the federal government must approve all transfers of ownership.

The case came to the Court on a certificate. The Ninth Circuit, "being in doubt," certified the case to the Supreme Court.

United States v. Jackson et al.

Certificate from the Circuit Court of Appeals for the Ninth Circuit

No. 57. Argued December 5, 1929—decided January 6, 1930.

280 U.S. 183 (1930)

[193]

Opinion of the Court, by Mr. Chief Justice Taft, announced by Mr. Justice Van Devanter.

It is a familiar rule of statutory construction that great weight is properly to be given to the construction consistently given to a statute by the Executive Department charged with its administration. . . . Applying this rule, we find . . . that it has long been the settled ruling of the Department of Interior . . . that Indian allotments and Indian homesteads are in all essential respects upon the same footing. . . .

* * * * *

[196] We find that the Indian Homestead Act of July 4, 1884, and the General Allotment Act of February 8, 1887, with its various amendments, constitute part of a single system evidencing a continuous purpose on the past of Congress. . . . It cannot be supposed that Congress. In any part of this legislation, all of which is directed toward the benefit and protection of the Indians, as such, intended to exclude from the beneficent policy which each Act evidences, an Indian claiming under the homestead act. . . . If there were any doubt on the question, the silence of Congress in the face of the long continued practice of the [197] Department of the Interior . . . must be

considered as "equivalent to consent to continue the practice until the power was revoked by Congress." *United States v. Midwest Oil Co.*, 236 U.S. 459, 481.

* * * * *

Omitted Taft Opinions

General Insurance Company of America v. Northern Pacific Railway Company, 280 U.S. 72 (1929)—dispute over insurance payment as a result of fire.

Luckenbach Steamship Company v. United States, 280 U.S. 173 (1930)—interpretation of the term "foreign port" in a federal statute.

Appendix 1

William Howard Taft's Statement and Testimony before the House Judiciary Committee, 1922

JURISDICTION OF CIRCUIT COURTS OF APPEALS
AND UNITED STATES SUPREME COURT

PAY OF SUPREME COURT REPORTER

Serial 33

Committee of the Judiciary
House of Representatives
Thursday, March 30, 1922

The committee met at 10:30 o'clock a.m., Hon. Leonidas C. Dyer presiding.

Mr. DYER. We have with us this morning the Chief Justice of the Supreme Court, who appears with reference to the bill (H. R. 10479) to amend the Judicial Code etc. Mr. Chief Justice, we will be very glad to hear from you.

STATEMENT OF HON. WILLIAM HOWARD TAFT, CHIEF JUSTICE OF THE SUPREME COURT OF THE UNITED STATES

Mr. Chief Justice TAFT. Mr. Chairman and gentlemen of the committee, I have been deputed by the Supreme Court to come here and present to your body this bill, which, in terms, is a bill "To amend the Judicial Code, and to further define the jurisdiction of the circuit courts of appeals, and of the Supreme Court, and for other purposes."

The bill has been the subject of very long discussion in the court itself. Before I came into the court a committee had been appointed for its preparation, consisting of Justice Day, Justice McReynolds, and, I suppose, ex officio, the Chief Justice. It was taken up again and a very careful and very much extended examination of it made by the committee, to which Justice Van Devanter was added. I suppose we have spent two or three months in its preparation. The care devoted to it was because of the importance that the court attributed to its passage. It is primarily a bill to bring within the jurisdiction of the Supreme Court all the business of the country in such a way that it can keep up with its docket. The business of the court is rapidly increasing, and unless the cases that are not important enough to occupy the time of the court are summarily disposed of it is impossible for the court to dispatch promptly, as it should, the important questions which it is organized to settle.

Primarily, it is a bill to do so just what I have said, and not to take away the right to go to the court with any case in which there is now a possibility of review by that court, but it is to change the method by which those cases reach the court, so that there may be promptly winnowed out by the court itself of all the cases which come those which deserve the court's consideration. That requires a reference to the method by which the cases are brought up for review in the Supreme Court. There are two methods, the second one being itself divided into two ways. One is what one might call the obligatory jurisdiction, which is a jurisdiction by writ of error at common law, or by appeal in equity or in admiralty. These are cases described by the statute as reviewable by the voluntary action of a party defeated in the court below if within the statute, and the court is bound to consider and dispose of them. Then, there is what may be called the discretionary jurisdiction of the court. That is exercised by a writ, either in the discretion of the Supreme Court or in the discretion of the court whose decree, order, or judgment is to be reexamined. The Supreme Court exercises its discretionary jurisdiction through the writ of certiorari. Now, if you will allow me, I will describe what is the procedure in respect to writs of certiorari in the court. An application has to be made within three months or six months, determinable by the question of where the case comes from, after final judgment in the court below. A petition for the writ of certiorari is filed, with the record and the briefs on behalf of the petitioner and the opposing party. These are considered by the court. Each member of the court takes the briefs and record. He examines both briefs and the record so far as the briefs may suggest the necessity of doing so.

In every conference on Saturday, the court takes up the cases and discusses them. Of course, it is impossible for the court or any member of the court, in reading the cases not to reach some conclusion, or at least, a curbstone conclusion, as to whether the case was decided rightly in the court below; but that is not the consideration that determines the action of the court. The question is whether the questions as presented are sufficiently important, considering the function that the Supreme Court has to play—to justify and require the court to let the case into the court for a full hearing on the merits. Now, the suggestion has been made, and I am anxious and my brethren are anxious to have me refute it, that certioraris are granted by favor. There is not anything of the kind done; every case is fully considered for the purpose of learning what kind of a case it is and its importance. Frequently there is a vote taken. Of course, if it is all agreed to, a vote is not taken. I have heard that one prominent gentleman suggested that each justice had a certain number of certioraris a term, and that they were allowed as a personal privilege. Of course, this has not the slightest foundation.

That reminds me of a story Mr. Knox told me. A Member of Congress called on him as Attorney General and said that he wanted a pardon in a certain case. Mr. Knox looked over the papers and said, "This is a plain case of stealing from the post office. How can we give a pardon in such a case?" "Why," replied the Congressman, "I have had only one pardon, and I understand that every Member of Congress is entitled to two pardons each term." That same absurd hypothesis has been entertained in some quarters as to the granting of certioraris. It does the court great injustice. We give every certiorari full consideration. It is one of the heaviest of our duties. I would like for a moment, now, to discuss the proper basis for determining the class of cases which should be reviewed by the Supreme Court. No litigant is entitled to more than two chances, namely, to the original trial and to a review, and the intermediate courts of review are provided for that purpose. When a case goes beyond that, it is not primarily to preserve the rights of the litigants. The Supreme Court's function is for the purpose of expounding and stabilizing principles of law for the benefit of the people of the country, passing upon constitutional questions and other important questions of law for the public benefit. It is to preserve uniformity of decision among the intermediate courts of appeal.

Whenever a petition for certiorari presents a question on which one circuit court of appeals differs from another, then we let the case come into our court as a matter of course. These being the considerations that govern our allowance of certioraris the question whether the case was rightly decided in the court below as a matter of first impression is one of minor consideration with us. A case may be a very important case financially; it may involve millions of dollars but it may turn upon a question of fact or principle of law, the exposition of which is not important because it is well settled. In such cases we reject the petition. It does not come in because it is financially important to the parties, or because it is important to the parties at all. Every case is important to the parties. It comes in simply because the principle involved is such that it is important to have a general exposition of it for the benefit of the lawyers, for the benefit of the inferior courts, and for the benefit of the public at large, especially with respect to any constitutional issues involved. With these principles clearly before us the proper basis for the distribution of jurisdiction among the courts, we came to the question of how are we going to limit the jurisdiction of the Supreme Court.

There have been a great many methods attempted. The method adopted by the House of Lords in England was to make the costs so heavy that nobody would come up who did not have a long purse. In that way the jurisdiction was very much reduced, and the cases were left largely to the chance of getting a litigant with a long purse who would carry up important questions on appeal. That was a very poor method. Then it was attempted to divide up the court into two bodies and hear every case. That has been done in some of the States with very poor results, because you change the personnel of the courts, and lawyers become interested to secure that division of the court before which they think they can succeed. That makes the arrangement very unsatisfactory. We could not adopt it because our Constitution provides that there shall be one Supreme Court, and it is doubtful whether you could constitutionally divide the court into two parts. Another method, of course, has been carefully to define the character of cases which shall come before the court. Of course, that must be done, but where you depend on definition of cases by classes it is a very difficult thing to include all the important cases and it is a very difficult thing to exclude the unimportant cases. Then, there has been the method of the limitation of amount, and that, too, is an unsatisfactory method.

Important cases are not determined by the amount involved. On the other hand, we should not be influenced by a desire to give every man a chance to go to the Supreme Court. The not infrequent view of State legislators, expressed in the declaration, "I want a system by which the poorest man can carry his case through to the highest court," is fundamentally erroneous in its practical operation. There is no class of litigants to whom the dispatch of business is so important as to the poor litigants. It is the rich corporation or the man with the long purse who, as a litigant in the court, is greatly advantaged by a number of appeals. Therefore, in the long run, quickness in disposing of business and the limitation of appeals are in the interest of the poor man. Only those cases should come to the highest court which are sufficiently important pro bono publico, without regard to the interest of the litigants. As I have said, two chances are enough for any litigated interest, whether it be the interest of the rich or the interest of the poor.

The present bill is proposing a change, not by reducing in any respect the review which the Supreme Court may have of every case that may come before it, but by transferring from the obligatory jurisdiction to the certiorari or discretionary jurisdiction a great number of classes of cases that will increase largely the work of the court in passing promptly on certiorari cases, and reduce the number of cases that the court is obliged to take under full and complete consideration.

I omitted to mention another method of review which is exemplified in this bill: In every case where a certiorari may be allowed the court below may certify the questions arising in any case before it that it deems of importance, or with respect to which it wishes the aid of the Supreme Court. That would place the question of review also in the discretion of the Circuit Court of Appeals, or the Court of Claims, or the Court of Appeals of the District of Columbia, as the case may be.

This bill has another object, and this is to state succinctly the jurisdiction of the court in one statute where it can be found by any lawyer, and I might say, by any judge. I am very much troubled in coming into the court to find a wilderness of statutes to be consulted in determining what the jurisdiction of the Supreme Court is. The purpose of the framers of this bill is to enable any lawyer, judge, or layman to look to one statute and be sure that it contains all there is on the appellate jurisdiction of the Supreme Court. Another object of the statute is to determine what the appellate jurisdiction of the Circuit Court of Appeals is, because, that, too, is involved in doubt and needs clarification.

Then, there are certain remedial provisions that I would like to bring to your attention. I furnished to Mr. Walsh, the introducer of this bill, a statement that I drafted, and I have given him a copy for each member of the committee. That statement is a general résumé of the bill without references. The bill is long, and the statement with the references and with the statement covering previous legislation is quite complicated. There is need, therefore, for a simpler statement to accompany the very comprehensive, accurate, detailed statement of the legislation which is affected by this bill. That statement I have handed to Mr. Walsh. I have other copies, and if the committee sees fit, no doubt it can have the statement reprinted. I venture to think that all the members of the committee except those who have a greater earnestness and desire for complications than I have will not look into that detailed statement but the shorter one. I think the shorter statement, without the references, is sufficiently full to enable anyone to understand what the bill accomplishes and what changes it makes.

The bill is printed in the order of the sections of the Judicial Code that are amended, and that necessitates the absence of any logical arrangement; but I propose to look at it in a little different way and to take up first the Supreme Court jurisdiction. That jurisdiction involves the review of six different courts.

There is one court that is not affected by the bill, and that is the Court of Customs Appeals. The cases that come from that court are so rare and there being no disposition to change the jurisdiction, it was thought that any man that got into the Court of Customs Appeals would find in the Court of Customs Appeals act a sufficient description of what the jurisdiction of the Supreme Court was; so that we need not load this bill with a somewhat lengthy description of the circumstances under which an appeal could be carried from that court to the Supreme Court. The other cases are, first, from State supreme courts; second, from the district courts of the United States, because there is some direct review of them by the Supreme Court without going through the circuit court of appeals; then, cases from the circuit courts of appeals; then, from the Court of Appeals of the District of Columbia; then, from the Court of Claims; and, finally, from the Supreme Court of the Philippines.

With respect to the State supreme courts, by the act of 1916, passed by Congress, the jurisdiction over the State supreme courts was divided.

Under old section 25 of the judicial act, as drafted by Oliver Ellsworth, it extended to cases that involved any constitutional question in which the question was decided against the claim based on Federal right by the State supreme court; but it was found that could be just as many frivolous cases on constitutional grounds as on any other grounds, and therefore Congress cut down the obligatory jurisdiction over the State supreme court decisions by requiring that it should be limited either to a case in which the validity of a statute or treaty or authority of the United States under the Constitution was drawn in question, and the case was decided against that validity by the State courts, or where the validity of a statute or authority of a State was drawn into question and its validity was sustained; but all the other cases, like those where a man asserts a title, immunity, privilege, or right under the Constitution, not involving the validity of a statute or treaty or authority of the United States or a State were put in the certiorari class and they are now, so that when a man comes up now claiming a right under the fourteenth amendment, or the abuse under the fourteenth amendment, if he has no statute to attack, he can not get into the court except by certiorari. That jurisdiction as it is now is substantially retained under the bill, except that the case in which an authority under a State or under the United States is drawn in question is put in the certiorari class. All the rest from the State supreme courts are certiorari cases.

There are now a considerable class of cases that come directly from the United States district courts to the Supreme Court of the United States, and over them the Supreme Court has exercised jurisdiction on appeal and on writs of error. For instance, questions going to the jurisdiction of the district courts and constitutional questions can come up to us directly from the district courts. That has been abolished in this bill, and under it they would take their way through the circuit court of appeals, just as other cases from the district courts do. There, however, are four instances under this bill in which that jurisdiction is retained, and they are special cases. They are cases arising under the antitrust law and under the interstate commerce law: cases of criminal appeals, where the indictment against the defendant is quashed, without subjecting him to jeopardy and without a verdict in his favor, which cases the Government is permitted to carry up and to submit to the Supreme Court the question whether the demurrer to the indictment was properly sustained. The fourth class of cases is where it is sought to enjoin the enforcement of a State statute or authority on the ground that it violated the United States Constitution. Three judges have to sit to grant a preliminary injunction in such cases. I have now reviewed the entire obligatory jurisdiction of the Supreme Court under the new bill.

No review is allowed of right from the Judgments of the circuit courts of appeals under this bill. Now there is no jurisdiction obligatory over final judgments in the court of appeals in diverse citizenship cases, in revenue cases, in patent cases, in trade-mark and copyright cases, and in admiralty cases. The only jurisdiction of this court over them is by certiorari or by certificate. By this bill all the cases from the circuit court of appeals must come to us in these two ways. A similar provision has been made as to the Court of Appeals of the District of Columbia. There have been a good many cases which could come as a matter or right from the Court of Appeals of the District of Columbia, but now all of those cases are put in the certiorari class. So, too, with respect to the Court of Claims, with its five judges, handling a great variety of subjects. There are a great many of those cases. Many are not important. Then there are the cases from the Supreme Court of the Philippines. That is a very small class of cases, and they can only come in now by writ of certiorari. From this statement you can see what the present jurisdiction of the Supreme Court is, and how it is going to be affected. All the cases in the circuit court of appeals that now come upon writ of error or appeal will become certiorari cases, and all the cases in the district courts of the United States which are now directly reviewable in the Supreme Court, except the four classes which I have mentioned, will only reach us by certiorari after first being reviewed by the circuit court of appeals. All the cases from the Court of Appeals of the District of Columbia will become certiorari cases; all those from the Court of Claims will become certiorari cases, and those from the Philippines are now certiorari cases. Of course, we can not say certainly how much this will reduce our jurisdiction, but looking over all the cases as they come, we feel very confident that if you give us that authority we can winnow out the cases in such a way that we can catch up with the docket and keep up with it, and that, of course, is most important. The effect of this change is to largely increase the final jurisdiction of the circuit courts of appeals throughout the country. It does not, however, increase the number of the cases they have to hear by a great many. The only increase is in those cases in which there are direct appeals from the district courts to the Supreme Court which are cut off by the bill.

(At this point Mr. Dyer yielded the chair to Mr. Volstead.)

Now, there is another source of appellate jurisdiction involved in our having gone into what has been called imperialism. We have a jurisdiction by review in one way or another over Porto Rican courts, the court of the Virgin Islands, those islands purchased from Denmark, the court of the Canal Zone, the courts of Hawaii, the court of Alaska, the court of the Philippines, and the United States Court in China.

This bill takes away all such direct jurisdiction of the Supreme Court as now exists over the courts of Hawaii and Porto Rico, the Alaska district court and review of them is assigned to different circuit courts of appeals. Under this new bill, the result is that in Porto Rico all cases, both from the Supreme Court and the United States district court, go to the Circuit Court of Appeals for the First Circuit at Boston; the cases from the Virgin Islands court go to the Third Circuit Court of Appeals at Philadelphia; the cases from the Canal Zone go to the Fifth Circuit Court of Appeals at New Orleans. The Hawaii cases, both from the Supreme and district courts, the Alaska court cases, and cases from the United States Court in China go to the Ninth Circuit Court of Appeals. They go as a matter of course, and not on writ of certiorari, to the court of appeals. The Philippine Supreme Court cases now come only on writs of certiorari to us without going through the Circuit Court of Appeals of the Ninth Circuit. That feature is retained in the bill.

Mr. MONTAGUE. Do you have many of those applications from the Philippines?

Mr. Chief Justice TAFT. The number varies, but not more than an average of five a year, I should say.

Mr. MONTAGUE. Are the records usually very large?

Mr. Chief Justice TAFT. Of course, that depends on the case. They can not apply for certiorari unless the case involves as much as $25,000 or some constitutional question. The records are usually cut down.

I want to say one thing in regard to the appellate jurisdiction that is omitted from this printed statement, and I will have it inserted. That is something that I think you will regard as quite important. As you know, the circuit court of appeals is pretty close to the district courts, and an order granting, refusing, or continuing a temporary injunction may, on a 30-day appeal, be carried to the court of appeals to decide whether the injunction was improvidently granted. There is also a provision that an order appointing a receiver may be carried in 30 days to the court of appeals. We have thought it wise to add a provision by which an order refusing the discharge of a receiver or refusing to take any steps necessary to end a receivership may also be appealed within 30 days. This offers an opportunity for quick examination by the court of appeals of any possible abuse by a district court in retaining a receivership.

I come now to the remedial features of the bill, which are not many, but some of them are really quite important: We have enlarged the time limit for application of writ of error or appeal or certiorari to the Supreme Court from the present limit of three months, and six months for the Philippines, by a provision for a further allowance of 60 days upon order of a Justice of the Supreme Court upon a proper showing. Three months is not a very long time and it occasionally happens, especially with the six months' provision for the Philippines, that parties have been delayed by excusable causes in completing their appeals or writs of error or petitions for certiorari.

Mr. WALSH. Are we to understand that cases from the Philippines go direct to the Supreme Court?

Mr. Chief Justice TAFT. Yes.

Mr. WALSH. Why do they not go to the Circuit Court of Appeals, the same as the others?

Mr. Chief Justice TAFT. It is so now. We did not disturb the present arrangement. There are only a few of them, and they come in by certiorari at any rate. Besides, we thought that probably the Ninth Circuit had enough to do without having those cases put on them, and that, as they came in by certiorari, we could dispose of them without very much difficulty.

Mr. WALSH. Are they any different in that respect from cases from Hawaii and Alaska?

Mr. Chief Justice TAFT. Not very different.

Mr. WALSH. I mean do those cases only come by certiorari?

Mr. Chief Justice TAFT. No, sir: those cases go as of course to the Circuit Court of Appeals, and then they only come to us by writ of certiorari from the Circuit Court of Appeals.

Mr. WALSH. But the Philippine cases do not come in that way?

Mr. Chief Justice TAFT. They come directly to us. I suppose it was thought that inasmuch as they have to come halfway around the world to get here they should go into a court that could finally dispose of their cases.

Mr. SUMNERS. Is there any special reason why cases from those several Territories controlled by this country should go to the courts to which you propose to respectively assign them? For instance, the Virgin Island cases, I believe, go to the Circuit Court of Appeals at Boston.

Mr. Chief Justice TAFT. No, sir: they go to the Philadelphia court. I don't know certainly why those courts were selected, but I suppose they were sent to the courts that have the most time to devote to them and that are the most convenient. I understand that the Porto Rican people like to go to Boston. Boston has not a large docket, and the cases can be promptly disposed of. None go to the second circuit, at New York, because that jurisdiction is so heavily loaded. The third circuit is not so heavily loaded, and neither is the fifth. It is more convenient to reach New Orleans from the Canal Zone than it would be to go to New York or some other place. Then, of course, on the Pacific coast the question of geography and time is one that is quite important.

Mr. SUMNERS. It would seem that the Porto Rican cases would go to New Orleans.

Mr. Chief Justice TAFT. I think they are as near to Boston, but however that may be, I think they were consulted about it, and they preferred to go to Massachusetts. We are disturbing as little as we can existing legislation.

The second remedial provision, a mere refinement of something that is now in the statutes, namely, that where the record does not show the amount involved in the controversy to be sufficient to give jurisdiction this fact may be shown, either in the court of first instance or in an appellate court. Many cases had been thrown out upon this ground.

The third remedial provision is quite important, and it is an amendment to the existing provision. An appeal is the form of review allowed in equity and admiralty cases, and a writ of error is the form of review allowed in common-law cases. Now, a case may come to the Supreme Court on appeal when it should have come on a writ of error, or on a writ of error when it should have come on appeal. In the old days that mistake would cause the appeal to be thrown out and if the time for filing the right writ had passed the complaining party would have been finally defeated. By the existing law, when a case comes up either on writ of error or appeal and it should have by appeal or writ of error, the court shall treat it as rightly brought. I think you have had an argument by the Bar Association, in which they propose to provide only one form of review by appeal. I think that would be a good thing. We have availed ourselves of the opportunity to put in something additional. A man under the act of 1916 finds it difficult to tell whether to come up under the obligatory jurisdiction of the Supreme Court—that is, by writ of error or appeal—or by petition for a certiorari. Now, if he come up on a writ of error when he should have come up on a writ of certiorari, we must defeat him. This has happened in a number of cases, and some very wise lawyers have not only taken out a writ of error but have also filed a petition for the writ of certiorari, so that if they miss on one they can catch it with the other. That condition ought not to be. It ought not to be. We have provided a remedy in this bill. Where one takes out a writ of error from the Supreme Court of the United States to a State Supreme Court, and it turns out that it should have been a certiorari, the writ of error may be considered by our court as an application for certiorari and acted upon as such.

The fourth remedial provision is for the substitution in suits in the Supreme Court for public officers who have ceased to be such, of their successors, as parties to suits brought by them or against them. For instance, a suit is begun by a public officer which goes to the Federal court. The suit is brought by a county officer, municipal officer, or State officer, or it may be that a suit is begun against such officer. It is fought out in the court below, and the case is decided there. Then it takes 18 months or two years to get the case up to us, and, in the meantime, the people have changed their county officer and elected somebody else, and when the case comes into our court we have no power to substitute for the old officer the newly elected one, and the case abates and is dismissed.

Mr. MONTAGUE. Not in case of death?

Mr. Chief Justice TAFT. Of course, there is the usual provision that the administrator or executor may be substituted for private litigants, but I am speaking now of public officers. As to them, their retirement or death abates the suit. This condition produced a great deal of inconvenience with respect to Federal officers until Congress passed a law providing that when officers of the United States, sued or suing in our Federal courts, cease to hold office, there may be substituted for them their successors in office. This provision does not apply to county officers, however. I have just written an opinion myself in an Arizona case in which county officers of Maricopa County were parties. It involved the taxability of homestead claims in a reclamation tract. The case was tried some two or three years ago, or in 1918, and all of the county officers connected with the collection of the tax were made defendants and were restrained. When the case got up here, the counsel for the plaintiff came in and moved with an air of confidence the substitution for them of the newly elected officers. There had been some changes in the officers. Not knowing the practice, or assuming that, of course, the law must be reasonable. I said from the bench, "You can take the entry," and the entry was made. Then my colleagues called my attention to a line of cases in which it had been held that there could be no such substitutions. This bill provides a remedy for that situation. You will find in section 11 of the bill the provision by which the rights of successors who are to be substituted are entirely provided for. That section provides—

"Similar proceedings may be had and taken [i.e. of substitution] where an action, suit, or proceeding, brought by or against an officer of a State, or of a county, city, or other governmental agency of a State, is pending in a court of the United States at the time of the officer's death or separation from the office.

"Before a substitution under this section is made, the party or officer to be affected, unless expressly consenting thereto, must be given reasonable notice of the application therefor and accorded an opportunity to present any objection which he may have."

You will observe that the defects in our present procedure might lead to bringing up a case, fighting it out in the court below, coming up to the Supreme Court, only to have it dismissed and all the litigation proved fruitless. It has been sometimes queried whether Congress has the right, but we have no doubt about that, because this concerns the procedure in a Federal court, and Congress can control it.

We have also enlarged the provision that takes away all rights of corporations organized by Congress to seek the Federal courts on that ground. There is now provision of law of similar tenor, but it applies only to railway corporations. This enlarges that provision, so as to make it apply to every corporation organized under Federal authority, so that if Congress desires to give it the privilege of removing cases to the Federal court or going into the Federal courts, it must expressly say so. Otherwise, under this provision, it would be treated just as if it were organized in a State.

Mr. WALSH. It is so now, without that provision, that a corporation organized under an act of Congress can go into the Federal courts?

Mr. Chief Justice TAFT. That has been decided in several cases. Of course, that depends upon the language of the statute, but this situation ought not to be, and there ought to be some real reason for going in.

Mr. WALSH. This would require that there be accorded any corporation the rights that are given to those chartered by Congress?

Mr. Chief Justice TAFT. Yes.

I have occupied enough of your time, but I shall be glad to answer any questions.

Mr. Sumners. Mr. Chief Justice, in your discussion of what I believe you classed as section 3 of your statement, dealing with the distinction between the methods of approach to your court, you referred to a suggestion that has been made by the bar association?

Mr. Chief Justice TAFT. Yes.

Mr. SUMNERS. Would you hesitate to suggest to us which would be preferable, if Congress should be inclined to look with favor upon the suggestion of the bar association, or whether that plan would be more desirable than the plan suggested here?

Mr. Chief Justice TAFT. I am sure that the court would be quite willing to accept the suggestion of the bar association. Do you mean the one abolishing all forms of review except by appeal?

Mr. SUMNERS. Yes, sir.

Mr. Chief Justice TAFT. I am sure the court would welcome that, but I venture to think that it ought to go through as a separate bill which would affect this one. We hope to get this bill through earlier than we are likely to get that bill. I am not sure, however, that the bar association bill refers review by certiorari. Ours does, by providing that when a writ of error or appeal is wrongly filed, it may be considered by the court as an application for certiorari.

Mr. MONTAGUE. Would you abolish the distinction between appeals, writs of error, and certioraris?

Mr. Chief Justice TAFT. I would abolish the distinction between writs of error and appeals, but not between them and certiorari, because it is necessary to maintain it.

Mr. MONTAGUE. When a case came up on appeal, you would treat it in one of those three aspects?

Mr. Chief Justice TAFT. Yes: if it came wrongly on appeal, I would allow the court to treat it as an application for certiorari.

Mr. SUMNERS. In view of that statement, it would seem to me that we ought to go further and provide some uniform or general method of approach to the court. Then, after the application had reached the court or after the appeal had reached the court, the court would be at full liberty to deal with the matter.

Mr. Chief Justice TAFT. I think you will find that the distinction between the method of appeal which is obligatory and that of certiorari is such that you should maintain that distinction. It would be quite embarrassing unless you did it. On the other hand, you could make it entirely uniform by providing that where an appeal would not lie, or if found by the court not to lie, then it could be considered as an application for certiorari. Those cases will not be so many under the present bill as they have been under existing law, because the existing law is a trap and is full of pitfalls.

Mr. GOODYKOONTZ. I was wondering if Congress could aid you or the court by furnishing additional personal assistance, such as law clerks, secretaries, etc.?

Mr. Chief Justice TAFT. The change might throw so much additional burden on us in the matter of certioraris that we would need another law clerk, but we could leave that to the future. I think probably that we have enough. There is, however, a bill that you have passed, and if it contains finally what you put in it, namely, a provision for meetings of the court with the senior circuit judges and the Chief Justice, and in which you put on the Chief Justice the business and correspondence all over the United States for the purpose of distributing the additional judicial force to places where it is needed, then I think that, perhaps, I might be allowed a clerk to attend to that particular business, but I am going to rely on the generosity of the appropriations committee.

Mr. MONTAGUE. Would the bill under consideration increase the duties of the circuit courts of appeals?

Mr. Chief Justice TAFT. Yes: to some extent. It would require them to take under their jurisdiction all the cases of the district courts, where those cases now go directly to the Supreme Court. Of course, the cutting off of the obligatory jurisdiction of the Supreme Court over judgments of the circuit courts of appeals does not increase at all the work of the circuit courts of appeals, but it only makes what they do final. As I say, the only difference that I can see with regard to the circuit courts of appeals would be in their jurisdiction over those cases that now go directly from the district courts to the Supreme Court. There may be, too, some cases from the courts of the dependencies that now go direct to the Supreme Court that would go to the circuit courts of appeals. I mentioned the first, third, fifth, and ninth circuits, but with those exceptions I do not think their work would be increased.

Mr. MONTAGUE. Is there any complaint from the circuit courts of appeals that they are overworked?

Mr. Chief Justice TAFT. That depends upon the circuit. They are not overworked in the Massachusetts circuit or the first circuit. They are very much overworked in the second circuit; but they have, I think, four circuit judges there, so that they get through with their work fairly well.

Mr. WALSH. That is the New York circuit?

Mr. Chief Justice TAFT. Yes. In the eighth circuit, which is a very heavy circuit, they have kept up remarkably well, considering that our circuit judge, Walter I. Smith, was incapacitated for several years. He is now dead, and Judge Kenyon has succeeded him. They have four regular circuit judges and a Commerce Court Judge. In the Philadelphia circuit I think they are up with their work.

Mr. MONTAGUE. How many judges do they have?

Mr. Chief Justice TAFT. They have three there. In the fourth circuit they have two and ought to have three. They have Judge Knapp, a Commerce Court judge, in that circuit.

Mr. MONTAGUE. I want to ask you, if it is not irrelevant to this bill, what your view is as to the other bill?

Mr. Chief Justice TAFT. You mean the bill giving the fourth circuit an additional circuit judge? I am strongly in favor of it.

Mr. MONTAGUE. You would have the circuit courts of appeals composed entirely of circuit judges?

Mr. Chief Justice TAFT. I think that one of the defects that have arisen in the administration of the circuit courts of appeals has been the change of the personnel of the courts. It has varied the uniformity of the decisions.

There is a good deal of human nature in judges, and it helps to have the same court sitting together. If you have four circuit judges who sit together, that defect is reduced a good deal, because they are always together; but where you call in district judges that condition is disturbed, and it is not as wise a method of providing for the court as where you have a solid court constantly sitting. As I say, I was very glad to see that in the Senate bill they added to what you have done in the additional judge bill by putting another circuit judge in the fourth circuit. Judge Knapp came here and urged that that be done. Though beyond the age of retirement, he is a most useful and active judge. He is conscientious and does not like to apply for qualified retirement unless he knows that the fourth circuit is fully equipped. When his place becomes vacant his office ceases, so that there ought to be another permanent judge.

Mr. MONTAGUE. He has rendered very fine service in that circuit.

Mr. Chief Justice TAFT. Yes: he is a most excellent judge.

Mr. MONTAGUE. My observation is that while there are some very fine district judges, they have not worked well in the circuit courts.

Mr. Chief Justice TAFT. I think they are better in the district court.

Mr. MONTAGUE. I think they lack the judicial environment, the judicial continuity, and other considerations that you have suggested.

Mr. Chief Justice TAFT. Yes.

Mr. DYER. Was there another matter you wished to present to the committee, Mr. Chief Justice?

Mr. Chief Justice TAFT. Yes. I hate to be in the attitude of a continual beggar from Congress, but I seem to have arrived at the court just when it was necessary. The matter to which I wish to bring your attention arises from the fact that the contract made by the reporter of the court with Banks Bros. for the reporting of our decisions has ended, and there is now no provision of law by which that work can be carried on in an effectual way at all. The price that Congress has fixed for the volumes is altogether too low, or at least too low for a private contractor. That price is $1.75 per volume, and the volumes as they should be published and have been published are worth fully $3. Therefore Banks Bros. have declined to renew the contract. It would be difficult to secure the publication of the reports by any private contractor at that price. The system has been a complicated one, involving the making of a contract by the reporter with the publisher, and his deriving a part of his compensation from that contract. It is not a good system. It is a system under which reporters in the past have made a great deal of money, but the present reporter has had the poorest pickings of the lot. He is in a very bad way now. He is trying to complete the last volume of the reports for last year, but our present opinions are not being made ready at all. As I recall the law you give him $4,500 and allow him something, or perhaps $1,500 for the second volume. After that he gets nothing, but he has to pay his expenses, and then he makes his profit out of the sales under his contract with the contractor.

Now, it has always been supposed that Banks was the one man who could give us a volume such as we wish to have.

It has been proposed that the Government should do the printing, and the Public Printer says he can do it at a reasonable price, below what the private contractors can do it for. I suppose that is, naturally, because the overhead charge does not have to be taken into consideration in the calculations of the Public Printer. We are not concerned, except as citizens, in the economic running of the Government, but we are very anxious that a permanent arrangement should be made. And, so far as we are concerned, we are quite willing—I brought this matter up in the court—we are quite willing to have the reporter paid as a Government official and free him entirely from any relation to the contract. But we would deprecate your cutting down his salary below a very substantial sum. The work is a most delicate and absorbing work, and it is most exacting.

He has now about three volumes a year to publish. He has to syllabize, as the expression is, every opinion. He has to go through every opinion when written and run down every reference in the original opinions, and correct them. And the number of corrections he has to make, even in a careful judge's opinion, you would hardly credit. And when you come to the opinion of a judge who is not so careful, who only tries to reach a conclusion, and is bothered with references, the number of corrections which the reporter has to make are very numerous and that adds greatly to the burden of his work. Then he has to prepare and furnish the references: he has to consult with the judges and go over the syllabuses, and the drafting of a syllabus is a very difficult matter in many cases.

Then he has to prepare the argument. Of course, as you undoubtedly know, it has been charged that the furnishing of the argument in the Supreme Court reports has padded the volume and increases the necessity for more volumes, increasing his compensation, as well as the compensation of the contractor, if he has a good contract.

If you should put the reporter on the basis of a regular Government salary, you should not only provide him with assistants and an office, but you should provide him with clerical help. He must have assistance: he must have one competent legal assistant, because comparison is the chief part of his work, and the only way by which he can verify his work, is by having competent persons go over the work and compare it. I can not exaggerate the importance of making that comparison and having those reports carefully prepared for publication.

Mr. GOODYKOONTZ. Does he prepare the index?

Mr. Chief Justice TAFT. Then he must prepare the index, and we should have an analytical index. You gentlemen who have consulted the reports know how very exasperating it is when you are looking for a reference not to find it in the index and have to go through the volume itself.

Mr. WALSH. The reporter has prepared a draft of a measure, at the suggestion of the chairman of the committee and myself, on which the subcommittee has had a hearing. He has prepared a bill which permits either printing under contract, or at the Government Printing Office, and fixes a definite salary for him, with assistants. His salary is to be $10,000 per year. Do you think that would be adequate?

Mr. Chief Justice TAFT. I went over that bill. He brought it to me—having a copy of what he furnished to you—at your suggestion. I cut out $1,500 for the additional work of preparing those advance sheets. I think he ought to be content with an adequate salary, not matter what work he has to do; his time will all be occupied; anyhow, he ought to do it. Therefore, I would not put in that provision. I think, on the other hand, you ought to be a little more generous with him in respect to allowances. I went over the bill and put in $3,500 for an assistant—$1,500 for clerical assistance, and $2,000 for those incidental expenses which are involved in the running of his office and for the various instrumentalities that have to be used in the work, such as stationery, and other things. Then it will be a clean business, and these allowances should be approved by the Chief Justice, I think, or by the Attorney General, if you prefer, although we know the work to be done rather more intimately. Then, I think, there ought to be a provision that the Attorney General should fix the price; or, perhaps, the Public Printer, with the reporter, should fix the price, subject to the approval of the Attorney General; or the Public Printer or the Attorney General alone, though the reporter would be pretty well advised on the subject, and, having no interest in the contract, would not be affected by the price.

Then, you ought to fix the price, as you have provided here, so that you shall get back out of the price half of what you pay the reporter in salary and for expenses—the other half being reimbursed to you by the number of reports you appropriate for public use. I do not know that anybody has the patience to go through the long list of persons who are to receive free reports. Therefore, there has been put in the measure a provision that if the Attorney General finds that some of those contributions can be wisely cut out, he may exercise his discretion to do so. They go all over the United States. You will find them kicking around in Government offices, where they are not used, and I should think there might be a good deal of economy exercised in reducing the number of volumes circulated in that way. Of course, there are some offices that do not now get them that ought to have them, and I think you might well provide for those cases. This is a pressing matter, gentlemen, and I urge you to take up the bill and adopt it in some form. We are not insistent that you include in it the right of the court or of the Chief Justice to make a contract with a private business firm. We are willing to try the Public Printer. He says he can make as good a volume as Banks. We can try him, and if he does not do it we could come to Congress again and ask for more authority. But if you are willing to give us the discretion, we do not decline it.

Mr. DYER. It would be better to let you have discretion in the matter, would it not?

Mr. Chief Justice TAFT. I should think it would be. I certainly would try the Public Printer, because I do not think we can get a contract now for the publication of these reports for anything that is reasonable. Having tried the Public Printer, we can then make up our minds as to the practical cost, after he has tried it.

Mr. BOIES. There is some criticism now with regard to the different prices put upon these reports.

Mr. Chief Justice TAFT. Yes; there is that criticism. And I want to speak to my good friend, the reporter, who is a very admirable man, in the highest terms. Mr. Knaeble is one of the best reporters the court ever had, but he is a nervous man. When he got before the subcommittee of the Committee on Appropriations, with Mr. Husted and Mr. Johnson asking him questions, the character of the examination was such that he practically lost his memory, and he could not answer questions on subjects ordinarily at his fingers' ends, and which he could have answered easily when he was in a calm state of mind.

Mr. BOIES. He did not know how much rent he was paying.

Mr. Chief Justice TAFT. No. He is a very loyal, honorable man, and he has made a great deal less out of this office than any other of the reporters which the court has had. He is now just skinning along under very little pay, doing the best he can.

You asked me about the charge. That was one of those cases that has grown up, doubtless, through a very strained construction of law that has always prevailed, that where a man bought and did not pay in cash—and also, I think, did not pay the express charges—the publisher might charge him $3 instead of $1.75. That is a thing which was brought about by too low a price fixed by Congress. That is the truth of it. I am not here to defend that, but that is the explanation of it.

Banks Bros. have gotten into such condition that they are not able to do it; they have a lost a good deal of money on the publication of the volumes.

Mr. WALSH. Referring to the bill, H.R. 10479, may I ask you a question—if you do not care to express an opinion—

Mr. Chief Justice TAFT. (interposing). If I have one you will get it.

Mr. WALSH. I do not know whether it is proper to ask the question, whether it is the view of the court that unless some relief is given in connection with this obligatory jurisdiction, that the rate at which the court's business is increasing it will be but a short time before the docket will be very badly congested and you will be very far behind with your work.

Mr. Chief Justice TAFT. Yes, Mr. Walsh. We took stock about three weeks ago, and we found that we were 40 cases behind where the court was at the same time last year. We have no doubt that unless we do get this relief the time within which cases can be reached on our docket will be increased. It now takes from 18 months to two years to reach a case on the docket. Of course, that is due to two circumstances: first, to the increase of business; and, second, to the necessity under which the court feels of responding to the motions of the Government to bring up for hearing and immediate dispatch important questions of constitutional law arising in connection with new acts of Congress and in other ways, the prompt disposition of which is in the public interest. If we could control our jurisdiction by the greater exercise of certiorari, we would feel very much less like granting motions to advance. The custom is when you make a motion to advance a case, and the motion is granted, the case is set for the first case on Monday, because we begin our business each Monday, and we are often occupied perhaps until Thursday, and sometimes during the entire week, with especially set cases and the docket is just pushed back that far. If we do not get at that docket, we can not get rid of it, but if we can get right at it we can get rid of it. Sometimes we do get a shot at it, and there are a lot of cases on it that are rotten, in the sense, as you gentlemen will understand, that they can be easily disposed of, cases that were possibly brought with the idea of delay. We are longing to get at the docket. If you give us a little more leeway in this matter, I am quite sure we can catch up and keep up with the docket.

Mr. WALSH. About how many cases are there on the docket, approximately?

Mr. Chief Justice TAFT. I insert a letter from the clerk showing the condition of the business of the court as of March 31, as compared with a corresponding date last year.

Office of the Clerk,
Supreme Court of the United States,
Washington, D.C., March 31, 1922

My Dear Mr. Chief Justice: Complying with your request, I beg to submit the following report as to the state of the docket at the present term up to this date. Also, by way of comparison, a report of the state of the docket at the last previous term to and including March 31, 1921:

	Cases docketed	Cases disposed of	Cases on docket undisposed of
1920 term, Mar. 31, 1921	840	434	406
1921 term, Mar. 31, 1922	844	390	454

Very respectfully,

Wm. R. Stansbury, Clerk

Hon. William H. Taft
Chief Justice of the United States
Washington, D.C.

Mr. MICHENER. Is it your thought, Mr. Chief Justice, that after you have disposed of what might be called war legislation, the work of the court will be normal, or do you think its work is going to increase, as it has in the last three or four years?

Mr. Chief Justice TAFT. Of course, the war increased that class of work to which I am referring on account of the necessity of having statutes immediately construed. But the result of the war has been to permanently increase the jurisdiction of the Federal courts—I mean the lower courts—and that naturally increases the amount of work that comes into the Supreme Court.

Mr. MICHENER. Is it your thought that that will continue?

Mr. Chief Justice TAFT. I think it will. Of course, I hope we can get the construction of the liquor laws settled; that is a subject that continues to be productive of a good deal of litigation. Then these other laws that are passed expand the character of Federal jurisdiction and create a good many new cases that we have to consider. I do not think there is any prospect of that kind of business substantially falling off as we get back into a normal condition.

Mr. BOIES. Congress at each session furnishes new work for the Court?

Mr. Chief Justice TAFT. Yes; it does.

I am very much obliged to you, Mr. Chairman and gentlemen, for giving me this full hearing.

The CHAIRMAN. The committee is obliged to you, Mr. Chief Justice.

(There follows a letter with further reference to the conditions of the docket of the Supreme Court:)

Office of the Clerk,
Supreme Court of the United States,
Washington, D.C., March 31, 1922

Dear Mr. Chief Justice: By way of continuation of my last report dated March 6, respecting the state of the docket, I beg to say that up to that time 796 cases in all had been docketed, leaving at that time 463 cases on the docket undisposed of. Since that time, 48 additional cases have been docketed, making 844 cases in all docketed at the present term.

Since March 6, 57 cases on the appellate docket have been disposed of. Adding these to the 333 cases previously disposed of, makes a total of 390 cases disposed of at the present term, so that there now remain 454 cases on the docket of which no disposition has been made.

Respectfully,

Wm. R. Stansbury, Clerk

Hon. William H. Taft
Chief Justice of the United States
Washington, D.C.

(Thereupon the committee adjourned.)

APPENDIX 2

William Howard Taft's Statement and Testimony before the House Judiciary Committee, 1924

JURISDICTION OF CIRCUIT COURTS OF APPEALS
AND OF THE SUPREME COURT
OF THE UNITED STATES

Committee on the Judiciary
House of Representatives
Thursday, December 18, 1924

The committee met at 10 o'clock a. m., Hon. George S. Graham (chairman) presiding.

The bill under consideration is as follows:

(H. R. 8206, Sixty-eighth Congress, first session)

A Bill To amend the Judicial Code, and to further define the jurisdiction of the circuit courts of appeals and of the Supreme Court, and for other purposes

* * * * *

STATEMENT OF CHIEF JUSTICE WILLIAM HOWARD TAFT

Chief Justice TAFT. Mr. Chairman, I do not intend to take much of your time and only intend to emphasize what has been so well said by my colleagues.

We have at one end of our conference room three or four gentlemen who are well versed in the complicated statutes giving jurisdiction to the Supreme Court. It is a great complex, this jurisdiction of the Supreme Court. I have been in the court only a short time, I am now on my fourth year, and I have yet to learn a great deal about the jurisdiction of the Supreme Court. Our court has an exceptional jurisdiction. When a man comes into our court he has to establish his right to be there. The consequence is too often that eager counsel come in all prepared for the merits of the case and are taken off their legs by a query from these three or four gentlemen to whom I refer, who show that the case has no reason for being there.

The jurisdiction of our court, I do not hesitate to say, is a trap in which counsel and litigants too often are caught, and that ought to be remedied by a single act. That is not the fault of the court, but it is the fact that the jurisdiction is to be found in dozens of statutes, and their construction by the court in an effort to reconcile them.

Now, that ought not to be. Every Federal court labors under the difficulty of the necessity of needing its jurisdiction proved. Otherwise it is an easy court to plead in. Lawyers have to show why they are there before they are heard. But when it gets to the Supreme Court it is confusion worse confounded. And this bill has been prepared not chiefly perhaps, but largely, in order to reduce all that to one statute, so that a litigant and his counsel may go to that statute and find whether he has a right to come, and how he can come to our court.

Now I do not want to dwell on the difference between the discretionary jurisdiction of the court and the obligatory jurisdiction, the first being by certiorari and the other by error or appeal; but I do wish to say one or two things about objections to our discretionary jurisdiction.

I heard the late Philander Knox, with whom I was on intimate terms, say, either to me or to some one in my hearing, a word or two indicating that he thought the question of whether a case got in by certiorari or not was governed by the temperament, the digestion and the good nature of the particular person in the court to whom the question was referred, that it was distributed in some way so that each member of the court had two or three certioraris that it could let in. I was able to recall the story that Knox himself told of being in the Attorney General's office when he was Attorney General and receiving a call from a Member of Congress who came in and said he would like to have a pardon.

Upon being asked for whom he wanted the pardon he replied "Well, for two men," naming a certain man and his son. He said that this man had been postmaster, and he and his son had connived in embezzling the funds of the Government. Knox asked the Congressman on what grounds he was asking pardon for such a crime as that, that ought to be punished severely. "Well," he said, "they are good friends of mine, they are good fellows, they were led off in this particular case, and I think if they are let out they will make good citizens" and then he said "I understood that each Member of Congress had two pardons per term, and I wanted to name these two men as my selection." [Laughter.]

And so I told Mr. Knox that we didn't distribute certioraris and their allowance on any such basis.

Now, the truth is, and I want to emphasize that because I think perhaps I have more do with certioraris in one way than any other member of the court, because I have to make the first statement of the case when a certiorari comes up for disposition: I write out every case that comes up for certiorari and I read it to the court. I think the members of the court are a little impatient sometimes because I give too much detail. Perhaps that is because I am a new member, or was a new member. And then having stated the case I go around and ask each member of the court, who has his memorandum, as to what view he takes. Then having discussed the case we vote on it.

Justice VAN DEVANTER. And sometimes it is put over to the next conference.

Chief Justice TAFT. Yes. After the index docket of each judge, certainly of my docket, you will find a note of how every man in the court voted in respect to the certiorari. And being a new member of the court and having a kind heart, I am inclined to grant probably more than is wise, and I am too often voted down on that subject to make me entirely confident that I am right.

Mr. MONTAGUE. I think it ought to be emphasized for the record, that when you ask for this large discretionary power you do not intend to relax close scrutiny on these cases.

Chief Justice TAFT. No; we do not. On the contrary, the proposition is that if we are given greater scope in this regard we may be able to give more time. We do not know whether we could, and I do not like to suggest the method proposed, but it is possible we could enlarge the time a little in that regard. But I do not think that anyone who has sat in the court as long as I have can be in the slightest degree influenced to the view that we do not give all the time necessary to these questions.

Mr. MONTAGUE. I did not intimate to the contrary.

Chief Justice TAFT. I know that; but a great many people do think it, and I think it is well to have that clearly understood.

The CHAIRMAN. The point is whether that would be relaxed in the future with an increase of applications.

Chief Justice TAFT. Of course with more cases we are likely to give more time to it. But it is an error to suppose that the scope of our investigation needs to be what a good many assume it must be, that we must decide a case in advance, that is not true. The decision of nice points in a case requires a great deal of time; but with the record before you, with the briefs on both sides, you can run through the case and determine what it means, I mean what kind of a decision it must be, and what the nature of the case is and what its importance is.

Justice VAN DEVANTER. Whether the questions are debatable?

Chief Justice TAFT. Yes; whether the questions are debatable and whether they are of such importance as to warrant an investigation, or whether they concern a question in which the circuit courts of appeals have differed, so that uniformity requires us to make a decision in the case; it is easy to determine as to those questions, whereas any final settlement of the case requires a great deal of time. That is the reason why we make a distinction; and it is the reason why we are able to dispose of as many cases as we have done on certiorari.

Then, as to the history of this bill, when I came into the court I found Mr. Justice Day at the head of a committee looking to the framing of a bill which looks to the betterment of conditions with respect to the jurisdiction of the courts. Mr. Justice Day was, as you know, ill toward the end of his term; but he took part, a good deal of part in the enlargement of this bill, because, when the suggestion made to the court to get up a bill to help was received and considered by the court, a full committee was appointed, and it was deemed wisest to codify—for that is what this bill does—codify the jurisdiction of the circuit courts of appeals and of the Supreme Court so that lawyers can go to this bill and determine from it whether the case is cognizable, and how cognizable in the courts of appeal of the United States.

Mr. MONTAGUE. Simplicity and certainty.

Chief Justice TAFT. That is it. I would hardly venture to call it simple, because the subject matter is not simple. My mother when I was a boy could not get my attention to the whole Bible and both Testaments, and so she got a book that she called a Bible for learners, and in the same policy I prepared for my own comfort a general review of this House bill, which I don't know whether you have or not.

The CHAIRMAN. We have copies. They have been distributed to members of the committee.

Chief Justice TAFT. And that I think is accurate. After that I had it commented on by others in our court informed on its jurisdiction, and I think it is exact; but it is for learners, and prepared by a learner, and if you are troubled by complications in a fuller statement perhaps if you will refer to this you will get a general idea more briefly.

Then I want to say about these statistics, I invite your attention to the fact that two bills were passed for the purpose of reducing and helping us in that regard, one in 1915, the act of 1915; and the other the act of 1916. The effect of those two bills is seen in the statistics that follow. But for those acts the court would have been completely overburdened before now.

But we are on the upgrade. We had, this year, on the 1st of October, 1924, 95 more cases than we had on the 1st of October in 1923. We are now behind a year, and from three to four months, according to the time when you take your calculations. So that it takes that time between the date when the case is filed in the court and our hearing of it.

Now, that ought not to be. We ought to be able to dispose of every case we have during the term, that is between October and June.

Mr. BOIES. Does not the Chief Justice feel he ought to donate that bible for beginners to the library, some of us who are puzzled with some provisions might be enlightened?

Chief Justice TAFT. Well, I am not going into the Bible just at present; this is difficult enough. I only want to emphasize another feature. Often in the legislature there is resounding eloquence on the subject that every poor man should have the opportunity to carry his case to the last court. There is no statement that is so unfounded as that. The truth is that it is in the interest of the poor litigant that litigation should be ended, and, my dear friends, there is nothing that offers such an opportunity for delay as a suggestion that a profound constitutional question is involved in sustaining a verdict in favor of the poor litigant when the rich litigant has a long purse with which to continue the litigation.

It is a mistake to suppose that the mere suggestion of a constitutional question is something that should require the case going right through. The court ought to be able shortly to say whether the suggestion has any real substance when tested by recognized constitutional principles. You can cite the fourteenth amendment and the fifth amendment and you can get up a great deal of fog, which it is the business of the court, and which it ought to have a prompt opportunity, to clear away by saying, "This case, although it purports to involve a constitutional question, really does not, and we cut it off."

I think I have said all, gentlemen. I am indebted to you, as I am sure the whole court is, for your kindness in listening to us.

Mr. MICHENER. Is it the judgment of each individual member of the Supreme Court that this legislation should be enacted?

Chief Justice TAFT. Well, I am told by all the members that I can say that the court is for the bill. There may be one member—I do not think there are more—who is doubtful about it, or, I should say, doubtful as to its efficacy: but he said to me that I could say the whole court were in favor of the bill. The only question that he has is as to how far this will be effective to accomplish all we hope for.

Justice VAN DEVANTER. I want to say that some have thought it ought to go farther than it does. May I say one thing more? To-day there is in the statute a provision whereby the circuit court of appeals may certify important questions of law in a case then pending before it to the Supreme Court for its decision in advance of one made in that court: that is, certify important questions in the case, separating them from the body of the case, and inviting a decision on them by the Supreme Court in order for that decision may be applied when the whole case is decided.

Now, this bill enlarges that statute: it applies it to the Court of Claims and enlarges it, and the point it this: It enables courts whose decisions are to be reviewed by us, or are subject to review by us, to avail themselves of decisions on distinct questions of law unassociated with all the other complexities of the case, and then to apply them instead of going ahead and making a decision and having the whole case come up to us.

That is a matter that rests in their discretion. Whenever they are so disposed this bill provides they can do that, but the questions certified must be questions of law. The provision applies to cases that are pending.

Mr. MONTAGUE. And you thereby expedite the administration of justice?

Justice VAN DEVANTER. That is the idea.

The CHAIRMAN. We thank the members of the Supreme Court for coming here and helping us.

(Adjourned.)

Index

ABC countries, **6**:135–40

Abraham, Henry, **8**:xxvi

Acton, John E. E. D., **5**:53–55, 114

Adams, Charles Francis, **6**:34

Adams, John, **6**:68

Adams, John Quincy, **6**:4; **7**:232

Addyston Pipe & Steel Company v. United States, **1**:171; **2**:47, 90–91; **5**:209–10, 212, 226

Adkins v. Children's Hospital, **8**:123–27

administration of justice, **1**:30–35, 340; **2**:7, 10; **3**:156, 158–59, 378–79; **4**:253; **5**:138. *See also* criminal law, administration of; judicial proceedings, reform of

Admiralty Courts, **5**:92

Africa: European involvement in, **3**:359, 403–4

African Americans: enslavement of, **3**:404; federal courts and, **1**:298–99; higher education and, **2**:54–55, 181; **3**:90–91, 93; industrial education and, **1**:244; **2**:53–54, 181–82, 217, 221; **3**:91–92; progress of, **1**:245; **2**:53, 180–81, 194–95, 218; **3**:29, 387, 404; religiosity of, **2**:200–201; in the South, **1**:248, 283–85; **2**:201–3, 217, 219; **3**:92; U.S. indebtedness to, **2**:57, 220; **3**:90, 93; violence against, **1**:299; **2**:56–57; voting rights of, **1**:245–48, 284–85, 299; **3**:52–54. *See also* racism

Aguinaldo, Emilio, **1**:249; **2**:59, 64

Aikens v. Wisconsin, **4**:367; **5**:185, 214

Alabama claims, **6**:171; **7**:45, 52, 175

Alaska: Controller Railway and Navigation Co. controversy, **4**:126–47; government of, **3**:222–24, 230–33, 257, 283; resources of, **3**:232; **4**:88–91; transportation needs of, **4**:359–65

Alberto v. Nicolas, **8**:367–73

Aldrich-Vreeland Act (1908), **3**:149–50

Alien Act (1920), **8**:163

aliens: Americans in China as, **1**:112–13; federal responsibility for, **3**:49; **4**:19; **6**:151–65; international law and, **6**:178; violence against, **6**:149–57, 163; as workers on Panama Canal, **1**:153, 185–86; **2**:163

Alsace-Lorraine, **7**:83, 118, 123, 157, 206

Altgeld, John P., **1**:321; **5**:147; **6**:75

Alverstone, Lord, **6**:197

American Bar Association, **1**:304, 323; **4**:41; **5**:17; **6**:154–55, 159–61, 163–64

American Federation of Labor, **1**:183, 185; **2**:153, 163, 164; **3**:115–19, 127, 129, 153

American Railway Union, **1**:321; **2**:89, 161; **3**:123–24; **5**:174, 185; **6**:75

Americans: characteristics of, **1**:33; **3**:273, 279, 303, 319, 336, 340; self-governing capacity of, **3**:141–42; **5**:193. *See also* United States of America

American Steel Foundries v. Tri-City Central Trades Council, **8**:xxv, 23–29

Ames, James Barr, **5**:188

amnesty, **6**:90

anthracite coal strike (1902), **1**:267; **3**:219; **6**:108–9

Anti-trust Act and the Supreme Court, The (Taft), **5**:168–242

Appleby v. City of New York, **8**:241–44

Appleby v. Delaney, **8**:244–45

appointments, Senate confirmation of, **1**:55; **6**:48–49, 52–54

arbitration: of boundary disputes, **3**:357; **4**:174–75; **6**:178, 197; of fisheries disputes, **1**:138; **3**:356–57; **4**:5–6, 298–99;

arbitration (*cont.*)

    international courts of, **6:**131, 180, 182, 186, 194–98, 200; in labor-management disputes, **1:**265–67; limits of, **6:**167; of states' debts, **6:**178–79; treaties of, **4:**173–74; **5:**156–59; **6:**82–83, 126–27, 169–71, 180–81; **7:**19, 44, 47, 166, 175, 203, 240, 243, 261, 289

Arizona: statehood of, **3:**279–83, 383; **4:**149–51, 157–58; **5:**6–7, 107–9; **6:**100

Arlington Hotel Co. v. Fant, **8:**351–53

armaments: limitation and reduction of, **7:**16, 106, 109–10, 166–67, 229, 241, 269–70, 296

Armenia, **7:**154, 207

Army, U.S.: administrative reorganization of, **1:**139–44; **3:**47–48, 375; **4:**208–10, 319–23; Brownsville Order and, **1:**228; cost of, **1:**144–45; **5:**153–54; and domestic tranquility, **1:**134, 136; **3:**62; **5:**146–47; engineering corps of, **3:**393–94; **4:**31; history of, **1:**134–38; **3:**96–99; **5:**149–50; and the Monroe Doctrine, **1:**135–36; National Guard and, **1:**141; **4:**29–30, 322; **5:**149, 152; in the Philippines, **1:**37–38, 133; **3:**292, 444–45, 447; regular branch of, **3:**96–99; **5:**147–48, 152–53; reserve corps of, **1:**144; **4:**321; responsibilities of, **4:**29; volunteer branch of, **1:**143–45; **4:**30, 322; **5:**148–50

Arnold, Matthew, **8:**17

Arthur, Chester A., **6:**95

Arthur case, **2:**87–89, 91, 124, 158–61; **3:**121–23, 125, 128

Articles of Confederation (1781), **6:**192

Article X of League of Nations, **7:**234, 246, 281, 297

Asquith, H. H., **7:**93

Atherton Mills v. Johnston, **8:**62–63

Atlantic Coast Line Railroad Co. v. Standard Oil, **8:**306–9

Bailey v. Drexel Furniture Company (Child Labor Tax Case), **8:**64–69

Bailey v. George, **8:**63–64

Balch, Thomas Willing, **6:**189

Baldwin v. Franks, **6:**163–64

Balkan states, **7:**123, 129

Ballinger, Richard A., **4:**133, 143–44

Baltic provinces, **7:**126, 129

Balzac v. Porto Rico, **8:**52–56

bank deposits: security of, **2:**111–21, 140–41

Barber, James David, **6:**5

Barclay & Co. v. Edwards, **8:**206–7

Bath-tub case, **5:**226–31

Beck, James: and the League of Nations, **7:**198

Belgium: neutrality of, **7:**85–86 violation of neutrality, **7:**85, 87

Bering Sea controversy (1902), **7:**47–48, 71, 222

Bernhardi, Frederick (German statesman), **7:**84

Bessarabia, **7:**129

Bethmann-Hollweg, Theobald (German political figure): favors League, **7:**93

Bill of Rights, **5:**86–87

Bismarck, Otto von (German chancellor, 1870–90), **7:**83, 86, 168

Blaine, James G., **5:**77; **6:**89

Bliss, Tasker, **7:**195

Blodgett v. Silberman, **8:**323–25

Board of Trade v. Olsen, **8:**127–31

body of delegates to League of Nations, **7:**243, 247, 267

Bohemia, **7:**129

Bolshevism (Bolsheviki), **7:**144, 163, 169, 170, 196, 248, 272, 277; **8:**xxxvi, 9, 10, 16, 17

Booth Fisheries Co. v. Industrial Commission of Wisconsin, **8:**240–41

Borah, William, **7:**75

Bosnia, **7:**207

bosses, political, **1:**306; **5:**70–71, 79

Boxer Rebellion (China, 1900), **6:**87; **7:**110

boycott: objections to answered, **7:**65–66; secondary, **1:**272–73; **2:**37, 87, 88, 158; **3:**19, 55, 115–23, 246; **5:**184–85, 223–24; blacklisting as form of, **1:**271, 273; use of to prevent war, **7:**98; when to institute, **7:**3, 24

Bradley, Joseph P., **1:**309

Brandeis, Louis D., **8:**xx, xxii, xxiii, xxvi

Brewer, David J., **1:**323; **5:**207–8, 218; **6:**165, 193

Brewer-Elliott Oil & Gas Co. v. United States, **8:**90–92

Briand, Aristide: favors League, **7:**70, 93

British Columbia Mills Tug & Barge Co. v. Mylroie, **8:**60–62

British League of Free Nations, **7:**190

Brooks v. United States, **8:**203–5

Brown, Henry B., **1:**304

Brown, James S., **7:**195

Brownsville Order (1906), **1:**228

Bryan, William Jennings: anti-imperialism of, **1:**181, 249; **2:**59, 65–66, 149; anti-trust proposal of, **1:**212; **2:**146; and League to Enforce Peace, **7:**93–117; and organized labor, **3:**118, 127, 129; as secretary of state, **6:**181–82; and silver issue, **2:**94–95, 138–39; Taft's criticism of, **1:**176, 181, 197, 212, 220–22, 249–54; **3:**39; in Taft's 1908 campaign speeches, **2:**43–44, 49–51, 59, 65–67, 79–84, 99–105, 140–41, 149–52; and tariff revision, **2:**77, 95

Bryce, James, **6:**188; **7:**70

budget: English system of framing, **6:**14–15; federal under Taft, **3:**465, 468–70; **4:**21, 313–14; U.S. practice of devising, **3:**464–65; **4:**244–46

Bureau of Indian Affairs, **4:**343–44

Burger, Warren, **8:**xviii

Burke, Edmund, **5:**32

Burns, James McGregor, **6:**4

Burton, David H.: quoted, **8:**50, 143

Butler, Nicholas Murray, **5:**6

Butler, Pierce, **8:**xx

cabinet, British, **6:**31

cabinet, U.S. president's, **1:**58–59; **6:**30–36, 48–49; Congress and, **4:**336–39; Supreme Court and, **6:**42–43

Calhoun, John C., **5:**89–90

Canada, Dominion of, **6:**191–92; reciprocity in trade with, **4:**104–10, 115–25; U.S.

relations with, **3:**357; **4:**8, 16–17; **7:**43, 63, 222, 242

Canning, George, **6:**135

Cannon, Joseph, **6:**79

capital, aggregated, **5:**240; abuses of, **1:**32, 168, 239, 269–70, 288–89, 300–301; benefits of, **1:**15, 168–69, 207, 212, 257; **2:**44; **3:**13; labor's relationship to, **1:**15–16, 256–62, 264–65, 318; **2:**41; legality of, **1:**208–9, 212, 252; **2:**48; **3:**14, 418–19, 424; private property and, **1:**14–16, 168, 257, 260; Supreme Court and, **4:**166–67. *See also* corporations; monopolies; overcapitalization; trusts; wealth

Cardozo, Benjamin, **8:**xxvi

Carroll v. United States, **8:**186–94

Carson Petroleum Co. v. Vial, **8:**359–63

Catholic Americans, **3:**250–51, 253

Catholic Church. *See* Roman Catholic Church

Cato the Elder (Roman senator and moralist), **6:**10

caucuses, party, **5:**70

Cecil, Lord Robert: quoted, **7:**260

Central Union Telephone Co. v. City of Edwardsville, **8:**230–32

Champlain Realty Co. v. Brattleboro, **8:**99–101

Charles Nelson Co. v. United States, **8:**110–12

Chesapeake & Ohio Railway Co. v. Stapleton, **8:**381–85

Chase, Samuel, **5:**129

Chicago & Northwestern Railway Co. v. Nye Schneider Fowler Co., **8:**81–83

Chicago Great Western Railway Co. v. Kendall, **8:**172–74

child labor, **2:**22, 86; **3:**54, 437; **5:**94; **7:**32; **8:**47, 62, 63

China: American investments in, **1:**113–14; **3:**366–67; **4:**10–11, 183–85, 289–90, 304–5. *See also* Open Door policy

Chinese: naturalization issue, **7:**64

Chisholm v. Georgia, **5:**87

Christianity: international missions of, **2:**207; **3:**276–77, 346–48, 400–404. *See also* Roman Catholic Church

church and state, **2**:188; **3**:252–53, 291
City of Boston v. Jackson, **8**:98–99
civil servants, **1**:58–59; **3**:371–72; **4**:73–74;
    6:50–52, 55–56, 67
civil service law, federal, **1**:58, 61; **4**:71;
    6:51–52
Civil War, U.S., **1**:122; **8**:36; analogy, **7**:81;
    Pennsylvania's role in, **3**:79–81, 98;
    Southern traditions and, **3**:332, 337,
    342; Ulysses S. Grant's role in,
    1:126–31
classes, social, **2**:40; **5**:67, 139
Clayton Antitrust Act (1914), **5**:168, 171; **8**:273
Clemenceau, George: quoted on League of
    Nations, **7**:198
Cleveland, Grover: biographical sketch of,
    3:58–63; and Gorman-Wilson Tariff,
    3:61; **6**:26; and interstate commerce
    laws, **1**:173; and Monroe Doctrine,
    1:138; and Pullman strike, **1**:322; **3**:62;
    5:147; **6**:75; and Sherman Antitrust
    Act, **1**:171; **5**:203; and silver issue,
    3:61–62
Cline v. Frank Dairy Co., **8**:291–95
coastlines, fortification of, **1**:138, 140–42;
    3:48, 256; **5**:151; Chesapeake Bay, **3**:352,
    376, 469
Cohens v. Virginia, **1**:298; **2**:8; **5**:89
Coke, Sir Edward (Lord Chief Justice of
    England), **5**:104
Colgate v. United States, **8**:390–91
Commission on Conciliation, **7**:47, 48, 50,
    56, 180
Commission on Economy and Efficiency,
    3:470–72; **4**:228–49, 260–71
common law: civil law contrasted with,
    1:325–28, 332; employers' liability
    under, **2**:17, 35, 86; **3**:54; **4**:252; federal
    procedure in, **1**:26; **3**:378; **4**:334–35;
    history of, **5**:187–88; individual inde-
    pendence under, **5**:139; inheritance
    under, **1**:34; judicial application of,
    5:170, 178; jury trial under, **1**:25–28,
    329; labor combinations under,
    5:182–84, 223; restraint of trade under,
    3:248, 419; **5**:168–82, 204–8, 210, 212,

216, 221; and Sherman Antitrust Act,
    4:160–61; **5**:218, 220, 232; in territories
    acquired from Spain, **1**:328–29, 331–32;
    in U.S. courts, **5**:119
*Compañia de Navegacion v. Fireman's Fund
    Insurance Co.,* **8**:328–30
compulsory military training, **7**:111
confederation of small states, **7**:37
Congress, U.S.: appropriation power of,
    1:60; **6**:27–28, 104, 437; and cabinet
    officers, **1**:60; **4**:336–39; expenditures
    by, **1**:57; **3**:392, 396, 465; **5**:97–98;
    6:14, 16; and foreign relations, **6**:81;
    incorporation of power of, **3**:424; in-
    vestigating power of, **1**:61; and juris-
    diction of federal courts, **1**:311, 317;
    limits on power of, **1**:59; **6**:95; states'
    powers and, **3**:436–37; and territories
    such as the Philippines, **1**:84. *See also*
    Senate, U.S.
Congress of Nations, **7**:190
Connelly v. Union Sewer Pipe Company, **4**:367
Conscription Law, **7**:91
conservation (of resources), **5**:96; definition
    of, **3**:213, 249; **4**:78; federal role in,
    3:302, 432, 438, 458; soils and, **3**:430;
    Theodore Roosevelt and, **3**:219–20,
    427, 458; **4**:79, 84–85. *See also* forests,
    preservation of; public lands; reclama-
    tion (of arid lands)
Constantinople: as mandatory, **7**:207
Constitution, U.S.: church and state under,
    3:252–53, 291, 349; criminal prosecu-
    tion under, **1**:332–37, 339; "general
    welfare" clause of, **3**:437; individual
    rights under, **1**:329; **3**:84; **5**:139; inter-
    state controversies under, **1**:303,
    309–10; **6**:172–73; liberal construction
    of, **1**:297; **5**:20–21, 87–89, 91; "neces-
    sary and proper" clause of, **6**:163;
    8:157; preamble of, **5**:19–22; and the
    presidency, **1**:55–56, 59; **6**:13; prize
    courts under, **6**:195; republican gov-
    ernment in, **5**:56–57, 59–60; separa-
    tion of powers under, **3**:60; **4**:152;
    5:108–9, 117, 123; **6**:11–12, 94–95,

99–104; slavery under, **5**:90; strict
construction of, **1**:297–98; **5**:86–87;
taxation under, **1**:34; **3**:197; treaties
under, **6**:83, 161–63. *See also* Bill of
Rights; *specific amendments*
Constitutional Convention, U.S., **5**:23–24,
86; **6**:13
constitutionality: determination of, **1**:297;
2:8; **3**:436; **4**:153; **5**:104–7, 118, 190;
6:23–25, 40–41; 101–3; of League of
Nations, **7**:251; of League to Enforce
Peace, **7**:55–62
constitutions: amendment of, **5**:40–42, 107,
192; as fundamental law, **3**:279,
283–83; written, **2**:8; **6**:50
Controller Railway and Navigation Company, **4**:129–32, 136–44
Cooke v. United States, **8**:213–16
Coolidge, Calvin, **6**:4
Cooper, In re, **6**:193–94
Coronado Coal Co. v. United Mine Workers,
8:217–22
corporations: benefits of, **1**:168–69, 258, 269,
299–302; federal charter and registration of, **1**:213; **3**:11, 181, 193, 421–25;
4:39, 168–71; in federal courts, **1**:213,
303–4, 307–10; **5**:127–28; federal excise
tax on income of, **3**:135, 180–81, 195,
197–99, 239–41; Fourteenth Amendment and, **1**:308; overcapitalization of,
1:232, 290, 299–300; **3**:15; political
power of, **1**:289, 300, 303–6; **2**:22;
5:34, 51, 70
Council of Conciliation, **7**:145, 189
County of Spokane v. United States, **8**:354–59
court cases. *See individual case names*
courts, international, **3**:357–58; **4**:6–7,
189–90; **6**:128–29, 131, 143, 172, 193–97
Covington Drawbridge Co. v. Shepherd, **1**:314
Cox, Archibald, **8**:xxx
Craig v. Hecht, **8**:151–54
criminal law, administration of, **1**:30–33, 35;
3:156; **5**:138; constitutional limitations
and, **1**:332–37, 339; in England,
1:336–40; in territories acquired from
Spain, **1**:329–32, 340

criticism of the League, constructive,
7:182–84
Cuba: integrity guaranteed, **7**:132; relation to
United States, **7**:60–61, 69
*Cumberland Telephone & Telegraph Co. v.
Louisiana Public Service Commission*,
8:95–97
Cushman, Francis, **3**:228–29
Czechoslovaks ("Czecho-Slovaks"), **7**:123,
126, 162, 202–3, 219

Dalmatian Coast, **7**:286
Danbury Hatters case, **5**:223
Danzig, **7**:277–78
Dardanelles, **7**:169
Daugherty, Harry, **8**:xvii
Day, William R., **5**:167, 226
*Dayton–Goose Creek Railway Co. v. Interstate
Commerce Commission*, **8**:154–57
Debs, Eugene V.: in *Phelan* case, **2**:89–90,
161; **3**:123–24, 129; and Pullman strike,
1:322–23; **2**:161; **3**:123; **5**:147, 174; **6**:75
Debs, In re, **1**:321, 323; **3**:126–27; **5**:147; **6**:76,
165
Decatur v. Paulding, **6**:42–43
deficit, federal, **3**:459, 465–66; proposed
remedies for, **3**:133–34, 195, 370–71,
454
Democratic Party: antitrust proposal of,
1:173–74; and federal power, **6**:166;
Grover Cleveland and, **3**:61–62; history of, **5**:86, 90–91; and organized
labor, **2**:153, 164; **3**:118; and revenue
tariffs, **2**:77, 100; **3**:17, 40, 196; and
the South, **1**:242, 245, 247–48; support
for the League, **7**:183; **2**:135, 137; Taft's
criticism of, **1**:176–77, 181; **3**:15, 17, 20,
25, 34–35; in Taft's 1908 campaign
speeches, **1**:69; **2**:23–25, 29, 39, 93
Díaz, Porfirio (Mexican statesman), **3**:285–87,
363; **4**:13, 176, 181; **6**:140
Dier v. Banton, **8**:132–34
Dingley Tariff: enactment of, **1**:222; **2**:101;
3:37; and Panic of 1907, **2**:33, 101;
Payne-Aldrich Tariff contrasted with,
3:170–73; revenue resulting from,

Dingley Tariff (*cont.*)
    3:465; revision of, 1:224–27, 287;
    2:102–4; 3:16–17, 45–46, 56, 237,
    451–52; schedules of, 3:169–70
Director General of Railroads v. Kastenbaum,
    8:149–51
direct primary: uses and abuses of, 5:69–82
disarmament, 7:132–33, 150–51, 221
disease control, 7:32
District of Columbia, 2:86; 3:54, 66–71, 380;
    4:65–70, 347–50
divine right of kings, 7:128
Dollar Diplomacy, 6:123
Donegan v. Dyson, 8:227–30
double jeopardy, 6:159–60; 8:101
Dred Scott v. Sandford, 5:91, 115–16; 6:102–3
Dreyfus affair (1894), 1:332
due process, 8:101, 330, 363
Dugan v. Ohio, 8:326–27

economic barrier: discussion of, 7:163
eight-hour law, 1:153, 182, 185–86; 3:18;
    4:61–62
election laws, federal, 1:299; 5:146–47; 6:58
electorate: exclusions from, 5:24–25, 29; role
    of regarding fundamentals of law,
    5:192–95
Eleventh Amendment, 5:87
Elkins Act (1903), 1:195–97, 210; 2:45
Ellsworth, Oliver, 5:102
Emancipation Proclamation, 1:283; 3:387;
    4:70; 6:110
Employers' Liability Act (1908), 1:182, 206–7,
    291–92; 2:17, 22, 35, 86; 3:18, 54, 416;
    5:128
Employers' Liability and Workmen's Com-
    pensation Commission: findings of,
    4:250–53
England: colonial management by, 1:47–48;
    constitution of, 6:11, 14–15, 16–18, 21,
    31; income tax in, 3:199; judicial his-
    tory and procedure in, 1:31, 35,
    275–76, 312–14, 336–39; 2:11; and her
    navy, 7:151; 3:439; 5:187–88; 6:186;
    Privy Council of, 6:191–92, 199; U.S.
    relations with, 7:45

equity: procedure in, 5:132, 234; history of,
    1:275–76, 312–14, 330; 5:188; principles
    of, 3:127; reform of federal, 2:11;
    3:158–59, 378; 4:334–35. *See also* re-
    ceivers (in equity)
Espionage Act (1917), 8:165
Essgee Co. v. United States, 8:135–37
Europe: rearranging map of, 7:130, 141
executive council: power of, 7:191, 269
Ex parte. *See name of litigant*

Falkland Islands, 6:89
Farrand, Max, 5:10, 86
Federalist, The, 5:57–58, 83–86
Federalist Party, 5:86–88; 6:39–40
Federal Trade Commission, 8:289
Federal Trade Commission Act (1914), 5:168,
    171
*Federal Trade Commission v. Claire Furnace
    Co.,* 8:288–91
*Federal Trade Commission v. Curtis Publishing
    Co.,* 8:108–10
*Federal Trade Commission v. Western Meat
    Co.,* 8:273–74
federation, international, 6:183–91, 198–200
fellow-servant rule, 1:206; 2:17, 35, 86; 3:18,
    54
Field v. Clark, 6:170
Fifteenth Amendment, 1:245, 247, 284–85;
    3:52–53
Fifth Amendment, 5:93; 8:107
Filipinos: goodwill of, 1:38–40, 52; readiness
    of for self-government, 1:40–44, 50,
    68, 249–50, 331; 2:60; 4:326–27;
    5:71–72. *See also* Philippines, the
Finland, 7:119, 219
First National Bank v. Missouri, 8:157–60
Fitch, James, 3:139–41
Fiume (Adriatic port), 7:272, 278, 285
Foch, Marshall, 7:272
Fong Yue Ting v. United States, 6:170
Foraker Act (1899), 3:72–78; 6:76–77, 141–42
force: discussion of, 7:97, 112, 145, 173; neces-
    sary for an effective League, 7:101, 119
Ford v. United States, 8:281–85
forests: and fires, 4:57–58; preservation of,

3:217, 300, 432–33; 4:52; 5:96; refor-
estation and, 3:433; 4:58; states' role
in, 3:214, 300, 334, 433; statistics on,
3:213, 260; 4:83–84; in U.S. history,
4:83
Four Aspects of Civic Duty (Taft), 1:3–61
Four Horsemen, 8:128
Fourteen Points, 7:126, 129, 132, 141, 143,
150–51, 153, 158–59, 163, 169, 198
Fourteenth Amendment: and African Americans, 1:244, 283; due process under,
3:85; equal protection under, 4:367;
8:106; individual rights under, 5:86–87,
193; property rights of corporations
and persons under, 1:302–3, 308
Frankfurter, Felix, 8:xxix
freedom of the seas, 7:147, 150, 163
French Association for the Society of Nations, 7:191
French Directory, 6:35
Freund v. United States, 8:85–87
fugitive slave laws, 1:298; 5:90–91
Fuller, Ex parte, 8:131–32
Fuller, Melville, 5:165, 200–203; 6:172–73,
193; 8:xxv

Gaines v. Washington, 8:330–32
Garfield, James A., 6:52–53
Garfield, James R., 1:172, 193; 6:105–6, 108
Germany: colonies of, 7:129, 152–53; mem-
bership in the League, 7:133–34; not
join League at once, 7:176; willingness
to join League, 7:101–2
Gilbert Bill, 1:183
Gitlow v. New York, 8:xxix
Goethals, George W., 3:51, 107; 4:331
Goltra v. Weeks, 8:253–56
Gompers, Samuel: and injunctions, 1:183–84;
2:155, 164; 3:115–18; and presidential
campaign of 1908, 2:153, 155, 164, 166;
and secondary boycotts, 1:185; 2:87;
3:115; 8:10
Gong Lum v. Rice, 8:299–303
Gorgas, William C., 1:150–51
Gorman-Wilson Tariff, 1:287; 2:19–20, 95,
100–101; 3:39, 61, 453; 6:26

graduated income tax, 5:99
Grand Army of the Republic, 3:136–38
Grant, Ulysses S., 1:30, 120–21, 125–31;
6:95–96, 98
Gray, Horace, 6:68, 69
Great Britain, representation of, 7:247. *See
also* England
Greater League, 7:95, 147–48
"Great Powers" and the League, 7:134,
147–48, 165, 176, 178–81, 186, 201–3
Greece: history of, 6:184–85
Greene, In re, 5:197–99, 206
Grey, Lord Edward: favors League, 7:70, 93
Grossman, Ex parte, 8:180–86

habeas corpus, 1:327; 3:84–85; 6:110; 8:151
Hague Conferences, 3:358; 6:126, 128, 190,
194–96, 198; 7:46
Haiti, 6:139, 143, 167
Hallanan v. Eureka Pipe Line Co., 8:118–19
Hamilton, Alexander, 5:83–85; 6:39; 8:xvii
Hammerschmidt v. United States, 8:165–67
Hampton & Co. v. United States, 8:319–22
Hampton Institute, 2:54, 197, 217, 221;
3:354–55
Hanover Fire Insurance Co. v. Harding,
8:270–73
Harding, Warren, 8:xvii
Harlan, John Marshall, 5:202, 210, 212,
218–22; 6:197
Harrison, Benjamin, 1:67, 171, 173; 3:87–88;
6:4, 21, 89
Harrison Anti-Narcotic Act (1914), 8:314
Hay, John, 6:86–87, 126, 169–71, 175–76
Hayashi, Count, 6:149
Hay-Buneau-Varilla Treaty (1903), 1:149;
6:73, 85
Hayes, Rutherford B., 6:27–28; 1876 presi-
dential election disputed, 7:145
Hay-Pauncefote Treaty (1901), 4:276–79, 282,
330
Heitler v. United States, 8:104–6
Henry, Patrick, 7:227
Hepburn "Railroad Rate" Act (1906):
amendment of, 1:172, 175–76,
200–203; 3:245; compared to Elkins

Hepburn "Railroad Rate" Act (1906) (*cont.*)
Act, **1**:195, 197, 211; consequences of,
1:172–73, 197–99, 289–90; **2**:45; **3**:7,
38; enactment of, **1**:236; **3**:186; objec-
tions to, **1**:193–94, 197; **3**:409–10; and
Panic of 1907, **1**:236, 238; provisions
of, **1**:192–93; **3**:244
Herzegovina ("Herzogovinia"), **7**:207
Hetrick v. Village of Lindsey, **8**:167–68
Hildreth v. Mastoras, **8**:21–23
Hill, Sarah Althea, case of, **6**:70–71
Hill v. Wallace, **8**:70–73
History of English Law, The (Maitland), **5**:187
Holden v. Hardy, **5**:195
Holmes, Oliver Wendell Jr., **2**:3; **5**:111–12,
167, 185, 207, 213–15, 228–30
Holt, Hamilton, **6**:122, 131–32, 133–47, 184
Holy Alliance, **7**:128
Holy Roman Empire, **6**:187–89, 198–99
Honduras, **6**:168
Hoover, Herbert, **6**:4; **8**:xxvi
House, Colonel, **7**:195
House Judiciary Committee: Taft's 1922 testi-
mony before, **8**:395–416; Taft's 1924
testimony before, **8**:417–22
Howat v. Kansas, **8**:46–47
Hughes, Charles Evans, **2**:77, 102; **5**:125, 167,
216; **7**:94
Hughes Bros. Timber Co. v. Minnesota,
8:268–70
Hungary, **7**:272–73

immigrants: federal responsibility for, **3**:49;
4:19; **6**:151–65; international law and,
6:178; violence against, **6**:149–57, 163;
7:291
immigration service, U.S., **8**:174
income tax: amendment for, **1**:215; **3**:134,
200–203, 239; constitutionality of,
1:215; **3**:32, 133–34, 196–97, 238–39;
corporate excise tax as, **3**:135, 180–81,
195, 197–99, 239–41; graduated, **3**:198;
5:99; immunity from, **5**:50; on individuals, **3**:201–2
incorporation, federal, **3**:11, 437, 460; **4**:39,
168–71

indemnities, **7**:271–72
individuals: character and conscience of,
5:64–65; Fourteenth Amendment and,
1:302; **5**:86, 193; private property and,
1:14–16, 256, 302; rights of, **1**:328–29;
2:66; **3**:84; **4**:150–53; **5**:21–22, 52, 65,
190–92
industrial education, **1**:49, 91; **2**:53–54,
196–97, 220; **3**:315, 355
inheritance: federal tax on, **1**:214–15; **3**:46,
133, 195–97; state jurisdiction over,
1:34, 213–14; **3**:202–3; **5**:99–100
initiative (for laws), **5**:45–52, 55, 137; **6**:100
injunctions, **1**:274–79; **3**:19–20; against corporations, **1**:274; **2**:90, 95; **5**:234; Interstate Commerce Commission and,
3:409; in labor disputes, **1**:183–85, 274,
321–22; **2**:92, 154–55; **3**:115–18, 121–22,
124–28, 185; notice of, **1**:183, 277–78;
2:39, 92; **3**:21–22, 40, 115–17, 154,
379–80; **4**:42; organized labor's campaign against, **1**:183–85, 279; **3**:115–18;
Supreme Court and, **2**:155; **3**:20, 21
In re. *See name of litigant*
Internal Revenue Service, **8**:79, 379
international army: need for, **7**:133
international bureaus, **7**:32
International Court, **7**:53, 56, 62–63, 94, 172,
179, 189, 209
International Labor Bureau, **7**:228
international law: conference to agree upon,
7:46, 48; definition of, **7**:62, 88,
112–13; method of formulating, **7**:5–6;
League to determine methods for
writing laws, **7**:94–95
International Prize Court, **7**:57
interstate commerce, federal jurisdiction
over, **1**:303, 310; **3**:437; **5**:92–94
Interstate Commerce Commission: appeals
of decisions by, **3**:187, 244–45, 408–9,
411; and the Panama Canal, **4**:280–82;
powers of, **3**:7–8, 10, 188–90, 456–57;
and railroad rates, **1**:172, 204; **3**:186,
189–90, 411–14; and railroad stocks,
1:200–201; **3**:189–90, 414–15, 457;
4:74–76; and receivership, **6**:58; and

worker safety, **3**:185, 416; **4**:75. *See also*
Elkins Act; Hepburn "Railroad Rate"
Act
*Interstate Commerce Commission v. United
States ex rel. Los Angeles*, **8**:391–92
isolation: inconceivable, **7**:285–86
Italy: entrance of into war, **7**:285–86

Jackson, Andrew, **5**:90; **6**:102, 114
Jackson, Howell E., **5**:198–99, 206
Japan, **1**:115–19; **4**:185–86; **6**:149, 157
Japanese immigration and naturalization,
7:52, 64, 243–44, 295
Jay, John, **5**:87–88
Jay's Treaty (1795), **6**:68–69, 97; **7**:57
Jefferson, Thomas: on the cabinet, **6**:35–36;
communication with Congress, **6**:38;
and judicial authority over the president, **6**:98–99, 102; and *Marbury v.
Madison*, **6**:39–42; as president,
6:98–99, 110–15; and slavery, **5**:90; and
strict construction of the Constitu-
tion, **1**:298; **5**:87–89; **7**:108, 161, 238
Jews: American, **3**:95; and religious liberty,
7:154–56; on Romania and Poland,
7:284
Johnson, Andrew, **6**:49–50, 90, 99
Joint Traffic case, **5**:205, 207, 210, 220
judges: appointment power of, **4**:216; **5**:130;
6:57–58; functions of, **1**:123; **5**:136–37,
190; history of, **6**:185; impeachment
of, **1**:298; **4**:157; **5**:128–30; in international law, **6**:200; in jury trials,
1:25–26, 28, 31; **3**:156–58; **5**:126; recall
of, **4**:150, 153–57; **5**:107–10, 124; selection of, **4**:155–56; **5**:119–22, 188–89; so-
called legislative powers of, **5**:136–39;
tenure of, **4**:155–56; **5**:102–3, 123–27;
6:40
Judges Act of 1925, **8**:xviii, xxi, 399
Judges Conference, **8**:xxii
judicial proceedings, reform of, **1**:30–33, 35,
340; **2**:10; **3**:378, 438–39; **4**:40–41;
5:115, 138–39. *See also* administration
of justice; criminal law, administration of; litigation, costs of

judicial review, **1**:297; **2**:8; **4**:153; **5**:104–7;
6:23–25, 40–41, 101–3
judicial settlement of international disputes:
history, **6**:183–200
judiciary, federal: and civil liberty, **3**:88; and
constitutionality, **1**:297; **5**:105–7; criticism of, **1**:295–99, 304, 306, 317,
323–24; establishment of, **5**:101–2; jurisdiction of, **1**:294, 297–99, 302–11,
314, 316–17, 319
judiciary, independent, **4**:152–53, 155;
5:108–9, 114–15, 123–24, 192; **6**:128
Judiciary Act (1789), **3**:116; **5**:102
Judiciary Committee, House: Taft's 1922 testimony before, **8**:395–416; Taft's 1924
testimony before, **8**:417–22
jurisprudence, sociological, **5**:144
jury trial: in antitrust cases, **1**:211; in civil
cases and territories formerly under
civil law, **1**:329–32, 340; under common law and U.S. Constitution,
1:329; in contempt cases, **1**:322–23;
2:39, 92–93, 150, 164–66; **3**:23, 40, 119,
129; in criminal cases, **1**:336–41; in employers' liability cases, **2**:16–17; in federal courts, **1**:26, 31, 329–30; **3**:22–23;
6:152–53; importance of, **1**:25–26;
judge's role in, **1**:25–26, 28, 304,
336–38, 340; right to, **8**:52
justiciable, definition of, **6**:173; **7**:3–4, 166

Kaiser Wilhelm, **7**:126–27
Kansas v. Colorado, **6**:172–73, 193
Kant, Immanuel, **7**:104
Keating-Owen Child Labor Act (1916), **8**:64
Keefe, Daniel, **2**:164
Keller v. Potomac Electric Power Co., **8**:119–23
Kelley v. Oregon, **8**:280–81
Knox, Philander C., **6**:127, 172–73; answered
by Taft, **7**:255–62; on League,
7:261–62

labor: improving condition of, **7**:31; relationship to capital of, **1**:15–16, 256–61,
264–65, 318; **2**:41; right to organize of,
1:181–82, 212, 262, 318–19; right to

labor (*cont.*)
    strike of, **1**:267–68, 318–19; **2**:36–37,
    125, 160; **3**:120, 122–23, 125; **5**:183–84;
    role of in safety legislation, **1**:263;
    Sherman Antitrust Act and, **4**:367–68;
    5:223–24; Supreme Court and rights
    of, **5**:194–95. *See also under* boycott;
    under injunctions; *names of organiza-*
    tions
Lamar, Joseph R., **5**:167
Lamar, Lucius Q. C., **3**:207–9
Lancaster v. McCarty, **8**:201–3
lands, public. *See* public lands
Laney, Lucy, **2**:194–95, 197, 219
Lansing, Robert, **7**:195
Lardy, M., **6**:190
Larson v. South Dakota, **8**:349–51
Laski, Harold, **6**:5
Latin America, U.S. relations with, **3**:363–66;
    4:12–15, 174–83, 288–93, 305–10
law: "judge-made," **5**:137; professional prac-
    tice of, **2**:17–18, 211–14; **3**:324;
    5:133–36, 142–44
Layne v. Western Well Works, **8**:xix
League of Nations: analogy to domestic gov-
    ernment, **7**:76; as barrier to war,
    7:237–40; constitutionality of,
    7:147–48, 255–62; covenants as re-
    vised, **7**:287–93; feasibility, **7**:176;
    functions, **7**:179–81; fundamental plan
    of, **7**:179–81; greatest step in history,
    7:263; objections to the League,
    7:63–64, 66–67, 182, 184, 192, 230;
    opposition to, **7**:269; reasons for join-
    ing, **7**:230–31; withdrawal from, **7**:296
League to Enforce Peace: constitutionality of,
    7:55–61; objections to, **7**:74–77;
    planks of platform, **7**:72–73; purposes
    of, **7**:73–74
Lederer v. Stockton, **8**:79–80
Lee, Robert E., **3**:343
legislatures, constitutional obligations of,
    6:25
Lehigh Valley Railroad Co. v. Board of Public
    Utility Commissioners, **8**:337–42
Leo XIII (pope), **2**:188; **3**:145, 252–53

"Lesser Powers" and the League, **7**:133–34
Liberty Oil Co. v. Condon National Bank,
    8:97
"Liberty under Law" (Taft), **8**:3–18
Lincoln, Abraham, **1**:125, 283; **2**:130–32; **5**:68,
    77; **6**:34, 36, 102–3, 107, 110; **7**:81
Lithuanians, **7**:162
litigation, costs of, **2**:10–17; **3**:158–59; **4**:39,
    217, 252; **5**:115, 131–32
Livingston, Edward, **6**:68–69, 110–15
Lloyd George, David: quoted, **7**:105, 202
Loan Association v. Topeka, **5**:52–53
Lochner v. New York, **5**:194; **8**:xxviii
Lodge, Henry Cabot, **5**:6; **6**:179–80; **7**:93–94,
    192, 198
Loewe v. Lawler, **5**:223–24
Long, Huey, **8**:95
Longborough, Lord: quoted, **7**:58
Longworth, Alice Roosevelt, **8**:xxix
Lurton, Horace H., **5**:167, 210, 227
lynching, **1**:30–31, 36, 341; **3**:378; **6**:151–57

Madison, James: and federal authority over
    interstate commerce, **5**:85; and *Mar-*
    bury v. Madison, **6**:40–41; and presi-
    dent's removal power, **6**:49; and
    republican government, **5**:57–59; and
    slavery, **5**:90; and strict construction
    of the Constitution, **5**:87, 89; **7**:233
Mahler v. Eby, **8**:163–64
Maine, Henry Sumner, **5**:11–12
majority rule, **3**:265–66, 323; **5**:21, 65; and
    tyranny, **4**:150–52; **5**:22, 53–55, 57
mandatories, **7**:207, 217, 240, 283, 289
Maple Flooring Manufacturing Ass'n v. United
    States, **8**:224–25
Marbury v. Madison: impact of, **2**:8; **5**:89,
    105; Taft's explanation of, **6**:39–42;
    8:xxvii
marriage: jurisdiction over, **3**:438; women
    and, **3**:314, 316
Marshall, John: as chief justice, **1**:298; **3**:436;
    5:88, 91, 122; as congressman, **6**:69;
    and *Marbury v. Madison,* **5**:89, 105;
    6:39–42; as secretary of state, **5**:88;
    and "We the People," **5**:20; **8**:xxvii

Martin v. Hunter's Lessee, **5:**20

Maryland v. Soper No. 1, **8:**232–36

Mason, Alpheus Thomas, **8:**xxv

Mason, Edward Campbell, **6:**20–21

Mason, George, **7:**227

McCulloch v. Maryland, **5:**89; **8:**xxvii

McKenna, Joseph, **5:**226; **8:**xxii

McKinley, William, **2:**26; **3:**36, 346; **6:**46; domestic policies of, **1:**173; **2:**173–74; international affairs under, **1:**287; **2:**59; **3:**446; **6:**87, 157

McReynolds, James Clark, **8:**xx, xxv

meat, inspection of, **1:**174–75

meat packers' trust, **5:**212–14

Mecklenburg Declaration (1775), **3:**83, 85–86

merchant marine: importance of, **3:**226, 235–36, 334; **4:**19; Panama Canal and, **3:**272; **4:**18; subsidization of, **3:**226–27, 234–35, 382; **4:**19

merit system, **4:**19–20, 286–87; **6:**51, 55

Mesopotamia, **7:**229

Mexico: Taft's administration and, **3:**363; **4:**175–82, 293, 299–300; Woodrow Wilson and, **6:**74–75, 86, 145. *See also* Díaz, Porfirio

Michel v. Reynolds: as example of Taft's ability to mass the Court, **5:**178

Miles Medical Company v. Park & Sons Company, **5:**216

militarism, **7:**87, 125–26, 129, 143, 152

military forces: analogy to domestic police, **7:**99; discussion of, **7:**94, 103; objections to, answered, **7:**59, 66; when to employ, **7:**3–4, 14, 47, 48–49

militia. *See* National Guard

Milyukoff, Pavel Nicholas (Russian statesman): quoted, **7:**121

Minimum Wage Act (Washington, D.C., 1918), **8:**123

Miranda ruling, **8:**62

Mississippi River: flood controls for, **3:**312, 391; **5:**97; navigation improvements to, **3:**310–12, 390–91, 434

Missouri River: improvements to, **3:**391, 494

Mogul Steamship Company v. McGregor, **5:**181–83, 205

monetary reform, **1:**285–86; **3:**39, 149–50; **4:**206–8, 314–17. *See also* silver, coinage of

monopolies: history of, **5:**176; illegality of, **1:**208–9; **2:**47–48; **3:**14, 191–92, 248, 417

Monroe, James, **6:**26

Monroe Doctrine: critics of, **6:**141–42, 146; history of, **1:**138; **5:**151; **6:**133–35, 138–39, 144; in international arbitration, **6:**179; limits of, **3:**363; **6:**122–23, 136–37, 139–41; and Mexico, **6:**145; as obligation, **3:**344–45; **6:**144; U.S. Army and, **1:**135–36; **7:**232, 234, 246, 249–50, 264, 295, 299, 300

Montesquieu, Charles Louis, **6:**11

Moody, William H., **5:**167

Moore, John Bassett, **6:**179

Moores & Company v. Bricklayers' Union of Cincinnati, **2:**87, 123, 158; **3:**119–20, 123

Morris v. Duby, **8:**285–88

Motor Vehicle Theft Act (1919), **8:**203

muckrakers, **1:**33–34

munitions, manufacture of, **7:**16

Myers v. United States, **8:**257–68

Myrdal, Gunnar, **8:**299

Napoleon, **7:**97, 128

Nash v. United States, **5:**230

national government: expanded power of, **5:**95–98

National Guard, **1:**141–43; **4:**29–30, 322; **5:**149; **6:**76

nationalism and the League, **7:**131

national isolation: impossible in future, **7:**120

National Union Fire Insurance Co. v. Wanberg, **8:**87–90

nations (or republics): creation of, **7:**xvii, 129, 160–63, 170–71, 219

Native Americans, **8:**116

naturalization, **7:**63–64

natural laws, **1:**16

Navy, U.S.: administration of, **3:**48, 375–77; **4:**47–49, 220–22, 332–33; cost of, **3:**469; **5:**153–54; growth of, **1:**138, 253;

Navy, U.S. (*cont.*)
  3:352, 469; 4:220–21, 331; merchant
  marine and, 3:226, 236; 4:18–19;
  Pacific base for, 3:376, 469; in the
  Philippines, 1:133; 3:376, 469; popu-
  larity of, 1:132–34
Neagle, In re, 7:104
New Mexico, statehood of, 3:383; 4:101–3,
  111–12, 149–50
New Nationalism (Roosevelt, 1910), 5:99
New York v. United States, 8:43–45
Nicaragua, 3:364–65; 4:182, 291–92; 6:75
Nigro v. United States, 8:314–18
NLRB v. Jones & Laughlin Steel Company,
  8:xxviii
Noble State Bank v. Haskell, 5:111–12
nonjusticiable questions, 7:52
Northern Securities Company v. U.S., 1:171;
  4:172; 5:167, 169, 207–8, 211–12

O'Connor, Sandra Day, 8:xxx
Ohio Constitutional Convention (February
  1912), 5:7
Ohio River: improvements to, 3:297, 311, 391,
  395–97, 433
Oklahoma: banking laws of, 2:119–21, 151–52;
  constitution of, 1:220–21; 2:140, 150;
  6:100
*Old Colony Trust Co. v. Commissioner of In-
  ternal Revenue,* 8:385–88
Old Court (pre-1937), 8:87, 131, 291
Olmstead v. United States, 8:xxix, 332–36
Olney, Richard: as attorney general, 1:171,
  322; 2:47; 5:200, 203; 6:75; as secre-
  tary of state, 1:54; 5:151; 6:125, 134–35,
  137; 7:58
Olney-Pauncefote Treaty (1895), 6:125
Open Door policy, 1:107–9; 3:366; 6:86–87
opium trade, 7:32
Oregon Steam Navigation v. Minon, 5:221
*Oregon-Washington Railroad & Navigation
  Co. v. Washington,* 8:236–39
Oriel v. Russell, 8:342–44
original package doctrine, 8:139
Orlando, Vittorio, 7:286
Osborn v. The Bank, 5:89

overcapitalization, 1:232, 290; 3:15; of railroads, 1:200–201; 2:50; 3:10, 37–38,
  190, 245, 415

Pacific States Company v. Oregon, 5:60
Paderewski, Ignace Jan, 7:284
Palestine: as mandatory, 7:207
Panama Canal: celebration of, 4:346–47;
  construction of, 1:166; 3:275, 393;
  4:34; cost of, 3:106–7, 110–11, 370,
  467; 4:21, 34; 5:156; debate over,
  3:102–13; effects of, 3:225, 259, 275;
  5:95; financing of, 1:149; 3:47, 370,
  466; fortification of, 4:35; 5:155–56;
  Hay-Pauncefote Treaty and,
  4:276–79, 282, 330; history of,
  1:146–66; 3:100–102; Interstate Commerce Commission and, 4:280–82;
  Spooner Act and, 1:148–49; 3:101, 370;
  4:211; tolls for, 4:35–36, 212, 280, 330;
  workforce on, 1:151, 153, 185–86; 2:94,
  157–58, 163, 220; 4:330
Panama Canal Zone, 1:149; 4:210–12; 6:73,
  85; 7:60, 72, 132
Panama Railroad Co. v. Rock, 8:175–77
Panic of 1907, 1:230–38; causes of, 1:231–32,
  236, 238, 261; 2:42, 101–2, 148; 3:15;
  effects of, 1:233–35; 2:149; 3:33, 46;
  remedies for, 2:98, 102, 138, 149; 3:16,
  41–42
parliamentary governments, 6:16–18
parties, political, 1:17–21, 56, 281–82; 2:169;
  3:179, 238; 5:33, 38, 70, 72–73, 79–82
patronage, political, 1:22, 306; 4:223–24; 6:51,
  55–58
Payne-Aldrich Tariff: corporate excise tax
  under, 3:135, 180–81, 195, 239–41;
  Court of Custom Appeals under,
  3:187, 410; Dingley Tariff contrasted
  with, 3:171–73, 452–53; enactment of,
  3:169, 174–75, 179, 238; 5:5; "maximum and minimum" clause of,
  3:180–81, 242, 373–74; 4:15–17, 193,
  295–96; and the Philippines, 3:64–65,
  181, 224–25, 233, 240; as a political
  issue, 3:462; Tariff Board under,

3:181–83, 374–75, 454–55; wool under, 3:176–77, 237, 454; 4:199–202, 273–75

peace, 2:7; domestic, 5:146–47; international, 4:7; 5:154–58; 6:183, 199–200; 7:80, 267, 291

Pearre Bill (1907), 3:115–16, 119

Peckham, Rufus W., 5:205–7, 220

Pennsylvania Railroad Co. v. United States Railroad Labor Board, 8:112–16

Pennsylvania Railroad System v. Pennsylvania Railroad Co., 8:199–201

Phelan, In re, 2:89, 91, 161–62; 3:123–25, 128

Philippine Act (1902), 1:41, 84, 99–102; 2:61; 6:77–79

Philippines, the: Chinese Bookkeeping Act challenged, 8:248; civil vs. common law in, 1:328–29, 331; cost of U.S. involvement in, 3:345, 446; economy of, 1:46, 78, 88, 97–98; 2:61; 3:27–28, 52; guerrilla insurrection in, 1:37–38, 44–45, 77, 86; 2:59; 3:28, 444–45; history of U.S. policy toward, 1:85–98, 287; inauguration of civil government in, 1:75–81; independence proposal for, 1:39, 42, 50, 86, 88; 4:324–27; National Assembly of, 1:99–105; Protestant missions in, 3:346–47; Roman Catholic Church in, 1:48, 87; 2:62–63, 185–88; 3:144–45, 252–53, 346; Taft's presidency and, 4:213–14; U.S. Army in, 1:xx, 37–38, 133; 3:28, 292, 345, 444–45, 447; U.S. guardianship of, 1:85; 2:60–63; U.S. Navy in, 1:133; 3:376, 469; U.S. responsibility for, 1:44–45, 107, 249–50; 2:59, 64–65; 3:27, 345, 445; 6:142; U.S. trade with, 1:39–40, 45–46, 79–80, 88; 2:65; 3:64, 181, 224–25, 233; 4:32. *See also* Filipinos; *under* Taft, William Howard

picketing, legal and illegal, 8:30

piracy, legal, 6:195

Planned Parenthood v. Casey, 8:xxix

Platt Amendment, 5:95; 6:69–70

Plunkett, Sir Horace, 7:226

pogroms, 7:154–55

Poincaré, Raymond, 7:197

Poindexter, Miles: answered, 7:135–36; quoted, 7:221

Poland, 7:154–55

Political Issues and Outlooks (Taft), 2:7–222

Polk, James K., 6:74

Pollack v. Farmers' Loan and Trust Company, 3:133–34

Ponzi scheme, 8:48

Ponzi v. Fessenden, 8:48–49

popular government: dangers of, 4:151–52; 5:53–55, 57; definition of, 1:18; 5:21–22, 24; and individual rights, 4:151; 5:139, 190–92; judicial branch of, 1:27; 5:117–18; limits of, 3:265–66, 323–24; 5:24–26, 29–30, 114–15, 190–91; merits of, 1:18; 5:21; parties and, 1:19, 56

Popular Government (Taft), 5:3–159

populism, 5:100, 163

posse comitatus, 5:146–47

postal savings banks: and federal authority, 5:95; inauguration of, 4:43, 218–19; operation of, 4:339–40; Taft's advocacy of, 2:108–10; 3:24–25, 162–66, 381–82, 455–56

Pound, Roscoe, 5:188–89

Preamble of the U.S. Constitution, 5:4, 19, 22

Present Day Problems (Taft), 1:65–341

president: appointment power of, 1:55, 59; 6:48–49, 52–56, 58–60, 95–96; as commander in chief, 1:85; 4:177; 6:74–77, 87, 97, 110; confidentiality rights of, 6:97; documents of, 6:34; and execution of treaties, 6:68–70, 169–70; executive functions of, 6:19; and foreign relations, 6:80–82, 85–89; foreign travel by, 6:45; inferable obligations of, 5:146–47; 6:60–74; judicial authority and, 6:99–103; legislative role of, 1:56, 59; 6:18–23, 32–33, 43–44; limits on power of, 1:54–55, 60; 3:323–24; 6:94–96, 104–6, 115–16; minor functions of, 6:30, 38–39, 43–44; official oath of, 6:18; pardoning power of, 6:89–93; powers of, 3:323; 6:12, 47; quasi-judicial powers

president (*cont.*)
of, **6**:64–66; quasi-legislative powers
of, **6**:64; removal power of, **1**:59; **6**:49,
57; statutory construction by,
6:63–64; Supreme Court and, **6**:43;
veto power of, **6**:19–28; visits to Congress by, **6**:37–38

President and His Powers, The (Taft), **4**:3;
6:3–117

Presidential Addresses and State Papers (Taft),
3:5–472

presidential cabinet: minor powers of,
6:30–47

presidential elections, **7**:170–71

press, freedom of the, **1**:51–54; **5**:71

primary elections, **5**:73–82, 121

prisons, reform of, **6**:92, 114

pro-German sentiment, **7**:88, 91

Progressive Party, **6**:187

progressivism, **1**:69, 71; **5**:4, 35–37, 163

Prohibition, **1**:29–30; **8**:80, 104, 212, 222, 232,
309, 326

property, right of, **1**:14–16, 216, 239–40, 256,
308; **5**:65–66

prorogation, **6**:43–44

prostitution, **3**:385; **5**:94

public discourse, **3**:205–7, 209

public health: federal role in, **2**:209–10;
3:334–36, 342, 385–86

public lands: appeals regarding, **4**:50; classification of, **3**:217; coal, gas, oil, and
mineral rights on, **3**:219–20, 249, 306,
428–29; disposition of, **3**:216–17, 306,
426–28; **4**:80–81, 342–43; **5**:96; railroads and, **4**:133; water-power sites on,
3:217–19, 249, 260, 307, 427–30. *See
also* forests, preservation of; reclamation (of arid lands)

public opinion, **1**:51–54; **3**:461; **5**:71–72

Puerto Ricans, **1**:331; **4**:324; **6**:76

Puerto Rico: criminal appeal from, **8**:303

*Puget Sound Power & Light Co. v. County of
King*, **8**:161–63

Pullman strike, **1**:321–22; **2**:89, 161; **3**:62, 124;
5:147, 185; **6**:75

pure food law (Federal Food and Drugs Act

or Wiley Act of 1906), **1**:175; **2**:21;
4:344–45

Queen's Bench Cases (1865–75), **5**:180–82

racial freedom, **7**:283–84

racism, **1**:242–46; **2**:56–57, 217, 221; **3**:49,
53–54, 443–44, 448

railroad brotherhoods, **1**:183, 185; **2**:85, 89–90,
124, 160–61; **3**:123, 128–29

*Railroad Commission v. Chicago, Burlington
& Quincy Railroad*, **8**:39–43

Railroad Rate Bill. *See* Elkins Act; Hepburn
"Railroad Rate" Act

railroads: economic importance of, **2**:97;
overcapitalization of, **1**:200–201, 290;
2:50; **3**:10, 37–38, 190, 245, 415; rates
of, **1**:204, 314; **3**:9–10, 186, 188–90,
244, 411–14; rebates by, **1**:172, 210,
270; receivership procedure for,
1:311–17; traffic agreements of, **3**:8; valuation of, **3**:9–10; waterways as competitors of, **1**:290; **3**:295, 298, 310–11,
394, 434; worker safety on, **2**:17, 22;
3:18, 54, 185, 416; **5**:128. *See also* Elkins
Act; Hepburn "Railroad Rate" Act;
Interstate Commerce Commission;
and specific court cases

Randolph, Edward, **6**:13

recall, **5**:61–63; **6**:154; of judges, **4**:150, 153–57;
5:107–10; of judicial decisions, **5**:7,
110–14

receivers (in equity), **1**:311–17; **2**:89, 133; **3**:124;
5:234; **6**:58

reclamation (of arid lands), **3**:214, 249, 260,
430–31; **4**:81–82; **5**:97; cost of, **3**:215,
340, 431–32; private role in, **3**:216

referendum, **5**:27, 40–45; **6**:100; shortcom-
ings of, **5**:45–52, 55; **7**:105–6

religions, tolerance among, **3**:140, 144,
266–67, 277, 400; **7**:154, 283, 301

representative government, **5**:30–39, 53, 58, 60

reprieve (presidential power), **6**:90

republican government, **5**:30–39, 53, 58, 60

Republican Party (Jeffersonian), **5**:86;
6:39–40, 42

Republican Party (modern): and African
Americans, **1**:285; conservatism in,
5:5–6, 8; dissension in, **3**:460–62; and
farmers, **3**:17; formative years of,
1:282–83; history of, **1**:282–83, 286–88;
2:68–72; and labor, **1**:181–87; **2**:35–36,
71, 85, 154; **3**:17–18, 117–18, 129, 185;
and liberal construction of the Constitution, **1**:282; **2**:29; and protective
tariffs, **1**:222–24, 286–87; **2**:99, 102;
3:16, 168, 177, 196, 451; and reform,
1:289–92; **2**:34–35, 72–73, 145; **3**:5–6;
in the South, **1**:244, 247, 288; **2**:27–30,
135, 137
Republican Party Platform of 1908: and Arizona's statehood, **3**:282; and conservation, **3**:458; and injunctions, **2**:92; and
the Interstate Commerce Commis-
sion, **2**:75; **3**:411, 414–15, 456–57; and
judicial reform, **3**:117–18, 154, 379,
457–58; and overcapitalization, **2**:74;
3:245, 467; and postal savings banks,
2:107; **3**:162, 455–56; and tariff revision, **2**:76–77, 99, 104–5, 146–48;
3:168, 172–73, 451–52; and Theodore
Roosevelt's policies, **2**:27, 73; and
trusts, **2**:74; **3**:459–60, 463
roads: federal jurisdiction over, **5**:98
Roman Catholic Church: in the Philippines,
1:87; **2**:62–63, 185–88; **3**:144–45,
252–53, 346; in the United States,
3:250, 253, 349
Roman Empire, **6**:185
Romania ("Rumania") and the Jews, **7**:183–85
Roosevelt, Franklin D., **8**:xix
Roosevelt, Theodore: and aliens' rights,
6:157–58; and arbitration treaties,
6:169; and conservation, **3**:219–20,
249, 295; and injunction issue,
1:183–85, 292; **3**:115–16; and labor,
1:181–87; and Monroe Doctrine,
6:137–39; and president's powers,
6:106–11; and public opinion, **1**:243;
3:461; and railroad regulation,
1:172–73; **2**:21–22, 34; **3**:37–38, 244; as
a reformer, **1**:216–19, 289, 291–92;

2:21–22, 175; **3**:6–7, 13, 44; and Sherman Antitrust Act, **1**:171, 235–36;
2:46; **3**:37–38, 247; **5**:166; and Taft,
3:243; **6**:107; Taft's praise for during
campaigns, **1**:177–79; **2**:2, 22, 33,
43–44, 71–72, 79, 139; **7**:74, 185–88
Root, Elihu: and arbitration treaties, **4**:6;
6:126–27; conservatism of, **5**:6, 10;
and federal power, **3**:436–37; and the
Philippines, **1**:101; **6**:77; and representative government, **1**:101; **5**:30; and the
U.S. Army, **1**:139; **7**:288–91
Round Robin (Senate group opposing the
Treaty of Versailles), **7**:279
Russia: discussion of its problems, **7**:183–85;
referred to, **7**:84, 87, 121, 129, 141, 162,
202, 277–78
Ryan v. United States, **8**:92–93

SAAR District, **7**:206
Salisbury, Lord, **6**:89
Samuels v. McCurdy, **8**:194–99
Santo Domingo, **6**:139, 143, 144
Schubert, Glendon, **8**:xx
seals: killing of, **4**:190, 297–98, 351–58; **6**:89,
194, 197
Secret Service, U.S., **6**:45–46
secret treaties, **7**:285
Segurola v. United States, **8**:303–5
self-determination, **7**:123
self-government: definition of, **7**:170–71
Selzman v. United States, **8**:222–23
Senate, U.S.: confirmation of appointments
by, **1**:55; **6**:48–49, 52–54; confirmation
of treaties by, **5**:158–59; **6**:37, 81–83, 88,
101, 169–70, 179–81. *See also* Congress,
U.S.
Seward, William H., **6**:134, 137
Sharswood, George (federal judge), **5**:24
Shaw, Lemuel, **1**:206
Sherman Antitrust Act (1890): amendment
of, **3**:191–92, 246, 420–22; criticism of,
4:167; **5**:222; enforcement of, **1**:32,
170, 210, 235–36; **2**:21; **3**:420, 423, 459;
4:333; and farmers, **4**:367–68; history
of, **1**:170; **2**:45–46; **3**:417–20, 422;

Sherman Antitrust Act (1890) (*cont.*)
4:171–72; 5:174–75, 240; and labor
unions, 3:246–47; 4:367–68; 5:223–24;
language of, 5:164; restraint of trade
under, 3:417; "rule of reason" and,
3:421–22; 4:161; 5:168–70, 219–21,
232–33; Supreme Court and, 2:46–47;
4:159–61, 166–67; 5:164, 167–71,
197–242; Taft's interpretation of,
1:207–12; 2:46–48; 5:168–70, 197–242
Shields v. United States, 8:278–80
short ballot, 5:46
Siebold, Ex parte, 6:164–65
silver: coinage of, 1:233, 286; 2:20, 95–96,
138–39; 3:39, 61
Sioux City Bridge Co. v. Dakota County,
8:106–7
Skowronek, Stephen, 6:4–5
small nations: protection of by the League,
7:176
Smuts, General Jan Christian, 7:218, 240
socialism, 1:14, 17, 216–17, 239–40, 302; 2:3,
140; 3:155–56; 5:65–66
socialists, 7:131, 138
social justice, 5:140–43
social sciences, 1:12–13, 17, 21–22; 5:144
Society of Judicial Settlement of International Disputes, 6:189–90, 193
Sonneborn Brothers v. Cureton, 8:139–42
Sonnino, Sidney (Italian minister), 7:272,
286
Souter, David, 8:xxx, 65
southern states (U.S.): development of, 2:28,
174; 3:319; political parties and,
1:242–48; 2:27–30, 135, 137, 173, 175;
public health in, 3:334–35, 342; racism
in, 1:242–48; 2:56–57, 217, 221; 3:49,
53–54, 443–44, 448; reconciliation
with, 1:249; 2:28, 135, 173–74; 3:353;
traditions of, 2:28, 135; 3:319, 332, 337,
353; in the U.S. government, 1:241–42;
2:137, 174, 177; 3:87, 337, 342
sovereignty, 7:132, 136, 174–75, 238, 252–53
Spanish-American War: aftermath of, 1:179,
249, 287; 6:76; causes of, 3:345, 445;
6:143; criticism of, 6:142; effects of,

1:249; 3:345, 401, 446–47; 5:95; fund-
ing for, 6:100; National Guard in,
5:149. *See also* Philippines, the
Spooner Act (1903), 1:148–49; 3:101, 370;
4:211
Stafford v. Wallace, 8:56–59
Standard Oil Company: prosecution of
under Hepburn Act, 1:172–73, 195,
210
Standard Oil v. United States, 4:159–66;
5:167–69, 217–22, 225, 235–38
Stanton, William, 6:49
State Department, U.S.: modernization of,
3:368–69; 4:286–87
states: attempts to restrict interstate businesses by, 1:302–3; 3:421–22; and conservation, 3:214, 300, 334, 433, 438;
and inheritance, 3:202–3, 238;
5:99–100; international debts of, 5:158;
6:178–79; as parties to federal litigation, 8:341; peace of, 5:146; and political corruption, 1:304–6; powers
relinquished by, 3:436–37; secession
of, 5:91; sovereignty of, 5:19–21,
87–89, 95, 148; uniformity of laws
among, 3:334, 438–39, 441
statutory law, judges and, 4:153; 5:190
Steele v. United States No. 1, 8:209–12
Steele v. United States No. 2, 8:212–13
Stephenson, Benjamin F., 3:136–37
Stone, Harlan Fiske, 8:xxvi
Story, Joseph, 4:338; 5:20
Straus v. the Publishing Company, 5:230–31
Stuart kings, 5:124
submarine warfare, 7:78, 86, 89, 143, 167
substantive due process, 8:195
sugar trust, 3:373; 5:164–65; prosecution of
under Hepburn Act, 1:173, 195, 210
Sully, Maximilien (seventeenth-century
French statesman), 7:185
Sumner, William Graham, 2:3–4
Supreme Court, U.S., 1:35; 5:102, 116; and
aliens' rights, 6:163–64; appeals to,
1:339; 2:13–14; 3:378; 4:40–41; and
corporate rights, 1:307–9; and domestic peace, 5:146–47; and foreign rela-

tions, **6:**81, 89; history of, **5:**192–93; and income tax, **1:**215; **3:**196, 238–39; and individual rights, **5:**141; and injunctions, **2:**155; **3:**20–21; and international controversies, **7:**44; as international tribunal, **6:**193–94, 199; **7:**39; judicial review by, **2:**8; **5:**104–5; **6:**23–25, 40–41, 43, 102–3; jurisdiction over states by, **1:**297–98, 307–8; **6:**172–73, 192, 194; and labor's rights, **5:**194–95; membership of, **4:**40; **5:**166–67; and other branches of government, **2:**8; **3:**196; **6:**11–12, 43, 77, 90, 99, 106; and the Philippine Act, **6:**78–79; restraint shown by, **5:**60; and Sherman Antitrust Act, **2:**46–47; **3:**419–20; **4:**159–61, 166–67; **5:**164, 167–71, 197–242; and treaty-making power, **6:**84; and war as a legal fact, **6:**74. *See also names of individual justices and specific cases*

Sutherland, George, **8:**xxv

Sutter Butte Canal Co. v. Railroad Commission, **8:**363–67

Swiss National Insurance Co. v. Miller, **8:**178–80

Swiss Republic, **5:**27; **6:**189–90, 199

Syria, **7:**229

Taft, Alphonso, **1:**120, 230; **2:**52, 133; **3:**115

Taft, Charles P., **4:**143–44

Taft, William Howard: as civil governor of the Philippines, **1:**67–68; **2:**163; **3:**346, 401; **6:**77; as Hampton Institute trustee, **3:**354–55; as Kent Professor of Constitutional Law at Yale University, **5:**9–10, 15, 168; **6:**121; messages to Congress, **4:**5–368; 1922 testimony before House Judiciary Committee, **8:**395–416; 1924 testimony before House Judiciary Committee, **8:**417–22; as political campaigner, **1:**66; **2:**25, 31, 134, 173; **3:**126–29, 153; **5:**9; as president, **3:**44; **4:**1–4; **6:**4–5, 92–93; as Red Cross head, **3:**406; as secretary of war, **1:**3, 6, 68; **2:**94,

157–58, 183–84; **3:**228, 338, 352, 393; **5:**154; **6:**61, 69, 73, 78, 85, 149; and Sherman Antitrust Act, **4:**333; **5:**166; as solicitor general, **1:**67; **3:**207; as superior court judge, **2:**87, 133; **3:**119–20; Supreme Court opinions of, **8:**21–394; and Theodore Roosevelt, **1:**71; **3:**243; **6:**107; as U.S. circuit court judge, **1:**67; **2:**16, 87, 134, 156–57, 161–63; **3:**114–15, 121–28, 152; **5:**210; **6:**58; works: *Anti-trust Act and the Supreme Court, The,* **5:**173–242; *Four Aspects of Civic Duty,* **1:**3–61; "Liberty under Law," **8:**3–18; *Political Issues and Outlooks,* **2:**7–222; *Popular Government,* **5:**3–157; *Present Day Problems,* **1:**65–341; *President and His Powers, The,* **4:**3; **6:**3–117; *Presidential Addresses and State Papers,* **3:**5–472; *Taft Papers on League of Nations,* **7:**3–302; *United States and Peace, The,* **6:**121–200

Taft Papers on League of Nations (Taft), **7:**3–302

Taney, Roger B., **1:**311; **3:**436; **5:**91–92, 122

tariffs, protective: benefits of, **2:**100–101; and farmers' interests, **2:**103–4; **3:**178; and laborers' interests, **2:**100; **3:**41, 178; periodic revision of, **1:**223; **2:**103; **3:**168, 451, 454–55; Republican support for, **1:**222–24, 286–87; **3:**16, 168, 177, 196, 451; and trusts, **1:**174; **2:**49–50. *See also* Dingley Tariff; Payne-Aldrich Tariff

tariffs, revenue: Democratic support for, **2:**77, 100; **3:**17, 40, 196; Grover Cleveland and, **1:**287; **3:**61; ill effects of, **2:**77, 102–3; **3:**41, 178; **7:**291, 298. *See also* Gorman-Wilson Tariff

Tennyson, Alfred Lord, **7:**185

Tenth Amendment, **8:**245

Tenure of Office Act (1867), **8:**38

Terral v. Burke Construction Co., **8:**36–37

Thayer, James B., **1:**332, 335; **6:**23–24

Thirteenth Amendment, **1:**244, 283; **3:**125

Thornton v. United States, **8:**245–48

Tilden, Samuel Jones: defeat in presidential election (by Hayes, 1876) disputed, **7:**145

Tillman, Benjamin, **3:**443–48
tobacco trust, **1:**173, 211; **4:**159–66; **5:**167–69, 218–19, 236–37
Tod v. Waldman, **8:**174–75
Transportation Act (1920), **8:**112
treaties: of arbitration, **4:**173–74; **6:**82–83, 126–27, 169–71, 180–81; constitutional status of, **6:**83–84, 87–88, 162–63; federal power to make, **6:**161; postal, **6:**101; Senate confirmation of, **5:**159; **6:**37, 81–83, 88, 101, 169–70, 179–81; **7:**56, 59, 66–67, 102–3, 220–21, 248, 254, 258–59. *See also names of specific treaties*
tribunals, executive, **2:**75; **6:**64–66
Trentino, Italy, **7:**123, 140, 152, 286
Triple Alliance, **7:**97, 285
Triple Entente, **7:**97, 285
Truax v. Corrigan, **8:**xxv, xxx, 30–35
Trustees of Dartmouth College v. Woodward, **1:**307
trusts: definition of, **1:**32, 168–70, 252; **3:**417. *See also* Clayton Antitrust Act; *individual trusts and antitrust cases;* Sherman Antitrust Act
Tumey v. Ohio, **8:**275–77
Turkey, **7:**123, 129

Ukraine, **7:**129, 219
United Leather Workers Union v. Herkert & Meisel Trunk Co., **8:**168–71
United Mine Workers of America, **8:**217
United Mine Workers v. Coronado Co., **8:**73–78
United States and Peace, The (Taft), **6:**121–200
United States Court of Claims, **8:**390
United States of America: influence of in League, **7:**178; should not join League, **7:**107; power and wealth of, **7:**68–69, 76; driven to war, **7:**143; purpose in war, **7:**120–22; as world police force, **5:**150–54
United States Postal Service: budget of, **3:**469–71; federal responsibility for, **5:**94–95, 146; management of, **3:**380–81; **4:**43–47; during Taft's presidency, **4:**218–20, 254–59, 339–42

United States v. American Tobacco Company, **1:**211; **4:**159–66; **5:**167–69, 218–19, 225, 236–38
United States v. Balint, **8:**47–48
United States v. Boston & Maine Railroad, **8:**388–89
United States v. Bowman, **8:**93–95
United States v. Butler, **8:**xxvii
United States v. E. C. Knight Co., **1:**170, 308; **3:**419; **5:**164–65, 199–202, 221–22; aftermath of, **1:**171; **4:**162; **5:**166, 169, 203, 209, 211–15; **8:**xxviii
United States v. Fruit Growers Express Co., **8:**377–79
United States v. Jackson, **8:**392–93
United States v. John Barth Co., **8:**379–81
United States v. Lanza, **8:**101–4
United States v. Murray, **8:**309–11
United States v. Pacific and Arctic Railway & Navigation, **5:**229–30
United States v. Patten, **5:**228
United States v. Reading Co., **4:**367; **5:**226–28
United States v. Trans-Missouri Freight Association, **5:**204–7, 210, 220
United States v. Union Pacific Railroad Co., **5:**226
United States v. Winslow, **5:**228–29
United Zinc & Chemical Co. v. Britt, **8:**50–52
Universalist Church, **3:**253
Upshur, Abel P., **6:**104–5
Upton, Emory, **5:**148–50

Van Buren, Martin, **6:**4
Van Devanter, Willis, **5:**167, 228; **8:**xxv
Venezuelan Boundary Dispute, **6:**125, 134
Versailles, Treaty of (1919), **7:**172–73, 273
veto, power of, **3:**441; **6:**19–28
victory obligations, **7:**128–37
victory program, **7:**5–6
victory with power, **7:**118–19
Virginia Military Institute, **3:**338
Vivani, René (French politician): quoted, **7:**121

Walker v. Gish, **8:**107–8
Wallace v. United States, **8:**37–39

war: delay of by investigation, **7**:102–3; right of Congress to declare, **7**:132

Washington, Booker T., **1**:244, 246; **2**:5, 181, 197, 218

Washington, George, **1**:124, 135, 145; **2**:214–15; **6**:37–38; advice regarding entangling alliances, **7**:68–69, 108, 117, 143–44, 161, 249

waterways, inland and inside: appropriations for, **3**:296–97, 307–8, 392–93, 466, 468; **4**:214–15; federal jurisdiction over, **4**:33; **5**:90; and railroad rates, **1**:290; **3**:295, 298, 310–11, 394, 434; systematic improvement of, **3**:390–94, 398–99; water-power sites on, **4**:328–29. *See also names of individual waterways*

wealth: accumulation of, **1**:11–12, 32–33, 213, 215, 300; as capital, **1**:168; duties of, **1**:11; inherited, **1**:11, 34, 213–15. *See also* capital, aggregated

Webb, Bill, **6**:24

Webster, Daniel, **6**:134, 136

Weedin v. Chin Bow, **8**:295–98

Western & Atlantic Railroad v. Georgia Public Service Commission, **8**:207–9

whisky trust, **5**:197–99, 206

White, Edward D., **5**:167–69, 217–20; **8**:xix, xxi

White, Henry, **7**:195

White House, **6**:44

Wichita Railroad & Light Co. v. Public Utili-ties Commission of Kansas, **8**:83–85

Wickersham, George W., **6**:193

Wiley Act (1906), **1**:175; **2**:21; **4**:344–45

Wilhelm (kaiser), **7**:126

Wilson, Woodrow, **6**:6, 8, 43, 75, 86, 102, 107, 110, 115; correspondence of, **7**:294–302; and Fiume, **7**:286; quoted, **7**:76, 87, 94, 121, 143, 201–2

Wisconsin v. Illinois, **8**:344–48

Wolff v. Court of Industrial Relations, **8**:143–47

women, **3**:314–16; **5**:25; appeal to, **7**:235–36

Worcester County National Bank, Ex parte, **8**:373–77

workers' compensation, **2**:86; **4**:63, 250–53, 335; **5**:128

workingmen: and the League, **7**:138–39

Work v. McAlester-Edwards Co., **8**:137–38

Work v. Mosier, **8**:116–18

world politics, **7**:120

World War I: purpose of United States in entering, **7**:130–31

writ of mandamus, **8**:232

Wuchter v. Pizzutti, **8**:311–14

Young Men's Christian Association, **2**:183–92, 199–200; **3**:211–12

Yu Cong Eng v. Trinidad, **8**:248–53

Yugoslavians ("Jugo Slavs"), **7**:123, 126, 129, 140, 162

zones, division of world into, **7**:199